GENRE AND HOLLYWOOD

In this important new book, Steve Neale provides a comprehensive introduction to genre and Hollywood cinema. He discusses all the major concepts,
theories and accounts of Hollywood and genre, and the key genres which
theorists and critics have tended to write about – from musicals to horror
films, from action-adventure to the western. He also offers detailed revisionist
accounts of melodrama and *film noir*, and puts forward new arguments about
the place and importance of genre in understanding Hollywood cinema.

Neale argues that many existing accounts of genre and Hollywood have
provided a partial and misleading account of Hollywood's output. He calls
for broader and more flexible conceptions of genre and genres, for more
attention to be paid to the discourses and practices of Hollywood itself, for
the nature and range of Hollywood's films to be looked at in more detail, and
for any assessment of the social and cultural significance of Hollywood's
genres to take account of industrial factors.

Assessing the place of genre and genres in new and old Hollywood alike,
Neale concludes that genre remains an important means of understanding
Hollywood, its history and its films, but that only an expanded conception of
genre can account for the variety and nature of its output.

Steve Neale is Research Professor in Film, Media and Communication
Studies at Sheffield Hallam University.

SIGHTLINES

Edited by Edward Buscombe, Southampton Institute and
Philip Rosen, Department of Modern Culture and Media,
Brown University, USA

Cinema Studies has made extraordinary strides in the past two decades. Our
capacity for understanding both how and what the cinema signifies has been
developed through new methodologies, and hugely enriched in interaction
with a wide variety of other disciplines, including literary studies, anthropology, linguistics, history, economics and psychology. As fertile and important as
these new theoretical foundations are, their very complexity has made it
increasingly difficult to track the main lines of conceptualization. Furthermore,
they have made Cinema Studies an ever more daunting prospect for those
coming new to the field.

Sightlines maps out the ground of major conceptual areas within Cinema
Studies. Each volume is written by a recognized authority to provide a clear
and detailed synopsis of current debates within a particular topic. Each makes
an original contribution to advancing the state of knowledge within the area.
Key arguments and terms are clearly identified and explained, seminal
thinkers are assessed, and issues for further research are laid out. Taken
together, the series constitutes an indispensable chart of the terrain which
Cinema Studies now occupies.

Books in the series include:

NARRATIVE COMPREHENSION AND FILM
Edward Branigan

NEW VOCABULARIES IN FILM SEMIOTICS
Structuralism, Post-structuralism and Beyond
Robert Stam, Robert Burgoyne and Sandy Flitterman-Lewis

CINEMA AND SPECTATORSHIP
Judith Mayne

UNTHINKING EUROCENTRISM
Towards a Multi-cultural Film Critique
Ella Shohat/Robert Stam

GENRE AND HOLLYWOOD
Steve Neale

GENRE AND HOLLYWOOD

Steve Neale

Routledge
Taylor & Francis Group

LONDON AND NEW YORK

First published 2000
by Routledge
2 Park Square, Milton Park, Abingdon, Oxon OX14 4RN

Simultaneously published in the USA and Canada
by Routledge
270 Madison Avenue, New York, NY 10016

Reprinted 2001 (twice), 2003, 2005, 2006, 2007 (three times), 2008, 2009

Routledge is an imprint of the Taylor & Francis Group, an informa business

© 2000 Steve Neale

Typeset in Bembo by
J&L Composition Ltd, Filey
Printed and bound in Great Britain by
the MPG Books Group

British Library Cataloguing in Publication Data
A catalogue record for this book is available from the British Library

Library of Congress Cataloging in Publication Data
A catalogue record for this book has been requested

ISBN 10: 0–415–02605–9 (hbk)
ISBN 10: 0–415–02606–7 (pbk)

ISBN 13: 978–0–415–02605–5 (hbk)
ISBN 13: 978–0–415–02606–2 (pbk)

This book is dedicated to my parents, Ron and Doreen Neale,
with love and thanks

CONTENTS

ACKNOWLEDGEMENTS

I would like first of all to thank Ed Buscombe, Phil Rosen and Rebecca Barden for commissioning this book and for their patience and encouragement during the lengthy period it has taken me to complete it.

Other thanks go to past and present colleagues, Ben Brewster, Elizabeth Cowie, Michael Grant and Murray Smith at the University of Kent, and Catherine Constable, Gerry Coubro, Sheldon Hall, Sylvia Harvey, Angela Martin, Geoffrey Nowell-Smith, Tom Ryall and Lynette Tan at Sheffield Hallam. Thanks also go to Frank Krutnik, whose work on comedy has been a considerable influence; to Richard Maltby and Ruth Vasey, for numerous discussions, ideas and roast meals; to Gerry Palmer, whose thoughts on genre in the early stages of this book had a major impact; and to Peter Stanfield for letting me have a copy of his exemplary thesis on the 1930s western.

I am grateful to Kent and Sheffield Hallam for periods of study leave, to the British Academy for a travel grant, to the librarians at Kent, Sheffield Hallam and the British Film Institute for their help, and to Deborah Allison for photocopying a decade's worth of reviews in *The Film Daily* in record time.

Portions of this book were delivered as papers and presentations at Glasgow, Kent, Sheffield Hallam, Oslo and Oxford Universities, at the University of Wisconsin-Madison, at the *Screen* conference, and at the BFI Conference on Melodrama. Portions have been published in *Screen*, *The Velvet Light Trap* and *The Cinema Book*. Thanks go to all concerned.

Finally, special thanks go to Kim and Clare Slattery and to Artemis, Dorothy, Nick, Olly and Turner, for putting up with all the typing, all the viewing, and the sustained period of absence upstairs when I should have been seeing them. The most special thanks of all, though, go to Kate Slattery, who has helped me throughout, and who has put up not just with these things but with everything else as well.

INTRODUCTION

After a lengthy period of neglect, there are signs of a significant revival of interest in the topic of genre and Hollywood. While this book has been in press, Rick Altman has published *Film/Genre* (1999), James Naremore has published *More Than Night* (1998), and Jonathan Munby has published *Public Enemies, Public Heroes* (1999). Altman explores a number of innovative ideas about genre in general. Naremore and Munby offer revisionist accounts of *film noir* and the gangster film respectively. All three take advantage of archival resources that were simply unavailable to those who pioneered the study of genre and genres in the 1960s and 1970s. And all three take on board some of the theoretical and ideological agendas that have been set since then. They show that genre remains as important and productive a means of thinking about Hollywood, its history, its audiences and its films as its pioneers and initial proponents always claimed. But because they each present new research and new thinking, they also help make the point that a fresh assessment of its strengths and weaknesses is long overdue.

In keeping with the other volumes in the *Sightlines* series, *Genre and Hollywood* is designed to review existing work and to present new ideas and new findings. Striking a balance between the two has not always been easy, particularly because I argue that the conventional wisdom embodied in many existing accounts is often open to question: that conventional definitions of genre are often narrow and restrictive, that traditional accounts of a number of genres are inaccurate or incomplete, that aesthetic and cultural theories of genre are prone to overgeneralization, and that accounts of the role played by genre and genres in Hollywood's practices, Hollywood's history and Hollywood's output are often partial and misleading. Like Richard Maltby (1995: 107–43), my own view is that many of these accounts have been driven by critical and theoretical agendas rather than by a commitment to detailed empirical analysis and thorough industrial and historical research. It is also that these accounts are usually underpinned by received definitions of genre, that these definitions are open to question on theoretical grounds, and thus that conceptual and empirical enquiry need, here as elsewhere, to inform one another.

1

It is in conducting these arguments that existing accounts are presented and discussed, and here I have sought to be as comprehensive as I can. Some accounts focus on definitions of genre, some on individual genres, some on the general characteristics of Hollywood's genres and some on the socio-cultural roles they perform as a whole. Other accounts focus on their commercial and industrial basis and on their role in Hollywood's output, others still on combinations of them all. The topic of genre and Hollywood is clearly multifaceted. I have therefore divided this book into three distinct parts. The first deals with basic definitions and general concepts, the second with individual genres, and the third with theories, descriptions and indust-rially oriented accounts of Hollywood's generic array.

Part I contains two chapters. The first is concerned with definitions. It focuses on fundamental concepts and points of debate within the context of an historically oriented account of their emergence inside and outside Film Studies. Here the work of major figures like Alloway, Altman, Buscombe, McArthur and Ryall is presented alongside basic concepts like iconography. It is noted that genre, a word meaning 'type', a word which is therefore logically applicable to all kinds of cultural forms, tends here to be associated almost exclusively with Hollywood and with mass-oriented commercial culture in general. The origins of this thinking are outlined, and the revisionist ideas of Tudor and Williams in Film Studies and of those working on genre in philosophy, literature and linguistics are presented and discussed.

These discussions provide the basis for number of arguments. One is that genre is a multi-dimensional phenomenon, a phenomenon that encompasses systems of expectation, categories, labels and names, discourses, texts and groups or corpuses of texts, and the conventions that govern them all. Another is that genre is ubiquitous, a phenomenon common to all instances of discourse: there is a generic aspect to all texts; all texts 'participate', to use Derrida's term, 'in one or several genres' (1992: 230). These two arguments dovetail with a third, which is that the concept of genre in Film Studies should logically expand to include categories, corpuses and terms like 'feature film' and 'documentary' as well as 'science fiction', 'horror' and 'western', and that on these grounds alone most films are multiply generic. The ramifications of these arguments for the traditional notion of 'the genre film' are explored and examined at the end of the chapter.

Chapter 2 looks in more detail at some of the dimensions of genre identified in Chapter 1. Beginning with the concept of verisimilitude, a concept which focuses on audience expectations and textual norms, Chapter 2 is concerned with the institutional role played by Hollywood and its 'inter-textual relay' (Lukow and Ricci 1984) in the generation of expectations, in the provision of generic images, labels, names, and hence in the provision of evidence as to the existence of genres, as to their prevalence in Hollywood's output at any particular point in time, and as to the meaning, application and use of genre terms. The term 'inter-textual relay' refers to the discourses of publicity, promotion and reception that surround Hollywood's films, and includes both trade and press reviews. It is argued that the role of this relay is a crucial one, and the issues raised here are explored by looking at the early westerns and the terms used to describe them, and by debating the arguments put forward by Altman (1987) in favour of a central role for the critic in identifying genres and in constructing on the corpuses of films they each embody and encompass.

The issues and arguments raised in Part I provide a framework for the rest of the book. Those concerning the respective roles of Hollywood's inter-textual relay and of genre theory and criticism form the backdrop to the opening chapter in Part II, Chapter 3, and come to the fore in the chapters that follow. Chapter 3 looks at the major genres critics have identified and discussed at some length. Summaries are provided of work on fourteen genres overall, from 'action-adventure' to 'westerns'. Queries and issues of debate are raised in the process. While the point is made that most of the genres discussed here correspond to those recognized and marked in Hollywood's inter-textual relay, the point is also made that they frequently hybridize and overlap, thus blurring the boundaries of the genres concerned, and that canons of critical preference, rather than those of empirical or historical enquiry, have often resulted in uneven degrees of attention, discussion and research.

Some of the issues at stake here are examined in more detail in Chapter 4, on *film noir*, and in Chapter 5, on melodrama and the woman's film. These categories and some of the films with which they are associated have generated an enormous amount of writing and research. However, melodrama and *film noir* in particular are revealed to be more problematic than is often acknowledged, especially when placed within the context of Hollywood's inter-textual relay and, in the case of *film noir*, especially when placed within the context of Hollywood's output in the 1940s and early 1950s. '*Film noir*' is a critical category. Despite numerous attempts to exemplify, define and explain it, it is argued here that the category is incoherent, that its proponents fail to provide criteria sufficient to distinguish between those films it includes and those films it excludes, and that its use tends to homogenize a number of distinct historical developments, tendencies and trends. However, as a result of the growing ubiquity of the term, and as a result of the fashion for producing films which draw on its image, it is also argued that *film noir* now has a generic status it originally did not possess in the past. It is thus a particularly interesting case, posing as it does questions about the nature of genres and about the purposes and effects of critical discourse.

As used within Hollywood's inter-textual relay, the term 'melodrama' is shown to have implied action and suspense, to have been used as a synonym for 'thriller', rather than applied, as Film Studies has assumed, to the woman's film. The roots of these meanings and uses are located in the history of melodrama on the stage on the one hand and in the history of Film Studies in Film Studies on the other. It is noted that 'drama' rather than 'melodrama' was the term used to describe woman's films, that work on their history may help to pinpoint some of the reasons for this, and that while domestic and romantic dramas – the traditional compartments of the woman's film – continue to be made, the term 'woman's film' itself has disappeared. Issues are therefore raised, once again, about generic identity and terminology, about the extent to which critical and industrial terms and definitions can differ from one another, and about the effects these differences can have on our understanding of Hollywood's output and Hollywood's history. It is argued that the heritage of nineteenth-century melodrama has been multi-generic and that, as Walker has suggested (1982), it may be best to divide that heritage into 'melodramas of action' and 'melodramas of passion'. While accounts of melodrama in Film Studies have focused on the latter, Hollywood itself has nearly always understood it to refer to the former.

Part III focuses on Hollywood's generic array and on the generic composition of Hollywood's output. Chapter 6 looks at general accounts of Holly-wood's genres from an aesthetic and socio-cultural point of view. Arguments concerning the formulaic and repetitive nature of Hollywood's genres are looked at in detail, as are theories and accounts of generic evolution and change. Adopting Altman's (1987) terminology 'ritual' and 'ideological' theories of genre, theories which attempt to link Hollywood's genres to cultural and ideological issues, trends and values, are looked at as well. The point is made that aesthetic and socio-cultural theories alike tend to under-play the elements of discontinuity, diversity and difference in Hollywood's output, to substitute a number of presumptions and generalizations for detailed empirical research, and therefore in effect if not in intention to isolate that output from the historical and industrial conditions and forces that underpin it. Arguments are made in favour of more specific, more industrially centred and more multi-dimensional forms of analysis.

Genre criticism and genre theory are often justified on the grounds that they acknowledge Hollywood's commercial and industrial nature and on the grounds that the genres they discuss correspond to the trends and divisions in Hollywood's output. These claims are examined in Chapter 7, which begins by looking at the naure and status of films as industrial commodities, at the conditions this status imposes on production and promotion, and at how these issues relate to genre. Every film is unique. Production and promotion are therefore governed by the need to recognize and celebrate difference as well as by the need to reuse capital assets and to recycle and signal the presence of tried and tested ingredients. These issues underpin the rest of the chapter, which focuses on the industrial role played by genre in the studio era and in the era of what is now usually called The New Hollywood.

By looking in detail at Hollywood's practices, structures and output in the mid-1930s and mid-1980s, traditional generic vocabularies are shown to be inadequate as means of charting Hollywood's output and of describing many,

4

if not most, of its films. In addition, a number of established tenets, accounts and assumptions are revealed to be misleading. The idea that film companies plan or planned their output in terms which correspond to traditional conceptions of genre is challenged. So too is the idea that they specialized in individual genres for any length of time in the studio era and that allusion and hybridity are features of the post-studio era alone. The strategies of the industry and its companies have always been plural and mixed, marked by an array of categories, formulas and combinations that overlap with, but often exceed, the categories that genre critics and theorists have tended to acknowledge hitherto.

In conclusion it is argued that only an expanded conception of genre, of the kind outlined in Chapter 1, can encompass the generic practices of the industry and its inter-textual relay on the one hand, and the diverse cyclic forms, trends, traditions and formulas that mark its productions on the other. More precise and more detailed historically, empirical and industrially informed research is called for. The concept of genre has for some time served as a means to link Hollywood's practices and Hollywood's output to Hollywood's audiences and to the socio-cultural contexts within which its films are produced and consumed. The conclusions drawn here suggest that its utility in all these respects needs to be re-examined, and that there is thus ample scope for more debate, more thinking and more research.

Part I

GENRE
Definitions and concepts

1

DEFINITIONS OF GENRE

'Genre' is a French word meaning 'type' or 'kind'. As we shall see, it has occupied an important place in the study of the cinema for over thirty years, and is normally exemplified (either singly or in various combinations) by the western, the gangster film, the musical, the horror film, melodrama, comedy and the like. On occasion, the term 'sub-genre' has also been used, generally to refer to specific traditions or groupings within these genres (as in 'romantic comedy', 'slapstick comedy', 'the gothic horror film' and so on). And sometimes the term 'cycle' is used as well, usually to refer to groups of films made within a specific and limited time-span, and founded, for the most part, on the characteristics of individual commercial successes: the cycle of historical adventure films made in the wake of *Treasure Island* (1934) and *The Count of Monte Cristo* (1934), for instance (Behlmer 1979: 12; Taves 1993a: 68–9), or the cycle of 'slasher' or 'stalker' films made in the wake of *The Texas Chainsaw Massacre* (1974) and *Halloween* (1978) (Clover 1992; Dika 1990).

As these examples illustrate, the definition and discussion of genre and genres in the cinema has tended to focus on mainstream, commercial films in general and Hollywood films in particular. Sometimes, indeed, genre and genres have been exclusively identified with these kinds of films. 'Stated simply', writes Barry Keith Grant, 'genre movies are those commercial feature films which, through repetition and variation, tell familiar stories with familiar characters in familiar situations.' 'They have been exceptionally significant', he adds, 'in establishing the popular sense of cinema as a cultural and economic institution, particularly in the United States, where Hollywood studios early on adopted an industrial model based on mass production' (1986b: ix). However, if (for the moment at least) we accept that genres are simply types or kinds of films, there is no logical reason for excluding either such non-American instances as the Indian mythological, the Japanese samurai film, or the Hong Kong *wu xia pan* or swordplay film, or such 'non-commercial' or non-feature length instances as the documentary, the animated short, the avant-garde film or the art film. Although writing can be found which considers these types of film from a generic point of view, most

9

of the writing on genre and genres in the cinema has focused on the commercial feature film and on Hollywood.[1]

There are a number of reasons for this. Most can be found either in the history of the study of the cinema, or in the history of genre as a concept within the fields of written fiction and drama. Given that this book will also concentrate on the feature film and on Hollywood, it is important to highlight these reasons at the outset, and to expose some of the limitations and problems to which they have given rise.

GENRE CRITICISM AND GENRE THEORY IN THE 1960S AND 1970S

In her survey of writing on genre in *The Cinema Book*, Christine Gledhill (1985a: 58) points out that books and articles on individual Hollywood genres began to be published in the US and in Europe (especially in France) in the 1940s and 1950s, notably by Bazin (1971a, 1971b), Chabrol ([1955] 1985), Rieupeyrout (1953) and Warshow ([1948] 1975a, [1954] 1975b). However, it was not until the late 1960s and early 1970s that the study of genre and genres began to establish itself more fully in Britain and in the US, in tandem with the establishment of Film Studies as a formal, academic discipline. As Gledhill goes on to indicate, there were two main reasons for the appearance of genre and genres on the agenda of theorists, critics, and teachers of film at this time. One was a desire to engage in a serious and positive way with popular cinema in general and with Hollywood in particular. The other was a desire to complement, temper or displace altogether the dominant critical approach used hitherto – auteurism.

There had always existed reviewers and critics (like James Agee, Manny Farber and Parker Tyler) who had discussed Hollywood films with some sympathy, intelligence and insight. But they had also always been the exception among those who wrote about film in the US and Britain. For the most part, intellectuals, critics and reviewers had been at best patronizing and at worst overtly hostile to Hollywood and its films – on the grounds that they were commercially produced, that they were aimed at a mass market, that they were ideologically or aesthetically conservative, or that they were imbued with the values of entertainment and fantasy rather than those of realism, art or serious aesthetic stylization.

During the late 1950s, the 1960s, and the early 1970s, a generation of intellectuals who had grown up with and who for various reasons liked and valued elements of commercial popular culture in general, and American popular culture in particular, began to debate and to re-assess its value.[2] By then the French film journal *Cahiers du cinéma* had pioneered an approach to the cinema that François Truffaut called 'la politique des auteurs' (Truffaut [1954] 1976), and that came in the US and in Britain to be known either as 'the auteur theory' (Sarris 1968) or else, more simply, as auteurism. *Cahiers'* auteurism was founded on three basic premises. The first was that despite the ostensibly collective and impersonal nature of film production, the cinema could be, and often was, a realm of individual and personal expression. The second was that in the cinema, the figure equivalent to the artist or author (*auteur*) in painting or in literature was – or could be – the director. And the third, and by far the most radical, was that directorial artistry and cinematic authorship were to be found not just within the culturally respectable realms of international art cinema (a common idea at that time), nor even, as far as Hollywood was concerned, solely within the realms of the occasional prestige or maverick project (another common idea), but also, perhaps especially, within the realms of its routine output (Hillier 1985b: 7).

Adapted, modified, reworked in various ways, these premises were adopted by Andrew Sarris, film critic for *The Village Voice* in the USA, and by *Movie* magazine, and later *The Brighton Film Review, Monogram* and *Cinema*, in Britain (Caughie 1981). The impact of auteurism on film criticism in general and on the criticism and appreciation of Hollywood films in particular was immense. It enabled both a systematic charting of a great deal of Hollywood's output, and much detailed discussion of form, style, theme and *mise-en-scène*. It thus provided those wishing to analyse – and validate – Hollywood cinema with a valuable critical stance and with a valuable set of critical tools. However, given its evaluative base (auteurs were preferred to non-auteurs and to mere '*metteurs-en-scène*'), and given its commitment to individual directors and hence to individualized corpuses of films, auteurism was of little help in dealing with the range of Hollywood's output overall, or in charting broader trends and developments within it. Moreover, the third of *Cahiers*'s premises in particular required the adoption of a 'perverse' attitude to Hollywood, a way of looking at and thinking about its films which neither Hollywood itself nor society at large encouraged. (Hence the tendency of *Cahiers* in particular and of auteurism in general to lapse into cultishness.) It thus encouraged an approach to Hollywood films which either ignored or defamiliarized their institutional status, their institutional conventions and the audiences to whom they were principally addressed. It is precisely for these reasons that the auteurism of *Cahiers, Movie*, Sarris and *Monogram* was – and is – of interest. However, it was for these reasons too that those interested in identifying these conventions and in taking account of the institution and its audiences found untrammelled auteurism unhelpful. Towards the end of the 1960s, they began to turn their attention instead to issues of genre.

As Gledhill has pointed out, an American art critic, Lawrence Alloway (1963, 1971), had already made the case for paying more attention to genres and cycles, arguing that they were fundamental not just to Hollywood cinema but to popular art as a whole. 'Alloway . . . resists the temptation to establish "classic" timeless dimensions in popular forms', she writes. 'He insists on the transitional and ephemeral character of genres, of cycles, and of any individual popular film (1985a: 59–60). In an overview of the writing on genre that followed, Tom Ryall restates the case against auteurism and reiterates Alloway's point about the nature of popular art: 'The auteur theory, though important and valuable during the 1950s and 1960s for drawing attention to the importance of the American cinema, nevertheless tended to treat popular art as if it were "high art"' (1975/6: 28). He also makes explicit the importance and the role of the audience. And he offers a definition of genre itself. 'The master image for genre criticism', he writes, 'is a triangle composed of artist/film/audience. Genres may be defined as patterns/forms/ styles/structures which transcend individual films, and which supervise both their construction by the film maker, and their reading by an audience' (ibid.).

I shall return to this definition in a moment. However, at this point it is worth stressing the extent to which Ryall is critical of some of the writing on genre that immediately preceded his own. 'By and large', he writes, 'genre criticism has confined itself to producing taxonomies on the basis of "family resemblances", allocating films to their position within the generic constellation, stopping short of what are the interesting and informative questions about generic groupings'. (1975/6: 27). To a degree these remarks are well-founded. Some of the writing that preceded (and followed) Ryall's article was indeed taxonomic, devoted to the discovery and analysis of the components of individual genres rather than to the pursuit of theoretical questions about the nature of genre as such. However, while writing of this kind has its limitations, it also has its uses, providing as it does an initial means of 'collating the range of cultural knowledge . . . genres assumed' (Gledhill 1985a: 61).

Moreover, not all the writing on genre in the late 1960s and early 1970s was taxonomic in kind. Both Buscombe (1970) and McArthur (1972), for instance, were concerned, among other things, to demonstrate the active role played by genre conventions in shaping the form and the meaning of individual Hollywood films. Here, for example, is Buscombe on *Guns in the Afternoon* (a.k.a. *Ride the High Country*) (1962), a western:

> Knowing the period and location, we expect at the beginning to find a familiar western town. In fact, the first few minutes of the film brilliantly disturb expectations. As the camera moves around the town, we discover a policeman in uniform, a car, a camel, and Randolph Scott, dressed up as Buffalo Bill. Each of these images performs a function. The figure of the policeman conveys that the law has become institutionalised; the rough and ready frontier days are over. The car suggests . . . that the west is no longer isolated from modern technology and its implications. Significantly, the camel is racing against a horse; such a grotesque juxtaposition is painful. A horse in a western is not just an animal but a symbol of dignity, grace and power. These qualities are mocked by it competing with a camel; and to add insult to injury, the camel wins.
>
> (Buscombe 1970: 44)

He later continues:

> the essential theme of *Guns in the Afternoon* is one that, while it could be put into other forms is ideally suited to the one chosen. The film describes the situation of men who have outlived their time . . .
>
> The cluster of images and conventions that we call the western genre is used by Peckinpah [the film's director] to define and embody this situation, in such a way that we know what the West was and what it has become. The first is communicated through images that are familiar, the second through those that are strange. And together they condition his subject matter. Most obviously, because the film is a western, the theme is worked out in terms of violent action. If it were a musical, the theme might be similar in some way, but because the conventions would be different, it would probably not involve violence . . . And if it were a gangster picture, it seems unlikely that the effect of the film's ending, its beautifully elegiac background of autumn leaves, would be reproduced, suggesting as it does that the dead Judd is at one with nature, the nature which seems at the beginning of the film to have been overtaken by 'civilization'.
>
> (Buscombe 1970: 44–5)

In this particular essay, Buscombe attempts also to advance a general theory about the aesthetic characteristics of popular genres. He borrows the concepts of 'inner' and 'outer' form from Warren and Welleck, who argued that 'Genres should be conceived as a grouping of literary works based, theoretically, upon both outer form (specific metre or structure) and also upon inner form (attitude, tone, purpose - more crudely, subject and audience)' (1956: 260). These particular concepts were not taken up by subsequent writers. But in illustrating the idea of 'outer form', Buscombe talked about 'visual conventions'. His work here thus drew on and fed into a concept that was to become much more influential – the concept of iconography.

ICONOGRAPHY

Along with its twin, 'iconology', the term 'iconography' derives from art history, and in particular from the work of Erwin Panofsky. Panofsky himself discussed the application of these terms to popular cinema ([1934] 1974), but it was Lawrence Alloway who sought to apply them in a systematic way to the analysis of genres and cycles (1963).

In 'Iconography and Iconology: An Introduction to the Study of Renaissance Art', first published in 1938 and reprinted in his *Meaning in the Visual Arts*, Panofsky distinguishes between three possible levels or stages in the analysis of Renaissance paintings, corresponding to three possible 'strata' of meaning (1970: 51–81). The first involves the identification and description of what he calls 'motifs' (essentially, the objects and events depicted through lines, colours and volumes). The second involves the identification and description of what he calls 'images' (the 'secondary or conventional' meanings conveyed by these motifs, as determined in particular by reference to the Bible and to other written sources. This for Panofsky is the realm of iconography). And the third involves the interpretation of these images. (This for Panofsky is the realm of iconology.)

In arguing for the application of the concept of iconography to the cinema, Alloway writes that

The meaning of a single movie is inseparable from the larger pattern of content-analysis of other movies. And the point is, that this knowledge, of concepts and themes, is the common property of the regular audience of the movies. It comes from 1) exposure to runs of related movies (soap opera, westerns) and from the fact that 2) the movies connect with other topical interests and activities of the audience. Such themes as kitchen technology and domestic leisure in soap opera and male outdoor leisure clothes, as well as attitudes towards violence in westerns, exist outside the movies, but aid identification with the movies once you are inside the cinema.

(Alloway 1963: 5)

He precedes this passage with another example, and with another facet of this argument:

iconography is not to be isolated from other aspects of film making. For instance, *The Thousand Eyes of Dr Mabuse* and *Rear Window* can be related to a persistent theme of American movies since World War II. There were the F.B.I. movies in which the Department of Justice kept spies under observation with a battery of voyeuristic electronic devices. Since *The Glass Web* television monitor devices of every kind have been brilliantly handled in urban films: for instance, a telephone wired with a bomb, as in *The Case Against Brooklyn* or the difficulties of telephone tapping in the '30s in *The Scarface Mob.*

(Alloway 1963: 4–5)

It should be noted that 'iconography' here tends to mean the objects, events and figures in films, as well as their identification and description. It should also be noted that Alloway tends to avoid interpretation. Partly for this reason, iconology does not even figure as a term. (It tends to disappear altogether in subsequent writing on genre. Only McArthur, in an unpublished paper written in 1973, briefly resurrects both the term and the conceptual distinction Panofsky originally designed it to make.) Finally, it should be pointed out that although Alloway discusses and exemplifies iconography

14

in relation to genres and cycles, he also discusses its application to stars and to star personae.

The concept of iconography was widely used by genre theorists and critics during the course of the next decade. There were two main reasons for this. One was the extent to which, in Alloway's formulation at least, it dovetailed with a sympathetic interest in popular films. The other was the extent to which it could be used to stress the visual aspects of popular films (in keeping with the stress placed on style and *mise-en-scène* by auteurism, and in contrast to the emphasis placed on character, plot and theme by more literary-minded theorists and critics). Hence Buscombe's synonym for iconography – 'visual conventions'. Hence his insistence on the argument that 'Since we are dealing with a visual medium we ought surely to look for our defining criteria on the screen' (1970: 36). And hence the stress placed on 'visual conventions' as well as on the 'relationship between genre and audience' in the chapter on the iconography of the 'gangster film/thriller' in McArthur's *Underworld USA*:

In *Little Caesar* (1930) a police lieutenant and two of his men visit a night-club run by gangsters. All three wear large hats and heavy coats, are grim and sardonic and stand in triangular formation, the lieutenant in front, his two men flanking him in the rear. The audience knows immediately what to expect of them by their physical attributes, their dress and deportment. It knows, too, by the disposition of the figures, which is dominant, which subordinate. In *The Harder They Fall* (1956) a racketeer and two of his men go to a rendezvous in downtown New York. As they wait for the door of the building to be opened they take up the same formation as the figures in the earlier film, giving the same information to the audience by the same means . . . In *On the Waterfront* (1954) and *Tony Rome* (1967) there are carefully mounted scenes in which the central figure is walking down a dark and deserted street. In each case an automobile drives swiftly towards him; and the audience, drawing on accumulated experience of the genre, realises that it will be used as a murder weapon against the hero. Both these examples indicate the continuity over several decades of patterns of visual imagery, of recurrent objects and figures in dynamic relationship. These repeated patterns might be called the iconography of the genre.

(McArthur 1972: 23)

McArthur goes on to categorize the genre's iconography, subdividing the patterns of its imagery into three basic types: 'those surrounding the physical presence, attributes and dress of the actors and the characters they play; those emanating from the milieux within which the characters operate; and those connected with the technology at the characters' disposal' (ibid.: 24). However, it is unclear as to whether this taxonomy is meant to be applicable to other genres as well. It is also unclear as to whether iconography is to be thought of as one of the defining features of a genre.

There are certainly traces of such a position in McArthur's book. He says at one point, for instance, that the iconographic patterns of a genre 'set it off visually from other types of film and are the means by which primary definitions are made' (1972: 24). However, he himself does not elaborate, and it is Buscombe who comes closest to arguing a position of this kind. Although stressing that not all generic conventions are visual in kind, he argues nevertheless that 'the major defining characteristics of a genre will be visual: guns, cars, clothes in the gangster film; clothing and dancing in musical (apart from the music, of course!); castles, coffins and teeth in horror movies' (1970: 41). This argument occurs during the course of a much more detailed discussion of the western. Nevertheless, the paucity of these examples (together with the taxonomic tendencies both of genre criticism in general and of iconographic analysis in particular) is strikingly apparent. One of the major reasons for this is that the possible connections between the items (or icons) listed is unclear. Another, more important, reason is that it is actually very difficult to list the defining visual characteristics of more than a handful of genres, for the simple reason that many genres – among them the social problem film, the biopic, romantic drama and the psychological horror film – lack a specific iconography.

It is no accident, therefore, that the genres discussed at some length by Buscombe and McArthur are the western and the gangster film, two of the genres which (along with the gothic horror film and the biblical epic) the concept of generic iconography seems to fit rather well. The failure to apply the concept productively to other genres suggests on the one hand that the defining features of Hollywood's genres may be heterogeneous in kind (some visual, others not). It suggests on the other that a number of fundamental questions – to do with definition, to do with identification, and to do with the nature and role of genre theory – still needed to be asked. They began to be asked first by Tudor (1974a: 131–52, 1974b: 180–220) and then by Ryall. They were displaced during the decade that followed as attention was turned to structuralism, to semiotics and to psychoanalysis – to general theories of method and meaning (Stam, Burgoyne and Flitterman-Lewis 1992). Structuralism, in particular, played a part in work on individual genres like the western (notably by Kitses 1969 and Wright 1975). However, although some or all of these theories were to have an impact on writing on genre in the 1980s, notably by Neale (1980) and Altman ([1984] 1986, 1987), and although feminist inflections and reworkings of these approaches were to find an important place in writing on hitherto neglected genres like the woman's film (see Doane 1987), issues and theories of genre as such were largely put to one side. Hence some of these questions remained unanswered and had to be re-raised, firstly by Alan Williams (1984), and then by Neale (1990a).

THEORETICAL QUESTIONS

The questions raised by Ryall derive from a distinction he draws between two types of analytical activity:

> The key to understanding the theoretical foundations of the concept of genre lies in pushing beyond . . . classificatory exercises and confronting the crucial distinction between, on the one hand suggesting that a film is a Western; and, on the other, suggesting that a film is a genre film. The former simply involves observing similarities between films, while the latter urges us towards a more generalised theoretical activity in which our conclusions would not merely link one film with another under some category such as 'Western'; but rather, would link the established genres (Westerns, gangster films, musicals, etc) under the more general concepts of 'convention' and 'expectation', and would explore the variety of questions associated with the area of 'reading' film.
>
> (Ryall 1975/6: 27)

Ryall goes on to note the multi-dimensional aspects of genre, insisting on the importance of audience knowledge and audience expectation on the one hand, and of the industry and film reviewers on the other. It is clear, therefore, that for Ryall genres are not simply groups of films linked by common characteristics. He argues in addition that the problem of defining genre as a term is exacerbated by its pervasiveness: 'its widespread usage by film distributors, by reviewers and critics, and by popular audiences, poses problems for criticism insofar as ordinary usage carries with it the implication that the concept of genre is clear and well-defined, non-problematic' (1975/6: 27).

Similar points are made by Tudor (1974a), who tends both to pursue them further and to raise other issues as well. He begins by raising questions about genre identification and genre recognition:

> most writers tend to assume that there is some body of films we can safely call the western and then move on to the real work – the analysis of the crucial characteristics of the already recognized *genre* . . . These writers, and almost all writers using the term *genre*, are caught in a dilemma. They are defining a western on the basis of analyzing a body of films that cannot possibly be said to be westerns until after the analysis . . . To take a *genre* such as the western, analyze it, and list its principal characteristics is to beg the question that we must first isolate the body of films that are westerns. But they can only be isolated on the basis of the 'principal characteristics', which can only be discovered from the films themselves after they have been isolated. That is, we are caught in a circle that first requires that the

films be isolated, for which purpose a criterion is necesary, but the criterion is, in turn, meant to emerge from the empirically established common characteristics of the films. This 'empiricist dilemma' has two solutions. One is to classify films according to a priori criteria depending on the critical purpose. This leads back to the earlier position in which the special *genre* term is redundant. The second is to lean on a common cultural consensus as to what constitutes a western and then go on to analyze it in detail.

(Tudor 1974a: 135–8)

This is a fundamental point. It raises questions about the nature and purpose of genre criticism. And, implicitly at least, it raises questions as to how 'a common cultural consensus' is established. What agencies and institutions are involved? What is the role of the film industry? What is the role of film critics, film reviewers and the like? On the one hand it helps underline Ryall's point about the importance of distributors, reviewers and critics. On the other it helps stress the culturally relative, and therefore the culturally contingent, nature of genres themselves:

In short to talk about the western is (arbitrary definitions apart) to appeal to a common set of meanings in our culture. From a very early age most of us have built up a picture of the western. We feel that we know a western when we see one, though the edges may be rather blurred. Thus in calling a film a western a critic is implying more than the simple statement 'This film is a member of a class of films (westerns) having in common x, y, and z.' The critic is also suggesting that such a film would be universally recognized as such in our culture. In other words, the crucial factors that distinguish a *genre* are not only characteristics inherent in the films themselves; they also depend on the particular culture with which we are operating. And unless there is a world consensus on the subject (which is an empirical question), there is no basis for assuming that a western will be received in the same way in every culture. The way in which the *genre* term is applied can quite conceivably vary from case to case. *Genre* notions – except in the case of arbitrary definition – are not critics' classifications made for special purposes; they are sets of cultural conventions. *Genre* is what we collectively believe it to be.

(Tudor 1974a: 139)

The stress here on culture and cultures, rather than just on films, leads Tudor, like Ryall, to stress the role and the importance of audiences too. And this leads him in turn (and for the first time in work on genre and genres in the cinema) not just outside the realm of Hollywood but outside the realms of mainstream cinema altogether:

the genre concept is indispensable in more strictly social and psychological terms as a way of formulating the interplay between culture,
audience, films and filmmakers. For example, there is a class of films
thought by a relatively highly educated middle-class group of filmgoers as
'art movies' [Tudor goes on to cite *The Seventh Seal* (1956), *L'Avventura*
(1960) and *La Dolce Vita* (1959) as examples]. Now for the present
purposes *genre* is a conception existing in the culture of any particular
group or society; it is not a way in which a critic classifies films for
methodological purposes, but the much looser way in which an
audience classifies its films. According to this meaning of the term,
'art movies' is a *genre*.

(Tudor 1974a: 145)

Thus, to reiterate, 'there does not seem to me to be any crucial difference
between the most commonly applied *genre* term – the western – and the art-
movie that I have been discussing. They are both conceptions held by certain
groups about certain films' (ibid.: 147).

It is here, in including art films under the rubric of genre, and in defining
genres as 'conceptions', that Tudor departs most radically from most of the
ideas and definitions of genre in the cinema advanced hitherto. The questions
he asks are radical ones. They challenge conventional notions as to the
cinematic and cultural site of genre and genres. They open up the issue of
groupings and classification. And they place spectatorial and audience activity
and the cultural and institutional contexts within which that activity takes
place firmly at the centre of theoretical debate. To that extent they are echoed
not just by Williams and Neale, but also by a number of linguists, philoso-
phers and literary theorists who have written on genre in recent years.

LITERATURE, LINGUISTICS AND GENRE

On a number of occasions in the 1960s and 1970s, writers on genre in the
cinema referred to definitions and theories of genre in literature. Some, like
Cawelti (1976), made use of particular literary theories (in Cawelti's case,
those of Frye 1957). However, while the existence of literary theory was
explicitly acknowledged, it was in practice usually ignored. One of the
reasons for this, as Ryall points out, was the apparent discrepancy between
generic terms and 'divisions' in literature, and the terms and divisions familiar
to critics and theorists of the cinema:

As well as the widespread usage within film, the critic also has to
contend with the term as it occurs in the discussion of other arts,
notably literature where genre divisions have been made on the basis
of formal distinctions (the novel, drama, poetry) compared with the
subject or content divisions more usual in film criticism. The term,

therefore, while having an apparent stability within the discussion of film becomes somewhat confusing in the context of, for example, genre definitions in literature.

(Ryall 1975/6: 27)

Hence while Buscombe, for instance, referred in passing to the divisions in Aristotle's *Poetics* between 'tragedy, epic, lyric, and so forth' (1970: 33), they were effectively forgotten by the time he turned to the gangster film, the western and the musical.

It was not until 1984 that this discrepancy was re-raised and discussed as an issue, during the course of Williams's review of Schatz's *Hollywood Genres* (1981):

> Perhaps the biggest problem with genre or genre criticism in the field of the cinema is the word *genre*. Borrowed, as a critical tool, from literary studies (or at least having resonances from that area – the word does have a life of its own in the film industry) the applicability of 'genre' as a concept in film studies raises some fairly tough questions. Sample genres are held to be Westerns, Science Fiction Films, more recently Disaster Films, and so on. What do these loose groupings of works – that seem to come and go, for the most part, in ten- and twenty-year cycles – have to do with familiar genres such as tragedy, comedy, romance, or (to mix the pot up a bit) the epistolary novel or the prose poem?
>
> (A. Williams 1984: 121)

Williams continues:

> For the phrase 'genre films', referring to a general category, we can frequently, though not always, substitute 'film narrative'. Perhaps *that* is the real genre. Certainly there is much more difference between *Prelude to Dog Star Man* and *Star Wars* than there is between the latter and *Body Heat*. It's mainly a question of terminology, of course, but I wonder if we ought to consider the principal film genres as being the narrative film, experimental/avant-garde film, and documentary. Surely these are the categories in film studies that have among themselves the sorts of significant differences that one can find between, say, epic and lyric poetry.
>
> (A. Williams 1984: 121)

The first point to make in response to this is to highlight the extent to which genres and genre categories in literature are by no means always as systematically coherent or long-lived as Williams – or Ryall – seem to suggest. Comedy, romance and tragedy are long-lived as terms, but the criteria that define them, along with the types of work they encompass, have in each case changed over time (see Beer 1970 on romance, and Koelb 1975 on tragedy). Moreover, comedy and romance, at least, are familiar as terms and as genres to critics and theorists of film. In addition, the criteria that define, say, the epistolary novel and epic poetry on the one hand and comedy and romance on the other are very different in kind, varying from the purely formal (in the case of the epistolary novel), to a mix of criteria involving form, content and tone (in the case of most of the others). And to switch the focus of the argument, the western and science fiction are both literary genres as well as cinematic ones. Even the disaster film of the late 1960s and early 1970s has its analogue – indeed its origins – in contemporary novels written by Arthur Hailey, Paul Gallico, Richard Martin Stern, and others.

This leads me to a second point, a point that is crucial for understanding why genre and genres have so often been identified with Hollywood (rather than, say, the art film), and hence why some of the contradictions and discrepancies to which Williams points have arisen. Within a great deal of modern writing on literature, the kind of fiction exemplified by disaster novels and science fiction is often the only kind labelled as generic. The rest is 'literary fiction' or simply 'literature' proper. The latter is the province of 'genuine' literary art and 'authentic' authorial expression. The former, by contrast, is usually considered formulaic, stereotypical, artistically anonymous, and therefore artistically worthless. Hence the following, from Sutherland's *Fiction and the Fiction Industry*:

> Another feature of the increasingly 'packaged' nature of all fiction – including the quality novel – is the advance of 'genre' or the categorised product. By 'genre' is meant such forms as Science Fiction, the detective novel, Gothic, etc. . . .
> Genre incorporates a high ration of familiar to strange elements. Habitually it eliminates the bewilderment associated with avant garde and experimentalism. It specialises in books without shock. If, as Ezra Pound says, the modernist's motto is 'make it new' then the genre author's motto is 'make it the same' . . . Genre fiction is, characteristically, convention-governed . . . There is a soothing quality to much genre fiction; a high incidence of what Q.D. Leavis calls 'living at the novelist's expense' . . . generally the material is bland, despite its claims to unbearable excitement. Similarly genre may have a superficially impressive specialised knowledge . . . But in the end there will be nothing to task the reader's capacities.
> (Sutherland 1978: 192–4. For a very different view, see Bloom 1996.)

It will be readily apparent that those writing on Hollywood's genres in the 1960s and 1970s decisively rejected – indeed often symmetrically inverted – the values and judgement evident in a passage like this. McArthur, for instance, argues that genre conventions can play a positive role in curbing authorial 'excess and self-indulgence' (1972: 94). However, the point to emphasize here is that they share its definitions and its terms, and that these definitions and terms, along with the values and judgements of someone like Sutherland, have a distinct and particular history. As Kress and Threadgold have pointed out:

> *Genre* is valorised very differently in different contexts. From the Romantics through modernism to postmodernism, *genre* is a devalued term in the dominant literary/aesthetic discourse. To be 'generic' is to be predictable and clichéd; within that ideology, literature and art generally has to be free, creative, individual . . . hence literature cannot be generic . . .
>
> In classical periods, for example the English Neo-classical period in the late seventeenth and early eighteenth centuries, or even before then in the Renaissance, the reverse was the case. Literature had to be generic to be considered literature (consider Dryden's famous essay on Dramatic Poesy), and notions of genre were so intimately tied up with what was to be literature that they overtly and in very conscious ways affected both the reading and writing of literary texts.
>
> (Kress and Threadgold 1988: 219–20)

Threadgold reiterates these points elsewhere, stressing the role of conceptions of genre within and across the cultural divisions in artistic practice, in particular those between 'high' and 'low', 'popular' and 'elite':

> Before Romanticism what was Generic was Literature. The rest, the 'popular culture' of political pamphlets, ballads, romances, chapbooks, was not only *not* generic; it escaped the law of genre, was excluded by that law, suffering a kind of rhetorical exclusion by inclusion in the classical distinction between high, middle, and low styles. It was seen as a kind of anarchic, free area, unconstrained by the rules of polite society and decorum, by *genre* in fact.
>
> (Threadgold 1989: 121–2)

Thus genre has undergone 'a fundamental shift of positioning' (ibid.: 120). And this shift runs parallel with shifts both in cultural and aesthetic production and consumption, and in the history of the term 'genre' itself. As Cohen has pointed out, the use of the term in English to refer to aesthetic practices and products is a nineteenth–century phenomenon (1986: 203). Thus although the concept is clearly much older, the term itself emerges with industrialization, mass production, new technologies, new capital, new means of distribution (notably postal systems and the railways), the formation of a relatively large literate (or semi-literate) population – and hence a potential market – at a point of profound transformation in the conditions governing cultural production and the discourses and debates with which it was accompanied.[3] Now it is the new popular culture, the new mass culture that is marked – with a new term – as 'generic'. Repetitive patterns, ingredients and formulae are now perceived by many cultural commentators not as the law of Culture, but as the law of the market. It is therefore hardly surprising that genre was – and still is – principally associated with an industrial, commercial and mechanically based art like the cinema, and with its most obviously industrial, commercial and popular sectors like Hollywood in particular. And it is thus particularly important to consider ideas, definitions and theories of genre which challenge conventional conceptions.

One source of and for such ideas is the literary critic E. D. Hirsch (a surprising source, perhaps, given his commitment to traditional literary values). Hirsch insists on the fundamental role played by genre – not just in the framing and interpretation of works of art but also in the framing and interpretation of any kind of utterance. He also insists on the fact that genres centrally include – even consist of – a set of expectations. A reader's or interlocutor's 'preliminary generic conception', he writes, 'is constitutive of everything that he subsequently understands, . . . and this [always] remains the case unless and until that generic conception is altered' (1967: 74). In elaborating this view at greater length, Hirsch makes clear that genre in this sense is as much a phenomenon of everyday discourse as it is of literary texts:

> quite apart from the speaker's choice of words, and, even more remarkably, quite aside from the context in which the utterance occurs, the details of meaning that an interpreter understands are powerfully determined and constituted by his meaning expectation. And these expectations arise from the interpreter's conception of the type of meaning that is being expressed.
>
> By 'type of meaning' I do not, of course, intend to imply merely a type of message or theme or anything so simple as content. The interpreter's expectations embrace far more than that. They include a number of elements that may not even be explicitly given in the utterance or its context, such as the relationship assumed to exist between the speaker and the interpreter, the type of vocabulary and syntax that is used, the type of attitude adopted by the speaker, and the type of inexplicit meanings that go with explicit ones. Such expectations are always necessary to understanding, because only by virtue of them can the interpreter make sense of the words he experiences along the way. He entertains the notion that 'this is a certain type of meaning,' and his notion of the meaning as a whole grounds and helps determine his understanding of details. This fact reveals itself whenever a misunderstanding is suddenly recognized. After all, how could it have been recognized unless the interpreter's expectations had

been thwarted? How could anything surprising or puzzling occur to force a revision of his past understanding unless the interpreter had expectations that could be surprised or thwarted? Furthermore, these expectations could have arisen only from the genre idea: 'In this type of utterance, we expect these types of traits.'

(Hirsch 1967: 72–3)

During the course of his discussion of genre, Hirsch draws in particular on the structural linguistics of Saussure ([1959] 1974). Issues of genre and parallels with Hirsch's position have been more apparent, however, in speech act theory and pragmatics. Speech-act theory and pragmatics are branches of linguistics and of analytical philosophy, respectively. They are both concerned with language in use, and in particular with the rules and conventions that govern the production, reception and comprehension of specific kinds of linguistic utterance in specific kinds of context.[4] Mary Louise Pratt (1977), for instance, has written a pioneering book on speech-act theory and litera-ture stressing the generic aspects of all forms of discourse, indeed of 'litera-ture' as such. More recently, in an essay on the short story, she highlights the role, importance and ubiquity of genre in literary and in non-literary dis-course alike. 'Genre is not solely a literary matter', she writes. 'The concept of genres applies to all verbal behavior, in all realms of discourse. Genre con-ventions are in play in any speech situation, and any discourse belongs to a genre, unless it is a discourse explicitly designed to flaunt the genre system' (1981: 176).

Speech-act-oriented theories of genre have recently been drawn on (and sometimes modified, extended or criticized, though always from within a recognizable similar ambit of concerns) by Derrida (1992), Freadman (1988), Hunter (1989), Reid (1989) and Ryan (1981). Derrida criticizes speech-act theories of genre on the grounds that texts can always exceed specific expectations, contexts and labels. He would therefore contest Pratt's notion that texts 'belong' to genres. He would also deny, though, that any text or instance of discourse could ever escape being generic. A text or an instance of discourse might be able to 'flaunt' a particular 'genre system', but they could never flaunt the 'law of genre' as such, for the simple reason that all texts, all utterances, all instances of discourse are always encountered in some kind of context, and are therefore always confronted with expectations, with systems of comprehension, and in all probability with labels and names. Freadman gives a good example of this:

When the title 'Untitled' started appearing beneath paintings, it cor-responded to the claim of abstract painting to be non-representational: to be 'painting', simply . . . It is a title that represents the non-representational. Now, since the titles of paintings – place-names, personal names, the names of historical or legendary events, or kinds

24

of subjects – designate not only their represented subjects but also, through the naming conventions themselves, their genres, the title 'Untitled' claims above all to transcend genre. Reflect on this. For 'untitled' paintings are themselves a genre; and the title 'Untitled' points to genre in the very act of its denial.

(Freadman 1988: 67)

A less spectacular example from the cinema would be a film like *Un Chien Andalou* (1928), which certainly flaunted the genre system predominant in Europe at the time it was made. It also flaunted the genre 'narrative feature film', and the genres of the contemporary European art film. One of its makers, Luis Buñuel, claimed it was not even an instance of avant-garde film-making, but rather 'a desperate appeal to murder' (Aranda 1975: 63). However, it is precisely for all these reasons that it is usually now understood, and now usually labelled generically, as an exemplary instance of Surrealism. Hence, to return to Derrida, 'Every text participates in one or several genres, there is no genreless text.' Although 'participation never amounts to belonging', 'there is always a genre or genres' (1992: 230).

Derrida's use of the phrase 'one or several genres', his stress on the possible plurality of generic participation, may not resolve the discrepancies between some of the genre terms used in literary studies and the terms that tend to dominate the study of the cinema. (Such discrepancies are historical in origin, and are thus not entirely susceptible to logical or conceptual resolution.) But it does point to a way of resolving Williams' dilemma about 'real' genres, and the validity of categories like the western and science fiction on the one hand, and 'narrative film, experimental/avant-garde film, or documentary' on the other. For from a Derridean perspective, this dilemma is ultimately false. Any film (like any text, utterance or instance of representation) can participate in several genres at once. In fact, it is more common than not for a film to do so. Thus, without trying to be too exhaustive (and leaving aside for the moment the issue of overt generic hybrids), both *Star Wars* (1977) and *Body Heat* (1981), to use two of Williams' (1984) examples, participate in the genres 'film', 'fiction film', 'Hollywood film' and 'narrative feature film'. The former also participates in the genre 'science fiction', and the latter in the genre 'thriller' (and possibly also 'neo-*noir*'). *Prelude to Dog Star Man* (1965), meanwhile, participates in the genres 'film' and 'avant-garde/experimental film' – and also, for some of its viewers at least, the genres 'mythopoeic' and/or 'visionary film', categories first suggested by the influential critic and historian of American avant-garde film, P. Adams Sitney (1979).

While challenging traditional definitions of genre, it is worth noting that there remains a degree of common ground between speech-act-oriented theorists like Pratt, Hirsch and Derrida and theorists like Tudor and Ryall. All agree that genre is a multi-dimensional phenomenon and that its dimensions centrally include systems of expectation, categories, labels and names, discourses, texts and corpuses of texts, and the conventions that govern them all. Some stress the primacy of expectations, others the primacy of texts, still others the primacy of categories, corpuses, the norms they encompass, the traditions they embody and the formulae that mark them. What seems clear is that all these dimensions need to be taken into account. What also seems clear is that they need to be distinguished one from another.

However, the argument that genre is ubiquitous, a phenomenon common to all instances of discourse, ignores or collapses the distinction between those instances which are relatively formulaic, relatively predictable, relatively conventional, and those which are not, between those produced in accordance with the conventions of a pre-signalled genre or genre system and those designed to flaunt them. It also ignores or collapses the boundaries between different ways of categorizing texts and of grouping expectations. The expectations triggered by the name of a star or director are as generic as those triggered by terms like 'western', 'thriller' or 'horror film'. One would normally want, though, to distinguish between the two.

These boundaries and distinctions underlie a great deal of traditional thinking about genres. They have often been tied, as we have seen, to issues of evaluation. They have often been linked to the establishment of aesthetic and cultural hierarchies. And they have often inhibited the development of genre theory. However, while it is important to question traditional thinking and to expand the definition, the meaning and the field of application of genre as a term, it is also important to recognize the differences these boundaries and distinctions serve to mark.

GENRE AND THE GENRE FILM

One way of acknowledging some of these differences without falling into the usual conceptual or cultural traps is to note that they apply to high art as well as to low: a sonnet is formulaic in a way that free verse is not; a Restoration comedy is conventional in a way that a modernist novel is not; and so on. In addition, it should be noted that when Warshow talked about the pleasures and characteristics of aesthetic 'types', he was referring to Restoration comedy and Elizabethan tragedy as well as to westerns and gangster films: 'For a type to be successful', he wrote

> its conventions have imposed themselves upon the general consciousness and become the vehicle of a particular set of attitudes and a particular aesthetic effect. One goes to any individual example of the type with very definite expectations, and originality is to be welcomed only in the degree that it intensifies the expected experience without fundamentally altering it.
>
> (Warshow [1948] 1975a: 129–30)

Within the realms of cinema, numerous movements or trends in art cinema and in avant-garde film-making are or become as predictable (and as typically pleasurable) as any Hollywood western. However, and conversely, there is a difference between academic or programmatic aesthetic formulae and formulae which arise as a result of commercial conditions. And there is a difference between films which are designed to conform, however broadly, to pre-existing categories, expectations and models, and those, like *Un Chien Andalou*, which are not. The latter may encounter expectations and those expectations may be based on previous films or on the tenets of a movement or a group. They may conform to labels or descriptions circulated in advance by critics, distributors, reviewers, perhaps even film-makers themselves. And they may all establish their own internal norms and hence become more familiar – and more predictable – as they unfold. But many of these norms are often unique to the films themselves. Thus the films are less predictable in advance, and at more or less every level. That does not necessarily make them better. But it does make them different.

Altman makes a further distinction. He points out that

> not all films engage spectators' generic knowledge in the same way and to the same extent. While some films simply borrow devices from established genres, others foreground their generic characteristics to the point where the genre concept itself plays a major role in the film.
>
> (Altman 1996a: 279)

Parodies are an obvious instance of the latter, as Altman goes on to indicate. So too are films like *Silverado* (1985), *Chinatown* (1974), *Scarface* (1983) and *Back to the Future III* (1990), films which pastiche, rework or in other ways foreground particular generic traditions, norms and conventions. Altman, following Schatz (1981: 16–18), goes on to propose two different terms, 'film genre' and 'genre film,' in order to mark this particular distinction:

> By definition, all films belong to some genre(s) . . . but only certain films are self-consciously produced and consumed according to (or against) a specific generic model. When the notion of genre is limited to descriptive uses, as it commonly is when serving . . . classification purposes, we speak of 'film genre'. However, when the notion of genre takes on a more active role in the production and consumption process, we appropriately speak instead of 'genre film', thus recognizing the extent to which generic identification becomes a formative component of film viewing.
>
> (Altman 1996a: 277)

While these terms and definitions are useful, Altman here tends to conflate genre as a category and genre as a corpus of films: *Stagecoach* (1939) is both a singular instance of the category 'western' and part of an expanding corpus that includes films like *Hell's Hinges* (1916), *Riders of the Range* (1923), *Bend of the River* (1952), *El Dorado* (1967) and *Tombstone* (1993). The two are distinct. He also tends, through the term 'self-conscious', to conflate routine generic production and routine generic consumption, both of which entail specific generic models and in both of which such models are 'active', with special and particular instances like parody and pastiche. In addition, he tends to imply that the activation of a generic model necessarily entails conformity or participation. But a model may be invoked in order to be reworked or rejected altogether, as is arguably the case with some of the 'revisionist' films of the late 1960s and early 1970s – films like *Chinatown*, *The Long Goodbye* (1973) and *Buffalo Bill and the Indians* (1976) – which rework or reject existing models of the detective film and the western, and as is certainly the case with *Un Chien Andalou*, which both invokes and decisively rejects the model of the contemporary narrative film. For all these reasons, the proposed term 'genre film' tends to evoke traditional definitions, thereby potentially reducing the multiplicity and scope of the phenomenon of genre itself. In order to avoid some of these problems, and in order to take some account of speech-act-oriented thinking, terms like 'generically marked film' and 'generically modelled film' might be preferable. The former would indicate films which rely on generic identification by an audience – and hence specific forms of audience knowledge – in order to make sense. (This would include parody, pastiche and other forms of self-consciousness. But it would also include less specialized instances as well.) The latter would indicate films which draw on and conform to existing generic traditions, conventions and formulae. In practice, of course, the two often overlap. But the former refers more to the moment of reception, and may include instances of generic reworking and generic rejection as well as instances of generic conformity. The latter refers to the moment of production, and by definition excludes generic rejection. Both remain distinct from genre as a category, and genre as a group or corpus of films.

What emerges from this overview is that genre as a term has been used in different ways in different fields, and that many of its uses have been governed by the history of the term within these fields – and by the cultural factors at play within them – rather than by logic or conceptual consistency. The questions raised by Ryall, Tudor and Williams are important ones, as are the questions raised by speech-act theory and pragmatics. The answers to these questions require thinking of genres as ubiquitous, multifaceted phenomena rather than as one-dimensional entities to be found only within the realms of Hollywood cinema or of commercial popular culture. Only then can some of the pitfalls identified by Ryall, by Tudor, by Williams and by others be avoided. And only then can the nature, the functions, and the general topic of genre in Hollywood itself be examined in more detail.

NOTES

1 On the Indian mythological, see Barnouw and Krishnaswarmy (1980: 11–23), and on the Hong Kong swordplay film, see Mo-ling (1981). On the documentary, see Barnouw (1974), Corner (1996), Guynn (1990), Nichols (1991), Renov (1993), and Winston (1995). On art cinema and art films, see Bordwell (1979, 1985), Neale (1981a) and Siska (1976).
2 See, for instance, Hall and Whannel (1964). On some of the reasons for a more positive response in Britain at this time to American popular culture in general and to Hollywood films in particular, see Bennett (1981), Nowell-Smith (1987b) and Strinati (1993).
3 On the growth and forms of industrial mass culture in the West in the ninteenth century, see among others, Allen (1981), Altick (1957), Barth (1980), Bianchi (1986), Birch (1987), Bold (1987, 1991), Denning (1987), Fullerton (1979), Gedin (1977), Hart (1963), McConachie and Freedman (1988), Mates (1985), Noel (1954), Pryluck (1986), Purcell (1977), Radway (1984), Reynolds (1955), Snyder (1970), Somers (1971), Sterne (1980), Toll (1976) and Wilson (1973).
4 On pragmatics and speech-act theory, see Blakemore (1992), Davis (1991), Leech (1983), Levinson (1983), Lyons (1981) and Mey (1993).

2

DIMENSIONS OF GENRE

The argument that genre is ubiquitous, a phenomenon common to all instances of discourse, clearly must modify the perception, and to some extent also the location, of Hollywood's genres. No longer the sole or even the principal site of genre in the cinema, Hollywood instead becomes just one particular site, its genres specific instances – not necessarily paradigms – of a much more general phenomenon. Genre in Hollywood also expands. It now encompasses 'the feature film', 'the newsreel', 'the cartoon', 'the B film', 'the A film' and 'the serial' as well as – and often at the same time as – 'the western', 'the musical', 'the gangster film' and the others. In addition, the argument that genre is multi-dimensional means that attention now needs to be paid as much to the factors that impinge on audience expectations, the construction of generic corpuses, and the processes of labelling and naming as to those that impinge on the films themselves. This chapter will pursue some of these points, and in doing so will introduce a number of further concepts, terms and topics of debate. The first of these is verisimilitude.

VERISIMILITUDE

To reiterate an earlier point. Genres do not consist solely of films. They consist also of specific systems of expectation and hypothesis which spectators bring with them to the cinema and which interact with films themselves during the course of the viewing process. These systems provide spectators with means of recognition and understanding. They help render individual films, and the elements within them, intelligible and, therefore, explicable. They offer a way of working out the significance of what is happening on the screen: a way of working out why particular actions are taking place, why the characters are dressed the way they are, why they look, speak and behave the way they do, and so on. Thus if a character in a film suddenly bursts into song, spectators (or at least spectators accustomed to Hollywood films) are likely to hypothesize that the film is a musical, a particular kind of film in which otherwise unmotivated singing is likely to occur. This hypothesis offers grounds for further anticipation: if a film is a musical, more singing is likely, and the plot is liable to follow some directions rather than others.

Inasmuch as this is the case, these systems of expectation and hypothesis involve a knowledge of, indeed they partly embody, various regimes of verisimilitude – various systems and forms of plausibility, motivation and belief. 'Verisimilitude' means 'probable', 'plausible' or 'likely'. In addition, it entails notions of propriety, of what is appropriate and *therefore* probable (or probable and therefore appropriate) (Brewster 1987; Genette 1969; Todorov 1977: 42–52, 80–8, 1981: 118–19. See also Aumont *et al.* 1992: 117–21). Regimes of verisimilitude vary from genre to genre. Bursting into song is appropriate, therefore probable – therefore believable – in a musical, but not in a war film or a thriller. Killing one's lover is possible in a gangster film, a thriller, or even a romantic drama, but unlikely in romantic comedy. And so on. As such, these regimes entail rules, norms and laws. Singing in a musical is not just probable, it is obligatory; it is not just likely to occur, it is bound to.

As Todorov (1981) has pointed out, there are two basic types of verisimilitude: generic verisimilitude, on the one hand, and social or cultural verisimilitude on the other. Neither equates in any direct sense with 'reality' or 'truth':

> If we study the discussions bequeathed us by the past, we realize that a work is said to have verisimilitude in relation to two chief kinds of norms. The first is what we call *rules of the genre*: for a work to be said to have verisimilitude, it must conform to these rules. In certain periods, a comedy is judged 'probable' only if, in the last act, the characters are discovered to be near relations. A sentimental novel will be probable if its outcome consists in the marriage of hero and heroine, if virtue is rewarded and vice punished. Verisimilitude, taken in this sense, designates the work's relation to literary discourse: more exactly, to certain of the latter's subdivisions, which form a genre.
>
> But there exists another verisimilitude, which has been taken even more frequently for a relation with reality. Aristotle, however, has already perceived that the verisimilar is not a relation between discourse and its referent (the relation of truth), but between discourse and what readers believe is true. The relation is here established between the work and a scattered discourse that in part belongs to each of the individuals of a society but of which none may claim ownership; in other words to *public opinion*. The latter is of course not 'reality' but merely a further discourse, independent of the work.
>
> (Todorov 1981: 118–19)

Drawing on Todorov's work, Jonathan Culler has gone on to propose five types of verisimilitude, five levels of *vraisemblance*, five ways in which a text may be brought into contact with and defined in relation to another text which helps make it intelligible. First there is the socially given text, that which is taken as the 'real world'. Second, but in some cases difficult to distinguish from the first, is a general cultural text: shared knowledge which would be recognized by participants as part of culture and hence subject to correction or modification but which none the less serves as a kind of 'nature'. Third there are the texts or conventions of a genre . . . Fourth, comes what might be called the natural attitude to the artificial, where the text explicitly cites and exposes *vraisemblance* of the third kind so as to reinforce its own authority. And finally, there is the complex *vraisemblance* of specific intertextualities, where one work takes another as its basis or point of departure and must be assimilated in relation to it.

(Culler 1975: 140)

Culler cites the detective story to illustrate the workings of generic *vraisemblance*, highlighting in addition the extent to which generic conventions are as much a property of expectations as they are of works themselves:

The detective story is a particularly good example of the force of genre conventions: the assumption that characters are psychologically intelligible, that the crime has a solution which will eventually be revealed, that the relevant evidence will be given but that the solution will be of some complexity, are all essential to the enjoyment of such books. In fact, these conventions are especially interesting because of the large place they grant to the irrelevant. It is only at the level of the solution that coherence is required: everything deviant and suspicious must be explained by the resolution which produces the key to the 'real' pattern, but all other details can at this point be set aside as of no consequence. The conventions make possible the adventure of discovering and producing a form, of finding the pattern amid a mass of details, and they do so by stipulating what kind of pattern one is reading towards.

(Culler 1975: 148)

Todorov (1977) also uses the detective story, and what he calls 'the murder mystery', to illustrate the concept of verisimilitude. One of the major points he makes is that the *generic* verisimilitude of the murder mystery entails a flaunting or trangression of *cultural* (or 'ordinary') verisimilitude, the second of Culler's categories of *vraisemblance*:

We find the same 'regularity' in any whodunit; a crime has been committed, the criminal must be found. Given several isolated clues, a whole is reconstructed. But the law of reconstruction is never the law of verisimilitude; on the contrary, precisely the obvious suspects turn out to be innocent, and the innocent are 'suspect.' The guilty man in a murder mystery is the man who does not seem guilty. In his summing up, the detective will invoke a logic which links the hitherto scattered clues; but such logic derives from a scientific notion of possibility, not from one of verisimilitude. The revelation must obey these two imperatives: possibility and absence of verisimilitude.

(Todorov 1977: 85)

Hence, if 'every discourse enters into a relation of verisimilitude with its own laws, the murder mystery takes verisimilitude for its very theme; verisimilitude is not only its law but also its object' (ibid.: 85).

The detective story and the murder mystery may well be special cases, instances in which the relationship, and in particular the gap, between generic and socio-cultural regimes of verisimilitude are brought to the fore in a systematic way. But as Culler points out, the *vraisemblance* of any artistic genre is always 'artificial' (1975: 140). This particular relationship and this particular gap are therefore always at stake, always in play. They are always at stake, for instance, in the musical, at those moments and points at which characters burst into otherwise unmotivated song. And they are always at stake, as Frank Krutnik and I have argued, in the comic events and moments that dominate most forms of comedy (Neale and Krutnik 1990: 83–94). Such events and such moments are founded on transgressions and gaps of this kind, whether they involve deviations from the norms of sense and logic, or departures from dominant cultural models of action, speech and behaviour.

It is arguably the case that most Hollywood genres, as traditionally defined, involve transgressions of socio-cultural verisimilitude – for the sake of particular kinds of aesthetic pleasure (as derived, for instance, from the song or from the gag), and in the name not of 'art', but entertainment. Nevertheless, there is in any individual genre always a balance between generic and socio-cultural verisimilitude, and some genres appeal more to the latter than to the former. Gangster films, war films and police procedural thrillers in particular often mark that appeal by drawing on and quoting 'authentic' (or authenticating) discourses, artefacts, and texts: maps, newspaper headlines, memoirs, archival documents, and so on. Other genres – sword-and-sorcery adventure films, space operas and supernatural horror films, for instance – appeal much less to this kind of authenticity. The discourses, artefacts and texts that they cite – like the Book of Revelations in *The Omen* (1974) or the lore of the Jedi in the *Star Wars* films – tend either to be blatantly fictional or else treated as such within our culture. Midway between these extremes lie such instances of science fiction as *Tarantula* (1955) and *Them* (1954), films which draw on the authentic, factual and verisimilitudinous status of science (and contemporary atomic technology) in order to motivate otherwise non-verisimilitudinous actions and events.

Of particular relevance here is Todorov's work on 'the fantastic' (1975), a category founded on the existence of different regimes of verisimilitude. For Todorov the fantastic is defined in relation to two neighbouring categories,'the marvellous' and 'the uncanny'. In the former, events are explained and understood as supernatural, in the latter in terms of the laws of the natural world. The fantastic involves a 'hesitation' between the two, often on the part of a fictional protagonist, but crucially always on the part of the reader:

> In a world which is indeed our world, the one we know, a world without devils, sylphides, or vampires, there occurs an event which cannot be explained by the laws of this same familiar world. The person who experiences the event must opt for two possible solutions: either he is the victim of an illusion of the senses, of a product of the imagination – and the laws of the world remain what they are; or else the event has indeed taken place, it is an integral part of reality – but then this reality is controlled by laws unknown to us. Either the devil is an illusion, an imaginary being; or else he really exists, precisely like other living beings – with this reservation, that we encounter him infrequently.
>
> The fantastic occupies the duration of this uncertainty. Once we choose one answer or the other, we leave the fantastic for a neighboring genre, the uncanny or the marvelous. The fantastic is that hesitation experienced by a person who knows only the laws of nature, confronting an apparently supernatural event.
>
> (Todorov 1975: 25)

It should be pointed out that although many works involve the hesitation to which Todorov refers, very few sustain it throughout. Todorov himself cites The *Saragossa Manuscript* and *The Turn of the Screw*. Aside from adaptations of these works, cinematic examples are few and far between. Examples include *Vampyr* (1928) (Nash 1976), *Martin* (1978) (Grant 1994: 114–15) and *The Birds* (1963).

Negotiating the balance between different regimes of verisimilitude plays a key role in the relations established between spectators, genres and individual films. In markedly non-verisimilitudinous genres these relations can be particularly complex – and particularly fragile (Neale 1980: 36–47, 1990b). The predominance of ideologies of realism in our culture tends to mean that, unless marked as high art, many avowedly non-realist genres are viewed as frivolously escapist, as 'mere fantasy', and thus as suitable only for children, or for 'mindless', 'irresponsible' adults. This, of course, is to refuse to acknowledge the generic status of realism itself (Todorov 1981: 18–20), and the element of fantasy inherent in all forms of artistic representation (Cowie 1984; Freud [1908] 1985a). However, such refusals have consequences. One is that adults who find themselves viewing examples of these genres have often to disown their enjoyment by maintaining that such genres – and such pleasures – are not really for them, but for children, teenagers, others less 'responsible' (less 'adult') than they are themselves (Bergala 1978). Another is that films which are modelled on these genres often take account of disavowals of this kind by overtly addressing the topics of adulthood and responsibility, childhood and the infantile, and credulity, fantasy and belief.

There are numerous manifestations and examples of this. Noel Carroll (1981) has identified two plot structures characteristic of horror films and of horror/sci-fi hybrids. The first he calls 'the Discovery Plot'. It has four main stages, 'onset', 'discovery', 'confirmation' and 'confrontation', and it is worth noting that as Carroll describes them, 'discovery' involves not just the testing – and failure – of responsibility and the capacity for belief of those in (adult) authority, but an identification of the one with the other, while 'confirmation' involves their eventual realignment. Thus the structure as a whole involves not only a 'play between knowing and not knowing', but an articulation of that play across themes and positions of responsibility, power and belief. It is also worth noting, particularly in the light of Carroll's concluding remarks, that 'teen horror' variants like *A Nightmare on Elm Street* (1984) nearly always insist on the adult status of those in authority, on the 'non-adult' status of those who really know and who are most under threat, on the culpability, irresponsibility and ignorance of the former, and on the extent to which the latter have to assume power themselves in order to survive:

> Perhaps the most serviceable narrative armature in the horror film genre is what I call the Discovery Plot. It is used in *Dracula*, *The Exorcist*, *Jaws I* and *II*, *It Came from Outer Space*, *Curse of the Demon*, *Close Encounters of the Third Kind*, *It Came from Beneath the Sea* and myriad other films. It has four essential movements. The first is onset: the monster's presence is established, e.g., by an attack, as in *Jaws*. Next, the monster's existence is discovered by an individual or group, but for one reason or another its existence or continued existence, or the nature of the threat it actually poses, is not acknowledged by the powers that be, 'There are no such things as vampires,' the police chief might say at this point. Discovery, therefore, flows into the next plot movement which is confirmation. The discoverers or believers must convince some other group of the existence and proportions of the mortal danger at hand. Often this section of the plot is the most elaborate, and suspenseful. As the UN refuses to accept the reality of the onslaught of killer bees or invaders from Mars, precious time is lost, during which the creature or creatures often gain power and advantage . . .
>
> After the hesitations of confirmation, the Discovery Plot culminates in confrontation. Mankind meets its monster, most often winning, but on occasion, like the remake of *Invasion of the Body Snatchers*, losing.

What is particularly of interest in this plot structure is the tension caused by the delay between discovery and confirmation. Thematically, it involves the audience not only in the drama of proof but also in the play between knowing and not knowing, between acknowledgement and nonacknowledgement, that has the growing awareness of sexuality in the adolescent as its archetype. This conflict can become very pronounced when the gainsayers in question – generals, police chiefs, scientists, heads of institutions, etc. – are obviously parental authority figures.

(Carroll 1981: 23)

The second plot is the Overreacher Plot. Where the Discovery Plot involves endowing childlike or adolescent credulity, rather than adult scepticism, with the virtues of true responsibility, the Overreacher Plot makes a virtue of childlike powerlessness and superstition, and vilifies adult, scientific knowledge:

Another important plot structure is that of the Overreacher. *Frankenstein, Jeckyll and Hyde* [sic], and *Man with the X-Ray Eyes* [sic] are all examples of this approach. Whereas the Discovery Plot often stresses the short-sightedness of science, the Overreacher Plot criticizes science's will to knowledge. The Overreacher Plot has four basic movements. The first comprises the preparation for the experiment, generally including a philosophical, popular-mechanics explanation or debate about the experimenter's motivation. The overreacher himself (usually Dr. Soandso) can become quite megalomaniacal here, a quality commented upon, for instance, by the dizzyingly vertical laboratory sets in *Frankenstein* and *Bride of Frankenstein*. Next comes the experiment itself, whose partial success allows for some more megalomania. But the experiment goes awry, leading to the destruction of innocent victims and/or to damage or threat to the experimenter or his loved ones. At this point, some overreachers renounce their blasphemy; the ones who don't are mad scientists. Finally, there is a confrontation with the monster, generally in the penultimate scene of the film.

(Carroll 1981: 23)

Films using neither of these plots are nevertheless marked by the same set of concerns. *Curse of the Cat People* (1943), for example, sets up an opposition between the imaginative sensitivity of a young girl and the prosaic matter-of-factness of her father. The girl believes she has an 'invisible companion' in the form of the ghost of her father's first wife. Her father refuses to believe her and threatens her with punishment. But his disbelief places her in danger when she subsequently runs away. It is thus seen not only as repressive and cruel, but also as irresponsible, a mark of failure in his role as adult and father.

37

Only when he tells his daughter that he believes her, only when he acknowledges her invisible companion, is he seen to be a truly responsible adult. Only then does he become a proper father – a *visible* companion for his child. In this way the film works to justify itself in terms of adult issues and concerns as well as in terms of childish or childlike ones.

A further set of remarks might be made at this point about non-verisimilitudinous genres and audience expectations. Viewers of horror or science fiction may expect the unlikely. But precisely for this reason they will often also be unable to anticipate the norms, rules and laws that govern the fictional world in any one particular instance. And this means that the films themselves will have to explain them. Of course, all fiction films involve exposition, the provision of information about the nature and state of the fictional world. But many films are able to rely on the norms, rules and laws – the systems of 'everyday knowledge' – embodied in regimes of socio-cultural verisimilitude in accounting at a fundamental level for the actions, events and behaviour they represent: most films do not have to explain the laws of gravity, or that humans are mortal, or that they are incapable of mutating into the life forms they ingest. However, in horror films and science fiction such laws may well not apply. Other laws, other norms, may have taken their place. Not only that, but these laws and norms may well be specific to one particular film, to one particular fictional universe. Thus they have to be explained; and thus the expositional burden carried by films of this kind is increased. Aside from their role in scenarios of scepticism, power, authority, belief and credulity, this is another reason why such films are so full of scientists, sages, doctors, seers and other experts in arcane norms and laws.

So far, verisimilitude, expectation and knowledge have only been considered in relation to genres as traditionally defined and conceived. However, in addition to the likes of the detective film, the horror film and science fiction, they are also relevant to the feature film, the documentary, the serial and the newsreel. For instance, if we know that the film we are watching is a feature film, we expect it to last a minimum – and also a maximum – amount of time. And certainly in the case of a Hollywood feature, we expect that time to be filled by a narrative. Thus if we were to go to a local commercial cinema and were to find ourselves watching *Empire* (1964), a film which is eight hours long, and which lacks narrative, characters and movement, we might well be nonplussed. For on these grounds alone, *Empire* would not qualify as a 'real' or 'proper' feature film. And even though it is essentially a filmed 'record' of the Empire State Building in New York, we would probably not consider it a proper documentary either – it is too long; its length appears to exceed the degree of interest or information its image track can provide; it lacks the conventional guidance usually provided by editing and a commentary; and so on.

Maybe, for all these reasons, we would not even consider *Empire* to be a real, a proper, a verisimilitudinous film at all. But this would depend upon the repertoire of genres with which we are familiar, and the institutional context within which we encountered the film. If instead of the local commercial cinema we were to encounter *Empire* at the Museum of Modern Art in New York or at the Filmmakers' Co-op in London, our expectations, and the generic systems around which they were organized, might well be very different. For in these contexts generic categories like 'the feature film' and 'the documentary' are not institutionalized as either dominant, or even particularly relevant. Here, the genres and regimes of verisimilitude associated with avant-garde art are more appropriate. The key term here is 'institutionalized'. These genres and regimes are made known to audiences in a number of ways: through statements, manifestos, programme notes, lectures, introductions, discussions and the like. Though different in many ways from the means by which Hollywood's genres are made known, they nevertheless perform a similar institutional function: they help provide a generic framework within which to comprehend films. It is important to bear this in mind when considering the institutional practices of Hollywood itself.

INSTITUTIONAL ASPECTS OF GENRE AND HOLLYWOOD

As John Ellis has pointed out, central to the practices of Hollywood is the construction of a 'narrative image' for each individual film: 'An idea of the film is widely circulated and promoted, an idea which can be called the "narrative image" of the film, the cinema's anticipatory reply to the question, "What is the film like?"' (1981: 30). As he goes on to note, the institutionalized public discourse of the press, television and radio often plays an important part in the construction of such images. So, too, do the 'unofficial', 'word of mouth' discourses of everyday life. But a key role is also played by the discourse of the industry itself, especially in the earliest phases of a film's public circulation, and in particular by those sectors of the industry concerned with publicity and marketing: distribution, exhibition, studio marketing departments, and so on.

Genre is, of course, an important ingredient in any film's narrative image. The indication and circulation of what the industry considers to be the generic framework – or frameworks – most appropriate to the viewing of a film is therefore one of the most important functions performed by advertising copy, and by posters, stills and trailers. In addition, reviews nearly always contain terms indicative of a film's generic status, while posters and trailers often offer verbal generic description – 'The Greatest War Picture Ever Made', 'The Comedy of the Decade', 'The Drama of the Year', and so on – as anchorage for the generically pertinent iconography they almost always also contain. Advertising campaigns, posters, stills and marquee displays in cinemas help comprise what Lukow and Ricci (1984) have called cinema's 'inter-textual relay'. They mention credit sequences and titles as well, and certainly it is hard from a generic point of view to think of the credit sequence of *The Wild Bunch* (1969) as the opening sequence in a musical, or of films with titles like *Night of the Living Dead* (1968) and *Fright Night* (1985) as anything other than horror films.

Cinemas, cinema programming and cinema specialization could also be considered components in the relay, especially if broader conceptions of genre, conceptions that include the short, the newsreel and the feature film, are taken into account. During Hollywood's studio era most cinemas in the United States showed mixed programmes of films: not just musicals or horror films, but also detective films, comedies and dramas; not just feature films, but also newsreels and shorts of various kinds. According to Douglas Gomery (1992: 137–54) and Barbara Stones (1993: 82–3, 119–23) there were cinemas, and even small circuits, which specialized in westerns and action films, and one or two cinemas, particularly in New York, which specialized in cartoons and newsreels. They and their names would thus have functioned as generic cues in their own right. But alongside cinemas and circuits which showed 'ethnic' films, 'art' films, and later – increasingly – pornography, they were, and are, the exception. The precise structure of the programmes shown in most cinemas during the studio era is unclear, and probably varied considerably. However, it *is* clear that if you had just sat through two feature films, a newsreel, short or trailer was likely to follow. Hence you would probably have had to adjust your generic expectations.

In addition to the provision of generic images for individual films, the industry's inter-textual relay also provides images of and for genres themselves. This is the case whatever the genre, feature film or short, musical or thriller. The former are genres which are, or were, exclusive to the cinema (they can now be found in television too). The latter also exist in the theatre and/or in popular fiction. Some can be found in television and radio. And some predate the cinema itself. The inter-textual relays that accompany the theatre, the publishing industry and other sectors of media thus also play a part in the circulation of such images. It is therefore worth drawing attention both to the general circulation of personnel from one institutional relay to another (an increasing phenomenon in an era of synergy and conglomeration), and to specific individuals like Warren William Baumgarter, Dean Cornwell, John Held Junior and William Rose, who not only designed film posters but also designed illustrations and covers for comic books, paperbacks and pulp magazines (and who were thus responsible in a literal sense for the images associated with a number of popular genres).

LABELS AND NAMES

In additition to images, Hollywood's inter-textual relay also circulates a number of generic labels, terms and names. The importance of labels and names has been touched on already. Their existence is one of the hallmarks of a genre, one of the signs of its institutional and social existence. This point has been stressed by Ryan (1981). During the course of her argument she refers to the work of Ben-Amos (1976) on folklore genres, and draws on the distinction he makes between 'ethnic' and 'analytical' categories, concepts and terms. Ben-Amos 'opposes the "ethnic genres" yielded by native taxonomy to the "analytical categories" made up by the specialist for their description and classification', she writes. In addition, 'he warns against the danger of "changing folk taxonomies, which are culture-bound and vary according to the speaker's cognitive system, into culture-free, analytical, unified and objective models of folk literature"' (1981: 113). Ryan herself reinforces this point. However, she goes on to propose a compromise, a way in which analytical categories and terms can still be of use:

> even if the generic system of every culture should be studied in its own right, there is no need to give up the possibility of describing its genres by means of cross-culturally applicable concepts. The gap between ethnic and analytical approaches to the problem of genre can be bridged by viewing analytical categories as building blocks for the characterization of genres, rather than as abstract generic concepts in themselves.
>
> (Ryan 1981: 113)

A similar compromise is adopted by Altman (1987) during the course of one of the few comparable discussions to be conducted in relation to the topic of genre in the cinema.

Altman is writing about culturally familiar – or 'native' – genres. His central concern is with the establishment of a generic corpus for subsequent analysis. In this context, he argues that the categories and terms provided by Hollywood and by the reviewers of its films have only a limited role to play. They may indicate the possible presence of a genre, but beyond that they are of little further use:

> The fact that a genre has previously been posited, defined, and delimited by Hollywood is taken only as *prime facie* evidence that generic levels of meaning are operative within or across a group of texts roughly designated by the Hollywood term and its usage. The industrial/journalistic term thus founds a hypothesis about the presence of meaningful activity, but does not necessarily contribute a definition or delimitation of the genre in question.
>
> (Altman 1987: 13)

Thus the location of industrial and journalistic terms is for Altman just the first step in a multi-stage process – and the only one in which such terms have a role to play. Having established an initial corpus, the task of 'the genre critic'

41

is to subject the corpus to analysis, and to find a means by which to define and describe the structures, functions and systems specific to most of the films within it. Thus far, institutional terms and analytical categories more or less dovetail with one another. However, the next stage that Altman proposes involves the redefinition and reconstruction of the corpus itself:

> Texts which correspond to a particular understanding of the genre, that is which provide ample material for a given method of analysis, will be retained within the generic corpus. Those which are not illuminated by the method developed . . . will simply be excluded from the final corpus.
>
> (Altman 1987: 14)

At this point, institutional and analytic categories begin to diverge. 'The genre critic' replaces the former with the latter and includes or excludes films on that basis. He or she, though, is at this point in danger of producing a version of the gap identified by Ryan and Ben-Amos and of separating genre and genre analysis from the conditions and the features that define genres themselves. To that extent he or she risks undermining the two final tasks that Altman proposes: the construction of a history of the genre itself, and an analysis of the ways in which it is 'moulded by, functions within, and in turn informs the society of which it is a part' (ibid.: 14–15). For genres, as Todorov (1990) has pointed out, are public and institutional – not personal or critical – in nature.[1] It is 'always possible', he writes

> to discover a property common to two texts, and thus to put them together in a class. Is there any virtue in calling such a combination a 'genre'? I believe we will have a useful and operative notion that remains in keeping with the prevailing usage of the word if we agree to call genres only the classes of texts that have been historically perceived as such. Evidence of such perception is found first and foremost in discourse dealing with genres (metadiscursive discourse) and, sporadically and indirectly, in literary texts themselves.
>
> (Todorov 1990: 17)

It is precisely because they 'exist as an institution' that genres can 'function as "horizons of expectation" for readers and as "models of writing" for authors' (ibid.: 17, note 9). (The term 'horizons of expectation' derives from Jauss 1982.)

It should be noted that Todorov's argument here is, as he himself points out, at odds with arguments he had previously made in favour of the notion of 'theoretical genres' – types or categories of work deducible as logical variants on the properties or conventions of particular forms of representation (Todorov 1975: 13–15; Ducrot and Todorov 1979: 149–52). Aside from

Todorov's own work on the marvellous, the uncanny and the fantastic (all of which are defined as variants on a set of motivational conventions), the notion of theoretical genres has rarely been explored. In her Ph.D. thesis on a category of films she calls 'the apocalypic', Sylvia Lynne Foil (1991) argues in favour of a 'conceptual approach' to genre, though in the end her own approach is closer to Altman's than it is to Todorov's. While further work in this area may be possible, it is probably best to distinguish theoretical genres from genres proper by renaming the former 'theoretical categories'.

In the passage cited above, Todorov is writing about literature, and High Literature at that. The 'metadiscursive discourse' to which he refers may therefore include the writings of critics and theorists, and the discourse produced by academies, universities, and other institutions of a similar kind. But as far as Hollywood is concerned, it is principally located in the industry's inter-textual relay. Testimony to the existence of genres – and evidence as to the boundaries of any particular generic corpus – is to be found primarily there. Moreover, it is only on the basis of this testimony that the history of any one genre and an analysis of its social functions and social significance can begin to be produced. For a genre's history is as much the history of a term as it is of the films to which the term has been applied; is as much a history of the consequently shifting boundaries of a corpus of texts as it is of the texts themselves.[2] The institutionalization of any generic term is a key aspect of the social existence – and hence the potential social significance – of any genre, the provenance or use of a term in Hollywood's inter-textual relay precisely an index of Hollywood's social presence and cultural power. In addition, sometimes the conjunction of a generic term, a corpus of films and the inter-textual relay can be of wider social and historical significance, a point exemplified by the early history of the western.

THE EARLY WESTERN

According both to Eric Partridge's *Dictionary of Slang and Unconventional English* (1961: 1345) and to the researches of Jean-Louis Leutrat (1987), the first use of the term 'western' as a generic noun (rather than as an adjective) occurred in or around 1910. Leutrat draws attention to the fact that this terminological event coincided with a number of important developments in the American film industry, among them the shooting of increasing numbers of 'western' films in and around California, and the increasing specialization of a number of companies, in particular Selig, Essanay, Bison and Flying A, in the production of such films. He also notes that it was not until the 1920s that the term itself was fully established:

> It was in that same year, 1910, that we encounter one of the first uses of the word 'Western' as a noun. The study of genres has as its point of departure testimony as to the existence of genres. A genre is what it is

43

collectively believed to be at any given point in time. Up until the mid-1920s, the word 'Western' mostly enabled one to be more precise about a traditional generic term. It remained an adjective. In his 1915 book, *Buck Purvin and the Movies*, Charles E. Van Loan includes a director named Jimmy Montague who 'had a reputation for making sensational cinematographic dramas'. These *dramas* are films which concern themselves indiscriminately with the civil war, with the circus, with Indians, with animals, etc. They are set just as effectively at sea as in the American West, the Great North, or the deserts of Africa and Asia. And in order to designate these groups of films, categories inherited from the theatre and the novel of the preceeding century are used: melodrama, drama, comedy, romance . . . 'Western' can further characterize any of these terms: it allows the specification of an atmosphere, a setting. In 1904, the Kleine Optical Company's catalogue proposed five generic categories – the Western was not among them. An article on nickelodeons published in the *Saturday Evening Post* in 1907 reprinted the publicity material produced by a film production company: each film title is followed by a brief phrase in parenthesis indicating its genre – the word 'western' does not appear at all. In 1910, an article in the *Moving Picture World* notes that 'There seems to exist among the exhibitors we questioned a powerful and increasing demand for [. . .] Indian and Western subjects [. . .].' In another article published in the same journal a year later, there is a report on films (Western and Indian films) being shot around Los Angeles: it is noted that most of Selig's, Kalem's and Biograph's films are 'westerns'.

(Leutrat 1987: 127–8; my translation)

One of the implications of Leutrat's research is that a film like *The Great Train Robbery* (1903), often retrospectively hailed as an early example of the western, is unlikely, in fact, to have been perceived as a western at the time the film was made.[3] Charles Musser makes a similar point, arguing that the contemporary success of *The Great Train Robbery* was due to its location within generic paradigms provided by melodrama, 'the chase film', 'the railway genre' and 'the crime film' rather than the western:

Kenneth McGowan attributed this success . . . to the fact that the film was 'the first important Western', William Everson and George Fenin find it important because it is 'the blueprint for all Westerns'. These, however, are retrospective readings. One reason for *The Great Train Robbery*'s popularity was its ability to incorporate so many trends, genres and strategies fundamental to the institution of cinema at that time. The film includes elements of both re-enactment of contemporary events (the train hold-up was modeled after recently reported

44

crimes) and refers to a well-known stage melodrama by its title. Perhaps most importantly, *The Great Train Robbery* was part of a violent crime genre which had been imported from England a few months earlier. Porter [the film's director] was consciously working (and cinema patrons viewing) within a framework established by Sheffield Photo's *Daring Daylight Burglary*, British Gaumont/Walter Haggar's *Desperate Poaching Affair* [*sic*] and R. W. Paul's *Trailed by Bloodhounds* . . . [Thus] When initially released, *The Great Train Robbery* was not primarily perceived in the context of the Western. Its success did encourage the production of other Westerns but other films of crime – Lubin's *Bold Bank Robbery*, Paley and Steiner's *Burned at the Stake*, and Porter's own *Capture of the Yegg Bank Robbers* . . . It was only when the Western genre emerged in the nickelodeon era that *The Great Train Robbery* was interpreted from this new perspective.

(Musser 1984: 56–7)[4]

The importance of 'the nickelodeon era' is also stressed in Robert Anderson's account of the early western (1979). Anderson is particularly concerned with the role played by the western in shifting the balance of power between American and non-American film companies in the domestic market in the US in the latter half of the 1900s. Like Leutrat, he stresses the role of companies like Selig and the American Film Manufacturing Company and the importance of shooting on location in the West. (An advertisement for the latter's Flying A westerns in the *Moving Picture World* (8 April 1911: 779) draws attention to the fact that they were 'made IN the West – OF the West – BY our Western Company'. Emphases in original.) And like Leutrat, he sees 1910 as 'a pivotal year' (1979: 25). The key period overall is the period between 1907 and 1911. It is then that the western emerges as a 'uniquely American product':

The explosive increase in production and popularity of perhaps the most definitively American type of narrative film, the Western, from 1907–1911 was accomplished through the successful manipulation of the American marketplace by domestic film companies who by self-consciously promoting a uniquely American product (in marked contrast to the stage dramas of European art photoplays), corralled the nickels and enthusiasm of motion picture patrons nationwide. By late 1909, in an article entitled 'An American School of Picture Drama', *Moving Picture World* referred to the Western as the 'foundation' of American dramatic narrative and recognized those pictures with Wild West or Indian themes as being 'the most popular subjects.'

(Anderson 1979: 22)

The emergence of 'An American School of Moving Picture Drama', and of a generic term for its product, is, then, coincident with the emergence of American film companies – and the American film industry in general – as the dominant force in the domestic market in America itself. It is coincident too, as Leutrat and as Abel (1998) point out, both with a resurgence of American nationalism and American imperialism and, in the wake of the official closure of the frontier in 1890, with the emergence of what Leutrat calls the 'synthetic' western (and a synthetic West) across an array of cultural practices in America, from rodeos and Wild West Shows to novels and pulp magazines, from comic books and paintings to the work of ethnographers, photographers, folklore societies and academic historians.[5] The appearance of the western as a body of films, and the appearance of 'the western' as a term at this time, is therefore of crucial and multiple national significance.[6]

The same kind of significance cannot, of course, be claimed for all generic terms. Nevertheless, the emergence and use of such terms is always of *some* significance, if only within the industry itself. Of significance too, as is implied by Musser's argument, is the distinction between terms used retrospectively by critics and theorists, and the terms in use within the industry's relay when a particular film – or when a particular group of films – is made. Two terms of particular interest here are '*film noir*', a critical term first used in the mid-to-late 1940s in France to describe a number of then contemporary Hollywood films, and 'melodrama', a term used both by Hollywood's relay and by a number of recent critics and theorists, though with rather different emphases and meanings, as we shall see later on in Part II.

NOTES

1 Of course, viewers, spectators and fans often devise their own 'unofficial' or improvised terms. Richard Maltby cites the example of a reader of *Picturegoer* magazine who expressed a preference for 'Love and Romance' films, but distinguished between 'Boy-meets-girl' romances and 'triangle stories' (1995: 108). As always, terms like these perform a generic function for the person – or the people – concerned. The same is true of the terms devised by critics and theorists. That does not mean, though, that they are always indicative of production trends or of genres as such.

2 Rick Altman unwittingly confirms this point when he notes that 'the first musicals built around entertainers and their music were not identified as "musicals",' that 'the use of "musical" as a free-standing term designating a specific genre did not achieve general acceptance until the 1930–1 season', and that 'Not until 1933, with the definitive merger of music-making and romantic comedy, did the term "musical" abandon its adjectival, descriptive function and become a noun' (1996a: 277). He himself argues that early musical films already constituted 'the type of category we call film genre', but that they had yet to become 'genre films'. However, it could be argued that early musical films were far too disparate in kind to constitute a genre, and that this is precisely reflected in the lack of a noun to describe them. See Barrios (1995), in particular the chapter headed 'Is It a Musical?' (309–22).

3 This does not mean, of course, that representations of 'the West' or of 'the

frontier' did not exist, or that these representations were unfamiliar to audiences in the early 1900s. Far from it. What it does mean is that they had yet to cohere into anything resembling a single genre. For a survey of the earliest films representing western scenes, views and activities, see Jones (1980). For a survey of representations of the West and the frontier prior to the advent of the western itself, see Buscombe (1988b: 18–22). For other short surveys, see the essays in Truettner (1991), in Aquila (1996: 21–105, 243–68), and in Milner, O'Connor and Sandweiss (1994: 671–833).

4 The references here are to MacGowan (1965: 114) and Fenin and Everson (1962: 49).

5 Leutrat's thesis is thus consonant with the work of Richard W. Etulain and Lee Clark Mitchell on the western novel. Etulain argues that 'the Western was born in the first twenty-five years of the present century' (1973: 76), and Mitchell that most of the fundamental codes of the western, especially those to do with landscape and gender, were either established or synthesized in recognizably modern generic form by Owen Wister in *The Virginian* in 1902 and by Zane Grey in *Riders of the Purple Sage* in 1912. He writes: 'Not until Owen Wister's *The Virginian* . . . does the Western reach its acknowledged embodiment, the first in a line of narratives that stretch throughout this century' (1996: 9). However, the extent to which these codes hegemonized all western films or only some, and hence the extent to which the synthetic western was – and is – a heterogeneous rather than a homogeneous phenomenon, remains a matter of research and debate. (See the section on the westerns in Chapter 3.)

6 The popularity of the western in Europe at this time, as noted by Vasey among others (1997: 274 n. 2), merely augments this significance: the western clearly helped establish a distinctively American presence in the European market and on European screens as well as American ones.

Part II

GENRES

3

MAJOR GENRES

Aside from *film noir* and melodrama, special cases which will be discussed at length and in turn in the next two chapters, genre critics and theorists have identified around a dozen major genres. Richard Maltby has suggested eight: 'The Western, the comedy, the musical, and the war movie are four uncontested categories', he writes. 'Different critics will then argue the relative independent merits of at least one of the thriller, the crime or gangster movie, and list the horror movie and science fiction as either one or two additional genres.' (1995: 116). To these I have added the detective film, the epic, the social problem film, the teenpic, the biopic and action-adventure. Most of these genres are uncontentious. The terms critics and theorists have used have generally coincided with those used by the industry itself, and the films categorized or discussed under the headings these terms have provided have for the most part been categorized or described in the same way by the industry's relay. However, anomalies and problems remain. The industry has often used a number of additional terms to describe and to sell its films. These terms have often been flexible, imprecise and hybrid rather than rigorous, pure and exact, and their application to individual films has often been transitory and opportunistic (Maltby 1995: 107–12). In addition, the feature film, the newsreel, the serial and the short have rarely been described or defined as genres.[1] And as will become apparent, many Hollywood films – and many Hollywood genres – are hybrid and multi-generic. This is as true of the feature film as it is of an obvious hybrid like musical comedy. Bordwell, Staiger and Thompson have examined the ways in which the Hollywood feature film combines romance with other kinds of stories and plots (1985: 16–17). And Barry Salt has noted the extent to which, since the 1910s, it has tended to alternate passages and scenes of pathos, humour and excitement ([1983] 1992: 111–13). In consequence, genres often overlap, and individual films are sometimes considered here under a number of different generic headings.

The quantity of writing on individual genres varies enormously. There are numerous books on the horror film and the western, very few on the epics, and fewer still on the biopic and the social problem film. This is a reflection in

51

part of theoretical and critical fashion, in part of the history of genre theory and the genres privileged within it, and in part of the history of Hollywood itself – of the genres dominant within its output at various points in time. Whatever the reasons, the consequence here is that the sections on individual genres, designed to summarize writing and research in the field as well as to pinpoint continuing issues, problems and gaps, are inevitably uneven in detail and length. This is not intended to imply that some genres are more important than others. The selectivity and unevenness of genre criticism, the extent to which it has canonized particular films or particular groups of films, and the extent to which it has tended as a result to produce a distorted picture of Hollywood's practices and Hollywood's output are issues which will arise a number of times during the course of this survey. They will be discussed in more detail in Chapter 7.

ACTION-ADVENTURE

The term 'action-adventure' is nowadays mainly used to describe what was perceived in the 1980s and 1990s to be a new and dominant trend in Hollywood's output, a trend exemplified by the *Alien* films (1979, 1986, 1993), the *Indiana Jones* films (1981, 1984, 1993), the *Rambo* films (1982, 1985, 1988), the *Die Hard* films (1988, 1990, 1995) and the *Terminator* films (1984, 1991), as well as by films like *Total Recall* (1990), *Point Break* (1991), *The Last of the Mohicans* (1992) and *Braveheart* (1995). This trend encompasses a range of films and genres – from swashbucklers to science fiction films, from thrillers to westerns to war films – and is thus a clear instance of Hollywood's propensity for generic hybridity and overlap. The term 'action-adventure' has been used, though, to pinpoint a number of obvious characteristics common to these genres and films: a propensity for spectacular physical action, a narrative structure involving fights, chases and explosions, and in addition to the deployment of state-of-the-art special effects, an emphasis in performance on athletic feats and stunts. The hyperbolic nature of this emphasis has often been accompanied by an emphasis on the 'hyperbolic bodies' and physical skills of the stars involved: Arnold Schwarzenegger, Sylvester Stallone, Dolph Lundgren, Bruce Willis, Brigitte Nielson, Linda Hamilton and others. It is thus not surprising that the two major books published to date on these films – *Hard Bodies: Hollywood Masculinity in the Reagan Era* by Jeffords (1994) and *Spectacular Bodies: Gender, Genre and the Action Cinema* by Tasker (1993) – both focus on the ideological implications of this emphasis and both contain the word 'bodies' in their titles.

In the wake of her previous book, *The Remasculinization of America: Gender and the Vietnam War* (1989), Jeffords' aim is 'on the one hand to argue for the centrality of the masculine body to popular culture and national identity while, on the other, to articulate how the polarizations of the body altered during the years of the Reagan and Bush presidencies' (1994: 13). Her argument in essence is that

> whereas the Reagan years offered the image of a 'hard body' to contrast directly to the 'soft body' of the Carter years, the late 1980s and early 1990s saw a reevaluation of that hard body, not for a return to the soft body but for a rearticulation of masculine strength and power through internal, personal, and family-oriented values. Both of these predominant models . . . are overlapping components of the Reagan Revolution, comprising on the one hand a strong militaristic foreign-policy position and on the other hand a domestic regime of an economy and a set of values dependent on the centrality of fatherhood.
>
> (Jeffords 1994: 13)

In arguing her case, Jeffords links a reading of the narrative structure of the films she discusses to the policy statements of Reagan, Bush and their spokespeople. However, she does not specify a mechanism through which the presidential ideologies she discusses find their way into the films. She is therefore forced to rely on analogy. This is a procedure – and a problem – common to numerous ideological analyses of genres and cycles as we shall see, though it should be said that in this case Jeffords's analysis dovetails with arguments made about 1980s action films by Britton (1986), Ryan and Kellner (1988: 217–43), Sartelle (1996), Traube (1992: 28–66) and Wood (1986: 162–88). However, others have taken a different view, both about the ideological significance and scope of 1980s action films, and about their aesthetic characteristics and values. Pfeil, for instance, argues that the category of 'white, heterosexual masculinity' that often underpins these analyses is not as monolithic as is often implied, that the films as a whole are often multivalent (combining appeals to the populist Left as well as the Right), and that distinctions need to be made among and between the films themselves, particularly between those produced by Joel Silver at Warners and Fox – the first two *Die Hard* films and the first two *Lethal Weapon* films – and others like *Batman* (1989) and *Total Recall* (1995: 1–36). For Pfeil the former are sites in which 'fantasies of class- and gender-based resistance to the advent of a post-feminist/post-Fordist world keep turning over, queasily, deliriously, into accommodations' (1995: 28), in which, within a 'very specifically white/male/hetero American capitalist dreamscape, inter- and/or multi-national at the top and multiracial at the bottom', 'all the old lines of force and division between races, classes and genders are both transgressed and redrawn' (ibid.: 32). While 'the rhythms of excitation and satisfaction in these films' assert male violence, 'their own speeded-up processes of gratification undermine any claim to male authority' (ibid.). The repeated spectacle of 'torn but still beautifully exposed slick-muscled bodies' raises rather than answers a number of questions: 'how do we distinguish between their (re)assertion of gendered difference and their submission to the camera . . . as objects of its gaze and our own? What, likewise, is the boundary line between the diehard assertion of rugged male individualism and its simultaneous feminization and spectacularization?' (ibid.: 29).

Similar points are made by Willis (1997: 27–59) and also by Tasker. Tasker points to the ambivalent populism of many of these action films, and to the fact that the muscular hero within them is often literally 'out of place': 'Increasingly . . . the powerful white hero is a figure who operates in the margins, while in many senses continuing to represent dominance. This is an important trait in many action pictures and is central to the pleasures of the text' (1993: 98). Equally central are style, spectacle, atmosphere and tone. Tasker is particularly interested in the knowing visual excess and the tongue-in-cheek humour characteristic of these films. She is therefore particularly insistent that ideological readings based solely on an analysis of their plots may be reductive, misleading, or both. As an example, she cites *Red Sonja* (1985), a sword-and-sorcery follow-up to Schwarzenegger's *Conan* films (1982 and 1984). Early on in *Red Sonja*, we learn that Sonja herself (Brigitte Nielsen) has rejected the sexual advances of Queen Gedren. She becomes a swordswoman, and it is in this guise that she encounters Schwarzenegger as Kalidor: 'An analysis of the ideological terms at work in a film like *Red Sonja* is not difficult – the film follows Sonja's journey to a "normal" sexual identity, or at least the rejection of lesbian desire. After the initial "threat" of lesbianism, Sonja becomes a masculinised swordswoman who refuses Kalidor/Schwarzenegger until he can beat her in a "fair fight"' (ibid.: 30). However, the comedy and the excess permeating the presentation of the fight and the 'texture' of the film as a whole 'call into question the very terms deployed – the "normal" sexual identity to which Sonja is led' (ibid.). Tasker continues, noting the extent to which exaggeration and parody are involved in the presentation of the body in these films. For her this means that the body and the terms of its gender can become the site of transgression and play, the focus of an attention that can make strange as well as reinforce norms of gender and sexual identity. Similar points are made by Holmlund in an article on *Lock Up* (1989) and *Tango and Cash* (1989), though while stressing the extent to which in these films heterosexual masculinity is presented as 'masquerade', she concludes by noting that 'Masculinity may be only a fantasy, but as the success of Sylvester Stallone's films, including their invocation by right-wing politicians like Reagan and Bush, so amply demonstrates, masquerades of masculinity are eminently popular, and undeniably potent' (1993: 225–6). Her conclusion thus dovetails as much with Jeffords's position as it does with Tasker's.

Related issues and disagreements are raised by the 'women warrior' films discussed by Tasker, films like *Fatal Beauty* (1987), *China O'Brien* (1988) and the *Alien* trilogy, and by what Brown (1996) and Willis (1997: 98–128) see as an increasing trend towards 'hardbody heroines' and 'combative femininity' in action films in the 1990s. An additional complication here is the fact that *Fatal Beauty* centres on a black female star, Whoopi Goldberg, and thus constitutes an exception to what most commentators have perceived not just as an ethnic bias in action-adventure, but as a systematic project of marginalization, demonization and subordination *vis-à-vis* non-whites whose immediate roots lie in the racist and imperialist policies of Reagan and Bush. (In addition to Jeffords, Ryan and Kellner and others cited above, see Marchetti 1989 and Ross 1990: 94–101.)

One way to contextualize, if not necessarily to resolve, these issues and debates is to contextualize the films themselves by locating them within a tradition. 'Action-adventure' is not a new term. It was used by *Film Daily* in 1927 to describe a Douglas Fairbanks film called *The Gaucho* (1927) (27 November 1927: 6). And it was used, among others, to categorize 'The New Season Product' in the *Motion Picture Herald* in 1939 (3 June 1939: 17). Used separately, the terms 'action' and 'adventure' have an even longer history, and films in the action-adventure tradition have been a staple in Hollywood's output since the 1910s.[2] With its immediate roots in nineteenth-century melodrama and in a principle strand of popular fiction, action-adventure has always encompassed an array of genres and sub-types: westerns, swashbucklers, war films, disaster films, space operas, epics, safari films, jungle films, and so on. As Thomas Sobchack points out, 'Although these groups of films may appear a disparate lot, their patterns of action and character relationships display characteristics which clearly link them together and distinguish them from other genres' ([1980] 1988: 9). 'In a sense,' he continues, echoing Cawelti (1976: 39–41),

all non-comic genre films are based on the structure of the romance of medieval literature: a protagonist either has or develops great and special skills and overcomes insurmountable obstacles in extraordinary situations to successfully achieve some desired goal, usually the restitution of order to the world invoked by the narrative. The protagonists confront the human, natural, or supernatural powers that have improperly assumed control over the world and eventually defeat them.

(Sobchack [1980] 1988: 9)

Set 'in the romantic past or in an inhospitable place in the present', the exotic milieux and the 'flamboyant actions of the characters' in the adventure film afford numerous opportunities for filmic spectacle (Sobchack [1980] 1988: 10). Its basic narrative structure, meanwhile, gives rise to two characteristic variations. 'One focuses on the lone hero – the swashbuckler, the explorer who searches for the golden idol, the great hunter who leads the expedition, the lord of the jungle.' The other, the 'survival' form, most apparent in war films, prison films and disaster films, 'focuses on a hero interacting with a microcosmic group, the sergeant of a patrol, the leader of a squadron, the person who leads a group of castaways out of danger and back to civilization' (ibid.: 12). As Marchetti points out, the plots in adventure films of all kinds are usually episodic, 'allowing for wide variations in tone, the inclusion of different locations and incidentally introduced characters, and moments of spectacle, generally involving fights, explosions, or other types of violence' (1989: 188). It might be noted that among the variations in tone to which Marchetti refers, tongue-in-cheek humour and tongue-in-cheek knowingness are as common in swashbucklers as they are in modern action-adventure films. And it might also be noted that even where locations are restricted, as they often are in prison and submarine films, space, the control of space, and the ability to move freely through space or from one space to another are always important.[3]

In his discussion of the swashbuckler, Sobchack notes that the hero is 'defined as much by his physical expressiveness as by his good deeds' ([1980] 1988: 13). He also argues that in the survival genres, 'women play a decisive role in the success or failure of the group', thus returning us to issues of gender and the body within the context of the adventure film as a whole. Displays of the male body and of the hero's physical prowess are traditional in all kinds of adventure films, especially those of the lone-hero variety. Swashbucklers themselves tend to rely more on costumes and *coiffeur* rather than muscles (though as Richards (1977: 15, 40) points out, displays of the naked male torso − often in scenes of torture or violence − are a regular feature of such films). But the reverse is the case in the Tarzan films and in epics like *Samson and Delilah* (1949). And just as modern performers like Schwarzenegger and Stallone are well-known for their physique, so too were Victor Mature, Burt Lancaster (who trained as an acrobat) and Johnny Weissmuller (who played Tarzan at MGM and Columbia, and who was once an Olympic swimmer).

These displays reach back beyond Elmo Lincoln's performances as Tarzan in the late 1910s and early 1920s and Douglas Fairbanks's performances in films like *The Three Musketeers* (1921), *Robin Hood* (1922) and *The Thief of Bagdad* (1924). (On the Fairbanks films, see Richards 1977: 12–13, 25–6, Koszarski 1990: 270–1 and Taves 1993a: 67–8). They include the performances of such muscular stars as House Peters, Richard Talmadge, Jack Tunney and Joe Boromo in the numerous adventure serials, 'railroad melodramas' and circus films that pervaded the 1920s, as well as those of Tom Mix, Ken Maynard and others in stunt-oriented westerns like *Riders of the Purple Sage* (1924) and *The Glorious Trail* (1928).[4] They also include performances of various kinds in the stunt-based aviation films of the late 1920s and early 1930s, the Errol Flynn films made at Warners in the mid-to-late 1930s and early 1940s, the Tyrone Power films made at Fox in the late 1940s, the post-war cycle of adventure films featuring the likes of Robert Taylor, Burt Lancaster, Alan Ladd and Cornell Wilde, such subsequent post-war epics as

Spartacus (1960), *Ben-Hur* (1959) and *El Cid* (1961), and the numerous adventure serials, Tarzan films and jungle melodramas that appeared through-out the 1930s, the 1940s and the 1950s.[5]

Hence, as Tasker points out, 'the appearance of . . . "muscular cinema" during the 1980s calls on a much longer tradition of representation' (1993: 1). The same might also be said of women warriors. As we have already seen, the 1910s were marked by the serial queens. And if 'the character of most successful serials after the war shifted to emphasize male heroics' (Koszarski 1990: 166), women warriors are by no means impossible to find. Texas Guinan, 'The Female "Bill Hart"' (*Exhibitors Herald and Motography*, 14 June 1919: 15), starred in a number of two-reel westerns in the late 1910s and early 1920s, successors to such earlier films as *Queen of the Prairies* (1910) and *A Girl of the West* (1911) and contemporaries of films like *The Girl Who Wouldn't Quit* (1918) and *The Crimson Challenge* (1922). In the early 1940s, Republic and Universal began to make westerns with Kay Aldridge and Jennifer Holt, and traces of these new roles for women were evident in a number of post-war B westerns as well (White 1996: 148–50). The adventure films of the 1920s included *Adventure* (1925), with Joan Lackland, and *Flaming Barriers* (1924), in which 'the heroine is required to play chauffeur to a fire truck' (*Film Daily*, 3 February 1929: 8). The aviation cycle included such films as *Flying Hostess* (1936), *Wings in the Dark* (1935), *Tail Spin* (1939) and *Women in the Wind* (1939) (Parks 1982: 114–16; Pendo 1985: 143–7). And the post-war adventure cycle included *At Sword's Point* (1952) and *Anne of the Indies* (1952) (Richards 1977: 18, 38; Taves 1993a: 29, 129–30).

There were specific contextual factors at work in each case. The female-centred adventure films of the 1910s were influenced by the advent of New Womanhood. The female-centred westerns of the 1910s and the 1920s were influenced in addition by the notion that women in the west were 'free and untrammeled by the conventions of society' ('Western Dramas Win Patrons', *Exhibitors Herald and Motography*, 4 January 1919: 89), and by a cultural tradition that included dime novel heroines, cowgirls, and female performers in Wild West Shows and in rodeos (Armitage 1981; Jones 1970; Savage 1996: 86–93). The reappearance of the western heroine in the 1940s was due in part to the departure of male stars like Gene Autry and Tim McCoy for military duty during the war ('Lady On Hossback Newest Fad In Westerns, But Will Fans Go for It?', *Variety*, 14 October 1942: 1, 55). And the advent of female-centred aviation films was partly due to the promotion by the aviation industry of an association between women and flying as a means of assuring the public that flying was safe (Cadogan 1992: 87; Corn 1979). However, as Taves points out, 'the traits and activities of the adventurer are possible for members of either race and either sex' (1993a: 122). In other words, there is nothing inherent in the structure and the stereotypes of the adventure film to specify its central protagonists as either male or female.

The same is arguably true when it comes to ethnicity and race. As Nerlich has pointed out, the word 'adventure' originally meant simply an unexpected or extraordinary event ([1977] 1987: 3–4). However, as he himself goes on to argue, the ideology of adventure in its modern sense – its association with the active seeking out of such events – was developed in conjunction firstly with the medieval cult of the courtly knight, secondly with merchant adventuring (and state-sponsored piracy) in the early modern period, and thirdly with the spread of empire during the course of the nineteenth century. Hence its links with colonialism, imperialism and racism, as well as with traditional ideals of masculinity, run very deep. These links have been explored in numerous books and articles on adventure films and adventure fiction.[6] They traverse an array of survivalist and lone hero genres, and are readily apparent in safari and jungle films, in 'lost world' adventure films, and in films about European empires and European imperial heroes as well as in westerns and war films.

However, they do so unevenly, and sometimes in contradictory and tension-filled ways. The connections between prison films and imperialism are tenuous to say the least, though they are clearly far less tenuous in prisoner-of-war films. The same is true of disaster films. Rhona Berenstein argues that the 'interstitial' role played by white women in many 1930s jungle films means that while the films themselves 'are complicit with the larger mappings of racist attitudes that punctuated the era as a whole', 'the racial mobility of heroines suggests that dominant culture's investment in a racial hierarchy, in asserting the primacy of whiteness and the mastery of white masculinity, is also tenuous at best' (1996: 197). And in his book on the historical adventure film, Brian Taves has argued that while imperial, colonial and ethnocentric assumptions underly the genre as a whole, its commitment to an ethos of altruism, liberty and justice, to 'the valiant fight for freedom and a just form of government' (1993a: 4) can generate all kinds of ideological contortions and an array of quite distinct political positions.

To an extent these positions correspond to those of the four major cycles Taves identifies as marking the genre's history, and to those of the five major sub-types he sees as comprising the genre as a whole. Following the production of early versions of *The Count of Monte Cristo* (1912) and *The Prisoner of Zenda* (1913), he argues that the first major cycle begins with the Douglas Fairbanks version of *The Mark of Zorro* in 1920. This cycle includes other Fairbanks films, like *The Iron Mask* (1929) and *Robin Hood* in (1922), and a series of adaptations of the novels of Rafael Sabatini – *Scaramouche* (1923), *The Sea Hawk* (1924), *Captain Blood* (1924) and *Bardeleys the Magnificent* (1926). It sets the pattern for a number of sub-types. A second cycle begins in 1934, with the release of *Treasure Island*, *The Lost Patrol* and *The Count of Monte Cristo*. It includes *Captain Blood* (1935), *The Adventures of Robin Hood* (1938), *The Mark of Zorro* (1940) and *The Sea Wolf* (1941), and although some of these films clearly deal in a displaced manner with the growth of fascism and the outbreak of the Second World War in Europe, America's entry into the war at the end of 1941 saw the end of the cycle. A third cycle begins in 1944 with the release of *Frenchman's Creek* and *The Princess and the Pirate*. Using the resources of colour much more frequently – and, after 1953, the resources of CinemaScope and other widescreen processes as well – the cycle encompasses such films as *Ivanhoe* (1952), *Moby Dick* (1956), *The Vikings* (1958) and *55 Days at Peking* (1963). It is marked as a whole by a 'loss of optimism' (Taves 1993a: 73), by more flawed and less virtuous heroes, and by an increase in the level of torment, torture and violence. The fourth cycle – whose films are often more cynical or tongue-in-cheek in tone, and which Taves describes as 'revisionist' (ibid.: 83) – begins with *The Three Musketeers* in 1974, and includes *Crossed Swords* (1977) and *Robin and Marian* (1976). (Arguably the success of *Robin Hood – Prince of Thieves* in 1991 inaugurated a fifth cycle, a cycle which includes *Rob Roy* (1995), *1492 – Conquest of Paradise* (1992) and *Braveheart* (1995).)

The sub-types Taves identifies are the swashbuckler, the pirate film, 'the sea adventure film', 'the empire adventure film', and 'the fortune hunter adventure film'. These sub-types vary not only in setting – from the castles of medieval Europe via the Spanish Main to colonial India and Africa – but also in the way they handle the topics of oppression, revolt and 'proper governance' (1993a: 13). Thus while some swashbucklers, including most of versions of *The Three Musketeers*, are conservative in implication, most, like *The Adventures of Robin Hood* and *The Mark of Zorro*, oppose what they characterize as tyranny, and often portray just – if limited – rebellions and struggles for freedom. By contrast, rebellions in empire adventure films, in films like *The Lives of a Bengal Lancer* (1935) and *Gunga Din* (1939), tend to emanate from the struggles of native populations against white colonial rule, and to be portrayed both as unjustified and as destructive, as far more tyrannical than any act or form of colonial government.

The politics of the other sub-groups tend to vary much more from film to film. Taves notes, though, that while in gender terms most historical adventure films tend to be firmly male-centred, the pirate film 'permits some of the most important roles for women in the adventure genre':

> The pirate adventure brings together diametrically opposed types of women, fellow adventurers and those who become objects and remain basically passive. The form is rife with women who occupy a background role, often abducted and won over by the pirate captain (*Raiders of the Seven Seas*). Yet the ranks of pirates also include unusually large numbers of fiery women of the sea who take active roles as the equal or superior of men (*Frenchman's Creek*; *Buccaneer's Girl*; *Anne of the Indies*; *Against All Flags*).
>
> (Taves 1993a: 29)

He goes on to argue that 'the independence of such characters is frequently undercut through their portrayals in situations where they become largely dependent on men' (ibid.). Here, the contradictions of the sub-group are as apparent as they are in the genre as a whole, where male codes of honour and dominance tend to rub shoulders with appeals to universal liberty and self-determination, where acts of rebellion tend to result in the institutionalization of benign but unelected regimes of authority,[7] and where 'while revolutionary movements are often valorized, many adventurers are also imperialists, who justify exploration and colonialism in the belief that they spread the benefits of their civilization to supposedly unenlightened lands' (ibid.: 222). Only occasionally have such contradictions been brought to the fore. But in that regard, as in its inherently contradictory (and ethnocentric) stance, the historical adventure film is no different from most other Hollywood genres.

BIOPICS

Despite being a regular if minor staple in Hollywood's output during the studio era, despite increasing steadily as a proportion of Hollywood's output since then, and despite its regular association with directors like Michael Curtiz, John Ford and Oliver Stone, very little has been written on the biopic. Custen's *Bio/Pics* (1992) is the only book-length study to date. This is largely because the biopic has lacked critical – rather than industrial – esteem. The target of historians and of film critics and theorists alike, it has been the butt of jokes rather more often than it has been the focus of serious analysis. (See a number of the entries in Carnes (1996) for some recent examples.) In consequence, only a handful of chapters and articles exist alongside Custen's book as published points of reference.

Custen defines the 'biographical film' as 'one which depicts the life of a historical person, past or present' (1992: 5), going on to argue that most biopics are 'minimally composed of the life, or the portion of a life, of a real person whose real name is used' (ibid.: 7). As Anderson, drawing on Bergen (1983), points out, the biopic is often hybrid and multi-generic: 'biographies of entertainers (*Funny Girl*) can be grouped together and also considered a subgenre of the musical, the lives of racketeers (*Al Capone*) share character-istics with the gangster movie, accounts of outlaws (*Left-Handed Gun*) follow the norms of the western, and so forth' (1988: 332). Studies of the hybrid nature of biopics are few and far between. But Hansen (1988) and Babington and Evans (1985: 114–40) discuss musical biopics. And Landy (1996: 151–90) discusses *The Scarlet Empress* (1932), McKee (1995) *All This and Heaven Too* (1940), and Landy and Villarejo (1995) *Queen Christina* (1933), both as biopics and as woman's films.

Landy (1996) and McKee (1995) help reinforce Custen's point that the biopic has been 'selective in its attention to profession, differential in the role it assigns to gender, and limited in its historical settings' (1992: 3). He notes that of the films in the 'purposive sample' he uses as the basis for his analysis, only 25 per cent centre on individual women, and of these the majority are entertainers, members of royalty, 'paramours', and members of caring professions like medicine. He also notes that the majority of biopics are set in the nineteenth and twentieth centuries, and that only 4 per cent centre on non-white Americans. Overall, he observes a division between biopics made before the Second World War, which tend to be dominated by figures associated with royalty, government and politics, and those made after the war which tend to be dominated by figures from the world of entertainment. One might argue on this basis that the pre-war biopic tends to address its spectators as citizens whereas the post-war biopic tends to address its spectators as consumers of popular culture (though of course there are exceptions like *The Mighty Barnum* (1934), on the one hand, and *Nixon* (1996) on the other). Within this schema, the numerous biopics of sporting figures made during the course of the 1940s, films like *Knut Rockne, All American* (1940), *Gentleman Jim* (1942) and *The Pride of the Yankees* (1942), would constitute an important transitional cycle, linking sport as an instance of popular culture to wartime populism and to martial values like fighting spirit, tactical awareness and the acceptance of loss and occasional defeat.

Custen's definition of the biopic is straightforward. It is one which corresponds, for the most part, to general and industrial usage. However, as is the case with most definitions of genres, there are one or two ambiguities and marginal cases. Films like *Scarface* (1932) and *Citizen Kane* (1941) have generally been understood as depicting the lives of historical persons – Al Capone and William Randolph Hurst respectively – but they do not use the persons' real names. In both cases this was because their biographical aspects could be, and were, disavowed. Custen is a little inconsistent here. *Scarface* and *Citizen Kane* are not included in the sample of films he discusses. But *The Star Maker* (1939) and *I Am a Fugitive From a Chain Gang* (1932) are included, despite the fact that they both invent fictional names for their real-life protagonists (Larry Earl for Gus Edwards in *The Star Maker* and James Allen for Robert E. Burns in *I Am a Fugitive From a Chain Gang*). Among other things, instances like this are indicative of the extent to which Hollywood sought to protect itself from certain forms of controversy – and from possible litigation, protest and any ensuing loss of revenue – during the studio era in particular.[8] They are also indicative of the extent to which Hollywood modelled the lives it depicted according to dramatic, generic and fictional formulae which it also used and applied to its fictions. Custen is well aware of both these points, as he demonstrates in his chapter on *Night and Day* (1946), which depicts the gay Cole Porter as a married heterosexual, in his references to the Hays Code, which was precisely linked to – and productive of – historical omissions and distortions and disavowable instances and forms of representation, and in his references to some of Darryl Zanuck's numerous memos. As a producer, Zanuck was something of a specialist in biopics. But he was constantly aware of the need to tailor the events they depicted and the stories they told so as to conform to what he saw as Hollywood's aesthetic values.

Hence his constant appeals to 'rooting interest', to finding ways of aligning audiences with biographical protagonists and involving them in their struggles. Hence his concern that in *Brigham Young – Frontiersman* (1940), 'we relieve the heavy drama by comedy, as was so effectively accomplished in *The Covered Wagon*' (1992: 159). And hence his oft-cited memo on *The Story of Alexander Graham Bell* (1939): 'The drama of the story does not lie in the invention of the telephone any more than the drama of Zola's life [in *The Life of Emile Zola* (1937)] was in his writing. Our main drama lies in Bell's fight against the world to convince them he had something great' (ibid.: 134). It is within these contexts that the inaccuracies and anomalies for which biopics are well known need to be placed and understood.

A second area of potential ambiguity arises where films centre on more than one real-life individual. *Bonnie and Clyde* (1967) centres on Bonnie *and* Clyde, *The Dolly Sisters* (1945) on The Dolly Sisters, and so on. These particular instances are unproblematic. But despite the indications in its title, a film like *Cleopatra* (1963) varies the focus of its attention quite considerably, beginning with Caesar, then moving on to Caesar and Cleopatra, Caesar and Mark Antony, and so on. Cleopatra herself (Elizabeth Taylor) is much less central to substantial portions of the film than might be expected. Similarly, the focus in *Words and Music* (1947) is much more on Lorenz Hart (Mickey Rooney) than on Oscar Hammerstein II (Tom Drake). The latter acts as the former's confidant and friend (a regular figure in the biopic, as Custen points out). He also functions as a point of comparison and contrast. But he is by no means as central to its drama.

This second area of ambiguity sometimes coincides with a third. Custen refers to 'the life' and to 'portions of the life' in his definition. As he himself points out, there are very few biopics which span any individual's life from beginning to end. Films like *The Adventures of Mark Twain* (1944) and *The Great Caruso* (1951) are the exception rather than the rule. Most biopics focus on the span of a person's career, the years that coincide with their rise to fame, rather than on his or her life as a whole. Alternatively, as with *Young Tom Edison* (1940) and *Young Mr Lincoln* (1939), they focus on the years that preceded and prefigured them. Films become more generically ambiguous when their span is more restricted, perhaps to a single episode, perhaps to a single, self-contained stage in a person's life. As biopics, *Frontier Marshal* (1939), *My Darling Clementine* (1946) and *Tombstone* are thus much more marginal than *Wyatt Earp* (1994).

As Custen points out, starting *in medias res* rather than at the beginning of a life allows for a focus on the individual as an autonomous agent and the construction of a model of causality and influence in which the role of the family is either downplayed or displaced (1992: 150–6). On the other hand, films which start at the beginning or which focus on the early years of a famous person tend to emphasize the family's role. Either way, in so far as the individual is 'gifted' or 'destined' rather than self-made, and in so far as he or she is also reliant on – or at the mercy of – fate or chance or a lucky or unlucky break, there can emerge a sense in which the individual is the instrument or pawn of forces over which they have in fact very little control. (This is markedly true of biblical biopics – *King of Kings* (1961), *Barabbas* (1962) and *The Ten Commandments* (1956), for instance – and of films about figures like Abraham Lincoln.) This sense is often augmented by the fore-shadowings and omens for which biopics are famous, and by the teleological structure with which the lives they represent are often endowed. It can also be augmented by the ways in which the nodal points in that structure – the turning points or 'epiphanies', to use Denzin's terms (1989) – are set up and handled.

Among the biopic's ideological and dramatic patterns, Custen highlights the tension between the innovative individual – the novel entertainer, the reforming politician, the ground-breaking scientist – and established institutions and traditions: 'A central conflict of the biopic . . . is the hero's antagonistic relations with members of a given community. One might even go so far as to postulate that within this conflict, the hero is attempting to reformulate the boundaries of a given community' (1992: 72). This conflict is often the basis for rooting interest. It helps give rise to characteristic scenes of confrontation and resistance, and to the added urgency with which events like 'the dramatic breakthrough' and 'the lucky break' are invested. The eponymous protagonists of biopics as diverse as *Sister Kenny* (1946), *The Court-Martial of Billy Mitchell* (1956) and *The Buddy Holly Story* (1978) thus spend as much time fighting those who police their fields of endeavour as they do pursuing those endeavours themselves.

Among the genre's formal conventions and motifs, Custen highlights the prevalence montage sequences, flashback structures and trial scenes: one in five of the biopics in Custen's sample contain at least one flashback; just under a half contain trial scenes, or scenes in which the biopic's protagonist addresses or performs in front of a crowd, a mob or some other manifestation of the public; and over 80 per cent contain montage sequences of one kind or another. (Custen's sample of a hundred films runs from the late 1920s to the late 1950s. Flashbacks were used in biopics earlier than that – in *The Lincoln Cycle* (1917), for instance, and in *Napoleon, Man of Destiny* (1909) – and by my calculations their use has increased since the 1960s to around one in four.) Flashbacks and montage sequences clearly serve several functional purposes. They help condense and abbreviate the presentation of the protagonist's life or career, and they help to mark, to motivate and to bridge the ellipses necessary in most biopics, even those which deal with only a part of a person's life.[9] (The use of voice-over, which is as common as the flashback in biopics, and which is often used in conjunction with it, usually helps serve a similar purpose.) In addition, they help endow the life with a pattern (whose significance a voice-over can help to articulate). And while flashbacks can also endow the events presented with the quality of 'historicity', montage sequences often help assert 'the qualities of greatness' and 'the teleology of fame' (Custen 1992: 185) through 'rapidly shifting headlines, theater posters, record labels, or charts to show box-office receipts' and other markers of public recognition. Along with trial scenes, auditions and performances, they thus also function as modes of display.

Trial scenes and their analogues function as markers, not just of public recognition but also of 'public judgement' (ibid.: 136). They offer 'a clear rooting interest in the roles of defendant and prosecutor' (ibid.: 186), a means of 'laying bare the narrative device, of telling the audience what the film is really about' (ibid.: 136), and a way of winning the audience over 'by the virtue of a case or the genius of an entertainer' (ibid.: 187). Custen here tends to assume that public judgement is always favourable. However, as Anderson points out, the biopic can accommodate variations of attitude and tone, 'with the hagiographic biopic offering a model of achievement [and approbation] . . . at one extreme, and a satire, such as *Buffalo Bill and the Indians, or Sitting Bull's History Lesson* (1976), with its attitude of aggressive debunking, at the other' (1988: 332). It also possesses what she calls a 'dark side' (ibid.: 336).

Anderson refers in this context to the 'success has a price' motif. But she also notes that the biopic 'accommodates itself as easily to the cautionary tale as to the sweep of the inspirational fable' (1988: 332–3). And it is here that emphasis should be placed on the fact that biopics deal with notoriety as well as with fame, with tyrants, villains and outlaws as well as with exemplary figures, with those who are willing to ignore or destroy the rules and the boundaries of communities as well as those who wish to reformulate them. This is particularly clear in gangster biopics, where innovation and opposition lead to a reformulation of the boundaries of gangsterdom but a breaking of the boundaries of law and order, where the atypical qualities of most bio-graphical protagonists are marked as deviant, and where the drive for success is coded as a form of megalomania.

This last point takes us to the heart of the fantasies with which the biopic usually deals and to the ambivalence with which they are often presented. The biopic centres on self-seeking or unwittingly finding fame and fortune, public attention, and success. This self nearly always finds gratification, often marked in the montage sequences and trial scenes to which Custen refers, in scenes of contrition, in which those who have doubted or opposed the biopic's protagonists come forward to apologize, and in scenes and displays of public recognition – the giving of medals in films like *Sergeant York* (1941) and *To Hell and Back* (1955), formal tributes like those in *With a Song in My Heart* (1952) and *Edison, The Man* (1940), commemorative services and funeral orations like those in *Joan of Arc* (1948) and *Alexander the Great* (1956), and sequences of the kind which end *Schindler's List* (1993) and *Malcolm X* (1992). In biopics of exemplary lives, of lives that are celebrated, the narcissism involved here tends to be downplayed (often through the 'success has a price' motif), disavowed (often by attributing ambition to others), or else treated as a temptation to be overcome (biopics are full of scenes like the one in which Sigmund Romberg (José Ferrer) in *Deep in My Heart* (1954) admits he has been 'a smart alec'. Each has 'his own ego, his own talent', he admits, but each also has 'his own limitations').

It is this ego that is allowed full rein in gangster biopics, and in biopics like *The Toast of New York* (1937), in which Jim Fiske (Edward Arnold) boasts at one point that 'nothing can stop me. Whatever stands in my way must go down.' As a consequence Fiske, like most gangsters, gets his come-uppance. But again like most gangsters his dynamism is presented as compelling, a point of potential attraction as well as repulsion. The resulting ambiguities are a hallmark of numerous biopics, particularly those, like *Custer of the West* (1968) and *Patton* (1970), which belong neither to the exemplary nor cautionary camps, but which seek instead to bring some of the ambiguities involved to the fore.

They remain a hallmark today. For despite Custen's claim that the biopic is now largely the province of television (where the ordinariness rather than the star-like qualities of its protagonists tends to be stressed, and where fame is persistently associated with suffering and victimization) (1992: 214–25), the biopic has increased rather than diminished as a proportion of Hollywood's output since the 1950s.[10] It thus remains an important, if still largely neglected, object of study.

COMEDY

The publication in recent years of a number of books on comedy – among them Gehring (1994), Horton (1991a), Karnick and Jenkins (1995a), Neale and Krutnik (1990), Palmer (1987), Rowe (1995a), and Sikov (1989, 1994) – is clearly indicative of a significant revival of interest on the part of film critics, theorists and historians. In its various guises, comedy has always been a significant staple in Hollywood's output. It has also, since the days of Chaplin, been a topic of critical debate, though generally within evaluative paradigms compatible with liberal humanist values, hence within frameworks of concern that have tended to focus on issues of aesthetic integrity, self-expression, and direct or indirect social and cultural worth. (See among others, Agee [1949] 1967, Mast 1976, McCaffrey 1968 and Robinson 1969, and to some extent also Kerr 1975 and Cavell 1981.) Aesthetics, evaluation and socio-cultural issues are by no means absent from more recent books. But the agendas within which they are working are in general rather different from those governing earlier writing and research. They include feminism, gender and sexual politics; structuralism, semiotics, post-structuralism and psychoanalysis; cultural studies, race and ethnicity; and the 1980s turn towards archival and historical research.

The diversity of topics addressed and approaches adopted in these books is at least in part related to the diverse and multifaceted nature of comedy itself.

Encompassing a range of forms, sites and genres (from jokes to intricately plotted narratives, from slapstick to farce, from satire to parody, from shorts and cartoons to features), comedy can also entail an array of defining conventions (from the generation of laughter to the presence of happy endings to the representation of everyday life), and is able in addition to combine with or to parody virtually every other genre or form (Neale and Krutnik 1990: 10–25). It is therefore hardly surprising that discussions of comedy have drawn on a variety of disciplines – from philosophy to narrative theory, from anthropology to psychology, and psychoanalysis – and that most comprehensive overviews tend to combine a multidisciplinary approach with a breaking down of the subject into a number of distinct topics, aspects and themes.

Most discussions of comedy begin by acknowledging a basic distinction between what might be called its comic units – gags, jokes, funny moments and the like – and the narrative and non-narrative contexts in which they occur. This distinction is important, both because it links to issues of film history, and because it raises questions about definition and hence about the criteria governing comedy as a genre. For many commentators, gags, jokes and funny moments are fundamental to all forms of comedy, and hence to definitions of comedy either as a single genre or as a diverse but related cluster of genres and forms. An initial distinction can then be drawn between those in which they occur outside, or are dominant over, narrative contexts and narrative concerns, and those in which they are not. Hence Horton's proposal that

> comedies are interlocking sequences of jokes and gags that place narrative in the foreground, in which case comedy leans in varying degrees toward some dimension of the noncomic (realism, romance, fantasy), or that use narrative as only a loose excuse for holding together moments of comic business (as in a Marx Brothers' film).
>
> (Horton 1991b: 7)

This proposal is made in response to Mast's emphasis on narrative in his book *The Comic Mind* (1976), and in particular to his thesis that 'There are eight comic film plots' (ibid.: 4). It echoes the proposals and critiques of Jerry Palmer, who argues that Mast's typology suffers from logical inconsistencies – it includes the 'parody of genres' and the 'sequence of gags' as plots – and avoids the issue of funniness by focusing on the 'maximum' units of comedy (like plots) rather than 'minimum' units like jokes and gags (1987: 28). To be fair to Mast, it is worth pointing out that he emphasizes 'comic climate', the ways what happens in a plot is signalled as comedy rather than drama (1976: 9–13), and that for some time in the West comedy was defined as a narrative with a happy ending, a definition which avoids the issue of gags, jokes and comic climate altogether (Neale and Krutnik 1990: 11–17). Nevertheless, Palmer's, Horton's and subsequent critiques – like those of Karnick and

Jenkins (1995c: 72) – clearly point to the inadequacies of Mast's typology, and of any approach to comedy which ignores its minimum units.

Palmer himself is concerned to argue not only that gags, jokes and funny moments are fundamental to comedy, but also that they exhibit similar structural and logical features. These include a preparation stage and a culmination stage (often in the form of a verbal or visual punchline), an instance or moment of shock or surprise (a peripeteia or reversal of fortune), and a system of logic – 'the logic of the absurd' – in which the plausible and the implausible always combine, but in unequal measure: while plausibility is always present, implausibility is always dominant, and it is this dominance that allows us to perceive the events, actions and utterances with which we are presented in comedy as comic (rather than poetic or tragic), and that endows them with what Palmer calls 'comic insulation'.

Palmer (1987) goes on to argue that these features mark comic plots and situations as well – that although comic units of all kinds have their own shapes and structures, they are susceptible to a degree, at least, of narrative integration. Elsewhere, Gunning (1995a, 1995b) and Crafton ([1988] 1995) have debated the extent to which such integration is possible, the extent to which gags, jokes and other comic units necessarily undermine or diverge from the narrative contexts in which they may be found. For Crafton, gags and jokes are inherently digressive. If narrative can be defined 'as a system for providing the spectator with sufficient knowledge to make causal links between represented events . . . the gag's status as an irreconcilable difference becomes clear. Rather than providing knowledge, slapstick misdirects the viewer's attention, and obfuscates the linearity of case–effect relations' (ibid.: 119). For Gunning, some gags are susceptible to narrative integration and can themselves be perceived as possessing narrative features, especially if narrative is itself reconceived as a 'process of integration in which smaller units are absorbed into a larger overarching pattern and process of containment' (1995b: 121). Neale and Krutnik, meanwhile, seek to identify degrees of integration, ranging from purely digressive gags and jokes to fully integrated 'comic events' (1990: 43–61). They also draw on the work of Coursodon (1964, 1986) and of other French writers like Lebel (1967), Mars (1964), Pasquier ([1970] 1973) and Simon and Percheron (1976) in drawing up a scale of structural complexity in gags, ranging from the simple 'comic effect' (a funny expression, a pratfall, a single, self-contained piece of comic action) to the elaborate 'articulated gag,' which may involve a multi-stage chain of events and effects. A great deal of attention has been paid to gags, jokes and other comic units. (In addition to those cited above, see Carroll 1991, Jenkins 1986 and Sweeney 1991.) Aside from their intrinsic interest, there are two fundamental reasons for this. The first is that they are points at which laughter is designed to occur, and can therefore act as a focus for ideas, theories and debates about laughter and humour. The second is that they are bound up with the early history of comedy in the cinema, and with a number of specialist producers, directors and performers, from Mack Sennett to Jerry Lewis, from Frank Tashlin to Woody Allen, from Laurel and Hardy to Hope and Crosby, and from Charlie Chaplin and Buster Keaton to Danny Kaye, Steve Martin, Jim Carrey and a number of others.

Laughter and humour have, of course, been discussed for hundreds of years. No single theory has dominated the study of these topics in the cinema. Mast occasionally draws on Bergson ([1900] 1911) and Freud ([1905] 1976, [1927] 1985b). Eaton (1981), Neale (1981b) and Neale and Krutnik (1990: 71–82) all also draw on – and to some extent modify – Freud's ideas. Neale and Krutnik draw on the work of Olson (1968). And Palmer (1987) draws on the work of Douglas (1968).

Douglas also features in Palmer's later book, *Taking Humour Seriously* (1995), an overview of theories of laughter and humour. His central argument here is that laughter and humour are multi-dimensional, hence that most theories of humour are partial. He considers these theories under four main headings: 'occasion' (theories which stress the contexts and rules which permit, encourage or solicit humour and laughter); 'function' (theories which stress the social and psychological purposes of humour and laughter); 'structure' (in which work on the shape and the logic of gags and jokes comes into play); and what he calls 'limits' – the points, psychic and social, at which humour or laughter can simply fail or disappear. In his discussion of structure, he notes that most modern theories of humour involve notions of incongruity, and this is certainly true of most theories of jokes and gags in the cinema, including his own. However, he also notes that such notions and forms may be historically and culturally 'local,' specific to the West in the modern era, rather than universal (ibid.: 143).

Local or not, gags, jokes, and slapstick humour in general have formed the basis for a tradition in film comedy that is virtually as old as film itself. (Gunning 1995a contains a lengthy discussion of what is perhaps the first example, the Lumières' *L'Arroseur Arrosé* (1895).) Derived initially from existing forms of variety entertainment, notably vaudeville and music-hall, but also the circus, the comic strip, burlesque and revue, and fed by later forms like radio, television and night-clubs, this tradition has been treated as a site within which a whole series of comic performers, including most of those listed above, have been able not only to present their skills but also to subvert or to question narrative values and conventions – and occasionally socio-cultural ones as well.[11]

A particularly influential account of this tradition can be found in Seidman (1981). Under the heading of 'comedian comedy', Seidman proposes an array of distinct – and eccentric – characteristics, themes and devices linking performers and films within this tradition and differentiating both from those found elsewhere in Hollywood comedy and in Hollywood cinema in general. Seidman starts from the premiss that nearly all the performers within this tradition began their careers, honed their skills and established their personae outside the cinema, in media and in forms of entertainment geared to live or quasi-live performance, and hence to the possibility – or the illusion – of direct interaction with an audience. He goes on to note the prevalence in their films of devices which draw on and foreground these contexts and characteristics, and which thereby conflict with, contradict or undermine the norms and characteristics of most other Hollywood films and hence of most other Hollywood genres – asides and direct address to camera, allusions to the artificial nature of films and their devices, and allusions to the world of show business outside the fictional universe of any one particular film.

The comedians in comedian comedy are thus privileged figures, able to step outside and to play with the rules governing most narrative films and their genres. But they are also anomalies and misfits. In the films they often portray eccentric or deviant characters, characters given to dreaming, to disguise, to regression and to bouts of madness. To that extent, the opposition between eccentricity and social conformity to be found elsewhere in Hollywood comedy is here internalized as an aspect of the comedian's character, one which is inextricably linked to his or her performance skills, and one which is therefore irresolvable.

In recent years, the concept of comedian comedy has been refined, extended and modified (Krutnik 1984, 1995a). It has also been criticized as ahistorical (Jenkins 1992; Karnick and Jenkins 1995b: 3, 1995d: 155–62). The male-centredness of comedian comedy has been noted. And the extent to which masculinism and masculinity are rehearsed, explored, endorsed or undermined has been looked at in detail (Bukataman 1991; Krutnik 1994, 1995b; Rowe 1995a: 102–6; Sanders 1995; Winokur 1996: 171–8). In response, several studies have recently appeared of Mae West (Curry 1995; Hamilton 1996; Rowe 1995a: 116–24). And in addition, given the 'low' – and popular – status of comedian comedy, and given the prevalence within it of Jewish performers and personnel, a number of studies have introduced (or reintroduced) issues of ethnicity and class (Jenkins 1992; Musser [1988] 1990b, 1991; Winokur 1996).

Meanwhile, a number of studies have appeared which either question any absolute distinction between comedian and narrative, situational, or 'polite' forms of comedy, or which seek to draw attention to the presence of the latter in early film and thus to question or modify the ways in which the early history of comedy in the cinema – and the careers of particular comic performers – have been written (Bowser 1990: 179–84; Gartenberg 1988; Kramer 1988, 1989, 1995; Koszarski 1990: 174–80; Musser [1984] 1990a; Neale and Krutnik 1990: 109–31; Riblet 1995). This can be seen both as a reaction to the canonic dominance of slapstick comedy and slapstick performers in accounts of early cinema, and as a sign of the revival of interest in narrative and in situational traditions and forms.

Of these, romantic comedy has received the greatest attention in recent years, at least in part because of its revival by Hollywood in the mid-1980s under the guise of what Neale and Krutnik have termed 'the new romance' (Neale and Krutnik 1990: 171–3; Krutnik 1990; Neale 1992). Neale and Krutnik argue that the emergence of the new romance, as exemplified by films like *Blind Date* (1987), *Roxanne* (1987), *When Harry Met Sally* (1989) and *Only You* (1992), constituted the revival not just of an 'old-fashioned' genre, but also of an ideology of 'old-fashioned' heterosexual romance and hence of the rituals, signs and wishes that mark it. Its appearance followed a period in the 1970s and early 1980s during which significant challenges had been mounted to that ideology, and during which romantic comedy itself seemed either to have taken the form of Woody Allen-like 'nervous romances' (Neale and Krutnik 1990: 171–2; Krutnik 1990), or else to have disappeared altogether (Henderson 1978).

Recent work on new romances like *Moonstruck* (1987) by Rowe and others suggests that the new romance may not be as ideologically homogeneous as Neale and Krutnik have proposed (Rowe 1995a: 200–9, 1995b; Evans and Deleyto 1998). Meanwhile many of these debates echo debates about the 'screwball' films of the 1930s and 1940s, about films like *The Awful Truth* (1938) and *Bringing Up Baby* (1938). The screwball cycle, which emerged in 1934 with *It Happened One Night* and *Twentieth Century*, has on the one hand been seen as one of the few 'genres of equality' to have emerged during the course of the studio era (Woodward 1991). On the other, it has been seen as a cycle which, in and through its aesthetic characteristics – an energetic mix of slapstick, wisecracks, intricately plotted farce and the comedy of manners combined with vividly eccentric characterization and a disavowable under-current of sexual innuendo – served to revivify the institution of marriage and traditional gender relations at a time when both were being bolstered by government policy following periods of intense turbulence, challenge and change during the Jazz Age and the early years of the Great Depression.[12]

In contrast to the screwball films, very little has been written on the 'sex comedies' of the 1950s and 1960s – films like *Pillow Talk* (1959) and *Lover Come Back* (1961) – aside from Neale and Krutnik (1990: 169–71) and some of the writing on Doris Day contained in Clark, Merck and Simmonds (1981). There are signs of a revival of interest in the 'sophisticated' comedies of romance, sex, marriage and remarriage that preceded the screwball cycle in the late 1910s and the 1920s, especially those directed by Cecil B. DeMille (Higashi 1994: 142–66; Musser 1995). However, there are as yet no histories of romantic comedy in Hollywood which encompass all these trends. Neale (1992) proposes a number of basic conventions, including 'the meet cute', 'the wrong partner', the learning process the couple nearly always have to undergo, and the initial hostility it eventually dispels. And Babington and Evans (1989) discuss a number of individual romantic comedies from a number of distinct periods and cycles.

The existence of comedies of remarriage (the term derives from Cavell 1981) suggests an area of overlap between romantic comedy and domestic comedy. However, like other forms of narrative comedy, and in curious contrast to the attention given to domestic and familial drama, domestic comedy remains largely unexplored. The same is true of parody and satire. Recent books by Hutcheon (1985) and by Rose (1993) are largely concerned with literature, or with art forms other than the cinema. Both note that parody and satire involve imitation, citation and reference. And both note that they are not always comic in intention or effect. Neale and Krutnik refer briefly to satire and parody in the cinema (1990: 18–20). And Crafton discusses the role of caricature and parody in Warner Bros cartoons (1993).

Satire – the debunking of prevalent social norms, institutions and mores – is clearly central to any theory or discussion of comedy's socio-cultural role and significance. Comedy has often been viewed as either actually or potentially subversive, or at least an inherently positive force for social renewal and social change. This view has long been influential in literary studies of comedy, and often finds an echo in the cult of slapstick, comedian and low forms of comedy in particular. It has been recently revived in and through the writings of Bakhtin (1965), and in and through the work of those, like Fischer (1991), Paul (1991, 1994), Perlmutter (1991), Rowe (1995a, 1995b) and Winokur (1995), who have used or adopted Bakhtinian ideas, especially their stress on the upturning of the social world and its rules in all forms of carnival comedy.

Others, however, have offered a different view. Neale and Krutnik argue that deviations from the norm are conventional in comedy and hence that 'subversion' is a licensed and integral aspect of comedy's social and institutional existence (1990: 83–94). And more recently, Purdie (1993) has explicitly attacked the views of Bakhtin and others, arguing that all forms of comedy involve a recognition of the norms whose transgression they entail, and hence a claim to social membership at the expense not only of those who are comedy's butts, but also of those who don't get its jokes. Either way, it is likely that, as is the case with most genres, comedy's ideological significance and impact varies from film to film, cycle to cycle, and audience to audience, and is probably best assessed at specific and local levels rather than at the level of universal generalizations.

CONTEMPORARY CRIME: DETECTIVE FILMS, GANGSTER FILMS AND SUSPENSE THRILLERS

Criminals, crime, victims of crime, and official and unofficial agents of law, order and justice have featured in films since the turn of the century. The earliest American crime films include *A Career in Crime* (1900), *The Bold Bank Robbery* (1904), *The Adventures of Sherlock Holmes* (1905) and *The Lonely Villa* (1909). They were followed in the early 1910s by films like *The Monogrammed Cigarette* (1910), *One of the Honor Squad* (1912), *Suspense* (1913) and *Detective Burton's Triumph* (1914). (For a comprehensive listing and description of early crime films, see Langman and Finn 1994.)

The Monogrammed Cigarette shows how the daughter of a famous detective solves her first case. *The Bold Bank Robbery,* as its title suggests, depicts the robbery of a bank by a gang of thieves. And *The Lonely Villa* shows a woman and her children besieged in their home by burglars and their eventual last-minute rescue by the woman's husband. Broadly speaking, the differences in focus and emphasis among and between these three films – the first with its focus on an agent of investigation and its emphasis on detection, the second with its focus on the perpetrators of crime and its emphasis on criminal activity, and the third with its focus on the victims of crime and its emphasis on their response – correspond to the differences in focus and emphasis characteristic of the three principal genres of crime as a whole: the detective film, the gangster film and the suspense thriller. As is often the case in the American cinema, these genres and their characteristics often overlap and cross-fertilize in individual cycles and films. *The Big Combo* (1955) for instance, can be seen as a hybrid gangster and detective film. And *Underworld USA* (1960), a gangster film, nevertheless involves a mystery, a process of investigation, and an (unofficial) agent of justice – elements normally characteristic of investigative thrillers. In addition, as Derry (1988) points out, the suspense thriller can focus on individual criminals as well as on victims, and can thus encompass films like *The Day of the Jackal* (1973). Nevertheless, all three genres remain distinct, at least as tendencies, and by and large can be charted with respect to three major figures, the criminal, the victim, and the agent of law and order, and two major aesthetic effects, suspense and surprise.

Detective films

Discussion of the detective film has been dominated by discussion and debate about *film noir,* and hence by discussion and debate about the hardboiled detective and the hard-boiled tradition in general. Even those like Cawelti (1976) and Schatz (1981) who neither use nor debate *film noir* as a term, tend to focus on the hardboiled tradition and hence on films, like *The Maltese Falcon* (1941) and *Murder, My Sweet* (a.k.a. *Farewell, My Lovely*) (1944), which as we shall are central to most versions of the *noir* canon. As a result, detective films made prior to the 1940s, and those which in general are considered neither as *noir* nor as hardboiled, have often either been ignored or mentioned merely in passing as inauthentic counterpoints to *noir* and the hardboiled tradition. And as a result, very little has been written about these films beyond the occasional enumeration of titles, cycles and dates.[13] *Films noirs* and the hardboiled tradition will be discussed at some length in Chapter 4. Here, attention will be paid to the presentation of ideas and findings relevant to all detective films and investigative thrillers, beginning with research into the origins of detective and investigative fiction and some of the theories put forward to explain its genesis, its socio-cultural role, and its popular appeal. Because of the preoccupation in Film Studies with *noir* and the hardboiled tradition, many of these findings and ideas derive from research on detective fiction rather than from research on the detective film as such.

Most commentators cite the following as key to the development of detective and investigative fiction in the late eighteenth and nineteenth centuries: the gothic mystery; William Godwin's novel, *The Adventures of Caleb Williams*; the *Memoirs of Vidoq*, and the memoirs, fictional and real, of other detectives and policemen; Edgar Allan Poe's Dupin stories; 'city mystery' fiction (books like Eugene Sue's *The Mysteries of Paris* and George Lippard's *The Quaker City)*; Victorian sensation fiction (especially the novels of Charles Dickens, Wilkie Collins, Charles Reade and Mary Elizabeth Braddon) and its counterpart on the stage; the American dime novel; American pulp fiction; the novels of Emile Gobariau, and, of course, Sir Arthur Conan Doyle's Sherlock Holmes stories.[14]

There are differences in emphasis among and between different commentators, depending on the extent to which stress is laid on the elements of enigma and investigation or on the figure of the detective. These differences, and the distinctions that underlie them, are important, both because the investigation of a criminal enigma need not necessarily be undertaken by professional detectives, as witness many of Hitchcock's films, and because narratives centred on detectives – or the police – need not necessarily focus on a process of investigation, as witness *Detective Story* (1951), *The Offence* (1973) and *The Onion Field* (1979). Moreover even if, like *Serpico* (1973) and *Prince of the City* (1981), they do, they need neither stress nor entail a central enigma. Indeed, it is a basic tenet of those like Hamilton (1993), Hoppenstand (1982) and Panek (1987, 1990), who have written specifically about the American tradition of crime fiction, that American detective stories, with their roots in the dime novel and pulp literature, have always been concerned as much with action and adventure as they have been with the solving of mysteries. And as Matthew Solomon (unpublished) has shown, dime novels, pulp fiction and the action-adventure tradition were as much a source of early American (and European) detective films as the tradition that placed the emphasis on ratiocination.

Among the conditions of existence of modern investigative fiction and the figure of the fictional detective, commentators have cited the emergence in the nineteenth century of the professional detective, professional detective agencies and a professional police force; the secularization of concepts of crime, sin and punishment (Cawelti 1976: 54–5; Knight 1980: 13–15); urbanization, population growth, and the reconfiguration of class (Cawelti 1976: 101–5; Hutter [1975] 1983: 234–5; Kaemmel [1962] 1983; Porter 1981: 151–4); concomitant shifts in attitudes towards criminals and the police (the heroization of the latter and the demonization of the former) (Mandel 1984: 1–11; Porter 1981: 147–56); and the introduction of scientific and bureaucratic procedures for tracking down and capturing criminals as part and parcel of what some, following Foucault ([1975] 1977), have seen as a

wholesale shift towards a mode of social control based – literally and figura-
tively – on a particular model of surveillance (Cawelti 1976: 57–8; Palmer
1978: 200; Porter 1981: 123–5). The weight of some of these factors –
together with the fact that in most detective stories the enigma is resolved,
the criminals caught and punished, and order restored – has led many to see
the genre as almost inevitably conservative. (See in particular, Hilfer 1990,
Kaemmel [1962] 1983, Mandel 1984, and Porter 1981.)

Foucault himself wrote that the nineteenth century witnessed a fundamental change in the dominant 'episteme' of punishment and crime, a change
in which 'we have moved from the exposition of the facts or the confession to
the slow process of discovery; from the execution to the investigation' (1979:
69), and of which the detective story itself is both product and sign. One way
of reading this change is in terms of the development of a post-Romantic cult
of mystery (Alewyn [1974] 1983). Certainly, the generation of mystery and
the provision of (rational) solutions to it have played a central part in accounts
of the pleasures and structures involved in investigative fiction. Callois, for
example, argues that 'At bottom, the unmasking of a criminal is less important than the reduction of the impossible to the possible, of the inexplicable
to the explained, of the supernatural to the natural' (1983: 3), while psycho-
analytic accounts stress the relationship between enigma and mystery, the
desire to know, and fantasies of the primal scene (Neale 1980: 42–3;
Pederson-Krag [1949] 1983; Porter 1981: 100–12).

The aesthetics of investigative fiction have been discussed in some detail,
especially by those working within a structuralist, Formalist, or Neo-Fomalist
framework. Drawing on remarks made by one of the characters in Michel
Butor's novel, *Passing Time*, Todorov makes the point that most whodunnits
contain not one story but two: the story of the crime and the story of the
crime's investigation. Using this point as a basis, he goes on to distinguish
between the whodunnit proper and the thriller. The latter, he argues, 'suppresses the first and vitalizes the second. We are no longer told about a crime
anterior to the moment of the narrative; the narrative coincides with the
action' (1977: 47). Instead of curiosity, the effect here is one of suspense, and
it is worth noting that its characteristics dovetail with the action-adventure
tradition mentioned above.

The Formalist concept of retardation, meanwhile, is central to Porter's
account of detective fiction. Here, emphasis is placed on the means by which
the revelation of the first story – the story of the crime – is forestalled by
various digressive means and devices. These include peripeteia, 'a discovery or
event involving a deflection or rebound from progress toward resolution.
Examples of this are parallel intrigues, including rival investigations or love
motifs that intermittently suspend the principal investigation, and false trials
and false solutions' (1981: 32). They also include 'the antidetective or criminal, who may remain passive and not impede the Great Detective's search or
actively intervene in a variety of ways to prevent unmasking or capture. There

are also other blocking figures, such as recalcitrant or confused witnesses, false detectives like Watson or Lestrade, who take time misrepresenting the evidence, and false criminals or suspects' (ibid.). In addition, they include the taciturnity of the detective, false clues, 'the episodes themselves, which, as in an adventure novel or odyssey, intervene in greater or lesser numbers between a given point of departure and a fixed destination' (ibid.: 33), and passages of extended description and dialogue.

In *Narration and the Fiction Film* (1985), David Bordwell draws on a number of Formalist concepts in his discussion of the detective film. He reworks the concepts of *syuzhet* and *fabula* to mean the narrative events and cues with which the viewer is actually presented, on the one hand, and the narrative as a whole, including those events and actions the viewer is left to infer, on the other. From this perspective, the *fabula* in the detective film is seen to consist both of the story of the crime, and also, depending on the nature of the film, of portions of the story of the investigation. The *syuzhet* is marked by the manipulation of information concerning the story of the crime, and by retardation in the story of the investigation.

For Bordwell, the crux of the detective film is knowledge, and in particular its suppression and restriction, and this accounts both for its modes, styles and tactics of narration, and for the 'emotional states' to which it often gives rise:

> The detective film justifies its gaps and retardations by controlling knowledge, self-consciousness, and communicativeness. The genre aims to create curiosity about past story events (e.g., who killed whom), suspense about upcoming events, and surprise with respect to unexpected disclosures about either story [*fabula*] or syuzhet. To promote all three emotional states, the narration must limit the viewer's knowledge. This can be motivated realistically by making us share the restricted knowledge possessed by the investigator; we learn what the detective learns, when she or he learns it. There can be brief marks of an unrestricted narration as well . . . , but these function to enhance curiosity or suspense. By restricting the range of knowledge to that possessed by the detective, the narration can present information in a fairly unselfconscious way; we pick up fabula information by following the detective's enquiry. Again, the narration can signpost information more overtly, but this is occasional and codified.
>
> (Bordwell 1985: 65)

In illustrating these points, Bordwell refers to *The Big Sleep* (1946) and *Farewell, My Lovely*, both of them generally regarded as hardboiled and *noir*. In her discussion of *Terror By Night* (1946) in *Breaking the Glass Armor* (1988), Kristin Thompson draws on a similar set of precepts and concerns but applies them instead to a Sherlock Holmes film, one in a series made at Universal in the 1940s. Thompson's aim here is neither to elucidate the workings of the

75

investigative thriller, nor to validate *Terror By Night* as a genre film. It is rather to validate the use of Formalist ideas as a means by which to illuminate the workings of what she calls 'the ordinary film'. Concentrating on the general issues of knowledge and retardation, she argues that the film is not a straightforward murder mystery, as might be expected, but rather a film that 'in its second half . . . becomes more oriented toward suspense; we wonder not, who is the murderer, but will the detective find out who he is in time?' (ibid.: 62). The film contains investigative material and an initial mystery, but these elements function as delaying mechanisms, as means by which to build up those forms of suspense associated with the thriller rather than the classic Holmes whodunnit as such.

The extent to which films like *Terror By Night* have been neglected is a function not only of the dominance of *noir* in academic writing on the detective film, but also of the dominance of neo-*noir* in Hollywood's output since the late 1960s. While detectives of a relatively traditional kind have appeared with regularity on TV, they have, unlike investigative thrillers, been almost completely absent from the cinema.[15] Partly in consequence, contemporary critics, theorists and historians have rarely been prompted to examine traditional detective films in more detail.

Gangster films

The gangster film occupies a privileged place in genre theory. Along with the western, it was, as we have seen, a major reference point for those writing on genre in the late 1960s and early 1970s. One of the reasons for this was that the gangster film and the western had been discussed with considerable intelligence, sympathy and insight by one of the few commentators writing seriously on film and popular culture in America prior to the 1960s, Robert Warshow. As a result Warshow's essays, 'The Westerner' ([1954] 1975b) and 'The Gangster as Tragic Hero' ([1948] 1975a) have had a considerable influence – direct and indirect – on writing on both these genres.

'The Gangster as Tragic Hero' is a piece of cultural commentary rather than an essay on film history, and as its title suggests, it is concerned as much with the significance of the gangster as a figure as it is with the films in which he appears. It is full of provocative arguments, insights and observations. It argues that the gangster film is the modern equivalent of tragedy, that the gangster embodies the dilemmas of a culture dedicated not only to happiness, but also to success, and that 'At bottom the gangster is doomed because he is under the obligation to succeed, not because the means he employs are unlawful' ([1948] 1975a: 133). It observes that 'No convention of the gangster film is more strongly established than this: it is dangerous to be alone' (ibid.: 132–3). And it proposes that 'The gangster's whole life is an effort to assert himself as an individual, to draw himself out of the crowd' (ibid.: 133), that the gangster is a 'man of the city' (ibid.: 131), and that 'the typical gangster film presents a steady upward progress followed by a very precipitate fall' (ibid.: 132). However, it is limited in two distinct but related ways. On the one hand it is very generalized. Only three films are mentioned by title, *Scarface*, *Little Caesar* and *Kiss of Death* (1947), and only two of these films – the first two – are referred to in any detail. On the other, it is highly selective. *Little Caesar* and *Scarface* are early 1930s films. No mention is made of silent gangster films, of other early 1930s films, or of subsequent films other than *Kiss of Death*, which is only referred to in a footnote, and which in attempting to inject a note of 'optimism and social constructiveness' (ibid.: 129) is viewed, tellingly, as an impure and unsuccessful exception.

Limitations similar in kind – and often in substance – mark many subsequent accounts of the gangster film. Although Shadoian's book *Dreams and Dead Ends* (1977), for instance, appears to be a history of the gangster film from the early 1930s through to the early 1970s, and although it draws attention to shifts and changes in structure and style, discusses far more films in far more detail, and contains numerous thought-provoking insights, it is still highly selective – only 19 films are discussed in any detail – and it is still dedicated to general propositions about the cultural significance of the gangster figure and the gangster film. For Shadoian, as for Warshow, the gangster is an urban figure whose drive for success embodies the contradictions of the American dream. A 'creature who wants' (ibid.: 14), the gangster is also both an outsider, an outlaw, and a product of society, in constant contact – and conflict – with many of its citizens, institutions, norms, laws and rules. As such, 'meanings emerge, whether deliberately or not, about the nature of society and the kind of individual it creates' in most, if not all, gangster films (ibid.: 3). And as such, changes in the nature of the gangster film are linked to changes in the nature of American society, from the world of the Depression in the early 1930s to the world of corporations and anonymous bureaucracy in the 1950s, the 1960s, and the early 1970s.

I have no quarrel with these particular propositions, though the extent to which rural gangsters like Dillinger and Bonnie and Clyde and the films made about them support or complicate the notion that the gangster is an urban figure is, perhaps, open to question. (On the significance of rural gangsters like these, see Kooistra 1989: 119–40.) What is more problematic is the extent to which so many films, and so many cycles of films, are ignored in accounts like this, accounts which purport to be history as well as theory, but which in their quest for social and aesthetic significance tend to by-pass routine productions and films which simply do not fit the models and theories with which they are principally concerned. Thus films like *They Gave Him a Gun* (1937) and *Prison Train* (1938), and cycles like the Chinatown gangster films of the late 1920s and the early 1930s and the rubber racketeer films of the early 1940s, are totally absent not only from Shadoian's book but also from books by Clarens (1980), McCarty (1993), and Rosow

(1978), who are in general much more comprehensive, and much less pre-occupied with theoretical issues and critical judgements.[16]

What is even more problematic is the extent to which critical and theoretical preoccupations have shaped the very definition of the gangster film, helping to decide in advance which films really qualify as gangster films and which do not. In his entry on 'Crime Movies' in *The Oxford History of World Cinema*, Phil Hardy asserts that the gangster film has its origins 'in the late 1920s and early 1930s' (1996: 305). Although 'the genre did not spring to life fully formed', it soon received definition in films like *Underworld* (1927), *Little Caesar*, *The Public Enemy* (1931), and *Scarface* (1932) (ibid.). Hardy notes that *Underworld* and *Scarface* were both scripted by Ben Hecht. 'Hecht wrote the first', he argues 'when the genre did not exist as such and the second when the ground rules of the genre had been established' (ibid.). Yet Hardy himself acknowledges the existence of at least one earlier film about gangsters and gangs, *The Musketeers of Pig Alley* (1912). *The Musketeers of Pig Alley* is by no means unique. It was one of a number of films made in the 1910s about crime, gangs and gangsters. However, for unspecified reasons, but presumably because it does not contain 'the underworld/overworld narrative strand . . . the rise-and-fall scenario [and] . . . the iconographical elements' characteristic of *Underworld* and *Scarface*, *The Musketeers of Pig Alley* clearly does not count as a gangster film 'as such' (ibid.).

The chapter on the gangster film in Schatz's *Hollywood Genres* is similar in approach, but differs in detail. Schatz, too, notes the existence of *The Musketeers of Pig Alley* and *Underworld*. For him, though, even *Underworld* is a mere 'precursor' of the gangster film (1981: 85), a genre whose 'narrative formula seemed to spring from nowhere in the early 1930s' (ibid.: 81), and whose 'conventions were isolated and refined in a series of immensely popular films' (ibid.) – a series which seems to consist, as usual, of just three films, *Little Caesar*, *The Public Enemy* and *Scarface*. 'Because of their overt celebration of the gangster-hero and their less-than-flattering portrayal of contemporary urban life,' he continues, 'these films were as controversial as they were popular, and threats of censorship, boycott, and federal regulation forced the studios to restructure the gangster formula by the mid-1930s' (ibid.: 82). As a result, 'the gangster film enjoyed possibly the briefest classic period of any Hollywood genre. Its evolution was disrupted by external social forces, and its narrative formula was splintered into various derivative strains' (ibid.) (Schatz's account here is similar to that put forward by Karpf 1973.) These strains included 'the gangster-as-cop variation (*G-Men*, *Bullets or Ballots*, *Public Enemy's Wife*, *Racket Busters*, etc.), in which [James] Cagney, [Edward G.] Robinson, and other former screen gangsters were recast as lawman',[17] and 'the Cain-and-Abel variation (*Manhattan Melodrama*, *Dead End*, *Angels with Dirty Faces*, etc.) which counterbalanced the gangster with an equally strong (or perhaps stronger) prosocial figure' (ibid.: 99). They also included 'the syndicate film, the caper film, the cop film, and so on' (ibid.: 82). All-in-all, then, a considerable number of cycles, forms and films. But only three films qualify as classic gangster films, only three films adhere to the gangster formula. The rest are either 'precursors', 'watered-down variations' (ibid.: 99), or 'derivative strains'.

Three points need to be made here. The first is that Hardy and Schatz ignore a number of other early 1930s gangster films, not just *The Finger Points* (1931), *The Last Parade* (1931), *City Streets* (1931), *Quick Millions* (1931) and *The Secret Six* (1931), but also *The Doorway to Hell* (1930), which preceded *Little Caesar*, which was the first film in the early 1930s cycle to be modelled on the career of Al Capone, and which functioned at the time as a touchstone for those films that followed (Clarens 1980: 53–83; Peary 1976; Rosow 1978: 181–210; Sarris 1977). They also ignore such late 1920s 'precursors' as *The Racket* (1928), *Alibi* (1929), *Born Reckless* (1930) and *Thunderbolt* (1929) (Brownlow 1990: 207–11; Clarens 1980: 33–47; Jacobs 1939: 408–10; McCarty 1993: 32–48; Peary 1975, Rosow 1978: 120–34; Sarris 1977). And they ignore numerous earlier films like *The Making of Crooks* (1914), *The Gangsters and the Girl* (1914), *Regeneration* (1915) – which director Raoul Walsh himself described as 'the first feature-length gangster picture ever made' (1974: 115) – and *The Penalty* (1920) (Brownlow 1990: 189–98; Everson 1978: 227–9; McCarty 1993: 5–8, 15–18; Rosow 1978: 79–80, 88). The second point is that in doing so they are led to view films like *The Musketeers of Pig Alley* and *Underworld* as isolated examples rather than as participants in distinct generic trends, and to underestimate the extent to which gangsters and gangster films had existed in various well-established forms prior to the advent of *Little Caesar*. As a result, they also tend to underestimate the extent to which the cultural and ideological significance of gangsters and gangster films had already undergone a series of transformations prior to the early 1930s, and the extent to which the 'classic formula' was itself 'strain', a 'variation' on formulae common in the late 1920s and early 1930s. Thirdly and finally, while it is perfectly true that the classic formula was abandoned for public relations and censorship reasons (for a detailed account, see Maltby 1993b), it is also true that the ensuing formulae were real, that they themselves were abandoned or modified, and that, like the classic formula itself, they were soon to take their place in a history marked more by abrupt and intermittent transformations and short-lived cycles than by smoothly evolving continuities.

Much of this history remains to be written. However, accounts of gangsters, gangs and gangsterdom prior to Prohibition can be found in Asbury (1927), Fried ([1980] 1993: 1–88), Prassel (1993: 167–93[18]) and Sante (1991: 197–235), and accounts of the shifting significance of the Prohibition gangster during the Jazz Age and the Depression can be found in Rosow (1978: 86–210), Ruth (1996) (who among other things has a number of particularly interesting things to say about the gangster's masculinity) and Woodiwiss (1990: 5–20). Early instances of films about gangs are briefly discussed and extensively listed in Langman and Finn (1994). Langman and Finn draw attention to the cycle of 'Black Hand' films that began with *The Black Hand* itself in 1906 (ibid.: xiv), and to the cycle of 'counterfeit films' that emerged in the mid-1910s (ibid.: xv). They also note the prevalence in the late 1910s and the 1920s of the topoi of 'redemption, reformation and rehabilitation' (ibid.: xvii). Traces of these topoi can be found in *Underworld*, *Thunderbolt*, *City Streets* and *The Doorway to Hell*, which perhaps explains why they are ignored or viewed merely as precursors by those attached to the classical formula. As Peary points out, one of the hallmarks of *Little Caesar* was its rejection of these topoi (1981: 20–1). The same is true of *The Public Enemy* and *Scarface*. However, their perpetuation in films like *Docks of San Francisco* (1932) and *Midnight Alibi* (1934), in *Angels with Dirty Faces* (1938) and *I Am a Criminal* (1938), in 'rural regeneration' films such as *Hide-Out* (1934), and in patriotic wartime films like *Lucky Jordan* (1942) and *Mr Lucky* (1943) suggests that they comprised a formula more deep-rooted, more long-lasting and thus more 'classical' than the classical formula itself.

William Everson, meanwhile, notes the longevity of another gangster formula, pointing out that *The Gangsters and the Girl* 'anticipates the basic storyline of not only hundreds of westerns but of key 1930's and 1940's gangster films (*Bullets or Ballots*, *The Street with No Name*, *White Heat*) as well – that of having the detective hero masquerade as a gangster and work from the inside to bring about the downfall of the gang' (1978: 228). As Everson's examples indicate, this formula can be found both in numerous 'G-man' films of the 1930s, and in numerous '*noir*' gangster films of the late 1940s and early 1950s. It overlaps with what Langman and Finn call 'the cops-and-robbers' formula (1995a: xv), a formula in which agents of law, order and government are pitted in open conflict against gangs and criminal syndicates.

Public investigation of criminal organizations of all kinds in the 1950s and 1960s formed the backdrop to a series of cycles and films, beginning with *The Enforcer* in 1951 and culminating in the *Godfather* films and their off-shoots in the early-to-mid-1970s (Cameron 1975: 138–69; Clarens 1980: 234–58, 276–92; McArthur 1972: 53–4; McCarty 1993: 167–207; Parrish and Pitts 1976: 12–13; Rosow 1978: 235–6, 272–5, 312–39; Shadoian 1977: 326–35). As Albini (1971), Friedman (1993: 272–3), Moore (1974), Nelli (1976) and Woodiwiss (1988: 96–162, 1990: 20–30) have all pointed out, evidence as to the existence of a single, nationwide syndicate, an alien criminal conspiracy that came increasingly to be labelled as 'the Mafia', was equivocal at best. Nevertheless, these investigations gave rise to a massive increase in government surveillance of crime, and a sense that criminal conspiracies and organized crime were all-pervasive.

These developments fed not only into the cycles mentioned above, some of them updated G-man films, some of them updated cops-and-robbers films, some of them dedicated to the exploitation in various ways of the 'Mafia mystique' (Smith 1975), but also into a series of 1950s films about city and small-town corruption (Cameron 1975: 60–1, McArthur 1972: 55; Parrish and Pitts 1976: 12). The 1950s, the 1960s and the 1970s also witnessed an intermittent series of heist films (Cameron 1975: 57–9; Kaminsky 1974: 101–3; McArthur 1972: 53; Parrish and Pitts 1976: 12; Telotte 1996: 163–6[19]), and at least three series of gangster biographies and Prohibition and Depression reconstructions (Cameron 1975: 131–5; Clarens 1980: 251–5, 259–66; McArthur 1972: 55–6; Parrish and Pitts 1976: 13–14; Rosow 1978: 235–6, 250–1). Like *High Sierra* (1941), *The Last Gangster* (1945), *White Heat* (1949) and *Key Largo* (1948) before them, the latter often trade – sometimes nostalgically, sometimes ironically – on an image of the gangster as the embodiment of a doomed individualism, as an outlaw maverick whose energies are finally destroyed or contained by an increasingly bureaucratic and corporate society which he himself defies, but which in some cases his own often increasingly organized acitivities serve to mobilize. In addition, and in tandem with some of the heist films, films like '*Bonnie and Clyde* (1967) and *The Godfather I* and *II* (1972, 1975) . . . portrayed a normative culture so lethally inimical to human needs that the only way to survive and find meaning within it was to create an alternative criminal society' (Raeburn 1988: 55).

Bonnie and Clyde drew on and fed into a trend towards youth-oriented gangster films that began in the late 1950s with films like *The Bonnie Parker Story* (1958), continued in the early 1970s with films like *A Bullet for Pretty Boy* (1970) and *Boxcar Bertha* (1972) (Clarens 1980: 259–69), and has reappeared since then in occasional brat-pack films like *Mobsters* (1991). The *Godfather* films drew on a trend towards self-conscious allusions to the gangster film's traditions that began in the post-war period with the gangster biopics of the late 1950s and has continued since then in movie-brat films like *Goodfellas* (1990), *Scarface* (1983) and *Casino* (1995). All have helped reinforce an association of the gangster film with the 'classical formula' of the early 1930s rather than with the topos of regeneration, though films like *Dillinger* (1973) and *The Untouchables* (1987) hark back as well – or instead – to the cops-and-robbers formula of the G-man films.

In the meantime and finally, two waves of black gangster films, 1970s blaxploitation films like *Superfly* (1972) and *Black Caesar* (1973) and more recent films like *Deep Cover* (1992), *Rage in Harlem* (1991) and *New Jack City* (1991), have highlighted the extent to which the gangster film has centred since the 1920s in particular on ethnic outsiders (Ferraro 1989; Rosow 1978: 103–5, 184–5),[20] and the extent to which, with the exception of the Chinatown films, those outsiders have hitherto been portrayed as exclusively white.[21] Rosow argues that the gangsters in the blaxploitation films 'fought racial and economic oppression . . . in the same proto-revolutionary fashion as Depression-era movie gangsters' (1978: 279). To that extent they and their successors exemplify at least one of Warshow's theses, that 'the gangster is the

"no" to that great American "yes" which is stamped so big over . . . [America's]
. . . official culture' (Warshow [1954] 1975b: 135).

Suspense thrillers

In part, perhaps because it has been so associated with the work of one
particular director, Alfred Hitchcock, the suspense thriller as a genre has
received very little attention. There *are* books on thrillers, suspense and
suspense films (Davis 1973; Gow 1969; Hammond 1974, for instance). But
most of them suffer from imprecision and from a tendency to focus on an
array of generically disparate films. An exception here is Derry's book, *The
Suspense Thriller: Films in the Shadow of Alfred Hitchcock* (1988). While marked,
as its title indicates, by Hitchcock's shadow, and while marred by a tendency
to concentrate almost exclusively on films made since the late 1940s, it is
rigorous, systematic and otherwise wide-ranging in its choice of examples.

Derry notes that suspense thrillers focus either on victims of crime or on
pursued and isolated criminals. One of their distinguishing features is therefore a lack of attention to official detectives or the police, and this is the basis
of Derry's definition: '*The suspense thriller*', he writes, is '*as a crime work which
presents a generally murderous antagonism in which the protagonist becomes either an
innocent victim or a nonprofessional criminal within a structure that is significantly
unmediated by a traditional figure of detection*' (1968: 62; emphasis in original).
Given that this is a broad – though precise – definition, a definition that
encompasses films as diverse as *North by Northwest* (1959), *The Manchurian
Candidate* (1962), *Wait Until Dark* (1967) and *The Postman Always Rings Twice*
(1946), Derry goes on to identify six major sub-types.

First is 'the thriller of murderous passions', which 'is organized around the
triangular grouping of husband/wife/lover. The central scene is generally the
murder of one member of the triangle by one or both of the other members.
The emphasis is clearly on the criminal protagonist . . . [and] . . . The
criminal motive is generally passion or greed' (Derry 1968: 72). Examples
include *Double Indemnity* (1944), *Blood Simple* (1984) and *Body Heat*. Second is
'the political thriller', a category which includes *Seven Days in May* (1964), *All
the President's Men* (1976), *The China Syndrome* (1979) and *Blow Out* (1981).
Films like this 'are organized around a plot to assassinate a political figure or a
revelation of the essential conspiratorial nature of governments and their
crimes against the people. These films generally document and dramatize
the acts of assassins, conspirators, or criminal governments, as well as the
oppositional acts of victim-societies, countercultures, or martyrs' (ibid.: 103).
And third is 'the thriller of acquired identity', which is exemplified by films
like *The Running Man* (1963) and *Dead Ringer* (1964). These films 'are
organized around a protagonist's acquisition of an unaccustomed identity,
his or her behavior in coming to terms with the metaphysical and physical

consequences of this identity, and the relationship of this acquisition to a murderous plot' (ibid.: 175).

Fourth and fifth are 'the psychotraumatic thriller' and 'the thriller of moral confrontation'. The psychotraumatic thriller is 'organized around the psychotic effects of a trauma on a protoganist's current involvement in a love affair and a crime or intrigue. The protagonist is always a victim – generally of some past trauma and often of real villains who take advantage of his or her masochistic guilt' (Derry 1968: 194). Examples include *Spellbound* (1945), *Marnie* (1964), *Hush, Hush, Sweet Charlotte* (1964) and *Body Double* (1984). The thriller of moral confrontation is exemplified by films like *The Window* (1949), *Strangers on a Train* (1951), *Sudden Terror* (1970) and *Outrage* (1973). It is 'organized around an overt antithetical confrontation between a character representing good or innocence and a character representing evil. These films often are constructed in terms of elaborate dualities which emphasize the parallels between the victim and the criminal' (ibid.: 217). The sixth, finally, is 'the innocent-on-the-run thriller', which is 'organized around an innocent victim's coincidental entry into the midst of global intrigue' and in which 'the victim often finds himself running from both the villains as well as the police' (ibid.: 270). Examples include *The Man Who Knew Too Much* (1955), *The Parallax View* (1974), *Three Days of the Condor* (1975) and *Into the Night* (1985).

In addition to constructing these categories, Derry also addresses the issues of thrills and suspense. In discussing thrills, he draws on the work of psychoanalyst Michael Balint (1959), and in particular on Balint's distinction between 'philobats' (lovers of thrills) and 'ocnophobes' (haters of thrills). He notes that thrillers tend to plunge ocnophobic protagonists into deadly – and thrilling – situations, situations in which familiar objects, spaces and activities are replaced by – or become – objects, spaces and activities which are unfamiliar and threatening.

In discussing suspense, he distinguishes between the role of surprise and the role of curiosity. He argues that suspense is not necessarily related to the resolution of enigmas or to 'the vague question of *what* will happen next' (Derry 1968: 31). It is dependent, instead, on 'the expectation that a specific action might take place': 'the creation of suspense demands that enough information be revealed to the spectator so that he or she can anticipate what might happen; suspense then remains operative until the spectator's expectations are foiled, fulfilled, or the narrative is frozen without any resolution at all' (ibid.: 31–2). In the interplay between expectation and narrative development, what becomes suspended in suspense is time: 'During those moments that suspense is operative, time seems to extend itself, and each second provides a kind of torture for a spectator who is anxious to have his or her anticipations foiled or fulfilled' (ibid.: 32).

In insisting on the importance of specific information and knowledge, Derry's argument parallels the argument put forward by Dove in *Suspense in the Formula Story* (1989). For Dove, as for Derry, suspense 'is dependent to a greater degree upon what the reader has been told than upon what he wants to find out. The more the reader knows (without knowing everything), the more he wants to know' (ibid.: 4). Dove, however, is less interested in sub-types than in broad generic variations on the structures that he sees as fundamental to all forms of suspense. These structures comprise four phases or states: '"cumulation" (the phase that accommodates the development of promises, clues, questions, tensions which will determine later developments); "postponement" (the phase in which the promise of early resolution is deferred); "alternation" (the period of doubt, where the chances regarding the outcome are uncertain); and "potentiality" (the crisis, in which the chances appear to be favoring a given outcome)' (ibid.: 50). These phases mark developments and shifts in the 'relational components of the story' (ibid.: 51), and it is here that generically specific variations tend to occur.

These components include a 'mover', 'A', an 'object', 'B', the tensions involved in the confrontation between them, 'C', and the exclusion of possible solutions or directions which would resolve the story too quickly, 'D'. In the thriller, where the basic issue is 'What is going to happen?', the identity of 'A' and 'B' are obvious: 'no question who or what is the menace, or the victim. "C" is generated by the conflict of "A" vs "B." The "D" component is clearly defined, as are the phases or states' (Dove 1989: 59). In the '"pure" or non-detectional mystery', the question is 'What is happening? "A" (the person, problem, menace) is not identified until late; "B" (the identity menaced) emerges somewhat earlier. "C" arises from the disturbance created by loss of security . . . [and] "D" is the vulnerability/inadequacy of "B" (ibid.: 60). In the detective story, the question posed is 'What really did happen? In this story "A" is the detective, the element that makes the story move . . . "B" is the problem, which would include the guilty person(s) . . . "D" is . . . the obscured past, which hold[s] the story in bounds . . . [and] "C" is the repeated revelation–frustration of the detective's pursuit' (ibid.). And in the 'tale of the Supernatural', the question is 'Is *anything* happening? "A" and "B" are customarily ambiguous, "A" often so until the end, and "B" may not emerge until late in the story . . . "C" is frequently present before "A" or "B" . . . [and] "D" is the irrationality–uncertainty–perversity–invulnerability of "A"' (ibid.: 61).

Dove's book concentrates on written fiction and his terminology (alphabetical and otherwise) is occasionally eccentric and difficult to follow. However, his formulae work as well for films as they do for novels, and he allows throughout for hybrids and combinations. The extent to which his formulae extend beyond the traditional realms of crime to encompass the supernatural is (yet another) indication of the extent to which popular genres are rarely tidy and self-contained, even, perhaps especially, from a structural point of view.

Further confirmation that this is the case can be found in historical surveys of crime films of the kind produced by Langman and Finn. As in Dove's – and

Derry's – book, categories and sub-types tend to abound. Here, though, they are founded less on form than on content, less on structural characteristics than on cyclical features and variations. They include 'The Courtroom Film' (Langman and Finn 1995a: xii–xiii), 'The Newspaper-Crime Film' (ibid.: xiii), 'The Exposé Drama' (Langman and Finn 1995b: xviii–xix) and 'The Social Conscience Drama' (ibid.: xix). While some of the films within these categories are marked by the structural features analysed by Dove and Derry, others are not. Whether regarded as genres or as sub-types, the point here is that they rarely feature in critical or theoretical discussions of the crime film as such.

EPICS AND SPECTACLES

'Epic' is essentially a 1950s and 1960s term. It was used to identify, and to sell, two overlapping contemporary trends: films with historical, especially ancient-world settings; and large-scale films of all kinds which used new technologies, high production values and special modes of distribution and exhibition to differentiate themselves both from routine productions and from alternative forms of contemporary entertainment, especially television. As such, there were at least two aspects to epics, two sets of distinguishing characteristics: those associated with ancient and historical films, and those associated with large-scale films. These two aspects normally coincided, as was true of *Ben-Hur* (1959), *Spartacus* and *How the West Was Won* (1962), and even of films with more recent historical settings like *The Longest Day* (1962) and *The Battle of the Bulge* (1965). But the production and special circulation of large-scale comedies like *The Great Race* (1965) and large-scale musicals like *South Pacific* (1958) and the production of more routinely scaled and circulated ancient-world films like *Helen of Troy* (1955) and *Hannibal* (1960) show that this was by no means always the case. The characteristics of the epic as a genre were therefore complicated and augmented by the generic characteristics of contemporary comedies, musicals, westerns and war films, among others. In addition, the trends involved were unevenly traversed by at least two further features: an emphasis on aural and visual spectacle (evident not just in the musicals and in the films with historical settings, whatever their scale, but also in the comedies, which were markedly slapstick and visual in character), and a dramatic and thematic concern with political and military power, political and military rule, and political and military struggle (a concern not so prominent in the musicals and comedies, but one which was persistently evident in the historical films, where it found articulation on national, international and sometimes global and cosmic scales).

I shall return to the specifics of a number of these trends in a moment. In the meantime, it is important to emphasize the extent to which at least some of them derive from generic and industrial traditions dating back to the early 1910s and beyond. In the period between 1910 and 1914, large-scale historical and ancient-world films, often made in Italy and elsewhere in Europe, helped establish the multi-reel feature as a format. Among these films were *The Fall of Troy* (1910), *Dante's Inferno* (1911), *From the Manger to the Cross* (1912), *Quo Vadis?* (1913) and *Cabiria* (1914). At a time when production, distribution and exhibition in the United States were geared to the rapid turnover of programmes of single-reel films in small, nickelodeon theatres, they were usually distributed on a 'road show' basis:

> Feature films could be road shown, as plays were, with stock companies playing in the provinces. This was the method used to distribute Helen Gardner's big feature film *Cleopatra* in late 1912. Numerous companies were sent out on the road with a print of the film, an advance man, a lecturer-projectionist, and a manager. Features were shown as special attractions in the local opera houses and town halls and legitimate theaters at advanced prices and stayed for as long as there was enough business to support them.
>
> (Bowser 1990: 192)

Many of the feature films with historical, biblical and ancient-world settings drew on nineteenth-century traditions of historical and religious representation, particularly paintings and engravings, toga plays, Passion plays, pageants, spectacular melodramas, and popular novels like *Quo Vadis?* and *Ben-Hur*. They also drew on nineteenth- and early twentieth-century preoccupations with Imperial Rome and early Christianity, on an association between religious and historical representation and nationhood and empire, and on a tradition of earlier films dealing with religious and historical themes, topics, stories and scenes.[22] These traditions and preoccupations were particularly prominent among the middle, upper and respectable classes at whom the new feature films in the US were pitched (Bowser 1990: 255–6; Urrichio and Pearson 1993: 111–94). They were augmented there by the production of films like *The Coming of Columbus* (1912) and *The Birth of a Nation* (1915), which dealt with aspects of American history. The films themselves helped found a tradition of large-scale, high-cost 'spectacles'. The way they were distributed helped found a tradition of road-showing lengthy, expensive and otherwise unusual or exceptional productions, a tradition which persisted even when the production, distribution and exhibition of feature films of all kinds had become routine. (Hall's Ph.D. thesis, in progress, contains a detailed history of road show productions in Hollywood.)

The spectacular values that characterized the historical feature films of the 1910s have been discussed by Bowser. She notes the importance of battle scenes, large sets and extensive casts. She emphasizes the extent to which these and other spectacular features were used to maintain the involvement of contemporary spectators in much longer films than they were used to. And she draws attention to two of the methods used to exploit 'big spectacle scenes to the greatest advantage: (1) a moving camera, as in *Cabiria*, offered a sense of great depth and solidity in enormous sets, or followed action over a broad geography; or (2) large scenes were dissected in editing, providing through a variety of details an otherwise inexpressible sense of a larger whole' (1990: 258). The other side of the coin was the use of large-scale sets and scenes to motivate and to frame devices like these, and the use of large-scale narratives of large-scale events to motivate, frame and sustain spectacle itself.[23]

Supported by the advent of the picture palace, road-shown spectacles remained an important component in Hollywood's output for the rest of the silent era. They included exotic adventure-romances like *The Thief of Bagdad* (1924). But films like *Robin Hood*, and in particular *The Covered Wagon* (1923), *The Iron Horse* (1925), *Ben-Hur* (1925), *The King of Kings* (1927) and *Wings* (1927), show that history, ancient and modern, remained their principal ingredient. However, despite their importance, and although there exists writing on some of these films in individual or auteurist terms, in terms of their stars, or in terms of their participation in more canonically central genres like the war film or the western, very little has been written about them either as a distinct generic group or as participants in cycles of the spectacle as such. This is even true of book-length studies of epics and spectacles, including those by Babington and Evans (1993), Elley (1984), Forshey (1992), Searles (1990) and Wyke (1997). It is a hallmark of most of these books that they focus on particular topics, like religion or Ancient Rome, or on particular periods of production, like the 1950s. It is a peculiarity of all of them that they organize discussion of the films around the periods in which they are set rather the periods in which they were made. This means that while some silent spectacles are discussed, and while sound and silent versions of the same story can sometimes be compared, any kind of contextual analysis tends to be rendered incidental and any kind of in-depth conjunctural analysis almost impossible. A lack of detailed attention to silent spectacles in general merely compounds this particular problem.

In consequence, the contextual attention paid to films like *Joan the Woman* (1917) and *The Ten Commandments* (1923) in Higashi's book on Cecil B. DeMille is unusual and useful, though also very particular in its focus on DeMille himself (1994). Higashi argues that throughout the silent era, DeMille was consistently concerned to make cinema part of respectable, middle-class culture, negotiating and addressing in and through his films the relationship between Victorian traditions and values on the one hand, and modernity – of which the cinema was a part – on the other. In contrast to his comedies, she sees his silent spectacles, drawing as they did on Victorian values and on traditions of Victorian pictorialism, as either straightforwardly anti-modernist, or else as engaged in a project of rendering aspects of Victorianism compatible with modernity itself. The extent to which the preoccupations that marked DeMille's films can be generalized or discerned across the array of Hollywood's silent spectacles as a whole is clearly open to debate and to future research, though it is worth pointing out that one of the devices he used in *The Ten Commandments* to articulate these preccupations, that of framing or counterpointing a modern story with a biblical or historical one, had been used by D. W. Griffith in *Intolerance* (1916), and was to be used again by Michael Curtiz in *Noah's Ark* (1928) (Elley 1984: 17; Hirsch 1978: 62). It is also worth pointing out that the elements of sensuousness and sexuality that link the modern and the historical in DeMille's films are common not only to most silent ancient-world films, but to many ancient-world films made in the era of sound as well.

DeMille's *The Sign of the Cross* (1932) and *Cleopatra* (1934) are two such films, though along with the *The Last Days of Pompeii* (1935) they constitute the only ancient-world spectacles made in Hollywood between 1928 and 1949. Aside from the early years of the Depression, the road-showing of expensive prestige productions continued. Indeed as Balio has shown, prestige productions were among the most popular box-office successes of the 1930s (1993: 179–211). However, as he has also shown, they tended to comprise comedies, dramas, war films, biopics and literary adaptations rather than traditional spectacles, though some of the prestige historical adventure films made in the second half of the decade, along with a number of late 1930s prestige westerns and films like *Gone With the Wind* (1939), clearly provided similar kinds of cinematic experience and possibly also served similar cultural and ideological purposes. Babington and Evans suggest that 'the crises of the Depression and the Second World War required more domestic inspiration' than could be provided by the traditional biblical spectacle (1993: 5). It might also be suggested that more modern history was cheaper to stage – Finler (1988: 38) notes that the profit margins on prestige films in the 1930s were actually rather small – and less likely, in the new sound era, to seem old-fashioned.

While Wyke locates *Cleopatra* in terms of DeMille's engagement with modernity (and his engagement in particular with the figure of the New Woman) (1997: 90–7), Forshey (1992) locates the other ancient-world films made in the 1930s in terms of a series of Depression-related issues. These included 'ethical behavior', 'social responsibility', luxury, wealth and poverty, and an opposition between urban and rural values. On *The Sign of the Cross* he writes that 'The eventual triumph of the good for those who hold fast to the "true faith" was a concept attractive to people experiencing hard times. The rural values are associated with Christianity, and Marcus' rejection of licentious urban attitudes intensifies the enjoyment' (ibid.: 17). On *The Last of Pompeii* he notes an insistence on the themes of money and class: 'Money, with its devaluation of human life (symbolized by richness, decadence and the arena) is opposed to Christianity, with the poor inheriting the earth and finding freedom from their poverty and oppression' (ibid.: 24). Wyke, on the other hand, sees the former as an endorsement of Americanism, with Nero (Charles Laughton) 'the embodiment of essentially *foreign* evils against which

a modern American crusade is to be fought' (1997: 133; emphasis in original). She sees the latter as a displaced 1930s gangster film, a 'success tragedy'
set in the city (ibid.: 174–80).

The successful re-release of *The Sign of the Cross* in 1944 – complete with a
prologue and epilogue showing US bombers flying over war-torn Rome –
helped re-launch the ancient-world spectacle in a new ideological and
industrial context after the war. DeMille himself followed it up with *Samson
and Delilah* in 1949 and with a remake of *The Ten Commandments* in 1956.
These particular films exemplify a number of the trends marking a cycle of
post-war ancient-world films that ran through to the release and the box-
office failure of *The Fall of the Roman Empire* in 1964. As already noted, this
cycle overlapped with other kinds of epics, spectacles and large-scale films.
With *The Greatest Show on Earth*, a circus film, DeMille contributed to
another of these trends as well.

The Ten Commandments was over four hours long. It was made in Vista-
Vision and Technicolor. It was shown with an intermission. And it was
released on a road-show basis in December 1956. It was therefore made at a
time when cinema attendances had fallen from their peak in 1946, when
the major studios had been forced to sell their theatre chains and focus
exclusively on distribution and production, and when competition from
television had begun to tell (Balio [1976] 1985: 401–38, 1990b: 3–9, 13–23).
It was also made at a time when large and widescreen processes like
VistaVision had been introduced (or reintroduced) as a means of renewing
and updating 'the cinematic experience', and at a time when the road-
showing of large-scale productions had been increasingly adopted as a
means of increasing rental charges and ticket prices and thus of maintaining
box-office income and profits in otherwise inhospitable market conditions
(Balio [1976] 1985: 422–33, 1990b: 23–8; Belton 1992: 69–210; Schatz
1993: 11–13). It is therefore exemplary of a number of the industrial
strategies and factors which, alongside the increasing use of foreign stars,
locations and facilities as a means of deploying blocked overseas income and
of gaining access to overseas subsidies and to relatively cheap plant and
personnel, were to sustain the epic as a production trend for nearly twenty
years.[24]

In the prologue to *The Ten Commandments*, spoken direct to camera by
DeMille himself, emphasis is placed on the fact that Moses learns he is
Hebrew, not Egyptian, prior to leading his people from slavery in Egypt to
freedom in the Promised Land. 'The theme of this picture', he states, 'is
whether men are to be ruled by God's law, or whether they are to be ruled by
the whims of a dictator like Rameses. Are men the property of the state, or
are they free souls under God? This same battle continues', he concludes,
'throughout the world today.' Attention is therefore drawn to a number of the
wider, socio-political conditions within which the post-war epic emerged,
and to a number of the ideological, political and cultural issues nearly all those

who have written on the trend have cited when discussing the films themselves. These conditions and issues include the Cold War, the post-war establishment of the state of Israel and concomitant tensions between the Arab world and the West (dealt with directly in *Exodus* in 1960), and the resurgence of Christianity and churchgoing in the United States, a resurgence accompanied and fed by the publication of some of the source novels used as a basis for some of the films, as well, of course, as the films themselves (Ellwood 1997: 10–12).

Readings of post-war epics in terms of the Cold War stress the thematic and dramatic oppositions between atheism and idolatory and a belief in one true God, and between religious, political and personal freedom and the repressiveness of 'totalitarian' empires, states and regimes, often represented in the ancient-world films by Egypt or Rome. However, as is often the case with films and readings that work by analogy, there are ambiguities, complications and contradictions. For one thing, as Wood points out, although

> All these stories invite our sympathy for the oppressed . . . the movies themselves, as costly studio productions, clearly take the other side. They . . . are all for tyranny and Rome, more imperialist than conqueror. The great scenes in these films, the reasons for our being in the cinema at all – the orgies, the triumphs, the gladiatorial games – all belong to the oppressors. The palaces, the costumes, the pomp . . . are all theirs.
>
> (Wood 1975: 184–5)

For another, as Cohan points out (1997: 130–5), the paranoid scenarios of Self and Other, Us and Them, characteristic of Cold War cinema can always be reversed: the imperial decadence of Egypt or Rome can always be read as 1950s or 1960s America, as Wyke's analysis of *The Fall of the Roman Empire* (1997: 185–8), Nadel's discussion of 'Corporate Egypt' (1995: 97–102), and Higashi's comments on the spectacle of consumption in *The Ten Commandments* all make clear (1996: 104–5).

An additional point is that in the early post-war period in particular, political tyranny was as likely to be associated with German fascism as with Soviet Communism. Wyke shows that both *Quo Vadis?* (1951) and *The Robe* (the film that launched CinemaScope in 1953) were originally planned with Mussolini and Hitler in mind (1997: 28–9, 139–40). And Lenihan's reading of such early 1950s costume films as *Ivanhoe* and *Julius Caesar* (1953) stresses these connections as well (1992). Also stressed are the parallels in these and other films and with the anti-Communist activities of HUAC (the House Committee on Un-American Activities), particularly in scenes and scenarios involving the infiltration of proscribed organizations (like the early Christian church) and the naming of names. Babington and Evans view *The Robe* in this light, emphasizing the liberal credentials of screenwriter Philip Dunne (1993:

210–13). Wyke makes a similar point about *Spartacus*, which was scripted by the hitherto blacklisted Dalton Trumbo from a novel by the Communist writer Howard Fast (1997: 60–72; see also Smith 1989). It might also be noted that the once-blacklisted Robert Rossen wrote, produced and directed *Alexander the Great*, a film which lays great emphasis on the betrayal of a long-standing friendship, while in self-imposed exile in Europe. A fourth and final point to note in this context, though, is that in *The Egyptian* (1954) and in other epics of extraordinary lives like *King of Kings*, *Barabbas* and *The Greatest Story Ever Told* (1965), Christianity undercuts or is presented as an alternative to engagement on any side in any kind of political struggle.

The increasing circulation in the US of Italian 'peplums', of films like *Hercules* [*Le Fatiche di Ercole*] (1958) and *The Warrior and the Slave Girl* [*La Revolta dei Gladiotori*] (1958), complicates the picture still further, particularly in so far as they mark a growing interchange between Hollywood and Italy (Elley 1984: 20–1; Frayling 1981: 68–102). On the one hand they emerge with a very different ideological agenda from a very different ideological and cinematic context. At the same time, they augment a specific trend towards displays of the muscled white male body as well as the general trend towards ancient-world spectacle. These displays in the peplum derive from a distinct Italian tradition (Dall'Asta 1992; Dyer 1997: 165–83; Wyke 1997: 44–5). But they mark Hollywood's spectacles too, drawing both on the tradition in action-adventure discussed above and on a strain in the post-war spectacle inaugurated by *Samson and Delilah* (Babington and Evans 1993: 227–37).

In addition to displays and to issues of masculinity (often linked in the Hollywood films to Cold War scenarios, to Orientalist discourses and to meditations to the figure of the warrior, as in *El Cid*, but also to meditations on the non-martial versions of masculinity represented by Christ and Christianity), many post-war historical spectacles also involve displays of the female body and a focus on contemporary gender relations. Forshey identifies a cycle of films concerned with 'sex and social responsibility' (1992: 59–82). The cycle includes films like *David and Bathsheba* (1951), *Salome* (1951), *Solomon and Sheba* (1959) and *Sodom and Gomorrah* (1963). It is specifically concerned with the temptations of hedonism, luxury, materialism and sex, and these temptations are frequently represented by women. Not always though. The constant in these films (and in nearly all the others) is the lure of alternatives to duty and the Law. Just as duty and the Law can be figured in martial or in non-martial terms, so the lure can be figured as male (as in *Ben-Hur*) or as female. It is another mark of the complications introduced by the peplum, though, that in films like *Aphrodite, Goddess of Love* [*La Venere di Cheronea*] (1958) and *The Bacchantes* [*Le Baccanti*] (1961), female pacifism, hedonism, sexuality and power are endorsed rather than condemned.

In part because of over-investment, overproduction, rising costs and falling profits, and in part because of changing audience demographics and increasing ideological divisions, the post-war cycle of historical spectacles came to an end in the late 1960s, together with large-scale musicals and comedies (Barra 1989; Elley 1984: 24; Forshey 1992: 163–82; Schatz 1993: 14–16). Traces remained in 1970s disaster films like *The Towering Inferno* (1974) and *Earthquake* (1974), as well as in stragglers like *Papillon* (1973) and *The Battle of Midway* (1976). But while television began to absorb some of the spectacle's traditional generic material, and while the peplum was revived in the guise of sword-and-sorcery films like *Conan the Barbarian* (1982), the heir to the spectacle in the cinema thereafter was the action-adventure blockbuster. The action-adventure blockbuster, however, differs in at least two respects from its traditional counterpart. On the one hand, its lavish budgets are usually expended on what in the studio era would have been programme, serial or B film material – space operas, cliff-hanging adventure films and the like. (Exceptions reminiscent generically of the traditional Hollywood spectacle have been made. They include *Heaven's Gate* (1980), an historical western, *Apocalypse Now* (1979), a war film, and *Gettysburg* (1993), an American Civil War reconstruction. However, most of them have failed at the box-office.) On the other, it is usually released not on a road-show basis, but on a multiple, simultaneous, 'saturation' basis in cinemas throughout the US, a strategy pioneered in the late 1950s not by major studios making large-scale spectacles for a dwindling adult or family audience but by small-scale independents making low-grade, low-budget films for a rapidly growing teenage population (Belton 1994: 304–5; Maltby 1983: 320–1, 1995: 75, 1998: 34–5; Schatz 1993: 17–36).

HORROR AND SCIENCE FICTION

As has often been noted, it is sometimes very difficult to distinguish between horror and science fiction. Not only that, it can at times be difficult to distinguish between horror and the crime film, and science fiction, adventure and fantasy as well. Films like *Frankenstein* (1931), *Psycho* (1960) and *Wait Until Dark* (1967), and *Star Wars*, *E.T.* (1982), *The Thing* (1982) and *The Hound of the Baskervilles* (1939) all in their own ways testify to the propensity for multiplicity and overlap among and between these genres in Hollywood. It is therefore hardly surprising that water-tight definitions of science fiction and horror – or for that matter fantasy, adventure and crime – are hard to come by. Nor is it surprising that articles and books on science fiction and horror often discuss the same or similar films. However, if there are areas and instances of hybridity and overlap, there are also areas and instances of differentiation – few would describe *Dracula* (1931) as science fiction, just as few would describe *Silent Running* (1972) or *Logan's Run* (1976) as horror films. In consequence, horror and science fiction will be treated here as related, but also as distinct.

92

Horror

Despite a long-standing intellectual interest in horror in France and elsewhere in Europe, there was comparatively little serious discussion of the horror film in Britain or America until the publication of books by Clarens in 1968 and by Butler in 1970. In consequence, as Gledhill points out, 'only in the second half of the 70s was the genre put on the agenda of film studies' (1985b: 99). In partial explanation, she goes on to cite Wood (1979), who refers to the low cultural status of the horror film, and to what she calls 'the special relationship' (1985b: 99) between the genre and its fans and 'aficionados':

> The horror film has consistently been one of the most popular and, at the same time, the most disreputable of Hollywood genres. The popularity itself has a peculiar characteristic that sets the horror film apart from other genres: it is restricted to aficionados and complemented by total rejection, people tending to go to horror films either obsessively or not at all. They are dismissed with contempt by the majority of reviewer-critics, or simply ignored.
>
> (Wood 1979: 13)

Gledhill also refers to the genre's 'mixed heritage and development in a wide range of different forms and cultures' (1985b: 99), and citing Tudor (1974b), Murphy (1972) and Ross (1972), to its principal aesthetic aim – 'to horrify' (1985b: 99).[25] While some have sought to legitimate horror in terms of a distinction between the horror of suggestion and the horror of Grand Guignol display, others have used its outsider status to claim it as subversive of dominant social and cultural norms. However, the 'chief route to cultural legitimation has been through popular anthropological or Freudian/Jungian references' (Gledhill 1985b: 99), and since the early 1980s, amidst a renewed interest in the genre on the part of film theorists and the advent of a new form of Grand Guignol known as 'body horror' (*Screen* 1986), through references to Baudrillard, Foucault, Kristeva, Lacan, Deleuze and other theorists of human subjectivity, discourse, and society. At the same time, amidst the development of feminist film theory and the advent of the slasher film, legitimation has often been displaced by the analysis of sexuality, gender and spectatorship.

There are echoes in all this of some of the debates that accompanied the advent of modern horror in the form of gothic fiction in the late eighteenth century in England. In his history of 'Scary Entertainment', Walter Kendrick relates the cultivation, generation and consumption of 'the pleasure . . . of fear' (1991: xxii) at this time to a number of factors. One was a profound shift in attitudes toward death, the past, and the mortal human body. Others included the beginnings of commercial mass publication and a relatively popular reading culture among the middle classes, and a connected – and partly consequent – cultivation of aesthetically generated sensibilities and feelings of all kinds. This cultivation represented a challenge to neo-classical aesthetic precepts by appearing to deprive improbable fictional occurrences and sublime or quasi-sublime aesthetic effects of any moral or social justification. It helped pave the way for High Romanticism (and eventually for forms of avant-garde modernism like Expressionism and Surrealism, both of which drew on the gothic tradition, and both of which fed into the development of the 'fantastique' in Europe). But it also posed questions as to the effects of this new aesthetic regime on a readership which at the time was presumed to be largely female. One of the consequences, as Clery points out, was the emergence of a division between high and low art, and the association of genres of all kinds with the latter rather than the former (1995: 139).

This last development flew in the face of the heterogeneity of gothic fiction, whose generic progeny included the detective story, the crime thriller and sensation fiction, as well as horror fiction as such (Varma 1957: 237–41). Some of its motifs, like graveyards and crypts, crumbling dwellings, demons, and decomposing corpses, are on occasion still deployed, and were, of course, actively invoked in most forms of horror in Hollywood in the 1930s and 1940s. But its 'figures of menace, destruction and violence' now tend to be 'mad scientists, psychopaths, extraterrestrials and a host of strange supernatural and naturally monstrous mutations' rather than depraved clerics or aristocrats, and they tend to appear in an array of 'different genres and media' (Botting 1996: 13; see also Hutchings 1996).

As well as being heterogeneous, the heritage of gothic fiction has also been discontinuous and intermittent. In addition to stressing this particular point, Kendrick emphasizes the extent to which, in the forms of melodrama as well as in the forms of Grand Guignol, it includes developments on the nineteenth- and early twentieth-century stage (1991: 101–33, 154–63, 201–6). This point is worth underlining, both because a number of discussions of horror and its history omit any mention of the theatre (see Botting 1996, Halberstam 1995 and Jancovich 1992a, for instance), and because as Hardy points out:

> theatrical horror is of special significance to the Anglo-American tradition of horror. It announced the kind of sensationalism that film-makers would seek to duplicate, and then to further intensify with apparatus and techniques newly available to them. Equally important, it was these theatrical versions of *Frankenstein* and *Dracula*, *not the novels themselves*, that were the models for the classic Universal interpretations of Mary Shelley and Bram Stoker's supreme gothic achievements. Indeed, there is a long theatrical tradition on Broadway of horror plays (and spoof horror plays, many of which were translated to the screen in the twenties).
>
> (Hardy 1995b: ix; emphasis in original)

Skal (1993) reinforces these points, adding the circus, the fairground and the freak show to the list of sources for horror in Hollywood, and detailing the stage to screen adaptation of *Frankenstein* and *Dracula* in the 1930s, *Dr Jekyll and Mr Hyde* in the 1920s and 1930s, and the influence of the circus, the fairground and the freak show on the work of Tod Browning and Lon Chaney in the 1920s and early 1930s. (On *Dracula*, see also Skal 1990.) Gordon cites the Grand Guignol as an influence on Browning and Chaney, Robert Florey, Paul Leni and Herschell Gordon Lewis ([1988] 1997: 40–3). Bowser refers in passing to the stage as a source for *The Devil* (1908) and *Dr Jekyll and Mr Hyde* (1908) (1990: 53). Clarens (1968: 54, 73–5), Kendrick (1991: 206–14) and Koszarski (1990: 186) note Broadway as the source for *The Cat and the Canary* (1927), *The Bat* (1926) and numerous other 1920s and 1930s 'old dark house' horror-farces and mysteries. And Balio cites the stage – as well as Europe and the German cinema – not only as a source for *Dracula* and *Frankenstein*, but also for a number of the actors, directors and production personnel involved in these and other 1930s horror films (1993: 298–301).

Balio notes that although 'almost every studio tried its hand' at the genre in the 1930s, and although the trend as a whole was numerically minor, 'one studio, Universal, specialized in the genre in an attempt to break into the first-run market' (1993: 198), banking on its relatively high production values as a means of according it 'premium-quality' industrial status (ibid.: 299). (For further details on Universal's horror films, see Schatz 1988a: 87–97, who stresses the extent to which they were nevertheless relatively cheap to produce.) Balio goes on to point out that Universal 'opted for product variation' rather than sequels (a policy which clearly changed in the 1940s when the studio produced numerous werewolf, mummy and Frankenstein films) (1993: 302). And he is careful to note the contributions made by MGM, Paramount, RKO and Warners, and the extent to which there were two distinct cycles, the first beginning with the release of *Dracula* and *Frankenstein* in 1931, the second with their re-release as a double bill in 1938.

In addition to the revival of Dracula, Frankenstein and Frankenstein's monster as figures, this second cycle saw a decline in the industrial status of horror, of which the more regular production of horror films as B films and the sequels, series, multiple-monster films and horror and comedy combinations of the 1940s are a mark (Clarens 1968: 125–9; Kendrick 1991: 221–5; Hardy [1986] 1995a: 74; Skal 1993: 213–18; Taves 1993b: 332–3; Tudor 1989: 33–5). This was the context in which Val Lewton's cycle of low-budget horror films emerged at RKO in 1942 (Gomery 1996a: 57). Though much praised and much discussed, these particular films are normally viewed as a relatively self-contained dead-end, at least as far as Hollywood is concerned (Clarens 1968: 137–45; Dyson 1997: 99–123, 133–51, 183–4; Siegel 1972; Telotte 1985). Thus while *I Walked With a Zombie* (1943) draws on an established tradition of Zombie films that was to be revived in the late 1960s, and while *Cat People* was remade in 1982, these revivals are marked much more by spectacular display than by the devices of evocation that characterized the Lewton films themselves. However, as Wood points out, although characterized by these devices, and although tending to retain the structural and connotational associations between horror and foreignness that were established during the course of the 1930s, it could be argued that by associating horror with the family, by on occasion setting horror within the everyday, contemporary world, and by emphasizing psychological and sexual themes, films like *Cat People* (1942), *The Seventh Victim* (1943) and *The Leopard Man* (1943) paved the way for a number of future developments (1986: 85–6).

The major hallmark of the 1950s are numerous sci-fi/horror hybrids and the international impact of Hammer's revival of Frankenstein and Dracula. The former persisted as a production trend into the early years of the following decade and the latter helped inspire the revival of gothic horror in the form of Roger Corman's 1960s Poe films at AIP (Hogan [1986] 1988: 122–37, 212–18; Tudor 1989: 190). However, the advent of *Psycho* in 1960 is generally regarded as a turning point, as the beginning of something new: as the film which located horror firmly and influentially within the modern psyche, the modern world, modern relationships, and the modern (disfunc-tional) family (Derry 1988: 163–4; Williams 1996: 15; Wood 1986: 87); as the film which marked a definitive *rapprochement* between the horror film and the psychological thriller and which helped inspire the slasher, stalker and serial-killer films of the 1970s, 1980s and 1990s (Clover 1992: 23–4; Schoell 1985; Tudor 1989: 45–6, 99–100); and as the film which marked the ending of 'classical' Hollywood, and with it the certainty and safety of classical narrative and generic conventions (Maltby 1995: 218–19; Tudor 1989: 190–5).

Writing about 1950s horror as a whole, and taking fiction as well as films into account, Jancovich (1996) disputes a number of these points, arguing that the features which appear to distinguish *Psycho* from earlier films should in fact be seen as the culmination of earlier trends, including those apparent in a number of sci-fi/horror hybrids. He also takes issue with the hitherto domi-nant view – a view expressed by Biskind (1983: 101–59), Luciano (1987) and Wood (1986: 86) among others – that these hybrids tend to be almost uniformly reactionary in their gender politics, in their militarism, in their Cold War hostility to aliens and Others, and even in their scenarios of nuclear mutation. Dividing the horror output of the 1950s into 'invasion narratives', 'outsider narratives' and narratives 'concerned with "crises of identity"', Jancovich places them within the context of an increasingly rationalized, bureaucratized and conformist US society (1996: 3). He goes on to argue that they frequently critique traditional masculine values, assumptions and images, that 'many 1950s invasion narratives and outsider narratives opposed "rationality" and saw the "irrational" features of emotion, intuition and spontaneity as potential sites of opposition to rationalisation' (ibid.: 4), and that *Psycho* should be seen in the context of crisis of identity narratives in particular.

In maintaining that 1960s and post-1960s horror should be viewed as a development rather a break from the 1950s, Jancovich takes issue with Andrew Tudor, who in *Monsters and Mad Scientists* (1989) argues that there is a fundamental difference between those horror films released in Britain between 1931 and 1960 and those released between 1961 and 1984:

> While the horror movies of the first three decades revolve around the twin poles of science and supernature, and their monsters threaten us largely, though not entirely, from 'outside', the second three decades bring the genre's central threat much closer to us. In these years the horror movie begins to articulate a radically different anxiety. The threat posed by post-1960s horror movies can be seen as expressing a profound insecurity about ourselves, and accordingly the monsters of the period are increasingly represented as part of an everyday contemporary landscape. That is why of all horror movie creatures it is the psychotic that is pre-eminent.
>
> (Tudor 1989: 48)

Tudor's argument is based on a survey of over 900 different films and on an operating model of horror narratives in which 'a monstrous threat is introduced into a stable situation; the monster rampages in the face of attempts to combat it; the monster is (perhaps) destroyed and order (perhaps) restored' (1989: 81). It is also based on a grid of variables which include the nature of the monster, the nature of its source, its powers and its threat, the nature of its victims and pursuers, and the nature of the settings in which the narratives take place. Both periods are divided into phases. The phases seen as marking the period 1931–60 correspond fairly closely to those used here (though Tudor is careful to note that sci-fi/horror hybrids – like gothic revivals – are much more prevalent in the second half of the 1950s than they are in the first). The period 1961–84 is divided into three phases: 'American Decline (1963–1966)', 'the Seventies Boom (1971–1974)' and 'Sustained Growth (1978–1983)' (ibid.: 25). As such it encompasses numerous cycles and short-term trends. These include the Grand Guignol melodramas that followed in the wake of *Whatever Happened to Baby Jane?* (1962) (Hardy 1995a: 128; Hogan [1986] 1988: 27; Kendrick 1991: 235; Tudor 1989: 50–1); the demon baby and demonic possession films that followed in the wake of *Rosemary's Baby* (1968) and *The Exorcist* (1973) (Derry 1988: 168–9; Hogan [1986] 1988: 19–23; Jancovich 1992a: 93–8; Skal 1993: 287–305; Sobchack 1987: 180–2; Tudor 1989: 63; Williams 1996: 99–128); and the slasher and stalker films that followed in the wake of *The Texas Chainshaw Massacre* (1974) and *Halloween* (Clover 1992; Dika 1990; Hogan [1986] 1988: 250–9; Jancovich 1992a: 104–9; Tudor 1989: 68–70. For a survey organized in detail around these and other trends, see Newman 1988). It also encompasses the development of a modern regime of special effects (Skal 1993: 307–31), the deployment of these effects in every kind and at every level of horror production (Hardy [1986] 1995a: 216), the ensuing dissemination of spectacularly explicit representations of violence, sex, and the human and monstrous body (Brophy [1983] 1986), and the changes in Hollywood's production policies and regimes of self-censorship – in particular the abandonment of the Production Code, the adoption of a ratings system, and the targeting in mainstream as well as marginal productions of niche, cult and teenage audiences – that have helped to bring them about (Waller 1987b: 5–6).

Tudor's thesis about the insecure, psychotic and everyday nature of post-1950s horror, even when based on gothic formats, and even when adopting supernatural conventions, echoes Polan ([1982] 1984), and has been echoed more recently by Crane (1994). All three see these developments as marking a profound, often nihilistic lack of confidence in established social institutions and in horror's traditional structures. Significantly, Tudor and Crane in particular arrive at these conclusions by treating the horror film as a multidimensional and historically variable phenomenon, by adopting an historical, empirical and multi-dimensional approach, and by explicitly rejecting one-dimensional definitions and all-embracing theories, especially those associated with psychology and psychoanalysis.

Although similar misgivings have been voiced in recent years by Grant (1994), by Prince (1988) and by others, definitions and theories of this kind have, as noted above, tended to dominate academic discussion of the horror film since the early 1970s. They are in general of three basic kinds: they seek to explain the meaning and the function of monsters, to account for the horror film's pleasures, or to elucidate the psychological and social significance of either or both. They include those of Tarratt ([1970] 1995), for whom monsters represent the unconscious forces of the id; those of Dadoun ([1970] 1989) and Neale (1980: 43–5), for whom monsters are fetishes, representing – and thereby disavowing – the anguish of castration; those of Twitchell, for whom 'modern horror myths prepare the teenager for the anxieties of reproduction' (1985: 7); and those of Grixti (1989), for whom horror propagates a sense of helplessness central to the maintenance of modern consumer culture. They also include those of Carroll, for whom monsters are 'anomalous beings' (1990: 191) who transgress categorial boundaries and who thereby elicit a mix of fascination and disturbance; those of Wood, for whom the monster is representative 'of all that our civilization represses or oppresses' (1986: 75) and for whom the horror film's 'basic formula' can be therefore be summed up as 'normality is threatened by the Monster' (ibid.: 78); those of Creed (1993), for whom the prototype of the monstrous is the reproductive female body; and those of Benshoff, for whom 'many monster movies . . . might be understood as being "about" the eruption of some form of queer sexuality into the midst of a resolutely heterosexual milieu' (1997: 4).

Creed's work in particular relates to a tradition of feminist scholarship that tends to view horror as profoundly misogynist. This tradition, which includes work by Williams (1984), Gledhill (1985b), Modleski (1986), Fischer and Landy ([1982] 1987), Lindsey (1996) and Hollinger (1996), focuses both on the extent to which female characters are victims in horror and on the extent to which the feminine is treated as monstrous. Much of this work presumes a masculine norm of spectatorship and that the audience for horror is principally male. This is as true of Clover's (1992) book on the slasher film – a book which argues that the 'Final Girl', the female survivor characteristic of most slasher films, is a point of identification for the male spectator – as it is of others cited here. However, while Berenstein draws on a number of empirical sources to suggest that women attended and enjoyed horror films in considerable numbers in the 1930s (1996: 60–87), Pinedo underlines the extent to which the claims made about the genre's male audience rely only on anecdotal evidence (1997: 144 n. 4). Taking issue with Clover, Creed and others, she argues that the slasher film 'is an imaginary staging of women who fight back with lethal force against male figures who stalk and try to kill them' (ibid.: 85). As such it may well appeal to women – and generate considerable anxiety in men.

Pinedo argues that some of the readings she disputes presuppose an equation between agency and masculinity: 'feminine means passive, so feminine agency is an oxymoron' (1997: 82). This is a point that applies to discussions of all action-oriented films. In the meantime, it is important to note that, like Berenstein (1996), Carroll (1984), Friedman (1984), Halberstam (1995: 77–84) and Wood (1986: 85), Pinedo is concerned with issues of ethnicity as well as with issues of gender, and hence with the extent to which horror films may identify the monster 'as a racial or ethnic Other.' (1997: 111).

Three points are worth making in conclusion. The first is that the forms and meanings of monsters are multiple: the monster 'is difference made flesh . . . Any kind of alterity can be inscribed across (constructed through) the monstrous body, but for the most part monstrous difference tends to be cultural, political, racial, economic, sexual' (Cohen 1996c: 7). The second is that 'the categories "human" and "monster" are coincident, mutually constitutive' (Cohen 1996b: xi), and that it is partly in so far as this is the case that there are grounds for the generic overlap between horror and science fiction, as we shall see. The third is that the category of 'nature' is at stake as well. This is both another reason for the sci-fi/horror overlap and also why Tudor is careful to specify that the source of horror in the horror film is not necessarily a monster, but a 'monstrous threat'. This threat can come from all kinds of sources and can take all kinds of different forms. As films like *Pulse* (1988) make clear, horror can stem as much from its monstrous effects as from any of its monstrous incarnations.

Science fiction

There are numerous definitions of science fiction. Some are normative and exclusive, designed to distinguish between 'good' and 'bad' science fiction or to promote a particular form or trend. This is especially true of those who commentate on written science fiction, and of those concerned to distinguish between its 'pulp' and its 'literary' forms on the one hand, and its written and filmic forms on the other. Some, like Richard Hodgens', are more descriptive and all embracing. 'Science fiction', he writes, 'involves extrapolated or fictitious science, or fictitious use of scientific possibilities, or it may be simply fiction that takes place in the future or introduces some radical assumption about the present or the past' (1959: 30). (This passage is cited during the course of a chapter on definitions of science fiction by Sobchack [1980] 1988: 17–63. See also Hardy [1984] 1995c: ix–xv; Kuhn 1990b; Tarnowski 1977.) What this means, among other things, is that in science fiction, science, fictional or otherwise, always functions as motivation for the nature of the fictional world, its inhabitants, and the events that happen within it, whether or not science itself is a topic or theme.

As a term, 'science fiction' was first used in the nineteenth century, but only became fully established in the late 1920s in and around American pulp magazines like *Amazing Stories*, and in particular *Science Wonder Stories* (James 1994: 7–11). It thus largely post-dated the vogue for 'invention stories', for 'tales of science', for 'tales of the future' and for the 'voyages imaginaires' which were associated in particular with Jules Verne, and which characterized the late nineteenth century and the early twentieth (ibid.: 12–30). This vogue coincided both with a second industrial revolution, a new machine age, and a cult of and for scientific invention, and with an acceleration of the processes of colonial expansion and imperial rivalry that had already fuelled a tradition of exploration stories, adventure stories, and stories of territorial conquest. It also coincided with the invention of film, itself seen, of course, as a new scientific and technical marvel.

The earliest generic vehicles for this vogue were 'trick films' like *The X-Ray Mirror* (1899) and Méliès' 'voyages imaginaires', both of which helped establish the bond between science fiction, special effects technology and set design that has remained a feature of the genre ever since (Barnouw 1981; Brosnan 1974; Finch 1984; Hammond 1974: 114–25, 1981; Hutchison 1987). In 1910, the first filmed version of *Frankenstein* helped establish a link between science fiction and horror in the cinema, a link that was to be reforged in gothic mode in the 1930s, in apocalyptic mode in the 1950s, and in body horror mode since the late 1960s. A little later, series and serials like *The Exploits of Elaine* (1914), *The Flaming Disc* (1920) and *Terror Island* (1920) helped cement a similar link between science fiction, action and adventure. This link was maintained in the 1930s and 1940s by low-budget serials like *Flash Gordon* (1936), *Batman* (1943) and *Superman* (1948) and revived in the form of the contemporary blockbuster by George Lucas and others in the late 1970s. Finally, a tradition of large-scale speculations on the future of modern society – and allegories in science fictional form about its current condition – was established in Europe by films like *Metropolis* (1926), *La Fin du Monde* (1930) and *Things to Come* (1936). It was revived in America, usually on a more modest industrial scale, during the course of the boom in science fiction in the 1950s, then again in the late 1960s and early 1970s with films like *The Day the Earth Stood Still* (1951), *On the Beach* (1959), *Planet of the Apes* (1968) and *Soylent Green* (1973). Since then it has tended to merge into the horror and action-adventure traditions, and to become ever more distopian in outlook (Franklin [1985] 1990; Glass 1989, 1990). These are the principal forms of science fiction in the cinema. They thus incorporate most but not all of the categories or 'templates' into which science fiction as a whole is divided in Pringle [1996] 1997: 21–37. These templates are listed as 'space operas', 'planetary romances', 'future cities', 'disasters', 'alternative histories', 'prehistorical romances', 'time travels', 'alien intrusions', 'mental powers' and 'comic infernos').

Although there are several books which detail the history of these trends (notably Baxter 1970; Hardy [1984] 1995c; Brosnan 1978), science fiction in the cinema has tended to lack a tradition of critical theory. There is a great deal of writing about individual films, periods and topics, but very little about science fiction as a genre. The major exceptions here are Vivian Sobchack's (1988) *Screening Space* (a reworking of her earlier book, *The Limits of Infinity*), the section on science fiction in Schatz's *Old Hollywood/New Hollywood, Ritual, Art, and Industry* (1983), and J. P. Telotte's *Replications* (1995).

Screening Space begins with a chapter on definitions, and moves on to consider iconography, and the genre's use of language and sound. She concludes on the one hand that 'Although it lacks an informative iconography, encompasses the widest possible range of time and place, and constantly fluctuates in its visual representation of objects, the SF film still has a science fiction "look" and "feel" to its visual surfaces' ([1980] 1988: 87). This 'visual connection' between SF films

> lies in the consistent and repetitious use not of *specific* images, but of *types* of images which function in the same way from film to film to create an imaginatively realized world which is always removed from the world we know or know of. The visual surface of all SF film [*sic*] presents us with a confrontation between a mixture of those images to which we respond as 'alien' and those we know to be familiar.
>
> (Sobchack [1980] 1988: 87; emphasis in original)

Thus '[t]he major visual impulse of all SF films is to pictorialize the unfamiliar, the nonexistent, the strange and totally alien – and to do so with a verisimilitude which is, at times, documentary in flavor and style' (ibid.: 88).

This relationship between the strange and the familiar is, she argues, as pertinent to the soundtrack as it is to the image. Vocabulary and language are often highlighted as issues in science fiction. In *2001 – A Space Odyssey* (1968), for example, 'we are constantly made aware of how language – and, therefore, our emotions and thought patterns – have [*sic*] not kept up with either our technology or our experience' ([1980] 1988: 177). And sound itself, the sound of machinery, the sound of natural forces, and 'the sound of the alien' (ibid.: 218), functions in films like *Five* (1951) and *The Thing* (1951) both as a generic marker, and as one of the points at which the strange and familiar meet.

Focusing almost exclusively on the 1950s, Schatz argues that 'The milieu of the science fiction is one of contested space, in which the generic oppositions are determined by certain aspects of the cultural community and by the contest itself' (1983: 86). The contest here is the contest between 'the human community' and some kind of 'alien or monstrous force' (ibid.). The milieu, whose attributes are usually 'a direct extension of America's technological capabilities' may be a small town, a city, or even the world as a whole (ibid.). However, the distinction between the human community and the alien force is by no means always straightforward. In films like *It Came from Outer Space* (1953) and *Invasion of the Body Snatchers* (1956), the distinction is blurred: 'the members of the community so utterly assimilate the group values that they are turned into automatons' (ibid.: 87). It becomes hard to tell alien and human apart. In this way, within a constellation of generic concerns that includes nature, science, technology, social and communal organization and that which is alien or other, the idea of the human, upon which the dramatization of these concerns centrally depends, is broached as an issue.

For Telotte (who here echoes Malmgren 1980 and Jancovich 1992b) the issue of humanness lies at the heart of science fiction, and it is focused in particular by the figure of the robot and by its most recent avatar, the cyborg. He traces the function and the meaning of these figures in films from *Metropolis* on, placing them within both their cyclic and cultural contexts. He thus sees such 1930s films as *Mad Love* (1935), *The Bride of Frankenstein* (1935) and *Island of Lost Souls* (1933) as depicting in the then current gothic horror mode 'violent efforts to redefine the human body as some sort of raw material' for scientific artifice and experiment (1995: 86), and hence as expressing contemporary concerns about the subjection of the human to the powers of technology and science. He sees the serials of the 1930s and 1940s as revealing 'a growing fascination with the technological and its potential for reshaping the human' (ibid.: 18), while at the same time drawing a line between the two through stories which 'repeatedly celebrate a *human* might and *human* feelings, particularly a human determination to say something other than a subject, serialized thing' (ibid.: 100; emphasis in original). He sees such 1950s films as *Forbidden Planet* (1956) as marking a 'newly recognized ability to duplicate anything, including the human body' (ibid.: 19), and such 1970s films as *Westworld* (1973), *Futureworld* (1976) and *Demon Seed* (1977) as expressing 'growing anxieties' both about 'our place' in a world in which that capacity has been enhanced by artificial intelligence (ibid.) and about the ensuing loss of 'all distinction between the private and the public' (ibid.: 146). And finally, in the 1980s and 1990s, as 'science fiction . . . returned to the level of popularity it enjoyed in the 1950s' (ibid.: 148), he sees films such as *Blade Runner* (1982), *Cherry 2000* (1986), *Total Recall* and *Terminator 2* repeatedly depicting the body 'as an *image* that is constantly being reconfigured and presented for display' (ibid.: 149; emphasis in original), and repeatedly using the robotic to interrogate, to blur and often to reverse the polarities between the artificial and the human. While the trend in the 1980s was 'toward showing the human as ever more artifical', the trend in the 1990s has been 'toward rendering the artificial as ever more human' (ibid.: 22).

As Telotte is well aware, the boundaries of the human and the issues of difference they raise are rendered more complex by the fact that they necessarily include issues of sexuality, ethnicity and gender. Following Haraway (1985), such issues have been explored by Berg (1989), Byers (1989), Penley ([1986] 1989) and Neale (1989), and in a number of essays edited by Kuhn (1990a) and by Penley *et al.* (1991). Nearly all these essays refer at least in passing to *Alien* and *Blade Runner*, films which have become canonic touchstones not just for discussions of difference but also for those engaged in debates about 'postmodernism' and the nature of 'postmodern' aesthetics and representation.

Aside from Bruno's essay on *Blade Runner*, an essay which touches on time, space, memory, history, simulacra, pastiche and the definitive absence of authenticity ([1987] 1990), the concluding chapter in Sobchack's book is probably the most sustained attempt to engage with some of these issues. Sobchack here argues that since the 1960s, science fiction in the US has undergone a number of fundamental changes. These changes

go much further than a simple transformation of the nature and manner of the genre's special effects or of its representation of visible technology. Whether 'mainstream' and big-budget or 'marginal' and low-budget, the existential attitude of the contemporary SF films is different – even if its basic material remained the same. Cinematic space travel of the 1950s had an aggressive and three-dimensional thrust – whether it was narrativized as optimistic, colonial, and phallic penetration and conquest or as pessimistic and paranoid earthly and bodily invasion. Space in these films was semantically inscribed as 'deep' and time as accelerating and 'urgent.' In the SF films released between 1968 and 1977 . . . space became semantically inscribed as inescapably domestic and crowded. Time lost its urgency – statically stretching foward toward an impoverished and unwelcome future worse than a bad present.

> (Sobchack [1980] 1988: 225–6)

With the release of *Star Wars* and *Close Encounters of the Third Kind* (1977), a further transformation occurred: 'technological wonder had become synonymous with domestic hope; space and time seemed to expand again' (ibid.: 226). Finally, during the course of the 1980s, postmodern norms take hold:

> most of today's SF films (mainstream or marginal) construct a generic field in which space is semantically described as a surface for play and dispersal, a surface across which existence and objects kinetically displace and dis-play their materiality. As well, the urgent or hopeless temporality of the earlier films has given way to a new and erotic leisureliness – even in 'action-packed' films. Time has decelerated, but it is not represented as static. It is filled with curious things and dynamized by a series of concatenated events rather than linearly pressured to stream forward by the teleology of the plot.
>
> (Sobchack [1980] 1988: 227–8)

Sobchack cites films like *Liquid Sky* (1983), *Strange Invaders* (1983) and *Night of the Comet* (1984) as examples of what she means. Whether her argument applies to films like *Aliens* and *Terminator 2* remains, perhaps, open to question.

Musicals

The Hollywood musical is a product of the advent of sound, of the industry's commitment to an ethos and to forms of entertainment represented, among other things, by the theatrical musical, by Broadway, and by Tin Pan Alley, of its stake in the music publishing, recording and radio industries (acquired during the conversion to sound in the late 1920s: see Hilmes 1990: 26–77; Jewell 1984; Millard 1995: 158–62; Sanjek [1988] 1996: 147–58; Shepherd 1982: 82–6), and of developments in and on the musical stage in America and elsewhere during the previous eighty to ninety years. Film versions of stage musicals like *The Merry Widow* and *The Student Prince*, and of operas like *Carmen* and *La Bohème*, had been produced during the silent era. So, too, had filmed records of dancers and dances (Hungerford 1951: 102–8). As Collins points out, these and nearly all other films were usually accompanied by live music, and were often shown in contexts and venues which included musical performances of one kind or another (1988: 269–70). As he goes on to argue, it was the presence and popularity of these musical acts that helped prompt the first experiments with sound in the mid-1920s, and that helped function as a model for the preludes and shorts produced by Warners and others at this time. And as he goes on to suggest, the ensuing 'tension between live musical acts and film presentation', between 'the increasing technological sophistication of the medium . . . and the sense of nostalgia for a direct relationship with the audience' has marked the musical ever since, providing the focus for such studies as those by Feuer ([1982] 1993) and Altman (1987), and the motivation for his own concentration on the 'ever-shifting relationship between performance, spectacle, and audience.' (Collins 1988: 270). In the meantime, as Wolfe (1990) has pointed out, the established nature and shape of the musical short helped govern the use of musical sequences in *The Jazz Singer* (1927), the film usually cited as the first feature-length musical. During the course of the next three years, over 200 musical films of one kind or another were made, and despite a decline in the number of musicals produced and released in the early 1930s, the musical had re-established itself as a routine component in Hollywood's output by 1934 (Altman 1996b: 294–7; Balio 1993: 211–18; Barrios 1995).

The musical has always been a mongrel genre. In varying measures and combinations, music, song and dance have been its only essential ingredients. In consequence its history, both on stage and on screen, has been marked by numerous traditions, forms and styles. These in turn have been marked by numerous terms – 'operetta', 'revue', 'musical comedy', 'musical drama', 'the backstage musical', 'the rock musical', 'the integrated musical', and so on. As we shall see, historians, critics and theorists of the musical sometimes disagree about the meaning of some of these terms. As we shall also see, some invent their own. Nevertheless, it is possible to provide some basic definitions, to indicate areas of debate and disagreement, and in the process to highlight the extent to which the musical has always been, despite its accessible and effortless image, multifaceted, hybrid, and complex (Collins 1988: 269).

Revue, to begin with, is usually and uncontentiously defined as a series of comic and musical performances lacking a narrative framework (lacking what in the theatre is called a 'book'), and unified, if at all, only by a consistent style, design or theme, a common set of comic targets, or a single producer, director or venue (Baral [1962] 1970; Bordman 1985; Kislan 1980: 78–92). Pure revue in the cinema is rare, though there was a vogue for revue in the late 1920s and early 1930s when as Balio, citing Walker (1979: 184), points out, it 'was used by producers to showcase stars and contract players and to offer "proof positive that everone could now talk, sing and dance at least passably well"' (1993: 211). And as Delameter points out, the influence of revue is evident in the backstage musical, where the show in preparation is usually a revue of one kind or another (1974: 122).

One of the distinguishing marks of operetta, by contrast, is the presence of a book. Important too, though, is the nature of the book, the nature of the setting, and the nature and importance of the music. (*Variety* argues that 'In operetta the score is the primary consideration . . . The book, dancing (if any), comedy (if any), production and acting (if any) are all secondary to the music and singing' ('This Is Operetta', 20 February 1946: 49).) To quote Rubin, 'operetta is characterized by its European origins, its elegance and sophistication of its tone, its use of melodic, waltz-time music, its picturesque and exotic settings, and its strongly integrative organization around a melo-dramatic, romance-oriented book' (1993: 48). In the cinema, operetta is usually exemplified by the films of Jeanette MacDonald and Nelson Eddy (*Sweethearts* (1938), *Rose Marie* (1936) and others, all based on stage hits by proponents of American operetta like Victor Herbert and Sigmund Romberg, and all produced as a series by Hunt Stromberg at MGM) (Balio 1993: 223–4), by a cycle of stage adaptations made in the late 1920s and early 1930s (ibid.: 211–12), and, as an offshoot of this cycle, by a group of four Jeanette MacDonald and Maurice Chevalier films made at Paramount: *The Love Parade* (1929), *The Smiling Lieutenant* (1931), *One Hour with You* (1932), and *Love Me Tonight* (1932) – all highly acclaimed by critics for their *risqué* wit, and for their inventive use of editing, space and sound (Altman 1987: 150–1; Balio 1993: 212–14; Knight 1985; Mast 1987: 123–4).

Operettas of a fairly traditional kind continued to be made in the 1940s and 1950s, some of them as vehicles for new musical stars like Kathryn Grayson and Howard Keel, and some of them also, like the remakes of *The Desert Song* (1953) and *Rose Marie* (1954), as contributions to a contemporary vogue for action, adventure and spectacle (always in colour, and often in CinemScope, Todd-AO or VistaVision too). However, the fact that so many of the 1950s film were remakes is significant. For most commentators argue that by then traditional operetta as a form capable of generating new work was moribund or dead (Bordman 1981: 144–8; Kislan 1980: 104–5). However, some, like Bordman (1981: 149–69) and Traubner ([1983] 1989: 377–421), argue that it had already given rise to a new form, 'musical drama' (or 'the musical play').

Musical drama is usually exemplified by a tradition of Broadway musicals that begins with *Show Boat* in 1927, and runs through *Oklahoma!* (1943), *Carousel* (1945), *South Pacific* (1949), and other works by Rodgers and Hammerstein, *Brigadoon* (1947), *My Fair Lady* (1956), and other works by Lerner and Loewe, and shows like *West Side Story* (1957) and *Fiddler on the Roof* (1964), all of which have been made into films, and many of which were road-show productions in the 1950s and 1960s, a period in which Hollywood increasingly turned to Broadway for pre-sold, prestige material (Collins 1988: 277).[26] Along with a tendency to use what Delameter calls '"big" voices' (1974: 123), one of the hallmarks of musical drama – one of the elements it derives from operetta – is the imporance of its storyline (one which could accommodate pathos, dramatic conflict, and even on occasion an unhappy ending), its attention to situation and character, and the 'sharply integrative' organization of its music, its singing and its dancing. Integration of this kind became an ideal not only among those who wrote, directed and choreo-graphed musical dramas, but also among critics, theorists and historians. It has tended to produce a canonic crest-line, a tradition of landmark films, shows and personnel. Although as Solomon points out 'there is no evident reason' for preferring integration (1976: 71), and although there are significant differences between Broadway's crest-line and Hollywood's, both have resulted on occasion in partial or distorted accounts of the musical's history.

The notion of integration and the idea of 'the integrated musical' appear at first sight to be quite straightforward. However, as Mueller (1984) has pointed out, things are not necessarily as simple as they seem. Focusing on the relationship between the musical numbers and the plot, he argues that there are at least six different possible permutations, from numbers *'which are completely irrelevant to the plot'*, to those *'which contribute to the spirit or theme'* (ibid.: 28) or *'which enrich the plot, but do not advance it'*, to those *'which advance the plot'* (ibid.: 29) either through their setting and narrative function – it is here that he tends to place the backstage musical – and/or through their lyrical content (emphases in original).

The precision Mueller seeks to bring to the concept of integration is unusual. Most uses of the term are rather vague. It can act as a synonym for almost any form of motivation, and sometimes even as a synonym for stylistic or aesthetic coherence. This is one reason why its history, both on stage and in the cinema, is also rather vague. There is no doubt that operetta and musical drama are important. But a number of the films and shows cited by Mueller and others are musical comedies. This is certainly true of the Astaire–Rogers films made at RKO in the 1930s, the principal focus of Mueller's article. It is also true of the Princess Theatre shows written by Guy Bolton, Jerome Kern and P. G. Wodehouse in the late 1910s, often cited as early examples of integration by historians of the musical on stage (among them Bordman 1982: 101–5; Kislan 1980: 113–16; Smith and Litton 1981: 122–3; Toll 1982: 133).

Issues of integration notwithstanding, musical comedy has always been much more heterogeneous than operetta or musical drama, as befits a genre – or sub-genre – whose origins lay as much in the minstrel show, vaudeville and other forms of variety entertainment as in turn-of-the-century farce (Bordman 1982: 3–77; Henderson and Bowers 1996: 7–36; Smith and Litton 1981: 2–87). What has remained constant has been a commitment to comedy and the comic, to popular and vernacular styles of music, song and dance, and a willingness to sacrifice coherence or integration for the sake of either or both. Most Hollywood musicals are musicals of this kind. Films like *College Holiday* (1936) and *Road to Morocco* (1942) have always outnumbered films like *West Side Story* (1961), *Swing Time* (1936) and *Meet Me in St Louis* (1944).

Alongside formal and sub-generic categories such as these, the musical has often been discussed under the headings provided on the one hand by the names of its producers, directors, choreographers and performers, and on the other by the names of the studios responsible for its production. Once again, though, treatment of these topics has been somewhat uneven, governed more by critical taste and ideological preoccupation than by historical precision.

During the studio era, for instance, most of the major and minor companies made musicals. But research into the production policies and output of these companies has been very uneven, and this is as true of the musical as it is of other genres. Thus while there is a whole book devoted to the output of the Freed unit at MGM (Fordin 1975), there are no book-length studies of the musicals produced by Fox, by RKO, by Warner Bros, or by Paramount, let alone those produced by Columbia, Universal or Republic. Moreover, while scholars like Morddern (1988: 234) and Schatz (1988a: 447) respectively document Warners' role in the revival of the musical in the early 1930s and MGM's numerical dominance of the genre in the post-war period, they are not really able to account for either. The same is true of Collins' account of Paramount's propensity for operetta and of Warners' propensity for contemporary settings and backstage conventions in the 1930s, and of MGM's propensity for self-reflexivity in the 1940s and 1950s (1988: 271–3, 275–7). And the same is also true of Rubin's observation that Fox's musicals in the 1940s tended on the one hand to feature big bands and exotic settings and on the other to eschew 'integration, coherent narrativity, consistent characterization, or even simply logic' (1993: 159). In addition, aside from Fordin's book on Freed, there are no detailed studies of the work of unit producers like Charles Rogers, Hunt Stromberg, Joe Pasternak or Pandro S. Berman, though it should be noted that Schatz (1988a: 237–42) contains references to all these figures, and a particularly interesting account of the roles played by Rogers and Pasternak in the development of a formula for Deanna Durbin's musicals at Universal in the late 1930s.

Pandro S. Berman is probably best known as unit producer of the Astaire–Rogers musicals at RKO in the 1930s. These films, and Astaire's role within them as choreographer and director of musical numbers as well as singer, dancer and star, have been subject to extensive analysis, not least as relatively early examples of integrated musicals on screen. Mueller's book-length study (1985) documents in detail the modes of integration in these and other Astaire films, Astaire's eclectic style as choreographer, the traditions of dance upon which he drew, and in particular his style as choreographer for the camera, filming and editing sequences of dance in such a way as to preserve the integrity of the body and the space within which it moves.

Along with the work of Ernst Lubitsch and Rouben Mamoulian at Paramount in the early 1930s, the Astaire–Rogers films are generally cited as important points of reference for the work of Vincente Minnelli, Gene Kelly, Stanley Donen, and others at MGM in the 1940s and 1950s. Minnelli's commitment to integration is well-documented, not least in his interviews and autobiography (Minnelli 1974 and Delameter 1981: 265–74). From this point of view, Elsaesser's account of Minnelli's work is exemplary ([1969] 1981). As he points out, the central characters in all Minnelli's films are engaged in a struggle to assert their identity, to articulate their vision of the world. In the musicals they succeed, and a key device in this respect is what Genne (1992) has termed 'the dance-drama', a lengthy sequence of dance in which the terms of the struggle are laid bare. Dance-dramas are also used by Donen and Kelly, who are both committed to integration too. Where they differ from Minnelli is in their preference for stories involving strong male friendships, in their deployment of a sparser, brighter and more evenly lit *mise-en-scène*, and in their use of what Genne calls 'street dances' (like 'Singin' in the Rain') in preference to the 'festive' or 'party' scenes that tend to figure in Minnelli's films. (For further discussion of Donen and Kelly, see Charness 1990.)

Minnelli, Donen, Kelly and Astaire all tend to contrast their work with that of Busby Berkeley, not least on the grounds of integration, motivation and display. However, as Rubin has pointed out, Berkeley's work – both on screen and on stage – belongs to a tradition that includes the circus, nineteenth-century extravaganza, the Wild West Show, and the spectacular revue, a tradition that has always eschewed integration, and one whose persistence leads him to argue that 'the history of the musical . . . [is] . . . not so much a relentless, unidirectional drive toward effacing the last stubborn remnants of nonintegration, but a succession of different ways of articulating the tension and interplay between integrative (chiefly narrative) and nonintegrative (chiefly spectacle) elements' (1993: 12–13). Rubin points out that in films like *The Gang's All Here* (1943), Berkeley sought 'to spectacularize the entire film' (ibid.: 161), to turn the conventional relationship between the narrative and the numbers inside out. Alain Masson ([1976] 1981) makes a similar point about George Sidney's work, arguing both that Sidney systematically exploited the artifice and the disjunctive potential of the musical and that his critical reputation has tended to suffer as a result.

Berkeley's work has also been criticized for what Lucy Fischer ([1976] 1981) has called its 'optical politics'. In an analysis of *Dames* (1934), Fischer points out that women literally become two-dimensional images, subordinated to a voyeuristic gaze whose instrument is the camera and whose source is resolutely male. In this context, it is worth noting that Berkeley made a number of musicals with Esther Williams in the 1940s and 1950s, and that along with Sonja Henie and Eleanor Powell, Williams is one of a trio of female performers whose films have been analysed by Faller in terms of what he calls their 'subversive power' (1992: v). In each case, Faller sees the relationship between the narrative and the numbers as the site of a potential contradiction between the powers and performance skills demonstrated in and through the numbers and the ideological work of the plot. Thus Henie's solitary skills as a skater and Williams's solitary skills as a swimmer so dominate the numbers in their films that narratives which seek to pair them up with men 'fail to contain' them (ibid.: 205). Meanwhile Powell's skills as a dancer result, almost uniquely, in narratives which centre as much on a successful career as on domesticity or romance.

The relationship between gender, narrative and spectacle in the musical has been explored in the case of male performers too. Cohan, for example, argues that Fred Astaire's 'male image' is grounded in 'the so-called "feminine" tropes of narcissism, exhibitionism, and masquerade' (1993: 48), while Rickard (1996) argues not only that the dance sequences in the Astaire–Rogers films serve to sexualize Astaire's masculinity, but also that this sexualization is authorized for the audience by Rogers's gaze. More traditional analyses of star personae and musical performance skills can meanwhile be found in Babington and Evans (1985), who discuss Jeanette MacDonald, Maurice Chevalier, Fred Astaire, Ginger Rogers and Gene Kelly. As well as Kelly and Astaire, Delameter (1981) discusses Alice Faye, Betty Grable, Danny Kaye, Bill Robinson and others, though principally as dancers rather than as actors, singers or stars. Reflecting the tendency to focus on dance rather than music and song, he also discusses such choreographers as Hermes Pan, Robert Alton, Jack Cole, Michael Kidd and Bob Fosse.[27]

This account has so far focused on the studio era. However, although the musical is often viewed as a quintessential studio form, and although the number of musicals produced has certainly declined since the 1960s,[28] it has by no means completely disappeared. But aside from occasional 'revisionist' musicals like *Nashville* (1975) and *All That Jazz* (1978) (viewed by Collins (1988: 277) as 'metafictional' extensions of the self-reflexive Freed unit films), and aside from even more occasional revivals of something akin to the traditional musical like *Evita* (1996), the numerically dominant form over the last 30 years has been the rock musical.

The rock musical was born in the 1950s with teenpics like *Jailhouse Rock* (1957) and *The Girl Can't Help It* (1956). Apart from research on the synergistic connections between the film and popular music industries and their effects on musical films (Denisoff and Plasketes 1990; Doty 1988; Sanjek [1988] 1996: 599–60), debate since then has tended to focus on the extent to which it has challenged or changed the values and conventions of the traditional Hollywood musical. For Grant, the anarchic rebelliousness and raw sexuality associated with rock'n'roll in the 1950s were potentially disruptive of the genre's commitment to romance and community. He argues, however, that by 'the stressing of rock's potential for community, and the taming of rock's energy through a deliberate moulding of its stars . . . rock 'n' roll changed much more than . . . the musical film' (1986c: 199). For Telotte, by contrast, the musical has changed fundamentally since the 1950s – not because of its music but because of a shift in the balance between its 'real' and its 'ideal' components. On the one hand musicals like *Grease* (1978) and *The Wiz* (1978) 'tend to integrate the musical components at the expense of a realistic plot. As a result they seem to deny or denigrate the reality of the world that has given birth to the music' (1980: 3). On the other hand, musicals like *Saturday Night Fever* (1977) and *The Buddy Holly Story* (1978) realistically motivate singing and dancing as diegetic action while setting them in counterpoint to a narrative world otherwise filled with difficulties, dangers and frustrations. In this way they address the limitations – as well as the potential – of music and dance as means of escaping, transcending or changing the everyday world.

The 'escapist' status of the musical has been addressed at length by Dyer, Feuer and Altman. For Dyer ([1977] 1981), musicals offer aesthetically 'utopian' solutions to real social needs and contradictions. The same is true for Feuer, who stresses the extent to which its artificial, quasi-modernist devices serve the conservative ends of show-biz by seeking to bridge the gap between producer and consumer and create in its stead an illusion of community. In this way the Hollywood musical can be seen as a form of modern industrial mass entertainment which nevertheless 'aspires to the condition of folk art' ([1982] 1993: 3).

For Altman, the resolution of contradictions and oppositions is not just a function of the musical, but also a method of analysis. Wishing to construct a rigorous critical definition of the musical, and a systematic history of its forms, its cultural functions, and its history, Altman constructs a corpus of films on the basis of perceived structural, stylistic and ideological character-istics, all of which entail opposition and mediation. Central to the corpus is a 'dual-focus' structure in which 'the text proceeds by alternation, confronta-tion, and parallelism between male and female leads (or groups)' (1987: 107), and in which a romance plot and a couple (or couples) provide the basis for the construction and reconciliation not just of differences of gender, but also – depending on the film – of differences of class, age, wealth, personality and outlook and so on as well. What this means, among other things, is that traditional narrative values like causality and motivation, and the conventional opposition between the narrative and the numbers, are displaced by structures and devices of comparison and contrast whose role is to articulate the dualities with which any particular film is concerned. Among these devices are 'the audio dissolve' and 'the video dissolve'. Where the former 'super-imposes sounds' (ibid.: 63) in moving from one portion of the soundtrack to another (from conversation, for example, to music and song), the latter serves to connect 'two separate places, times, or levels of reality' (ibid.: 74). Both devices thus serve to mark and to bridge oppositions.

Altman also constructs a new typology of musical forms. Using the rela-tionship between the musical's romance plot and its ideological oppositions as a basis, he suggests that there are three basic musical types: 'the fairy tale musical', in which 'restoring order to the couple accompanies and parallels . . . restoration of order to an imaginary kingdom', 'the show musical', in which 'creating the couple is associated with the creation of a work of art (Broadway show, Hollywood film, fashion magazine, concert, etc.)', and 'the folk musical', in which 'integrating two disparate individuals into a single couple heralds the entire group's communion with each other' (1987: 126).

Altman's book is to date the most sustained and detailed attempt to provide a theoretically rigorous account of the Hollywood musical. However, while it encompasses an impressive array of films and examples, and while its typology is convincing, it is not without its problems. Like Dyer and Feuer, Altman tends to argue that the musical always resolves the contradictions with which it deals. This position is not uncommon among theories of genre, as we shall see. But it tends on the one hand to obviate the need for further research, since the answers to questions about ideology in particular are always known in advance. On the other, it tends to underestimate the extent to which musicals like *Brigadoon* (1954) blatantly signal their resolutions as unreal, and the extent to which musicals like *West Side Story* and in particular *It's Always Fair Weather* (1955) (Babington and Evans 1985: 166–86; Wood 1975: 146–64) lay the costs of their resolutions uncomfortably bare.

Altman's insistence on the centrality of romance and a dual-focus structure is also problematic, both because romance and a dual-focus structure characterize romantic comedies as well as musicals, and because some musicals lack either or both. Aside from *The Wizard of Oz* (1939), an example acknowledged by Altman himself (1987: 104), one might cite *Ziegfeld Follies* (1946), which as a revue lacks an overarching plot, *Hold That Co-Ed* (1938), in which the dual cultural values of skilful hard work and entrepreneurial flair are embodied in the alliance between a football coach and a local politician rather than in the film's perfunctory romance, *Poor Little Rich Girl* (1936), a Shirley Temple film which lacks both a romance and a dual-focus structure, *Jupiter's Darling* (1955), which is triply rather than dually focused, and *Meet Me in St Louis*, which contains two romances, neither of which is dual focus in nature, and neither of which embodies the film's central opposition between domestic and familial harmony and domestic and familial discord.

Responding to an earlier version of these ideas (Altman [1978] 1981b), Babington and Evans cite *Gold Diggers of 1933* (1933) and *Easter Parade* (1948) as exceptions as well (1985: 80). While less ambitious than Altman, their own discussions of these and other musicals tend to be more attentive to the genre's multifarious nature as well as to the films' specificities. To that extent, their book shares the virtues of those ideologically oriented analyses which, like Dyer (1993), Gabbard (1996), Henderson (1981–2), McLean (1997), Roberts (1993), Rogin (1992), Roth ([1977] 1981), Smith (1991) and Woll (1983), are rather more localized and context-specific, rather more focused on particular issues, aspects, periods, performers and films than a book like Altman's. However, in their preoccupation with ideological significance, even these studies sometimes lose sight of the musical's basic aesthetic materials.

SOCIAL PROBLEM FILMS

The term 'social problem film' is essentially a critical invention. Labelled 'sociological', 'message' or 'thought' films by the industry (Brownlow 1990: xix, xxi), the films themselves have been grouped and described in ways which are recognizable and consistent, but also somewhat problematic. Writing about the British cinema of the 1950s and 1960s, Marcia Landy argues that 'The social problem film was directed toward the dramatization of topical social issues – capital punishment, prison life, juvenile delinquency, poverty, marital conflict, family tension, and, to a lesser degree, racism' (1991: 432). She goes on to quote Roffman and Purdy, who in their book on *The Hollywood Social Problem Film* maintain that 'The problem film combines social analysis and dramatic conflict within a coherent narrative structure. Social content is transformed into dramatic events and movie narrative adapted to accommodate social issues as story material through a particular set of movie conventions' (1981: viii).

'These conventions', they argue, 'distinguish the social problem film as a genre.' Central to them is a 'very specific' narrative focus: 'the central dramatic conflict revolves around the interaction of the individual with social institutions (such as government, business, political movements, etc.)' (1981: viii). This focus is sufficient to distinguish most of the films they discuss. But they themselves note that 'there is an extensive crossing of genres' (ibid.), and they themselves discuss gangster films, prison films, biopics, comedies and westerns, among others. They also consciously exclude 'historical "message" pictures' like *Juarez* (1939) and *Viva Zapata* (1952) (ibid.) and unconsciously exclude exploitation films, whose stock-in-trade was sensational topicality (see the section on teenpics, pp. 118–25). In addition, they recognize that 'there is only an indirect concern with broader social values' (ibid.) in social problem films, hence implicitly at least that all issues in all films are social. But they do not centrally address the extent to which the 'problems' with which the films deal are themselves constructed as such from the socio-cultural material upon which all films necessarily draw and by which they are all necessarily surrounded (Hill 1986). Nor do they fully address the extent to which they are selected from an array of potential 'problems' on offer.

Roffman and Purdy focus on the 1930s, the 1940s and the early 1950s. Drawing on Jacobs (1939: 67–77), they note the existence of a tradition of social problem and campaign films in the Progressive era of the early 1900s and the 1910s (1981: 9–11). But their book was written prior to the appearance of studies by Brownlow (1990), Sloan (1988) and Ross (1998), which deal with this era and its films in much more detail, which all note the role and the prevalence of melodramatic conventions and traditions in the gangster, labour, slum, suffragette and white slave-trade films they discuss, and which all remark on the extent to which these films – films like *Capital vs. Labor* (1910), *Votes for Women* (1912), *The Jungle* (1914) and *Why?* (1913) – were often openly radical in character.

Beginning with the early years of the Depression, Roffman and Purdy themselves discuss gangster, prison, fallen woman and 'shyster lawyer' films, films about ordinary people, politics and power, and films about the unemployed, the rural poor and the dispossessed. Focusing on the impact of the

New Deal, there is a chapter on Frank Capra's films, on workers, on juvenile delinquents, on lynching, and on the growing influence of fascism both at home and abroad. The war period is dealt with only briefly. But there are lengthy chapters on the cycle of post-war films about returning veterans, on post-war films about ethnic minorities, and on films about post-war labour problems and the alienation of individuals from American society. Most of these films are seen as influenced by the trend toward psychological motivation and the depiction of neurosis. Most of them are also seen as influenced not just by the advent of the Cold War, but also by the activities of the House Un-American Activities Committee (HUAC) in Hollywood in the late 1940s and early 1950s. Indeed, although they refer in closing to the late 1950s, the 1960s and the early 1970s, a period in which, they argue, films of all kinds were increasingly infused with 'an explicitly antisocial subtext' (1981: 298), it is one of the principal theses of Roffman and Purdy's book that HUAC brought about 'the end of an era' (ibid.: 284) by attacking and destroying the strand of liberal-left opinion built up in Hollywood during the years of Roosevelt's presidency and with it a tradition of liberal-left social problem films. (Similar ground is covered, with more attention to the Second World War and a sharper focus on the careers of liberal-left writers, producers, director and actors, in Neve 1992.)

It is an additional thesis that this tradition and its conventions were conditioned by the studio system and the 'Formula' that governed most Hollywood films at this time. Central to the Formula were predictable star personae and genres. Beyond that, narratives were to be 'linear', 'with the straightest line of action' and centred on individuals 'with whom the audience could identify' (Roffman and Purdy 1981: 3). Dramatic conflict was to be structured 'around two opposing poles definitively representing good and evil, with a readily identifiable hero and villain' (ibid.: 3). Conflict and emotion were to be 'generally expressed in terms of violent action' (ibid.: 3–4), while the 'good–evil morality called for a clear-cut, gratifying plot resolution – the Happy Ending, in which evil was destroyed and good rewarded' (ibid.: 4). As far as the social problem film is concerned, this meant a specific generic pattern with specific ideological effects:

> arouse indignation over some facet of contemporary life, carefully qualifying any criticism so that it can in the end be reduced to simple causes, to a villain whose removal rectified the situation. Allusions to the genuine concerns of the audience play up antisocial feelings only to exorcise them on safe targets contained within a dramatic rather than a social context.
>
> (Roffman and Purdy 1981: 305)

The studio system came to an end in the 1950s. It could therefore be argued that the demise of the system was as much a factor in the demise of the traditional social problem film as the Cold War and HUAC. But that would be to accept the aesthetic and historical parameters of Roffman and Purdy's account, at least some of which are open to question.

Roffman and Purdy themselves acknowledge that 'there are a surprising number of films which manage somehow to subvert Formula values' and that 'there are frequent examples' in the social problem film of a 'tension between a conventional form and a radical vision' (1981: 7). These examples include *I Am a Fugitive From a Chain Gang, You Only Live Once* (1937), *Body and Soul* (1947) and *Force of Evil* (1948). They also acknowledge that there are a handful of films, for the most part industrially exceptional productions like *Our Daily Bread* (1934), *Modern Times* (1936) and *The Great Dictator* (1940), which appear to 'evade' the Formula altogether. However, there are also a number of less obviously exceptional films which simply lack a number of the Formula's features. *The Power and the Glory* (1933), *Crossfire* (1947) and *The Snake Pit* (1947) lack linear narratives. *Mr Deeds Goes to Town* (1936), *The Best Years of Our Lives* (1946) and *Gentleman's Agreement* (1947) lack violent conflict. And *A Man's Castle* (1933) and *The Grapes of Wrath* (1940) both lack villains. (When the Joads are tractored off their land in *The Grapes of Wrath*, Muley (John Qualen) asks 'Who do I shoot?' It is part of the point that there is no clear-cut or obvious answer.) The 'crossing of genres' obviously plays a part here. Comedies like *Mr Deeds Goes to Town* and dramas like *The Best Years of Our Lives* tend to lack violent conflicts or villains or both. But in so far as the crossing of genres is a feature of the social problem film, and in so far as comedies and dramas were staple ingredients in Hollywood's output, greater account needs to be taken of its effects. Given their commitment to melodrama, it is arguable that the Progressive era films adhere much more closely to these aspects of the Formula than the films of the studio era. (One of the questions raised by this argument would then be how it relates to Ross's view that the studio system helped destroy the radical traditions of those Progressive era films made inside as well as outside the mainstream industry.) In the meantime, films like *The Public Enemy* and *Gabriel Over the White House* (1933) both raise issues about endings which apply to a number of other social problem films as well.

The Public Enemy, as is well known, involves the spectator in an increasingly irresolvable double-bind by inviting 'identification' with a gangster who is at the end presented in rapid succession as an ordinary human being who loves and is loved by his mother, then as a monstrous corpse (the consequence of his outlaw status and career), then in the closing titles as 'not a man', but 'a problem that sooner or later we, the public, must solve'. These words mark an ending which cannot be unequivocally described as happy (Cowie 1998: 184–5). They also help highlight the difference, indeed the disjunction, between the resolution of a plot and the resolution of a social problem, something commentators on social problem films often ignore. Disjunctions like this are very common in social problem films, which tend as a rule to insist that the problems they deal with are *not* resolved, and which often replace the possible resolution of social problems with the actual resolution of personal ones. (*The Defiant Ones* (1958), for instance, resolves the personal conflict between its black and white protagonists, leaving the general issues of race it raises unresolved and replacing them with a scenario in which male bonding and differences of gender become increasingly important.) However, unlike *The Public Enemy*, whose 'problem' remains irresolvable and almost openly contradictory, what they often do is to present problems in ways which promote a particular understanding of the issues at stake, and what they sometimes also do is provide a model or example of the kinds of things that can be done.

Gabriel Over the White House is an extreme and unusual example. It addresses a number of the problems facing the country in the early years of the Depression, among them unemployment, homelessness, gangsterdom and corruption. It identifies the lack of solutions to these problems with a lack of effective presidential leadership and with a corrupt and moribund political establishment. Following a car crash, the unconscious president (Walter Huston) is visited by the spirit of the angel Gabriel. The next morning he wakes up transformed. Full of ideas which are constantly blocked, he suspends Congress and declares martial law. Free of the normal protocols of American presidential government, he is also free to solve the country's problems. He forms an Army of Construction to help solve unemployment, repeals Prohibition, creates a special federal police force to wage war on recalcitrant gangsters, and insists that all the world's major powers repay their debts and stop making arms. Unusually, then, the problems with which this particular film deals are resolved within the fictional world. They are resolved by a benevolent dictator who adopts specific policies and measures. However, these resolutions do not end the film, which concludes when the president collapses, when Gabriel's spirit departs, and when the president briefly reverts to his former self and dies. The ending is thus again not particularly happy. Moreover, and more importantly, it is an ending which serves to reiterate the blatantly unreal nature of its central device. This does not undermine the solutions it proposes. But it explicitly marks them as fantasy. And it reminds the viewer that they have not (or not yet) actually taken place.

The politics of *Gabriel Over the White House* have been discussed at some length by Roffman and Purdy, who characterize the film as fascist, and who place it within the context of other contemporary right-wing social problem films (1981: 68–73), and by Matthew Bernstein, who notes its parallels with Roosevelt's election compaign (1994: 82–7). Either way, both *The Public Enemy* and *Gabriel Over the White House* were made prior to Roosevelt's election, prior to the New Deal, and therefore prior to the establishment of anything resembling a liberal-left consensus either in Hollywood or in the US at large. Neither is untouched, though, by the traditions of populism which Roffman and Purdy emphasize as a central ideological component in most social problem films, whether of the left, the right or the centre.

Populism is also discussed by Maltby, who notes its agrarian and small-town dimensions, its emphasis on cooperative individualism (on 'men of good-will'), its influence on the New Deal, and its place not just in social problem films like *Our Daily Bread* and *Mr Smith Goes to Washington* (1939), but in all 1930s and 1940s films which appealed to these values (1983: 153–71). These included westerns like *Drums Along the Mohawk* (1939), biopics like *Young Mr Lincoln*, and rural and small-town comedies and dramas like *Min and Bill* (1930) and *A Family Affair* (1937). Even gangster films like *The Public Enemy* were informed by a populist view of the city, while the man of good will (conspicuous by his absence from many early 1930s gangster films) was in many ways the model for most Hollywood heroes at this time.

Like Roffman and Purdy, Maltby (1983) argues that Hollywood's populism complicates any attempt made to attach conventional political labels to its films. At the same time, its promulgation in films of all kinds in the 1930s and 1940s complicates the idea of a totally separate social problem genre. Maltby notes that producer Darryl Zanuck, a specialist in such apparently radical social problem films as *The Grapes of Wrath*, voted Republican. (On Zanuck's social problem films, see Campbell 1978 and Custen 1997: 103–13, 229–39, 272–4, 294–308, 335–7.) And Bernstein (1994) notes that Walter Wanger, producer of *The President Vanishes* (1935) and *You Only Live Once*, as well as *Gabriel Over the White House*, viewed himself not as fascist but as a left-leaning liberal. Zanuck's campaigning style can also be found in his biopics, in films like *Wilson* (1944) and *The Life of Emile Zola*, and Wanger also produced *Stagecoach*, an overtly populist western, in the 1930s. Whether films like these can or could be considered social problem films is perhaps a moot point. But they clearly articulate populist values and they clearly make marked interventions into their contemporary socio-cultural contexts.

Both Zanuck and Wanger continued to produce social problem films after the war. (The war itself conditioned and influenced all kinds of films, imbuing spy films, war films and home-front films alike with a social urgency even as the treatment of domestic social problems was actively discouraged by the US government as bad propaganda (Koppes and Black 1987).) Zanuck produced *Gentleman's Agreement* and *Pinky* (1949). And Wanger produced *Riot in Cell Block 11* (1954) and *I Want to Live!* (1958). *Gentleman's Agreement* and *Pinky* were part of a distinct cycle of late 1940s social problem films as well as part of a longer-term trend towards films of all kinds about race relations and ethnic minorities.[29] It is the abrupt curtailment of the former and its apparent replacment by a series of anti-Communist thrillers that prompts Roffman and Purdy (1981) to identify the Cold War, the activities of HUAC, and the blacklisting of left-liberal production personnel as responsible for the demise of the left-liberal social problem film. However, *Riot in Cell Block 11*, *I Want to Live!* and numerous other 1950s films (like *On the*

Waterfront (1954), *The Blackboard Jungle* (1955) and *The Defiant Ones*) testify to persistence of the social problem film. According to Maltby (1983), some of them testify too to the persistence of a liberal tradition in Hollywood's films, a tradition modified not so much by HUAC as by the demise of Hollywood populism and mutations in the nature of its liberalism.

Maltby argues that liberalism after the war became increasingly detached from populism and increasingly attached instead to a vision of society equally governed by the principles of consensus and cooperative individualism, but managed from above by professional elites rather than led from below by the instincts and traditions of the people. These elites possessed reason and knowledge rather than populist faiths or fundamentalist beliefs. In an efficient, just and tolerant society managed by people of reason as well as good will, social problems were caused by social deviants, and social deviance was a psychological condition characterized by irrationality and ignorance. These were the enemies of the new liberal hero. They were also temptations against which he himself was forced to struggle. Their ultimate incarnation was the psychopath. The answer to the psychopath, as to all social deviants and the problems they caused, was unstinting opposition, implacable determination, sensitive understanding and remedial action, for the sake of which the liberal hero was prepared if necessary – and all too frequently – to martyr himself (1983: 224–96).

Maltby argues that the new post-war liberalism can be found at work in westerns like *High Noon* (1952) and *The Magnificent Seven* (1960), as well as in a tradition of social problem films that runs through to the late 1960s. This tradition clearly includes films like *Pressure Point* (1962), *The Chase* (1966) and *In the Heat of the Night* (1967). Running alongside it, though, are films like *Beyond a Reasonable Doubt* (1956), *Shock Corridor* (1963) and, indeed, *Riot in Cell Block 11* and *I Want to Live!*, which manage to avoid at least some of its conventions and assumptions.

Despite Hollywood's alleged espousal of counter-cultural values in the late 1960s and early 1970s, and despite its alleged turn to the right in the 1980s, liberalism of one kind or another continued and continues to dominate Hollywood's social problem films, from *All the President's Men* (1976) to *The China Syndrome* (1979), from *Brubaker* (1980) to *The Accused* (1988) to *Philadelphia* (1993). However, films like *Falling Down* (1993) on the one hand and *Do the Right Thing* (1989) on the other pose questions of the category and its governing assumptions in ways which have recently been explored by Willis (1997: 13–19, 163–7). Along with the fate of the social problem film in the 1920s, they still require further thought and further research.

TEENPICS

A period in life between childhood and adulthood has been marked by most societies in most periods of history (Graff 1995: 2, 8). However, during the

course of the twentieth century in America and elsewhere in the industria-
lized West, this period has tended to increase, and alongside a series of social
policies, practices and institutions which have increasingly treated those under
20 as both distinct and separate from adults, two key terms have emerged in
America to mark it: 'adolescence' (a term first coined by psychologist G.
Stanley Hall in 1904), and 'teenager' (a term first used in the popular press in
the 1920s, and first fully established during the course of the Second World
War) (Kett 1977). According to Maltby, a '"self-conscious subculture" of the
young developed during the 1920s and 1930s as a largely urban white
middle-class response to the increasing leisure opportunities afforded by
changing social attitudes' (1989: 140). But as he himself goes on to argue,
the first fully commercialized, cross-class, transnational – though for the most
part equally white – forms of teenage culture emerged in America in the
1950s, as significant numbers of young people with increasing amounts of
disposable income and leisure time comprised for the first time in the West
both an increasing proportion of the population as a whole and an expanding
sector of the market for services and goods.

In parallel fashion, Hollywood has always made films about young people
(Considine 1981). It has also always made films designed or presumed to cater
for what it called 'the juve trade' – juvenile spectators. (There is a distinction
between the two. Films about the young are not necessarily addressed to the
young; films presumed to address the young do not necessarily focus on or
feature young characters. The 'bad boy' films of the late 1890s and 1900s
were presumed to appeal to nostalgic middle-class men (Kramer, 1998b),
while B westerns and action serials, which featured adult characters and
actors, were often presumed to appeal to young teenage boys, and animal
films like *National Velvet* (1944) and *The Yearling* (1946) were aimed at an
audience of families.) However, the teenpic itself is normally held to emerge,
like modern teenage culture, during the course of the 1950s.

One of the conditions underlying its emergence was a growing awareness
on Hollywood's part of the importance of the teenage audience. Flying in the
face of the industry's presumption that 'Everyone who was not too young,
too old, too sick, or living in the remotest backwoods' attended most movies
most of the time (Quigley 1957: 21), audience research conducted in the late
1940s indicated that 'age [was] the most important personal factor by which
the movie audience is characterized' and that 'the decline of movie attendance with increasing age is very sharp' (Lazarsfield 1947: 162–3). Coming at
a time when the industry faced unprecedented challenges and changes in the
form of divorcement and divestiture, competition from television and other
leisure pursuits, suburbanization and a shift in audience demographics, and a
precipitous decline in ticket sales and audience attendance, these findings
reinforced the growing importance of the teenage market for films and of
targeting this market by drawing on aspects of teenage culture and by catering
for teenage interests, tastes and concerns (Doherty 1988: 20–5, 45–66).

A reflection in part of the industry's uncertainties, the teenpic was at this point heterogeneous, multi-dimensional, and often contradictory in its forms, concerns and modes of address. A number of genres, traditions and production trends, some of them quite distinct, contributed to its initial development. Firstly, there were mainstream dramas and social problem films like *The Wild One* (1954), *The Blackboard Jungle* and *Rebel Without a Cause* (1955), each of them produced by mainstream studios (Columbia, MGM and Warner Bros respectively), and each of them drawing on a tradition of films about juvenile delinquency, juvenile wildness and juvenile crime that stretched back as far as the 1920s and 1930s and that included films like *Flaming Youth* (1923), *Youth Astray* (1928), *Dead End* (1937) and *Wild Boys of the Road* (1933). However, their immediate origins lay in two separate cycles of juvenile delinquency films made during and just after the Second World War and that included films like *Where Are My Children?* (1944) and *I Accuse My Parents* (1944) on the one hand, and *City Across the River* (1949) and *Knock on Any Door* (1949) on the other. The idea and the image of the juvenile delinquent continued to colour films of all kinds made about teenagers in the 1950s and early 1960s, from sensationalized crime dramas and social problem films like *Teenage Crime Wave* (1955), *Girls in Prison* (1956) and *Juvenile Jungle* (1958) to musicals like *Jailhouse Rock* and *West Side Story*, though distinctions need to be made between those films which sought, at least ostensibly, to condemn juvenile delinquency, those which sought to understand it, and those which sought, either way, to use it to appeal either to a teenage or adult audience.

The cultural context within which delinquency emerged as an issue at this time has been explored by Gilbert (1986), the industrial context within which the films emerged by McGee and Robertson (1982), Doherty (1988: 105–41) and Betrock (1986). Gilbert stresses the extent to which a realignment of the relations between the media, the market, the teenage consumer, teenage tastes and teenage behaviour threatened hitherto dominant patterns of cultural authority. McGee and Robertson, Doherty and Betrock stress the heritage and the growing influence of independent production and 'exploitation'.

The term 'exploitation' originally referred both to the publicity techniques used to maximize a film's commercial potential and to the making of films which drew on topical, controversial or otherwise easily saleable subjects. During the studio era, both types of exploitation were common. But they were governed and controlled by the industry's organizations, notably the MPPDA (the Motion Picture Producers and Distributors of America) and its successor, the MPAA (the Motion Picture Association of America), and those films which exploited topics banned by the Production Code were refused a seal of approval and denied access to the theatres controlled by the majors (Langer 1994; Schaefer 1994). However, films which deliberately flouted the Code were produced by small-scale independents for independent distribution and exhibition, and many of these films – among them *The Burning*

Question (a.k.a. *Assassin of Youth, Reefer Madness* and *Tell Your Children*) (1936), *High School Girl* (1935), *The Road to Ruin* (1934) and *Girls of the Underworld* (1932) – used youthful deviance as a framework for dealing with exploitable 'adult' topics like drugs, prostitution, unmarried motherhood and venereal disease (Muller and Farris [1996] 1997: 13–31). Following divorcement, the MPAA found it much more difficult to enforce the Code. Meanwhile, the decline in audiences and in the number of films produced by the majors meant that many exhibitors were crying out for films to show, preferably films with exploitable potential, and films which would appeal to those still going to the cinema on a regular basis and to those whose tastes were not catered for by television. As a result, a number of small independent producers and production companies like Samuel Arkoff, Allied Artists and American International Pictures (AIP), together with a handful of unit producers at mainstream studios, like Sam Katzman at Columbia and Albert Zugsmith at Universal, began to tailor their films for the teenage market and for 'marginal' (rather than mainstream) adult audiences, to adopt the techniques and the practices of exploitation, and in the process to defy or at least test the limits of the Production Code and the bounds of 'good taste' as established by the MPAA. Many of these films were about juvenile delinquency and juvenile crime, and the resulting mix of mainstream and independent productions, practices and genres, and of adult, marginal adult and teenage components and points of appeal, is just one index of the 'ambivalence' Hay sees as fundamental – not just to the teenpic but to teenage culture in general (1990: 336).

A similar ambivalence marks other 1950s and early 1960s trends and genres, not least 'weirdies' and rock'n'roll and pop films and musicals, and not least because a similar mix is characteristic of them all. '"Weirdie" was inexact nomenclature for an offbeat science fiction, fantasy, monster, zombie and/or shock film, usually of marginal financing, fantastic content, and ridiculous title' (Doherty 1988: 146). Developing alongside cycles of 'adult' science fiction and low budget monster films made by the majors, produced both by the majors themselves and by independents like AIP, weirdies in particular sought to capitalize on the popularity of horror and science fiction with teenage spectators. Hence the appearance alongside *The Incredible Shrinking Man* (1957) and *The Deadly Mantis* (1957) of films with titles like *I Was a Teenage Werewolf* (1957) and *Teenagers from Outer Space* (1959).

Films like this drew on and fed into a wider teenage culture that included horror and fantasy comics. Other films drew on pop and rock'n'roll. Following the use of 'Rock Around the Clock' over the credits on *The Blackboard Jungle*, Sam Katzman produced the first rock'n'roll musical, *Rock Around the Clock*, the following year. Unlike *The Blackboard Jungle*, an adult-oriented social problem film, *Rock Around the Clock* was, as Doherty points out, 'the first hugely successful film marketed to teenagers *to the pointed exclusion of their elders*' (1988: 74; emphasis in original). It was arguably, therefore, the first modern teenpic, as well as the progenitor of a cycle of rock'n'roll films that included *Shake, Rattle, and Rock* (1956) and *Rock, Rock, Rock!* (1956), which were both produced by independents, and *The Girl Can't Help It* and *Rock, Pretty Baby* (1956), which were both produced by the majors.

These cycles and genres were soon joined by hot rod films like *Dragstrip Riot* (1958) and *Hot-Rod Girl* (1956), by calypso and beatnik films like *Calypso Joe* (1957) and *The Rebel Set* (1959), and by what Doherty calls 'clean teenpics', musicals and light romances like *April Love* (1957) and *Gidget* (1959) which recall a tradition stemming back to the Deanna Durbin, Mickey Rooney and Judy Garland films of the late 1930s and early 1940s (Considine 1981: 124–6), which parallel what some have seen as the incorporation and neutralization of rock'n'roll by the white musical establishment (Martin and Segrave [1988] 1993: 103–8), and which Doherty himself argues addressed teenagers and teenage concerns within an unambiguously white, middle-class, adult framework of values. 'In the clean teens baroque phase, AIP's *Beach Party* cycle (1963–65), parents were banished altogether,' he writes. 'As compensation, though, there was little in this portrait of teenage life that would disturb a worried father. Adults were usually absent, but their values were always present. Fulfilling the best hope of the older generation, the clean teenpics featured an aggressively normal, traditionally good-looking crew of fresh young faces, "good kids" who preferred dates to drugs and crushes to crime' (1988: 195).

Doherty's views are echoed by Morris (1993). However, there are a number of unspoken and perhaps rather glib assumptions at work here, not just about the relative merits of preferring dates to drugs and crushes to crime but also about the relationship between teenage and adult values, about the ethnic politics of early rock'n'roll, about rebellion and deviance as hallmarks of teenage authenticity, and, indeed, about the authenticity of teenage culture itself. As Graff points out, despite 'striking legacies, images, and myths to the contrary', there are numerous 'paths' to growing up, not just one (1995: xiii). And as Lewis points out, 'When we are talking about youth we are talking about a fundamentally mediated culture, one that continues to represent itself in terms of the products it buys, the art that defines it, and the art it defines as its own' (1992: 4). It is this 'dialectic of cultural autonomy and media appropriation' (ibid.: 4) that lies at the heart of the teenpic, and that helps generate the ambivalence noted by Hay, and the conflicts and contradictions to which that ambivalence gives rise.

Underlining the extent to which marginalized films, marginalized film-going practices and marginalized venues like drive-in cinemas 'contributed to the formation of teen spectators and a "teen culture"' in the 1950s, (Hay 1990: 335), points out that teen films often 'co-opted, parodied or resisted' the preferred genres and 'narrative practices of U. S. film culture' (ibid.: 336). However, he also points out that teen films and teen culture were never 'wholly autonomous' (ibid.). They too could be co-opted and resisted. The ensuing conflicts and contradictions often found articulation in 'rites of passage' narratives, in stories which placed their protagonists 'betwixt and between' (ibid.) adulthood and childhood, and which explored issues of autonomy, identity, allegiance and difference in the context of the teenage peer group on the one hand and adult society on the other, and in the ways in which – and the extent to which – hitherto dominant generic norms were inflected or reworked in the process:

> these films in some fashion involve narrative conflict *both* over finding one's place within a relatively autonomous society of youths and over defining, negotiating and resisting differences between youth and adulthood. In the sense that teenpics were given to modelling conflict in this manner and through generic conventions that also deterritorialized and reterritorialized the conventions of traditional Hollywood genres, they can be said to define doubly the relation of 'the minor' to a 'parent' culture.
>
> (Hay 1990: 336)

The clean teens films of the late 1950s and early 1960s are particularly exemplary of the problems and issues at stake here, especially in so far as they tend to centre on female characters, and especially in so far as they share a number of the features and concerns of contemporary woman's films like *Picnic* (1955) and *Peyton Place* (1957), as Hay points out. But subsequent teenpics are exemplary too, not least because, for demographic reasons, teenagers have since then comprised 'the primary battleground for commercial motion picture patronage in America' (Doherty 1988: 231), not least because 'Since 1960, teenpics have been an industry staple, if not the dominant production strategy for theatrical movies' (ibid.), and therefore not least because the relationship between what is marginal and what is central, what is minor and what is mainstream, has shifted and changed.

There have been important variations in the nature and volume of teenpics since the early 1960s. In the late 1960s and early 1970s, 'youth movies' drew much more on an image of counter-cultural rebellion than on an image of irresponsible juvenile delinquency. And as 'the boundaries between counter (film) culture and mainstream (film) culture all but evaporated' (Doherty 1988: 233), films like *The Graduate* (1967), *Bonnie and Clyde*, *Easy Rider* (1969) and *Five Easy Pieces* (1970) mounted serious critiques of the parent culture (Davis 1997: 107–10). Following a crisis wrought by overproduction in the late 1960s and early 1970s, and in the wake of a counter-culture in general decline, the industry resumed production of teenpics in regular numbers in the late 1970s and 1980s. Some, like *Halloween* and *Night of the Comet* were low-budget horror, sci-fi and slasher films. Some, like *Caddyshack* (1980) and *National Lampoon's Animal House* (1978), were 'gross-out' or 'animal' comedies. Some, like *Sixteen Candles* (1984), *Pretty in Pink* (1986) and *The Breakfast Club* (1985), were teen-centred dramas and romances. And some, like *Rumble Fish* (1983) and *River's Edge* (1986), were teen-centred art or social problem films. They were joined by brat-pack westerns like *Young Guns* (1988) and *Young Guns 2* (1990) and by musical biopics like *Great Balls of Fire!* (1989) and *La Bamba* (1987). (For an overview of teenpics since the late 1970s, see Bernstein 1997.)

Despite their generic diversity, these films can all be defined as teenpics because they all focus on teenage characters. However, issues of definition are complicated by the fact that since the early 1970s, Hollywood has been decisively 'juvenalized' (Doherty 1988: 235): not only do most Hollywood films aim to cater for a teenage audience, but directors and producers like George Lucas and Steven Spielberg, who as Doherty points out were 'Reared on the teen-oriented fare of the 1950s' (ibid.), have through films like *Star Wars* and *Raiders of the Lost Ark* helped establish a teen-friendly trend toward big-budget action, adventure and fantasy films, and through films like *American Graffiti* (1973) and *Back to the Future* (1985) a trend towards the recycling of 1950s teenage culture. They are further complicated by the fact that Doherty and Lewis both detect what Doherty describes as a 'palpable desire for parental control and authority' in post-1960s teenpics (ibid.: 237), and by the fact that so many teenpics are marked by what Doherty terms 'double vision':

> As teen-oriented movies have become the industry's representative product, the throwaway, unconscious artistry of the 1950s has been supplanted by a new kind of calculated and consciously reflexive teenpic . . . Thus films aimed at teenagers are not only more carefully marketed and calculating [*sic*] created, they also function more explicitly on two levels. *Fast Times at Ridgemont High* (1982) and *Risky Business* (1983) are teenpic-like in their target audience and content, but their consciousness is emphatically adult.
>
> (Doherty 1988: 236)

Points like these recall and refocus some of the questions raised by Hay (1990) and some of the points raised by Speer (1998). When reference is made in *Clueless* (1995) to a 1970s tennis player, an early 1960s epic and an eighteenth-century novel, who are these references aimed at? When in *Back to the Future* a rites of passage narrative is set in the 1950s, and focused not on the young male protagonist but on his father, and when in *Stand By Me* (1986) a rites of passage narrative, set again in the 1950s, is narrated by an adult male in retrospect, whose fantasy is being enacted? To whom is that fantasy addressed? What process of negotiation and exchange, of deterritorialization and reterritorialization is taking place? Along with developments like the advent of black teenage films, the trend towards pre-teens films in the early 1990s (Bernstein 1997: 220), and a recent decline in the proportion of teenagers in America's population, in the proportion of teenagers attending

Hollywood's films (Davis 1997: 142), and therefore in the volume of teen-oriented films, questions like these testify to the complexity and interest of a genre which has for years been important to Hollywood, but rarely, it seems, to genre critics, theorists and historians.

WAR FILMS

For the most part, the category 'war film' is uncontentious: war films are films about the waging of war in the twentieth century; scenes of combat are a requisite ingredient and these scenes are dramatically central. The category thus includes films set in the First World War, the Second World War, Korea and Vietnam. And it excludes home front dramas and comedies and other films lacking scenes of military combat. However, as with most generic categories, there are a number of ambiguities, some stemming from the generically untidy nature of some of the films, others from changes in their dominant conventions, still others from changes in the way films have been labelled or defined.

For example, the term 'war film' was first used in the industry's relay to describe films set in the Civil War or in the Indian Wars of the nineteenth century. These films included *The Empty Sleeve* (1909), described as a 'war picture' by the *Moving Picture World* (5 June 1909: 754), and *Clarke's Capture of Kaskaskia* (1911), advertised in the *Moving Picture World* as 'A new kind of War picture, taking us back to the pioneer days on the Frontier' (29 April 1911: 9). Films about the Indian Wars soon came to be treated as westerns. Some Civil War films did too, though films with a Civil War setting tended to form distinct and different generic alliances, and later Civil War films like *The Red Badge of Courage* (1951) and *Advance to the Rear* (1964) are in fact closer in look, tone and structure to contemporary war films than they are to contemporary westerns. (On early Civil War films, see Bowser 1990: 177–9 and Koszarski 1990: 186. On Civil War films in general, see Kinnard 1998. The term 'alliances' derives from Leutrat 1985.)

The criterion of combat, meanwhile, has exercised a number of theorists, critics and historians. Taking his cue from the inclusive nature of the surveys of war-related films conducted on behalf of the Office of War Information (OWI) by Jones in the 1940s (1945), Shain has argued for a broad definition of the war film. 'A war film', he writes, deals 'with the roles of civilians, espionage agents, and soldiers in any of the aspects of war (i.e. preparation, cause, prevention, conduct, daily life, and consequences or aftermath).' War films therefore 'do not have to be situated in combat zones' (1976: 20). Service comedies can be included, but 'not all films with military characters are on the list' (ibid.). On the other hand, Basinger, like Kagan (1974) and Kane (1976, 1988), argues that broad definitions are too vague. Proposing that 'The war film does not exist in a coherent generic form' (1986: 10), she restricts herself to films with a Second World War setting and substitutes the term 'combat film' for war film in order to mark combat itself as a central defining criterion: '"War" is a setting, and it is also an issue. If you fight it, you have a combat film; if you sit home and worry about it, you have a family or domestic film; if you sit in board rooms and plan it, you have a historical biography or a political film of some sort' (ibid.).

Issues of terminology have also been raised by those wishing to distinguish between films in terms of their attitudes to war. Chambers (1994), for example, suggests that 'antiwar film' might be a more appropriate term than 'war film' for films like *All Quiet on the Western Front* (1930). Thus there seems to be an assumption in some of the writing on war films that generic terms and definitions should be governed by logic: that the category 'war film' should logically include all films with a wartime background, that 'combat film' is the logical term for war films which focus on combat, and that 'antiwar film' is the logical term for films with an antiwar attitude. However, as Basinger in particular is otherwise the first to acknowledge, Hollywood's genres and terms are governed by custom, convention and history rather than logic. And custom, convention and history dictate that 'war film' implies a degree of focus on combat whatever attitude to war is adopted (Belton 1994: 164; McArthur 1982: 881; Springer 1988a. Belton compares the role of combat scenes in war films with the role of musical numbers in musicals; Springer discusses them in terms of their formal characteristics and of the ideological ambivalence their 'excess' can often generate). They also dictate that service comedies, spy films and home front dramas possess their own separate conventions and terms.

Some of the confusion here may stem from an awareness of the extent to which generic overlap can occur, of the extent to which a service comedy like *The Wackiest Ship in the Army* (1960) can culminate in scenes of serious combat or to which a 'combat film' like *Battle Cry* (1955) can include scenes of personal drama. Some may stem from the fact that scenes of combat can occur in other genres and films, that their dramatic functions can therefore differ, and that war films themselves can vary the number of combat scenes they include, as well as their duration, location and scale. In war films, combat with the enemy, however infrequent, usually determines the fates of the principal characters. That is why films like *Pride of the Marines* (1945) and *Coming Home* (1978), in which combat determines the physical condition of the central male characters but not their ultimate fates, are not normally considered as war films. That is why combat scenes nearly always occur towards the end of war films, at the point of dramatic climax. (Films like *All Quiet on the Western Front*, *Apocalypse Now* and *Paths of Glory* (1957) vary convention by having the fates of major characters determined by the actions of a single sniper, by the actions of a covertly commissioned assassin, and by the actions of a military court respectively. However, the ironies involved are in each case dependent on an awareness of generic convention, and this awareness is cued by the presence of extensive scenes of combat earlier on.)

And finally, given the life or death outcome of combat in particular and of wartime conditions in general, that is why writers like Kaminsky (1974: 229) and Belton (1994: 164–5) argue that war films are as much about the fragilities and conditions of physical survival as they are about war – or wars – as such.

Confusion may also stem from the tendency to focus on films with a Second World War setting. Basinger suggests that 'Different wars inspire different genres' (1986: 10). Like Kane (1976, 1988), she is concerned with the distinctive conventions of the 'World War II combat film'. Thus although she herself maintains that 'At bottom, both WWI and WWII films are about death' (1986: 87), she argues that their differences outweigh their similarities and that they should be treated as separate genres. However, aside from noting Koszarski's argument that *The Big Parade* (1925), a First World War film, helped establish the convention of 'the variegated platoon' (1990: 186), and aside from noting Isenberg's argument (1981: 89–90) that this particular convention, which Basinger and others associate specifically with Second World War films, was established even earlier, during the course of the First World War itself,[30] it is possible to mount an alternative argument. It is possible to maintain that the Second World War film, however specific its conventions, is and was a variant on the same basic genre, and that the foundations of this genre were laid during the course of the First World War, when the criterion of combat inherent in earlier uses of terms like 'war picture' first came to be focused on films about modern war.

Two books have been written on the First World War and Hollywood's films, by Isenberg (1981) and by DeBauche (1997). Neither is straightforwardly focused on fictional war films. And both have specific agendas. Isenberg is interested in the relationship between film and public opinion. He therefore spends some time detailing the history of government involvement in film production during the war itself, the activities of the Committee on Public Information (the CPI or 'Creel Committee') as the government's principal propaganda agency, collaboration with the military (especially in terms of the provision of advisers, extras and equipment, a key aspect since then of nearly all Hollywood's war films as Shain (1976), Suid (1978, 1979) and others have noted), and the nature and production of documentaries and training films as well as of fictional features. Like most commentators, he argues that there was a transition from pacifist antiwar films like *In the Name of the Prince of Peace* (1915) and *Civilization* (1916) to bellicose anti-German propaganda films like *Daughter of France* (1918) and *The Kaiser, The Beast of Berlin* (1918). He also notes, though, that the apparently straightforward nature of this transition was complicated by the early production of martial adventure and 'war prepared-ness' films like *The Battle Cry of Peace* (1915) and *The Hero of Submarine D-2* (1916). (A number of war-preparedness serials were made in 1916, most of them featuring action heroines and serial-queens. Examples include *The Secret of the Submarine* and *Pearl of the Army*. See Dall'Asta 1995.) Isenberg (1981) suggests that all three of these strands were governed by Victorian codes of gentility, manifest in the general avoidance of bloodshed and carnage, in the emphasis on honour, duty and valour in the second and third of these strands, and in the influence of contemporary liberal values in the first. He also argues that democracy and democratization were common themes and points of reference in films made both during and after the war, at their strongest in films about the army and at their weakest in films about the air force.[31]

Isenberg goes on to discuss the influence of changing attitudes to the First World War in the 1920s and 1930s, the extent to which the revisionist accounts produced by novelists, poets and playwrights affected Hollywood's films, the extent to which Victorian codes were challenged or had broken down, and the extent to which the war itself featured as background in romances like *The Enchanted Cottage* (1924) as well as foreground in war films as such. He argues that Victorian codes were by no means totally rejected, its codes of valour, honour and duty often co-existing with a revisionist ver-isimilitude in the treatment of battle scenes and in the use of 'hardboiled' language, and that 'Not until 1930, and then in only a very few films, did moviemakers come to realistic grip with modern war in a mood of disillu-sionment which approached that of literature' (1981: 114–15). Until then, routine 'war-inspired regeneration' films like *Dangerous Business* (1921) and *Dugan of the Dugouts* (1928) were produced in great numbers alongside road-shown specials like *The Big Parade* and *Wings*, films in which the contradictory effects of the interaction between Victorian codes and revisionist devices are, he argues, especially apparent.

Both here and elsewhere (1975), Isenberg suggests that revisionism remained only partly and intermittently visible in Hollywood's films. Even amidst the pacifism and isolationism of the 1930s, films like *Journey's End* (1930), *The Road to Glory* (1936) and both versions of *The Dawn Patrol* (1930 and 1938) continued to manifest contradictions like these, while a cycle of heroic aviation films that included *Hell's Angels* (1930) and *Hell in the Heavens* (1934) served to perpetuate the tradition of war as adventure. By the end of the decade, as the adventure tradition continued with films like *Submarine Patrol* (1938), a series of preparedness films for a new war began to appear (Basinger 1986: 110–13; Dick [1985] 1996: 65–100; Leab 1995).

DeBauche covers similar chronological ground, though she focuses in more detail on the 1910s. This is in keeping with her parallel aims: to deal not only with films with a First World War setting, but also with the impact of the war on the US film industry and with the history of the industry itself. As a result, she pays as much attention to the activities of the National Association of the Motion Picture Industry (NAMPI) as she does to those of the Creel Committee. She is keen to stress the commercial advantages of 'practical patriotism' (1997: 29). And she is much more precise than Isenberg about the nature of the industry's output and its relationship to the industry's practices. She notes that 'War-related feature films' did not become 'a significant factor in "List of Current Film Release Dates," until September 1918, two months before the signing of the Armistice' (ibid.: 38). (It was in March 1918 that *Daughter of France* and *The Kaiser, The Beast of Berlin* were released, to be followed in subsequent months by *To Hell with the Kaiser* and others. The most extreme anti-German propaganda films were therefore seen by the American public at, near or even after the end of the war.) However, while 'a minority of all films in distribution in 1917 and 1918 were war-related' (ibid.: 48), about half of these were specials and road shows and would thus in publicity and public-relations terms have been disproportionately visible.

The nature and duration of production schedules meant that over fifty war-related feature films were released in 1919. Numbers dropped severely in 1920 and 1921, increased slowly between 1922 and 1924, then increased rapidly in 1925 and 1926. For DeBauche, the war films of the 1920s 'displayed striking innovations. They were told from the soldier's point of view and foregrounded battle over any other wartime experience' (1997: 171). In addition, they 'eliminated or significantly reduced the role of women as causal agents in their narratives' as 'a clear divide was created between the "love story" and the war scenes' and as 'war was defined as combat' (ibid.: 172). Thus they came increasingly to resemble war films made later, in the 1930s and 1940s, though it should be noted that Isenberg argues that in films like *The Mad Parade* (1931) and *She Goes to War* (1929) 'women were almost indistinguishable from men as warriors' (1981: 198).

Basinger provides the most detailed account of the war film and its history from the 1940s through to the late 1970s. However, although she discusses films about the First World War, the Korean war and Vietnam, and although she also discusses musicals, dramas and comedies, her account is centred on the Second World War, not just as subject matter but also as the period during which the conventions she identifies as basic to her principal concern, the 'World War II combat film', were forged. Moreover, despite her willingness to discuss marginal examples, exceptions, and hybrids, to recognize variations, and to acknowledge the generic untidiness of Hollywood's output, she is wedded to a very particular notion of the combat film. 'I had a prior conception of what the genre would be', she writes,

> What I knew in advance was what presumably every member of our culture would know about World War II combat films – that they contained a hero, a group of mixed types, and a military objective of some sort. They take place in the actual combat zones of World War II, against the established enemies, on the ground, the sea, or in the air. They contain many repeated events, such as mail call, all presented visually with appropriate uniforms, equipment, and iconography of battle.
>
> (Basinger 1986: 23)

As a result, she treats the combat film not as a particular generic paradigm but

129

as the only true genre of war; as a result, for all its apparent comprehensive-
ness, her account is very specific in its focus; and as a result, the films she sees
as central are often outweighed by those she sees as marginal, especially (and
ironically) when she comes to consider those made during the Second World
War itself.

Basinger begins here by noting 'how few actual combat films were
released': 'From December 7, 1941 to January 1, 1944, the primary list of
pure combat films . . . contains only five films, and none of these appears
before 1943' (1986: 24). Because they lack an exclusive setting in combat
zones, an appropriate iconography and/or a hero, group and military objective, films like *Wake Island* (1942) and *Desperate Journey* (1942) are not
considered 'pure combat'. Pure combat only begins to emerge, and is in
fact only truly represented prior to 1945, by just two films, *Air Force* (1943)
and *Bataan* (1943), the former serving as the template for films marked by
journeying, movement and victory, the latter for those marked by stasis, last
stands and defeat. Thus *Action in the North Atlantic* (1943), *Destination Tokyo*
(1944) and others serve principally as further examples of generic impurity
until *Air Force* and *Bataan* are joined in 1945 by *Objective, Burma!*, *They Were
Expendable* and *The Story of G.I. Joe* and in 1946 by *A Walk in the Sun*. These
films are canonic. For Basinger they are important because they are the first to
display and exploit generic awareness, an awareness 'that they are all one type'
(ibid.: 123). They also provide the focus of Kane's book, which uses them
along with *Guadalcanal Diary* (1943) and *Air Force* to construct a structural
model of the combat film in which narratives can result in victory or defeat
and in the integration or disintegration of the combat group, and in which
dualities such as war and peace, savagery and civilization, democracy and
totalitarianism, humanity and inhumanity and duty and self-interest are
played out within and across a basic conflict between Americans and their
allies and their enemies. (Usually Japan and Germany rather than Italy, as
Fyne 1992: 311, among others, points out.)

With the coming of peace, the production of war films of all kinds
promptly ceases until the appearance of *Fighter Squadron* in 1948 and of
Command Decision, *Battleground* and others in 1949. These films inaugurate
a 'third wave' of combat films which persists in large numbers until 1959.
This third wave is marked by the purity of its conventions and by various
forms of generic awareness. It is also complicated and augmented by the
Korean War and the Cold War. In the Korean films, iconography is adjusted
to accommodate Korean terrain and the use of new weapons like jet planes,
the mixture of the group is adjusted to accommodate a wider variety of
minorities, and narrative patterns are changed to focus for the most part on
stalemate or retreat. Basinger argues that an uncertainty about war aims and
the necessity of leaving recently established homes and families to fight
overseas is accompanied by 'a new cynicism toward war and those who
plan it and lead it' (1986: 188). However, this effect is felt as much on First

World War films like *Paths of Glory* (1957) and on Second World War films like *Attack!* (1956) as it is on Korean films themselves, and it is preceded in the early years of the Cold War by films like *Twelve O'Clock High* (1949) and *The Caine Mutiny* (1954) which, like a number of contemporary novels and plays, focus sympathetically on the stresses, strains and values of command (Jones 1976: 67–86; Kane 1988: 95; Lundberg 1984: 386; Walsh 1882: 138–42). Shain argues that the realignment of allies and enemies brought about by the Cold War and the consequent realignment of Hollywood's overseas markets brought about changes in the depiction of the Japanese and the Germans and thus indirectly encouraged revisionist trends (1976: 92–128). He also argues that these trends were accompanied by changes in the image of hero, that the 'socially responsible citizen' of the 1940s and the 'professional warrior' of the 1950s increasingly gives way to depictions of a hero who rejects 'long range political, social, and military goals in favor of immediate personal considerations' (ibid.: 210).

Trends like these are especially marked in the fourth and fifth phases, which run overall from 1960 to 1975. Here an augmented cynicism, evident as satirical comedy and generic deconstruction in films like *What Did You Do in the War, Daddy?* (1966), in the stress on the waste and absurdity of war in films like *None But the Brave* (1965), and in the undermining of conventionally selfless motives in 'dirty group' films like *Kelly's Heroes* (1970), runs alongside 'epic reconstructions' like *The Longest Day* (see Ambrose 1994) and large-scale 'war-as-adventure' films like *The Guns of Navarone* (1961) and *Where Eagles Dare* (1968). Reactions to the war in Vietnam help further augment revisionist trends. However, depictions of armed combat in Vietnam itself are few and far between. Following *China Gate* (1957), *A Yank in Vietnam* (1964), *To the Shores of Hell* (1966), *Marine Battleground* (1966), *The Green Berets* (1968) and *The Losers* (1970), most of them both generically and industrially marginal, are the only films to represent combat in Vietnam in any form and to any great extent until the late 1970s.

Basinger discusses some of the films set in Vietnam towards the end of her book (1986: 212–13). Alongside the observations she herself makes there now exist numerous studies of Hollywood's films and the Vietnam war, and with them a set of standard explanations for the paucity of Vietnam war films prior to the late 1970s and a standard account of the evolution and characteristics both of films which refer to the war and of Vietnam war films as such. It is generally argued that Hollywood was reluctant to make war films with a Vietnam setting in the 1960s and early 1970s because the war was publicly divisive, because the industry was in crisis and seeking to appeal to younger sectors of the population who were largely hostile to the war and because the military were unwilling to provide facilities for films which criticized the war. Defeat and withdrawal from Vietnam in the early 1970s challenged the tenets of America's 'victory culture' (Englehardt 1995), ensured that its participation in the war remained deeply controversial, posed questions as to how the war could or should be represented, and rendered the paradigms associated with the Second World War combat film at least temporarily inappropriate. For all these reasons, the war was alluded to in neighbouring genres like the western and in figures like the maladjusted veteran far more often than it was represented directly on screen (Adair 1986: 7–76; Auster and Quart 1988: 23–55; Berg 1990: 47–60; Klein 1990: 19–22; Martin 1990: 134–57; Richman 1991: 1–105; Scarrow 1991: 1–67; Suid 1991: 100–98; Walker 1991).

Along with *Apocalypse Now,* the appearance of *Go Tell the Spartans* (1978), *The Boys in Company C* (1978) and *The Deerhunter* (1978), all of them independently financed and produced, put Vietnam back on Hollywood's agenda. These particular films varied widely in form and convention and are often seen as experimenting with ways of representing the war in the light of America's defeat. Some were modelled on the more cynical combat films of the 1950s and 1960s. Others echoed much more distantly some of the films set in the First World War or attempted to find a format of their own. However, along with a further cycle of films about veterans, they all tended to stress loss and impairment – the loss or impairment of American moral, political and military superiority as well of the lives, bodies, innocence or sanity of its troops – as fundamental hallmarks of the war and its aftermath (Adair 1986: 77–120; Auster and Quart 1988: 55–73; Berg 1990: 55–6; Klein 1990: 22–3; Martin 1990: 148–68; Richman 1991: 106–202; Scarrow 1991: 68–73, 121–3; Suid 1991: 199–233).

Finally, in the context of a decisive political turn to the right in the 1980s, the American military, the Vietnam war, victory culture and the Vietnam veteran were rehabilitated in an array of cycles which included sc-fi action-adventure films like *The Empire Strikes Back* (1980), films about the training and ethos of military officers like *Taps* (1981) and *The Lords of Discipline* (1983), films about the rescue by Vietnam veterans of American prisoners-of-war in Southeast Asia like *Uncommon Valor* (1983) and *Rambo: First Blood Part II* (1985), and later in the decade, a short-lived though much-debated series of films which revived and modified the conventions of the combat film, and which included *Platoon* (1986), *Hamburger Hill* (1987) and *Full-Metal Jacket* (1987).[32]

Rehabilitated too, some have argued, was a traditionally defined masculinity (Britton 1986: 24–7; Jeffords 1989, 1994; Ryan and Kellner 1988: 217–43; Wood 1986: 172–4). Coinciding with a renewed interest in the topic of masculinity in Film, Media and Cultural Studies, war films of all kinds have been studied since then, not only in terms of their Oedipal dynamics and their sado-masochistic scenarios, but also in light of the fact that the war film is one of the few genres in which, as *Saving Private Ryan* (1998) has recently confirmed, male characters are regularly permitted to weep as a means of expressing their physical and emotional stress and hence their physical and emotional vulnerability (Belton 1994: 167–9; Easthope 1986:

61–8; Fuchs 1990; Jeffords 1988; McMahon 1994; Modleski 1988; Neale 1991: 53–7; Newsinger 1993; Scarrow 1991: 161–78; Springer 1988b; White 1988). This is not the only conventional but otherwise unusual feature of the Hollywood war film. Its close relationship to US foreign policy, its regular stress on cooperative goals, its frequent critiques of extreme individualism and its routine emphasis on the extent to which its characters lack knowledge and control of their environment, their activities, their enemies and their fates all tend to make it the exception rather than the rule among Hollywood's genres.

WESTERNS

Westerns have occupied a pre-eminent place in writing of all kinds on genre in the cinema. Warshow ([1954] 1975b) and Bazin (1971a) wrote influential essays on the western in the 1940s and 1950s. And as we have already seen in Chapter 1, the western was central to the theoretical work of Buscombe, Ryall, Tudor and Cawelti in the late 1960s and early 1970s. It was central, too, to the work of Schatz in the early 1980s. As such, and despite the severe decline in the number of westerns produced since the early 1970s, the western still features centrally in introductory accounts and in introductory courses on genre in the cinema, fed in part by occasional attempts to revive it in Hollywood and by the resurgence of scholarly interest evident in books written or edited by Buscombe (1988a), Buscombe and Pearson (1998), Cameron and Pye (1996), Coyne (1997), Mitchell (1996), Slotkin (1992) and others. Its centrality can be measured by its prominence, not just in conventional accounts of genre but in otherwise unorthodox accounts (such as that provided by Maltby 1995: 107–43) as well. It is precisely for this reason that I want to stress here both the problematic consequences of the western's centrality to accounts of genre and Hollywood and the problematic aspects of conventional accounts of the western itself. This is not meant to imply that these accounts lack value, interest or importance. But given their prevalence elsewhere – and given the space available here – it is important to highlight their limitations and their blindspots as well as their merits and strengths.

Firstly, then, the western's occupation of a prominent, often paradigmatic place in discussions of genre can be a problem because many of its putative characteristics are unusual rather than typical, specific to westerns rather than characteristic of Hollywood's genres as a whole. This is especially true of its visual conventions, of its relationship to US history and US culture, and hence of its susceptibility to various methods of formal, cultural, ideological and thematic analysis. As we have already seen in Chapter 1, the western was the principal point of reference for theories of iconography in the late 1960s and early 1970s. As Buscombe demonstrated clearly in 1970, the visual conventions of the western are both highly distinctive and highly coded. However, as he has argued more recently, the western is in this respect the generic exception rather than the rule, and this is a point that applies not just to its dress, its decor and its landscape, but also to other aspects of its generic world – its use of language, its modes of transport, and so on (1988b: 15–17). In all these ways, the 'consistency and rigour' of the western's world is 'remarkable' (ibid.: 16). For all these reasons, and although I shall attempt below to draw attention to some of its non-standard aspects and trends, it is hardly a suitable model for general conceptions and theories of genre. It would be interesting to speculate on how different current accounts of genre might be, had biopics or comedies been taken as a central point of reference by theorists of genre in the late 1960s and early 1970s rather than westerns. In the event, those who sought to build on the idea of iconography have been forced, as we shall see in Chapter 6, to distinguish between genres which possess and genres which lack iconographies. Meanwhile, those attempting to write on the iconography of the gangster film, the thriller and the musical have usually been far less detailed, and therefore in my view far less convincing, than those writing on the iconography of the western itself.

Buscombe goes on to note the western's 'imaginative' relationship to America's geography and to America's history (1988b: 16–17). These relationships are not only generically unique, they blend, focus and participate in various ways and to varying degrees in what is often termed a 'mythology', a mythology that has itself been uniquely central to US history, US culture and US identity. This mythology is grounded in the notion (itself as imaginative as it is real) that there existed a moving western frontier in the US between the seventeenth and the late nineteenth centuries. One of its basic tenets is that this frontier served to distinguish and to mark the meeting point between Anglo-Americans and their culture and nature and the cultures of others, and between the Anglo-American West and the Anglo-American – and European – East. Others included the idea that frontier existence and frontier encounters were characteristically marked by opportunity and danger, hardship and bounty, adventure and violence; that the frontier served to cultivate unique national characteristics, particularly among those who inhabited, crossed or helped extend its borders; that its westward movement served to chart the path of Anglo-American settlement and hence to mark the 'Manifest Destiny' and the racial and cultural superiority of Anglo-Americans while at the same time increasingly ensuring its own disappearance; and that contact with the frontier, or at least with the land, the conditions and the ways of life which once marked its existence, was and is a means of personal and national renewal and regeneration.[33]

The term 'mythology' sometimes seems inappropriate – too grandiose, too abstract or too coy – particularly when used to obscure the racial and imperial aspects of the events, the ideologies, the images and the stories it is usually used to identify. However, powerful arguments have been made in its favour. It usefully indicates the interrelated nature of its various components, and in Film Studies it suggested and sanctioned the application to western films of the structuralist methods developed by anthropologist Lévi-Strauss (1967) for the study of the myths of 'primitive' societies. Its best-known example is the antinomial grid proposed by Kitses to identify the nodal terms and oppositions in the western's thematic structure, a grid whose elements derive directly from frontier mythology and which relate to one another in shifting, dynamic and dialectical ways rather than in rigid or fixed ones:

THE WILDERNESS	CIVILIZATION
The Individual	*The Community*
freedom	restriction
honour	institutions
self-knowledge	illusion
integrity	compromise
self-interest	social responsibility
solipsism	democracy
Nature	*Culture*
purity	corruption
experience	knowledge
empiricism	legalism
pragmatism	idealism
brutalization	refinement
savagery	humanity
The West	*The East*
America	Europe
the frontier	America
equality	class
agrarianism	industrialism
tradition	change
the past	the future

(Kitses 1969: 11)

Lacking the ethnic or racial terms which underpin most aspects of frontier (or western) mythology – and the gender terms stressed by Kolodny (1975, 1984), Mitchell (1996), Tompkins (1992) and others as fundamental too – Kitses' grid nevertheless serves to emphasize the points he makes about its basic ambiguities. Kitses himself underlines the extent to which these ambiguities help generate the western's dramatic and ideological variety, as well as the variety of its historical and geographical settings.[34] Buscombe and others have underlined the extent to which its pre-cinematic history is marked by the variety of its aesthetic traditions and forms (see note 3 to Chapter 2, pp. 46–7). However despite this variety, there remains a tendency among those who use frontier mythology as a basic framework for discussing the western to

135

view the latter solely as a vehicle for an unambiguous version of the former, to stress the former's overarching characteristics and centrifugal pull rather than the latter's local features and centripetal tendencies. (Slotkin, as Buscombe points out (1995b: 128), is a case in point.) Frontier mythology in all its forms is indeed the framework within which most westerns were (and occasionally still are) produced. But frontier mythology is by no means confined to westerns, as Drinnon (1981), Slotkin (1992), Tan (1998) and others have shown. And some westerns draw on its most tangential features or participate in its promulgation in only the most indirect of ways, while others have sought from time to time to revise or to challenge its tenets. It would be as misleading to ignore these and other aspects of the western as it would be to ignore frontier mythology itself.

Take as an example some of the accounts put forward to explain the production of hundreds of Indian westerns in the late 1900s, the 1910s and the 1920s. So numerous were these films in the late 1900s and the 1910s that historians like Bowser argue that they constituted a genre in their own right (1990: 173). Linking the appearance of *The Aborigine's Devotion* (1909), *The Redman's View* (1909) and others to contemporary interest in Native Americans, Bowser stresses the extent to which Indians were portrayed in these films as noble and tragic. As such films like these, as well as later examples like *The Vanishing American* (1925), have also been linked not just to a long-standing component of frontier mythology, the Indian as Nature's noble (or ignoble) savage, but also and specifically to a contemporary instance of equally long-standing perceptions of a disappearing frontier and a dying race of people (Abel 1998: 79–95; Aleiss 1991; Dippie 1982; Dixon 1913; Leutrat 1985: 192–9; Mitchell 1981; Wrobel 1993). Films like *Lone Star* (1916) and *The Red Woman* (1917), about the difficulties faced by Indians who have been educated in Anglo-American colleges and schools and who have adopted Anglo-American values and codes of behaviour, can be seen as a variant on this theme, a variant concerned with the question of the Indian's future. The same is true of films like *The Indian Land Grab* (1910), *The Flower of the Tribe* (1911) and *The Red, Red Heart* (1918), which from a variety of perspectives and with a variety of outcomes explore the topic of miscegenation. Meanwhile, *Red Wing's Gratitude* (1909), *The Good Indian* (1913) and other films about the loyalty and devotion of Indians to whites are for the most part straightforward vehicles for white supremacist attitudes, as of course are captivity narratives and films about historical conflicts between Indians and whites like *The Early Settlers* (1910), *A Frontier Girl's Courage* (1911), *Geronimo's Last Raid* (1912) and *The Call of the Blood* (1913). All can be related in various ways to central aspects of frontier mythology. But they remain distinct from one another. And those with contemporary settings made during the late 1910s and the 1920s can be related also, and much more specifically, to debates occasioned by the involvement of Native Americans in the First World War (Aleiss 1991: 468–70). Moreover, while the tropes of noble and ignoble savagery, of tragically vanishing Americans, and of white supremacy can be found in the foreground of many, perhaps most, of these films, they can be found only in the background of a number of others. *The Legend of Scar Face* (1910), *The Cheyenne's Bride* (1911), *The Song of the Wildwood Flute* (1911), and others like them, focus solely on Indian characters. Although some are imbued with the poeticisms associated with noble savagery, they are neither nostalgically concerned with the disappearance of a race nor preoccupied with relations between Indians and whites. Rather they are small-scale comic or dramatic romances in Indian dress and in natural surroundings.[35]

The heterogeneity of Indian films in the silent era is matched by the heterogeneity of films about whites. This heterogeneity has been stressed in the Leutrat book on the 1920s western, *L'Alliance Brisée* (1985), and is readily apparent in Langman's *A Guide to Silent Westerns* (1992). For Leutrat the 1920s western is neither a fixed nor substantive entity. It exists instead in and as an array of differently stressed and diverse components, in and as an ever-shifting and always provisional articulation of elements whose various 'objectifications' derive from the numerous alliances it forms with other genres, cycles and trends and from the specific and plural traditions these alliances call into play. These alliances are evident in the variety of formats in which the western existed at this time (from shorts to serials, from features to specials), in the variety of audiences to which it sought in various ways and at various times to appeal (from children to adults, from rural spectators to those who lived in cities), and in the variety of often hybrid terms used to describe the films themselves (from 'romantic western' to 'western comedy drama', from 'western farce' to 'western mystery melodrama' (1985: 157)). Principal among them are the alliance between the western and childhood, evident in the young protagonists of films like *The Boy and the Bad Man* (1929), in the young sidekicks of stars like Tom Tyler, Frank Rice and Gary Cooper, and in numerous animal-centred westerns like *The King of the Herd* (1927) and *Just Tony* (1922); the alliance between the western, visual action and acrobatic athleticism, evident both in the chases and stunts engaged in by Tom Mix and others and in rodeo and sports-centred westerns like *Under Western Skies* (1926); the alliance between the western, history and 'realism', evident both in the production of frontier epics like *The Covered Wagon* (1923), with their stress on period detail and period consistency, and in the traditions and techniques of psychological characterization and moral decision-making associated in particular by William S. Hart; and the alliance between the western and comedy, evident not just in the regular appearance of comic sidekicks, comic butts and comic situations of all kinds, nor even just in the traditions of parody and satire that at one point encompassed a cycle of films about the making of westerns, but also in the deployment in stunt and action westerns of regimes of bodily gesture, movement and space similar to those used by contemporary comedians like Buster Keaton and Harold Lloyd.

Traversing some or all of these alliances, as Langman's book makes clear, are cycles of films about encounters between the West and modernity (a modernity embodied in flappers, telephones, airplanes and cars and in cities like Chicago and Los Angeles), the activities of cowboys on the Western front, the rehabilitation of veterans from the First World War, the hardships and dangers faced by women in the West, the regeneration of young men and women from the East, and the activities of the occasional female gunslinger, sheriff or mayor. Traversing them too are plots that hinge on religious conversion and racial prejudice, as well as on revenge, on the activities of land-grabbing villains, and on false accusations of crime.

The silent western as a whole is therefore diverse. While most of its trends, components and alliances can be related in one way or another to frontier mythology, that relationship is often either distant or complex. Moreover as Palmer (1995) and Podheiser (1983) have shown, the uses to which it is put are diverse as well. Thus while for Palmer a film like *Hell's Hinges* (1916) deploys the traditional antinomies of frontier mythology – East and West, Law and Nature, and so on – in such a way as to demonstrate the corruption of both sets of terms and hence to undermine its utopian dimensions (1995), for Podheiser the attributes of the traditional Westerner are deployed in Douglas Fairbanks's 'parody-westerns' in order to 'rid the national hero of his old-fashioned primitivism' and in order to pave the way 'for a more "sophisticated" Westerner' (1983: 129).

Similar points are made in a Ph.D. thesis on the 1930s western by Peter Stanfield (1999), only portions of which have so far been published (1996, 1998). Seeking to consider the characteristics, the significance and the fluctuations in production of A and B westerns in the 1930s, Stanfield relies neither on the received wisdom of existing accounts nor on the 'abstract modelling of generic archetypes' (1999: 1). He relies instead on a detailed examination of contemporary trade and newspaper sources, of the films themselves, and of cultural histories of the US and its popular culture in the nineteenth and twentieth centuries. He argues on the one hand that the B western, aimed as it was at rural and small-town audiences, functioned as the site in which relationships between the old and the new, between capital and labour, and between rural and urban values, practices and lifestyles were explored in a variety of guises and forms. One of these forms was the singing western, a form which played a decisive role in reconfiguring rural Southern culture as Western (indeed as Country and Western), in attracting female audiences, and in staging successful confrontations with modernity (whose positive incarnations were usually represented by the heroine) and with large-scale economic and industrial forces (whose oppressive and threatening incarnations were usually represented by villainous businessmen, bankers and local politicians) during the years of the Great Depression. (For further discussion of B westerns and singing cowboys, see Everson [1969] 1992: 153–

86, 224–34, 243–8; Malone [1985] 1987: 137–75; Miller 1976; Nevins 1996; Taves 1993b: 334–5; White 1996.)

The fortunes of the A western, on the other hand, were conditioned by the need to appeal both to metropolitan audiences and metropolitan concerns and to a general – rather than to a specifically rural – female audience. A successful cycle of Zane Grey and 'South of the Border/Old California' westerns in the late 1920s, westerns in which romantic intrigue and the successful marketing of romantic male leads to women were especially prominent, was followed in the early 1930s by the failure of large-scale productions *The Big Trail* (1930) and *Billy the Kid* (1930). These films were marked by the ill-judged deployment of new widescreen and big-screen technologies and by a lack of romantic ingredients. Coinciding with the Depression and with the subsequent lack of government pressure on the major companies to cater to independent rural and neighbourhood exhibitors, the A western fell into decline until attempts were made to revive it in the mid- and the late 1930s. Fuelled by renewed government pressure on the majors to cater for these exhibitors, the A western was relaunched in various guises. *Three Godfathers* (1936), *Ramona* (1936) and other films designed to appeal specifically to women were followed by a cycle of city westerns which included the likes of *Dodge City* (1939) and *Destry Rides Again* (1939), which featured male and female stars with proven appeal, and which sought to introduce modern, 'adult' ingredients like drinking, gambling and sex. The sexual trends evident in some of these films were to lead to the production of films like *The Outlaw* (1943) and *Duel in the Sun* (1946) in the 1940s. In the meantime, some of the city films overlapped with a cycle of historical westerns which included *Drums Along the Mohawk*, *Stagecoach*, *Jesse James* (1939) and *Billy the Kid* (1941). These films capitalized on a general move towards action pictures of all kinds. They enabled the industry to promote them as Americanized engagements with large-scale historical and political themes and thus to counter growing accusations that its censorship codes prevented an engagement with serious issues. And they found successful ways of integrating romantic storylines and prominent female stars, often alongside matinee idols with proven female appeal. In addition, they often perpetuated the engagement with the South and with Southern culture which had enabled (and which continued to enable) the B western to address the concerns of rural and working-class audiences and which had in doing so represented the modern West and the old frontier alike as spaces in which social tensions of various kinds are played out, rather than as sites in which the nature of these tensions are initially defined.

Given these conclusions, it is hardly surprising that Stanfield (1999) finds accounts of the western premissed on frontier mythology alone less than helpful, particularly in so far as they regularly marginalize not only most 1930s B westerns, but most 1930s A westerns too. It is hardly surprising either that, like Podheiser (1983), Palmer (1995) and Leutrat (1985), he finds the models and terms advanced by Cawelti (1970), Warshow ([1954] 1975b) and Wright (1975) to describe the 'classic' western formula, the 'classic' western hero and the 'classic' western plot unhelpful too. For these are all based on the frontier myth. Thus for Cawelti the classic formula entails a setting 'on or near a frontier' (1970: 35), 'at a certain moment in the development of American civilization, namely at that point when savagery and lawlessness are in decline before the advancing wave of law and order, but still strong enough to pose a local and momentarily significant challenge' (ibid.: 38). It entails three central roles, 'the townspeople or agents of civilization, the savages or outlaws who threaten this group, and the heroes who are above all "men in the middle"' (ibid.: 46). And it entails narratives in which violent confrontations of various kinds are central and in which, equally central, are various patterns of 'chase and pursuit' (ibid.: 66). For Wright the 'classic western plot' articulates a specific version of this formula, a version in which the hero uses his savage skills to combat savagery, hence to protect and defend the interests of a civilized community which eventually accepts him and which he eventually decides to join (1975: 32–59). For all three, as for others like Parks (1982), the hero is quintessentially male. He is a figure who possesses the violent skills necessary to defeat the forces of savagery, and a code of values, the Code of the West, which ensures that these skills are ultimately used to advance civilized causes, and which hence help to establish civilization in the very wilderness in which these self-same skills had been honed – terms of description which in some or in all respects simply do not apply to the 'lavender cowboy' incarnated by Gene Autry (Stanfield 1998: 106–12) or to Fairbanks's '"sophisticated" Westerner', let alone to some of the characters played by female western stars like Louise Lester and Edythe Sterling.[36]

These models and terms were devised at the beginning of the post-war era (in Warshow's case) or at the end of what is often considered the western's Golden Age (in the case of Cawelti and Wright). It is therefore no accident that along with the 'revenge' and 'professional' variants noted by Wright, variants in which the hero's relationship to civilized society undergoes considerable modification and in which images of a troubled or untrammelled masculinity are especially prominent, they are much more straightforwardly applicable to westerns of this period – and to prewar westerns, like *Stagecoach*, which acquired their canonic status at this time – than they are to many, if not most, earlier films. For during this period – during the Cold War, during an era of increasing international tension and intervention, during the final flowering of victory culture and the era of counter-cultural agitation that coincided with the Vietnam war, the struggles of other Third World countries abroad and the struggles of ethnic minorities at home – frontier mythology served as an increasingly central reference point not only in westerns, but in other forms of national discourse too (Carroll 1998; Coyne 1997; Deloria 1998: 128–80; Englehardt 1995: 3–259; Lenihan 1980; Slotkin 1992: 347–643).

Even here though, and quite apart from the well-documented revisionism that increasingly marked westerns deploying frontier mythology in the 1960s and early 1970s (aside from a number of those cited above, see Belton 1994: 221–3; Buscombe 1996: 292–3; Cawelti [1973] 1974; Nachbar 1974b; Park 1974; Pye 1996a: 15; Schatz 1988b: 33–5), specific and diverse cycles and trends and local industrial and ideological circumstances need to be taken into account. The need to cater for 'mining, agricultural and other sectors' continued ('Swing to "A" Horse Operas', *Variety*, 30 August 1944: 3). So too did the need to produce westerns which appealed to women, as is evident in musical westerns like *The Harvey Girls* (1946) and *Annie Get Your Gun* (1950), western romances like *Flame of the Barbary Coast* (1945) and *The Redhead and the Cowboy* (1951), female pioneer and action films like *Cattle Queen* (1951), *Montana Belle* (1952) and *Westward the Women* (1952) (Evans 1996), and family comedies, dramas and sagas like *Take Me To Town* (1953), *Giant* (1956), *Cimarron* (1960) and *How the West Was Won*.

The topic of Southerners and the South continued as well, in singing westerns and B films, and in a series of post Civil War films like *The Raid* (1954), *Rio Conchos* (1964) and *Count Three and Pray* (1955) which clearly helped articulate a number of contemporary post-war and Cold War themes – racism, the place of the returning veteran, the issue of national allegiance, and so on. The Elvis Presley western, alongside the deployment in westerns of other young musical stars like Ricky Nelson, Frankie Avalon and Fabian, marked the attempts made by Hollywood to cater for a growing teenage market. At the same time the advent and influence of television, evident in increasing budgets, in the increasing use of widescreen technologies, in the adoption of a new brand of 'adult' ingredients, and in the demise of the B film and the increasingly two-way exchange of actors and formats, has been much discussed (Anderson 1994; Boddy 1998; Buscombe 1988b: 46–8; Delameter 1996; Everson 1978: 240–59; Hall 1996; MacDonald 1987; Taylor 1989: 32–7; Yoggy 1996). Much discussed, too, has been the revisionist treatment of ethnicity and race (Cripps 1993: 280–3; French 1973: 76–99; Lenihan 1980: 55–89; Neale 1998; Pines 1988: 69–71; Slotkin 1992: 347–78, 628–33), and the influence in the 1960s of international developments and trends (Buscombe 1988b: 48–51; Everson 1978: 261; Frayling 1981; Hardy 1984: 272).

The intensely male orientation of many post-war westerns has been discussed as well (Bingham 1994: 49–68; Coyne 1997: 84–104; Lusted 1996: 69–74; Mitchell 1981: 189–238; Pye 1996b). This was a real and growing phenomenon, finding its articulation in films about male business empires and patriarchal families like *The Big Country* (1958) and *Broken Lance* (1954), as well as in films about fathers and sons like *The Tin Star* (1957) and in those films about wanderering loners, unattached mercenaries and all-male groups which clearly echoed the contemporary male 'flight from commitment' noted by cultural historians like Ehrenreich (1983). However, despite this apparent consonance between western theory and Hollywood practice, it is at least worth asking whether the male-oriented versions of frontier mythology promoted by post-war western theorists are borne out in full by the industry's output, or whether the critical preference for films like *The Searchers* (1956), *Ride Lonesome* (1959) and *The Wild Bunch* has tended to obscure the existence of some of the other trends and titles mentioned above.

Masculinity and gender, along with ethnicity, race and the other ideological dimensions of frontier mythology, have dominated such discussion as there has been of Clint Eastwood's recent westerns, of what Lyn Tan has called the 'post-revisionist' western (*Dances with Wolves* (1990), *Silverado* and the like), of TV mini-series like *Lonesome Dove*, and of westerns like *The Ballad of Little Jo* (1993) and *Posse* (1993) which have sought to modify the ways in which some of these dimensions have been handled (Bingham 1994: 231–54; Fore 1991; Gallafent 1994: 102–37, 217–28; Grist 1996; Kelley 1995; Modleski 1995/6; Prats 1995; Smith 1993: 47–54, 263–268; Walker 1996; Worland and Countryman 1998). However, despite their awareness that there is a lot more to say about the western's recent – and not so recent – history, and despite their awareness that there have been a number of previously premature forecasts of its imminent demise, most commentators now argue that as a major component in Hollywood's output the western is now and has for some time been a thing of the past. What this means among other things is that its role as a generic paradigm, as a model or starting point for the study of Hollywood's genres, is even more problematic now than it was before.

NOTES

1 See Bordwell, Staiger and Thompson (1985: 1–84, 155–240) and Salt ([1983] 1992) on the single-reeler and the feature film, Gunning (1991) and Musser ([1984] 1990a) on the single-reeler, Bowser (1990: 53–7, 191–215) and Brewster ([1982] 1990, 1991) on the single-reeler and the early feature film, and Elsaesser (1971, 1975), Jenkins (1995: 104–5, 113–17) and Maltby (1995: 107–360) on the feature film in the studio and post-studio eras. On shorts, see Maltin (1972). On serials, see Barbour (1970), Cline (1984) and Lahue (1964, 1968). On the newsreel, see Fielding (1972). And on animated shorts and cartoons, see Crafton (1982), Klein (1993), Maltin ([1980] 1987) and George (1990).

2 One reason for this was audience preference, particularly in foreign markets, and particularly in the era of sound. As Maltby and Vasey point out: 'it was an influential truism of foreign distribution that movies reliant on dialogue to explain their plot and develop their story, known in the industry as "walk and talk" pictures, fared substantially less well in the non-English-speaking market than did action pictures' (1994: 90). See also Wyatt (1994: 80).

3 It is no accident that spaces and locations, in particular 'open' and 'closed' spaces and locations, often form the basis of systematic patterns in action-adventure films. In *Red Heat* (1988), for example, the hero is vulnerable to attack in interior spaces, but either safe or victorious out of doors; the first and the second halves of *The Great Escape* (1963) take place respectively inside and outside the prison

camp; and *Silverado* is founded structurally on a repeated motif of imprisonment, confinement and escape into an open natural landscape. It is tempting to map this preoccupation with space onto the preoccupation in many adventure films and stories with what Phillips has called 'The geography of adventure, a cultural space opened up by European encounters with the non-European world' during the era of colonialist and imperialist expansion (1997: 13). While there are connections in numerous instances, it is probably best to avoid collapsing the one into the other. For further discussion of colonialism, imperialism and adventure, see below. For the particular significance of geography, landscape and space in the western, see Basinger (1994: 116–20), Buscombe (1995a), Bush (1988), French (1973: 100–12), Mauduy and Henriet (1989), Mitchell (1996), Saxton (1988), Shohat and Stam (1994: 116–18), Short (1991: 178–96), Szanto (1987: 23–39), Wexman (1993: 109–11), and the discussions of landscape in the reviews of *Dead Man* (1996) by Jones (1996: 46) and Levich (1996: 41).

4 On the serials in particular, see Edmonds (1977), Koszarski (1990: 164–6), and Lahue (1964: 70–152 and 1968). On the westerns, see Buscombe (1988b: 30–3), Everson ([1969] 1992: 84–7, 103–26) and Koszarski (1990: 288–91).

5 On the aviation films see Paris (1995: 55–83) and Pendo (1985: 1–150). On the Errol Flynn films, see Balio (1993: 203–5), Richards (1977: 18, 26–7), Roddick (1983: 235–47), Schatz (1988a: 208–10) and Taves (1993a: 69–72). On the Tyrone Power films, see Richards (1977: 18, 30–1). On the post-war adventure films, see Richards (1977: 18–24) and Taves (1993a: 72–4). On the male body and masculinity in the post-war epic, and in these films in particular, see Cohan (1997: 141–63), Hark (1993), Hunt (1993), Neale (1993b: 18) and Willemen (1981). On the adventure serials and the Tarzan films, see Barbour (1970: 11–156), Cheatwood (1982), Cline (1984), Essoe (1979), Lehman (1991) and Morton (1993). For further general discussion of adventure and the white male body, see Dyer (1997: 145–83).

6 Aside from those cited already, see Bederman (1995: 170–239), Bristow (1991), Cheyfitz (1989), Dawson (1994), Denning (1987), Drinnon (1981), Engelhardt (1995), Fiedler (1968), Green (1979, 1984), Kaplan (1990), Kolodny (1975, 1984), Lears (1981), Leverenz (1991), Saxton (1990), Shohat ([1991] 1997), Shohat and Stam (1994: 55–177), Slotkin (1973, 1985, 1992), Tompkins (1985), Torgovnick (1990: 42–72) and White (1968). Engelhardt's thesis is particularly interesting, and demonstrates the merits of grouping various kinds of adventure films together. He argues that a 'national war story' common to westerns, war films and other tales of adventure, whose basic motifs and whose fundamental ideological framework date back several centuries, reached a peak in the 1950s and early 1960s. Shattered by the Vietnam war, it was revived by *Star Wars* in 1977 and by 1980s war and adventure films set in Vietnam itself. However, he goes on to argue that by then the motifs of the war story had become detached both from their ideological and historical moorings and from their place within a cohesive – and triumphant – political narrative. In consequence, the 'new war story . . . had only a mocking relationship to a national story, for all "war" now inhabited the same unearthly, ahistorical commercial space. Even Rambo, transformed into an action-figure team for children, found himself locked in television combat with General Terror and his S.A.V.A.G.E. terrorist group . . . and everywhere the boundary lines between us and the enemy, the good team and the bad team, threatened to collapse into a desperate sameness' (1995: 284).

7 Another way of reading these scenarios is in terms of the Oedipal fantasies they stage and exemplify, fantasies in which an unjust paternal regime is replaced by a

just one, and in which in the process the central protagonist is granted status and recognition (often marked in royal or noble terms). For male protagonists, the fantasy is often further marked by eventual – and officially sanctioned – marriage to an aristocratic heroine whom the hero has rescued or captured from the unjust regime. Fantasies like this bear a marked similarity to the 'family romances' described by Freud ([1910] 1977: 239–42). Their origins in childhood, and their appeal to children, are perhaps echoed in the putative juvenile appeal and status of adventure films themselves. Within this context, female-centred adventure films – and perhaps pirate films in particular – can be seen as engaging the 'tomboy pleasures' discussed by Laura Mulvey in her (1981) article on *Duel in the Sun* (1946). Either way, the social and political themes of historical adventure films in particular might in this light perhaps best be viewed as material for the activation and articulation of the fantasies and pleasures concerned.

8 However, the changing of names in biopics is not confined to the era of the Hays code. In *Goodfellas* (1990), which is based on an autobiography by Nicholas Pileggi, and which is otherwise remarkably close to it in incident, vocabulary, structure and tone, the name of the central protagonist is changed to Henry Hill, possibly because Pileggi himself co-wrote the script.

9 This feature was often remarked on in the industry's press, which frequently noted or complained about the episodic tendencies of biopics and the potential confusions to which an excessive use of flashbacks could give rise. *Variety* complained that the script of *The Story of Will Rogers* (1952) 'is a rather sketchy affair, spanning as it does the long period in Rogers' life from the 1900s through to August, 1935' (16 July 1952: 6), that *The True Story of Jesse James* (1957) was 'Poorly plotted with confusing flashbacks' (20 February 1957: 6) and that the writers of *Sutter's Gold* (1936) 'were required to cover too much ground. They start too far back and end beyond the climax, such as it is. Footage is wasted telling of Sutter's flight from a murder charge in Switzerland and his excursion to the Hawaiian Islands. The result is that there is scant opportunity to put over a cohesive and well-conceived plot' (1 April 1936: 16).

10 According to my calculations, the percentage of biopics made in the 1950s as a proportion of Hollywood's output was 3.5, an increase on 1 in the 1930s and 2.2 in the 1940s. In the 1960s, it increased again to 4.3, decreased in the 1970s to 3.9, then increased once more in the 1980s to 5.3, its highest ever point.

11 The literature on this tradition and its sources is enormous. Aside from those cited already, see Adamson ([1973] 1974), Allen (1980), Barr (1967), Brunette (1991), Dardis (1979, 1983), Donnelly (1971/2), Edmonds (1991), Gehring (1983, 1984, 1987, 1990), Huie (1975), Kamin (1984), Levy (1997), Louvish (1997), Maltin (1982), McCaffrey (1976), McCann (1993), McLean (1965), Moews (1977), Rheuban (1983), Robinson ([1969] 1970, 1986), Sobel and Francis (1977), Telotte (1988), Toll (1976 and 1982: 211–43), Weales (1985) and Wertheim (1979). A distinct but important site for this type of comedy in the studio era was the animated short. See Klein (1993), Maltin ([1980] 1987), and Peary and Peary (1980) for initial collections, overviews and histories. One of the figures whose career spans these sites is Frank Tashlin, whose work is discussed in Johnston and Willemen (1973), Sikov (1994: 179–242) and Garcia and Eisenschitz (1994).

12 Other writing on screwball comedy, and other participants in this particular debate, include Balio (1993: 268–79), Belton (1994: 150–5), Bergman (1971: 132–48), Byrge (1987), Gehring (1986), Harvey (1987), Henderson (1978), Kay (1977), Kendall (1990), Lent (1995), Neale and Krutnik (1990: 150–69), Schatz (1981: 150–85), Sennett ([1973] 1985), Shumway (1991), Sikov (1989), Sklar

(1975: 187–8), Weales (1985: 187–297) and Winokur (1996: 179–234). Winokur's is essentially a study of William Powell and Myrna Loy as stars who functioned as vehicles for what he calls 'a fantasy of [ethnic] assimilation' (1996: 179). Two other stars who have been associated with screwball films and other kinds of romantic comedy, and who have been assessed as manifesting ambiguities of sexuality and gender which are clearly of relevance in this context, are Cary Grant and Katharine Hepburn. See Britton (1983, 1984).

13 There is some discussion of the detective film in the silent period in Bowser (1990: 185–6), Kozarski (1990: 184–6) and Langman and Finn (1994: xiii, xv, xviii). For discussion of the detective film in the 1930s, 1940s and 1950s, see Langman and Finn (1995a: xvi, 1995b: xi). For intermittent discussion of the B detective film in the 1930s, see Taves (1993b: 336–41). And for discussion of a specific detective series, the Sherlock Holmes films made at Universal in the 1940s, see Haralovich (1979).

14 See, among others, Hamilton (1993: 320–1), the Preface to Hoppenstand (1982), Knight (1980: 8–37), Ousby (1976), Palmer (1978: 107–35), Panek (1987: 12–95, 1990: 1–114), Porter (1981: 12–23), Stewart (1980) and Symons (1972: 31–89).

15 Although not unique in this respect, the extent to which, like detectives in the cinema and in written fiction, detectives on TV tend to appear in series is worthy of note. It suggests that the personality of the detective is as much a source of pleasure, interest and attraction as the structure of the narratives in which he or she appears, that the unravelling of enigmas and the catching of criminals function as much as generically specific touchstones of character as they do markers of a fascination with crime or the shifting of distribution of narrative knowledge.

16 The Chinatown cycle includes films like *Chinatown Nights* (1929), *Law of the Tong* (1931) and *The Hatchet Man* (1932), which stars Edward G. Robinson. The rubber racketeer films are mentioned in passing by Langman and Finn (1995b: xiii).

17 For discussion of the role of J. Edgar Hoover and the FBI in the promotion of the figure G-man during and after the 1930s, see Powers (1983). For discussion of the reconfiguration of the careers and images of Robinson and Cagney, see Karpf (1973). It is worth drawing attention to the fact that other performers, like Akim Tamiroff and Leo Carillo, were consistently associated with gangster roles throughout the 1930s. Robinson and Cagney were by no means the only ones.

18 Prassel points out that the word 'gangster' 'was based on an English word for a group of workers and Americans began associating it with criminals in the nineteenth century. It even became a verb, to gang, indicating a mass attack on a victim. By the 1890s *gangster* was appearing in print and received prompt acceptance in England as well as the United States. It applied to membership of any violent criminal association, including those of the closing frontier, but the early motion-picture producers seized and consistently used it in reference to 'urban hoodlums' (1993: 185). It is worth noting in this context that although 'gangster' and 'gang' were frequently used as descriptive terms in the industry's relay in the 1910s and the 1920s, 'crook melodrama' was the commonest generic term by far. 'Melodrama' continued to be used (usually in conjunction with 'gangster') until the 1960s.

19 Taking *Reservoir Dogs* (1992), a particular notion of *film noir*, and a quote from Baudrillard (1990: 188) as his starting point, Telotte is especially interesting on the interplay between planning and chance, the fatal and the accidental, that marks both the heist film and its dominant motifs of gambling, mortality and time.

20 The marking of gangsters as ethnic outsiders in films coincided with a shift in the cultural role of the gangster from Jazz Age hero to Depression scapegoat (Maltby 1993b: 144–9; Peary 1981: 9–12). However, as Ruth points out, the Prohibition gangster had always been open to xenophobic and nativist readings (1996: 73–4), and as most commentators on the gangster films of the early 1930s have pointed out, the non-dominant ethnic identity of the gangster merely added a further layer of ambivalence to an already ambivalent – and volatile – mix. For further discussion of ethnicity and organized crime, see Bell (1960: 138–50) and Woodiwiss (1990: 25–6).

21 On the blaxploitation films, see Bogle ([1979] 1991: 234–42), Clarens (1980: 295–7), Guerrero (1993: 86–103), James (1995), Leab (1975: 247–63), Pines (1975: 118–27, 1996: 505–6), Rosow (1978: 279–80) and Ross (1996: 61–4). On the more recent films, see Chan (1998), Guerrero (1993: 186–8), McCarty (1993: 225–7), Pines (1996: 507–9), Reid (1995: 470–3), Ross (1996: 71–6) and Winokur (1995).

22 On the former, see Babington and Evans (1993: 118–19), Forshey (1992: 4), Higashi (1994: 117–23), Hirsch (1978: 14, 31), Mayer (1994a), Morsberger and Morsberger (1974), Reynolds (1992) and Vardac (1949: 211–13). On the latter, see Elley (1984: 16–17), Gaudreault (1992), Keil (1992), Mayer (1994b), Musser (1990c: 208–21 and 1993), Vance, N. (forthcoming), Vance W. L. (1989) and Wyke (1997: 14–17).

23 In an unpublished paper on the 1925 version of *Ben-Hur*, Ted Hovet suggests that sequences and shots of incidental detail serve to complement and underpin 'the larger spectacles of size and splendor'. The latter need to supplement the former 'in order to reinforce the text's representational prowess'. One might argue that that prowess finds a parallel in narratives which constantly lay claim to what Sobchack has called 'historical eventfulness' (1990: 28), and, along with Sobchack herself, that that eventfulness is often mimed in the status of the films themselves as special events. Babington and Evans, meanwhile, provide a tax-onomy of spectacle in biblical films which includes the spectacle of architecture, geographic and cosmic spectacle, the spectacle of the body, the spectacle of orgy, the spectacle of presentations, ceremonies and gift-giving, the spectacle of costumes, fabrics, ornaments and jewels, the spectacle of forbidden gods, reli-gions and rituals, the spectacle of ancient warfare, the spectacle of slavery, the spectacle of sadism, masochism, punishment and torture, and the spectacle of 'the act of God' – miracles, destructive acts and other forms of spectacular transformation (1993: 64–5). Large-scale narratives not only provide a frame-work for forms of spectacle like this. They also allow for similar forms to be repeated and varied and for different forms to be mounted across an extensive, though finite, span of screen-time. (The argument here echoes that of Holland (unpublished) on the chase film.)

24 These factors affected the production of films of all kinds. For primary sources on their relationship to historical, biblical and ancient-world films in particular, see among others, 'Hollywood's Foreign Splurge' (*Variety*, 9 July 1947: 15), 'Join Hollywood And See The World' (*Variety*, 20 July 1949: 5, 20), 'Announcing The Sales Plans For MGM's *Quo Vadis*' (*Variety*, 21 November 1951: 16–17), 'Announcing The Sales Plan Of MGM's *Ivanhoe*' (*Variety*, 17 September 1952: 16–17), 'A Statement From Columbia Pictures On Its Sales Policy For The Screen Achievement of the Year' (*Variety*, 21 January 1953: 12–13), '3–D Keys New Roadshow Pix Biz' (*Variety*, 1 April 1953: 1, 29), 'Flood of Outdoor, Biblical Spects To Flow Into Widescreen Horizon' (*Variety*, 29 April 1953: 4, 18), 'Whole Economy of Film Industry Changing With "Epic" Trends; No

More Poor Man's Peepshow' (*Variety*, 14 October 1953: 3, 18), 'Marathon Pix Runs Gaining' (*Variety*, 25 August 1954: 5, 18), 'H'Wood Taps Ancient History To Out-Spec TV But B. O. Stamina Test Looms for "Alex," "Conqueror," "Helen"' (*Variety*, 4 April 1956: 3, 18), 'Gear "Ben-Hur" To Run Two Years' (*Variety*, 17 June 1959: 1).

25 Some horror theorists – and some psychologists – distinguish between horror, terror, fear and disgust. As Tamborini and Weaver (1996: 2) point out:

> Edwards (1984) suggested that a clear separation between horror and fear lies in the distinction between external threat and the idea of threat, but to this she added that terror is associated with extreme fear, whereas horror couples extreme fear with disgust. Thus one may feel terrified by the impending danger that could result in death, but horrified by the thought of being dead and the disgust of corruption and decay. This designation of horror is similar to that found in literature on emotion . . .

Distinctions between all these reactions and shock, suspense and surprise need to be borne in mind as well, as does the persistent association of horror with comedy and laughter, especially, but by no means exclusively, in modern 'splatter' or 'gross-out' films. (See Arnzen 1994; Brophy [1983] 1986; Conger and Welsch 1984; Hoxter 1996; Paul 1994: 49–81, 409–30; Pinedo 1997: 46–50. Pinedo argues that comedy in horror films serves 'a double, paradoxical function; it creates both distance and proximity' (ibid.: 46). She also argues (ibid.: 17) that horror films are dedicated to the production of what she calls 'a bounded experience of fear'.

26 For discussion of *Show Boat* and its various adaptations, see Kreuger (1977). For comparisons between all these shows and their film adaptations, see Aylesworth (1985).

27 For discussion of the songs and songwriting deployed in the Hollywood musical of the studio era, see Brahms and Sherrin (1984), Furia (1990), Hamm ([1979] 1983), Mooney (1968) and Wilder (1972), among others. For further writing on choreography and dance, see Kislan (1987) and Stearns and Stearns ([1968] 1994).

28 One reason for this may be the dismantling of the infrastructure provided by the system of studio production. Another may be the alleged unpopularity of Hollywood musicals with foreign audiences at a time when the foreign market had been growing in importance as a source of income and profit. See 'Hollywood's Tune Recession' (*Variety*, 28 January 1959: 43, 48), and 'O'Seas Chill Reducing U. S. Musicals' (*Variety*, 20 January 1960: 3, 25).

29 The writing here is extensive. See among others, Bogle ([1979] 1991: 143–93), Burke (1988), Cripps (1979: 45–7 and 1993), Erens (1984: 173–87, 223–8), Leab (1975: 145–68), Lenihan (1980: 24–81), Marchetti (1993: 78–201), Neale (1998), Nesteby (1982: 235–56), Pines (1975: 63–88 and 1996: 501–2), Slotkin (1992: 347–78, 441–73) and Wallace (1993).

30 Given the importance accorded the collective and variegated nature of the combat group in writing on war films, its history as a convention is clearly important. Most commentators see it as a Second World War invention, stressing the role of the OWI in its promulgation. However, while it is clear that the OWI played a part in advocating cooperative devices and multi-ethnic variegation (Koppes and Black 1987), it is also clear that small-scale combat groups and variegation of one kind or another can be found in at least some films made before the Second World War. What seems to change is the nature and extent of

the variegation involved and the role allotted the individual within the group and its various activities.

31 This point dovetails with Basinger's acute observations about

> the various spaces assigned . . . to the three basic formats of combat: air, sea, and land. Those who fly can return to safe havens and the occasional foray into nightclubs or private homes . . . The spaces they occupy tend to be *professional*: offices, barracks, briefing rooms. On the ocean when not in combat, men occupy *domestic* spaces: their bunks, bedrooms, kitchens, galleys . . . On land, men occupy foxholes or tents, which are purely *combat* spaces. Consequently, the air force film is often about *professionalism*, the pressure of duty, the responsibilities of leadership. The navy film is often about *domestic strife*, not only the kind that grows up among men on board (as in family life), but also the kind they left behind with women who resent their long months at sea. The land/infantry film is about *combat*.
>
> (Basinger 1986: 21–2; emphases in original)

Basinger makes these points about Second World War combat films, but it applies (with one or two modifications) to films with a First World War setting as well.

32 The literature here is extensive. It includes Adair (1986: 121–86), Auster and Quart (1988: 92–147), Berg (1990: 61–3), Corrigan (1991: 39–47), Doherty (1988/9), Haines (1990), Klein (1990: 23–36), McMahon (1994), Martin (1990: 168–93), Porteous (1989), Richman (1991: 203–48), Rist (1988), Ryan and Kellner (1988: 194–216), Scarrow (1991: 123–60), Studlar and Desser (1990), Traube (1992: 39–66), Waller (1990), Walsh (1988) and Whillock (1988: 249), who argues that because of the heterogeneity and paucity of the films, there is 'no Vietnam war genre' as such.

33 There is an enormous amount of writing about western and frontier mythology. Aside from a number of those cited in notes 3 and 6 above, see Athearn (1986), Berkhofer Jr. (1995: 172–6), Billington ([1981] 1985), Butler (1994), Countryman (1988), Goetzmann and Goetzmann (1986), Grossman (1994), Hyde (1990), Nash ([1967] 1982), Nash (1991), Shohat and Stam (1994: 114–21), Smith ([1950] 1971), Truettner (1991), Turner ([1920] 1962), and Weinberg ([1935] 1979). As revisionist historians like Jennings have pointed out (1993: 172–9), there never existed a single moving frontier at any point in American history. Instead there existed shifting and multiple populations and shifting and multiple zones and types of contact (some violent, others peaceful) among and between Indian peoples before and after colonization, and among and between Indian peoples, slaves and ex-slaves from Africa and the Caribbean, and Europeans and Euro-Americans from various countries and of various kinds thereafter. See also Nobles (1997).

34 As Kitses points out, what is important is 'the idea of the West' (1969: 8). The West has in this sense never been confined to a single location: different places, spaces and regions in America have served as its incarnation (see note 3); and different periods in American history have served as its temporal site. Given that the idea of the West can be evoked by the signs of any period in which frontier conditions obtained, and by any landscape, region, mode of behaviour, speech or dress associated with it, worries over whether or not westerns set in the eighteenth or twentieth centuries or East of Missouri or South of the Mexican border are really westerns therefore tend not only to be restrictive, as Buscombe (1988b: 17) points out, but to miss the point.

35 For further discussion of all these films, see Aleiss (1995), Brownlow (1979: 327–54, Everson ([1969] 1992: 47–9, 79–81, 97–8), Friar and Friar (1972: 69–177), and Griffiths (1996). For discussion of the depiction of Native Americans in later films and in general, see Barker and Sabin (1995), Berkhofer Jr. ([1978] 1979), Churchill (1992), Friar and Friar (1972: 178–203), Hilger (1986, 1995), Lenihan (1980: 24–89), Maltby ([1992] 1996), Neale (1998), O'Connor (1980), Rollins and O'Connor (1998), Shohat and Stam (1994: 115–21), Slotkin (1992: 347–78, 628–33), Strickland (1997: 17–45) and Wilson (1996).

36 Louise Lester starred in a series of Calamity Anne westerns in the 1910s, Edythe Sterling in westerns like *The Arizona Cat Claw* (1919) and *The Girl Who Dared* (1920).

4

FILM NOIR

With the advent of the Second World War a new mood was discernible in film drama – an atmosphere of disillusion and a sense of foreboding, a dark quality that derived as much from the characters depicted as from the cinematographer's art. These films, among them such classics as *Double Indemnity, The Woman in the Window, Touch of Evil* and *Sunset Boulevard*, emerged retrospectively as a genre in themselves when a French film critic referred to them collectively as *film noir*.

This, from the blurb on the back of Bruce Crowther's book *Film Noir: Reflections in a Dark Mirror* (1988), is as good a summary as any of what *film noir* is generally taken to be – and as good an example as any of some of the problems associated with *noir*, especially in so far as these problems centre on issues of genre.

Crowther's book is just one of many essays, articles and books on *film noir* to have appeared in English over the last 25 years. Following a chapter on 'Black Cinema' in Higham and Greenberg's *Hollywood in the Forties* (1968: 19–36), the 1970s witnessed the initial publication of studies by Durgnat ([1970] 1996), Schrader ([1972] 1996), Place and Peterson ([1974] 1996), Porfirio ([1976] 1996), Karimi (1976), Damico ([1978] 1996), the first edition of Silver and Ward (1979), and the collection of essays on *Women in Film Noir* edited by Kaplan (1978a). The 1980s saw the consolidation of this trend, with books by Ottoson (1981), Hirsch (1981), Selby (1984), Tuska (1984) and Telotte (1989), in addition to Crowther's book, a second edition of Silver and Ward (1988), numerous articles, and chapters in books on more general topics. This trend has continued into the 1990s, which have seen the publication of a third edition of Silver and Ward (1992) and new books by Krutnik (1991), Palmer (1994) and Christopher (1997), as well as collections edited by Cameron (1992), Copjec (1993), and Silver and Ursini (1996). (For an excellent account of writing on *film noir* from the 1960s through to the early 1980s, see Root 1985; for reasonably complete bibliographies, see Ottoson (1981) and Silver and Ward).

A key feature of nearly all these essays, articles, chapters and books is an acknowledgement of the heterogeneity of the films, and hence the potentially problematic nature of the 'phenomenon' the term '*film noir*' has been used to label (Krutnik 1991: 24), coupled with an insistence, nevertheless, that there *is* a phenomenon, that it can be described and accounted for, and that it is in one way or another – aesthetically, culturally, ideologically or historically – important. As Michael Walker points out:

> The cycle of 'forties and 'fifties Hollywood films that retrospectively became known as *films noirs* seem at first sight to be rather too diverse a group to be constituted with any precision as a generic category. Nevertheless, various critics have sought different unifying features: motif and tone (Durgnat, 1970), social background and artistic/cultural influences (Schrader, 1971 [*sic*]), iconography, mood and characterisation (McArthur, 1972), visual style (Place & Peterson, 1974), the 'hard-boiled' tradition (Gregory, 1976), narrative and iconography (Dyer, 1977), a master plot paradigm (Damico, 1978), conditions of production (Kerr, 1979), paranoia (Buchsbaum, 1986 . . .) and patterns of narration (Telotte, 1989).
>
> (Walker 1992: 8)

Despite these difficulties and differences, Walker goes on to note that *noir* 'continues to fascinate' (ibid.). This element of fascination has also been noted by Cowie, who in addition reiterates the problematic nature of *noir* as a category, and the talismanic nature of *noir* as a term:

> whether it is a genre, a cycle of films, a tendency or a movement, *film noir* has been extraordinarily successful as a term . . . The term has succeeded despite the lack of any straightforward unity in the set of films it attempts to designate. Unlike terms such as the 'western', or the 'gangster' film, which are relatively uncontroversial . . . *film noir* has a more tenuous critical status. Yet this is matched by a tenacity of critical use, a devotion among *aficionados* that suggest a desire for the very category as such, a wish that it exist in order to 'have' a certain set of films all together. *Film noir* is in a certain sense a fantasy . . .
>
> (Cowie 1993: 121)[1]

This does not mean, though, that there was no phenomenon – or set of phenomena – no trend or trends in Hollywood's output in the 1940s and 1950s at least partially identified by the term '*film noir*' and by the critics, writers and theorists devoted to it, as Cowie herself goes on to argue. The problem has been that the *noir* canon, and indeed the very term '*film noir*', has obscured as well as illuminated the nature and extent of the phenomena it alone is said to embody or to name, that it has discouraged rather than invited a thorough survey of Hollywood's output for traces of the elements only it is presumed to exemplify or label. The *noir* canon, and its core films in particular, has been used either as the sole or principal basis for establishing the key features, the antecedents, and the contextual factors at stake in a phenomenon whose unity and coherence are presumed in the single term used to label them rather than demonstrated through any systematic, empirical analysis.

This problem stems in large part from the fact that *film noir* was not a genre in the sense used in this book. As Cowie points out, the term was used neither by the industry in America, nor by contemporary English-speaking audiences, reviewers or critics. It is in essence a critical category. This means that its corpus can only be established by means of critical observation and analysis; its constituents and contours cannot be verified by reference to contemporary studio documents, discussions or reviews, or to any other contemporary inter-textual source. This is not in itself an insuperable problem, provided that the nature and status of the term are acknowledged, and provided that the canon is established by applying a clear and consistent set of criteria to as broad an initial corpus of films as is possible. Unfortunately, many of the proponents of *film noir* have on the one hand been unable to decide on the nature of the phenomenon with which they are dealing. As Frank Krutnik points out, 'Higham and Greenberg and Paul Kerr refer to *film noir* as a genre; Raymond Durgnat and Paul Schrader see it as defined more by "mood" and "tone"; Janey Place and Robert Porfirio decribe it as a "movement"; while, most confusing of all perhaps, is Jon Tuska's position that *noir* is "both a screen style . . . and a perspective on human existence and society [1984: xv]"' (1991: 17). On the other, they have tended to seek to derive their criteria from a small group of films – those initially identified or labelled as *noirs* – while trying to privilege the genres with which those films were associated and to extend the corpus numerically and chronologically in order to substantiate *noir*'s existence and *noir*'s significance. The result has been considerable dis-agreement about basic criteria, about the overall contours of the larger *noir* canon, and about some of the antecedents, roots and causes of *noir*. Most important of all, *noir* critics have been unable to define *film noir*, even though there is considerable agreement as to the films that constitute *noir*'s basic canon.

This is odd. With a small core corpus of films, the identification of a set of basic characteristics – and hence basic criteria – should be much more straightforward. The problem – or at any rate the problem for *noir*'s pro-ponents – is that the systematic application of many of the criteria they have advanced as definitive tend either to necessitate the exclusion or margin-alization of films and genres generally considered as central, or else to necessitate the inclusion of films and genres generally considered as marginal. This in turn has knock-on effects for those who ascribe a socio-historical significance to *noir*, or who wish to explain and interpret its ideological features and functions. By looking in some detail at the range of explanations, interpretations and definitions of *noir* I hope here to highlight some of these problems. I shall ultimately argue that these problems are insuperable, principally because as a concept *film noir* seeks to homogenize a set of distinct and heterogeneous phenomena; it thus inevitably generates contradictions, exceptions and anomalies and is doomed, in the end, to incoherence. Paradoxically however, both *film noir* and neo-*noir*, a phenomenon of the 1970s, 1980s and 1990s, have, as we shall see, both acquired a much more secure generic status over the past three decades as the term '*noir*' itself has become more ubiquitous.

THE INITIAL PROPONENTS OF *NOIR*

The term '*film noir*' – or to be more precise '*films "noirs"*' – was first applied to a group of American films by the French film critic Nino Frank in 1946 (Frank 1946: 14). The circumstances of war and occupation had prevented the screening of American films in France for several years. Many of these films were released in great numbers in France once the war was over. A number of films made in Hollywood early on in the 1940s were thus first shown in Paris in the summer of 1946 alongside more recent films. Frank discusses four of them: *The Maltese Falcon* (1941), *Double Indemnity* (1944), *Laura* (1944) and *Murder, My Sweet* (a.k.a. *Farewell My Lovely*) (1944). He claimed to detect a new trend in the Hollywood crime film, one which echoed the emergence of Dashiell Hammett and Raymond Chandler within the field of the American crime novel. Suggesting 'criminal adventures' ('*aventures criminelle*') as a more suitable descriptive term than the traditional '*policier*,' Frank notes the emphasis in these films on 'criminal psychology', violence, misogyny, and everyday realism ('*vecu*'), and the extent to which the use of first-person narration and multiple flashbacks serve to fragment their narratives.

The term '*films "noirs"*' occurs in passing towards the end of the article. However, it is picked up and used by others. Jean-Pierre Chartier discusses *Double Indemnity, Murder, My Sweet* and *The Lost Weekend* (1945) in an article entitled 'Les Americains aussi font les "noirs"' (1946). He stresses the elements of pessimism, disgust, and fatal sexual attraction in these films, and as James Naremore has pointed out, 'was appalled by the moral effect of the series as a whole' (1995/6: 17).[2] Two years later, Henri-François Rey (1948) discusses *Double Indemnity, The Lost Weekend, The Woman in the Window* (1945) and *Scarlet Street* (1945) in an article entitled 'Demonstration par l'Absurde: les films noirs'. Rey similarly notes the elements of pessimism and anxiety in these films. He also stresses the extent to which they provide an unflattering picture of contemporary America.

Finally, in 1955, Raymond Borde and Etienne Chaumeton published a book, *Panorama du Film Noir Américain*. In the preface to this book, Marcel Duhamel links the term '*film noir*' to 'Série Noir,' the trade name under which a series of detective novels and crime thrillers – including those written by

Americans like Hammett and Chandler – were published in France. He also draws attention to the general connotations of *noir*, in particular its association with death, though the extent to which he is claiming that these links and connotations underlay the adoption of the term by critics of film remains unclear. Borde and Chaumeton themselves describe the films they identify as *noirs* in much the same terms as Frank, Rey and Chartier. They stress the importance of crime, violence and death (in particular cruel or gratuitous violence and death); and they underline the sado-masochistic character of *noir's* eroticism. In addition, they lay great emphasis on the nightmarish qualities of *noirs*, and on the moral ambivalence of *noir's* protagonists. Ultimately, the key term for them is '*insolite*' (which usually translates as 'unusual,' 'unforeseen' or 'unexpected') and the key effect the generation of anxiety, insecurity and 'malaise':

> moral ambivalence, criminal violence and the contradictory complex-
> ity of situations and motives combine to give the audience a genuine
> sense of anxiety or insecurity, and this is the hallmark of film noir in
> our era . . . The vocation of film noir was to create *a specific malaise*.
> (Borde and Chaumeton 1955: 15; my translation)

The cultural factors in France predisposing the identification and description of *noir* in these terms have been discussed by Arthur (1990: 2–5), Naremore (1995/6: 14–24), Palmer (1994: 7–20) and Vernet (1993: 4–6). Leaving aside for the moment the extent to which the terms themselves are applicable, it is worth noting, first of all, that the number of films cited by the French proponents of *noir* is actually fairly small. This has subsequently helped secure the cult status of the phenomenon they claim to have identified, but it casts doubt on aspects of at least some later accounts of the phenomenon itself.

THE DIMENSIONS OF THE *NOIR* CANON

Between them, Frank, Rey and Chartier cite seven films as *noirs*. Writing nearly a decade later, and therefore able to include a number of subsequent films, Borde and Chaumeton list 22 films under the heading of 'Films Noirs' in an appendix to their book, and an additional 62 films under other principal headings (1995: 205–9. See the appendix on pp. 259–61 of this book). It is important to put these figures into perspective. If what is being identified is, first and foremost, a trend in Hollywood's output, it is important to gauge its dimensions. According to Joel Finler (1988: 280), 5,325 American films were released in the United States between 1940 and 1952, the period covered by Borde and Chaumeton. The seven films mentioned by Frank, Rey and Chartier represent 0.13 per cent of this total, the 22 films in Borde and Chaumeton's core canon 0.41 per cent, and the 84 films they list overall 1.6

per cent. For Borde and Chaumeton the 'Grand Epoch' of *film noir* is the period 1946–8. The 13 core films they list for these years constitute 1.2 per cent of a total of 1,113, the 32 films they list overall 2.9 per cent.

Many subsequent writers on *film noir* have added to these lists. The most extensive additions can be found in the 1992 edition of Silver and Ward (333–6, 393–7). They list 248 films for the period 1940–52, 4.7 per cent of the total. According to them, the highest annual number of *noirs* were released in 1950. Thirty-nine films are listed for this year, 10.2 per cent of a total of 383. For the years 1941–58 (generally reckoned by writers like Walker to be the basic chronological parameters of *noir*), Silver and Ward list 312 films, 4.9 per cent of a total of 6,359.

The figures for Frank, Rey and Chartier are obviously negligible. However, they were commenting – often in the context of reviews of specific films – on a trend they saw as recently emerging, and were hardly in a position to provide a definitive overview. The figures for Borde and Chaumeton, who *were* providing an overview, are less negligible, but hardly impressive. The figures for Silver and Ward, and in particular the figure for 1950, though still not overwhelming, are clearly more significant. The question, though, is whether they are capable of sustaining the weight of significance – and the weight of interpretation – placed upon *noir* itself by its commentators, writers and critics.

NOIR'S SIGNIFICANCE

The significance of any trend in Hollywood's output need not necessarily depend on its numerical dimensions. The cycle of 'pro-Indian' westerns that emerged in the late 1960s, for instance, consists of just a handful of films, among them *Tell Them Willie Boy is Here* (1969), *Little Big Man* (1970) and *Soldier Blue* (1970). What matters is that they departed from convention in being critical of white society in general – and the white military in particular – and that they thus shared an 'anti-establishment' ethos both with other contemporary films like *The Graduate* and *M.A.S.H.* (1970) and with broader movements, trends and currents of opinion in the US itself. For many commentators, *noir*'s significance also lies in its departures from convention. As Belton points out, 'What struck French critics about film noir was its essential *difference* from earlier American films' (1994: 190). The nature and extent of this difference will be discussed in more detail below. The point here is that for some *noir*'s significance resides not, or not just, in its difference, but in what this difference reveals about America's social, political, and ideological condition at a particular point in time, and here, in contrast to the 'pro-Indian' westerns cited above, matters of interpretation are much less straightforward, in part because the period covered is much more extensive, in part because the terms of interpretation, however plausible, tend to be much less susceptible to any form of verification.

The following, from Crowther's book, is fairly typical of traditional inter-pretations of *noir*, both in its chronological scope, and in its stress on alienation, dislocation, paranoia, disillusion and fear:

What the French critics had spotted was that makers of these movies had exposed an inner core of darkness in American society which closely resembled that which engulfed Europe during the war and the immediate post-war years. Of course, there was no counterpart in America to the physical damage and wholesale death and destruction which had devastated Europe, but there was fear, alienation and both physical and psychological dislocation. A few years later, as red scares and witch-hunts damaged America, greatly affecting the nation's popular culture, disillusion set in and, more significantly for both American people and Hollywood film-makers, fear turned into paranoia.

It was during these post-war years, including the period of 'police action' in Korea, that most of the classic *films noirs* were made.

(Crowther 1998: 12)

Foster Hirsch makes similar arguments:

Noir never insisted on its 'extracurricular' meanings or its social relevance. But beneath its repeated stories of double and triple crosses, its private passions erupting into heinous crimes, the sleazy, compromised morality of many of its characters, can be glimpsed the political paranoia and brutality of the period. In its pervasive aura of defeat and despair, its images of entrapment, the escalating derangement of its leading characters, *noir* registers, in a general way, the country's sour postwar mood. The darkest, most downbeat of American film genres traces a series of metaphors for a decade of anxiety, a contemporary apocalypse bounded on the one hand by Nazi brutality and on the other by the awful knowledge of nuclear power.

(Hirsch 1981: 21)

It is possible to find some corroboration for theses of this kind both in contemporary comments on some of Hollywood's films and in books on American history. Producer John Houseman argued that the 'current "tough" movie is no lurid Hollywood invention; its pattern and its characteristics coincide too closely with other symptoms of our national life . . . The "tough" movie presents a fairly accurate reflection of the neurotic personality of the United States of America in the year 1947' (1947: 161). And historian William H. Chafe writes that the period just after the war in America 'was a time of anxiety and fear' ([1986] 1991: 30). However, as Jane Root has pointed out, theses like these offer 'few clear suggestions' as to how some-thing as vague as a national mood – or even how something more specific like a knowledge of Nazi brutality or nuclear power – '[is] actually articulated' in the films themselves (1985: 95). In addition, as writers like Schindler (1979: 107) and Nachbar (1988: 72–3) have pointed out, Hollywood was making cheerful and optimistic films like *Road to Utopia* (1944), *The Bells of St Mary's* (1945), *The Egg and I* (1947) and *The Bachelor and the Bobbysoxer* (1947) at the same time as it was making angst-ridden thrillers, and by and large these were the biggest successes at the box-office. At least one contemporary commentator disputed Houseman's thesis, pointing to the diversity of Hollywood's output and cautioning against any 'technique of interpretation' in which 'a broad generalization of universal application is induced from an isolated and deliberately selective instance' (Asheim 1947: 414). And historians can be found who argue that the immediate post-war era was marked by a sense of 'exhilaration' (Goldman [1961] 1973: 12), and that 'fears about the future of war contrasted with another mood in 1945 – pride, exuberance, even arrogance about American power' (Sherry 1995: 115).

A further index of problems like this is that commentators on *noir* some-times interpret similar social and cinematic data in diametrically opposite ways. For instance, while for Durgnat 'late '40s Hollywood is blacker than '30s precisely because the audience, being more secure, no longer needed cheering up' ([1970] 1996: 37), for Schrader, 'The disillusionment many soldiers, small businessmen and housewife/factory employees felt in returning to a peacetime economy were directly mirrored in the sordidness of the urban crime film' ([1972] 1996: 55). In addition, while some, like Hirsch and Schrader, see *noir* as expressive or symptomatic of dominant ideological trends or national moods, others, like Belton and Telotte, see it as marked 'by a subversive strain of behavioral deviance' (Belton 1994: 184). Most commen-tators tend to hover between these positions. This means that at times they find themselves arguing that *noir* registered a dominant ideological mood that was at the same time subversive of dominant values. Such a position is hard either to sustain or to verify, particularly when it is taken to apply to a decade and a half of Hollywood's output and America's history.

Those who recognize some of these problems have adopted a number of different strategies. Some, like Belton, see *noir* as one – subversive – trend among others. Others, like Nachbar, see it as 'the flipside of the postwar baby boom and the middle-class flight to the suburbs' (1988: 73). Another strategy has been to relate the *noir* phenomenon to more specific factors and trends. Telotte, for instance, sees *noir* as a site for expressing and exploring the problems of communication and representation in a changed post-war world. Dana Polan's arguments are similar. For him the defamiliarizing heterogeneity of *noir*'s devices relates it to numerous crises and struggles within America's social and symbolic order in the 1940s, in particular to those concerning the socio-cultural authority of Hollywood's classical narrative system itself (1986). More specifically still, Arthur sees *noir* in terms of a 'confrontation of individuals and networks of corporate/collective control' (1990: 46) during

158

a period – the first decade of the Cold War – which witnessed an increasing politicization of issues of loyalty, allegiance and betrayal.

The Cold War, and the general realignment of the political landscape in America in the immediate post-war period, features centrally in the chapter on *film noir* in Neve's book, *Film and Politics in America* (1992: 145–70). The book as a whole centres on a generation of left-wing and liberal writers, directors and producers, many of whom began work in Hollywood in the 1940s. Neve cites Edward Dmytryk, Orson Welles, Jules Dassin, John Huston, Albert Maltz, Dore Schary, Irving Pichel, Abraham Polonsky, Robert Rossen, Adrian Scott and a number of others. Prompted in part by comments made by Andersen (1985), Clarens (1980: 195), Davis (1990: 37–44), Kemp (1986) and Thompson (1990: 21), he notes the extent to which they were involved in the production of numerous films subsequently labelled as *noirs*. He also notes the extent to which the films themselves were pervaded by themes of class difference, class power and the corrupting influence of money, by sympathetic portrayals of lower class characters and lower class milieux, and often also by warnings about the continuing presence of fascism and fascists both abroad and in America itself.

Neve's account is judicious and grounded in evidence – he cites contemporary sources and participants as well as the ideas of subsequent writers on *film noir*. Precisely because of this, he is careful to avoid arguing either that liberal and left wing concerns were restricted to *noirs*, or that *noir* itself was an ideologically uniform phenomenon. For on the one hand, as he himself indicates, left-liberal sentiments and left-liberal personnel can be found at work in westerns like *Broken Arrow* (1950), war films like *Destination Tokyo* (1945), and in post-war social problem films like *Pride of the Marines* (1945) and *Home of the Brave* (1949). And on the other, there exist anti-communist *noirs* like *The Woman on Pier 13* (a.k.a. *I Married a Communist*) (1949) and *I Was a Communist for the F.B.I.* (1951). In addition, as Maltby has pointed out ([1984] 1992), a number of contemporary leftists and liberals were hostile either to individual *noirs* or to the phenomenon of which they were a part – John Houseman's views on 'tough' films would be an example. One reason for this was a perception that Hollywood's thrillers incarnated rather than diagnosed distinct fascist tendencies in post-war America. In his critique of Houseman, Asheim cites Kracauer's warnings that 'aside from the genuine and constant affinity between sadism and fascism, it seems probable that the sadistic energies in our society at the present moment are specifically suited to provide fuel for fascism' (1947: 415). These warnings were later echoed by John Howard Lawson, who argued that the 'pattern of sex and violence' in these films was evolving towards 'direct propaganda for war and fascist regimentation' (1953: 24).

Once again, then, we encounter problems in characterizing *noir* from an ideological point of view and in relating it to its socio-cultural context. These problems stem in part from the methods and interests of its commentators, critics and theorists. But they also stem from its critical status, from its dependence on the criteria and perceptions of its critics, and from a consequent haziness about the contours of larger *noir* canon in particular – neither *The Woman on Pier 13* nor *I Was a Communist for the F.B.I.* appear on Selby's list of *films noirs*, and while the latter appears in the latest edition of Silver and Ward, it does not appear in earlier ones. Similar problems bedevil one of the most influential strands in the ideological analysis of *noir*, the analysis of sexuality and gender.

GENDER AND SEXUALITY

For many commentators, the principal hallmarks of *noir* include a distinctive treatment of sexual desire and sexual relationships, a distinctive array of male and female character types, and a distinctive repertoire of masculine and feminine traits, ideals, characteristics and forms of behaviour. For some these elements can be related directly to contemporary social and cultural trends and factors; they help not only to define *film noir*, but also to account for its existence.

Most of these commentators argue that desire in *noir* tends to be marked as dangerous or destructive, and that it tends to be represented from a male point of view. They argue in addition that *noirs* typically centre on male characters who aspire, sometimes successfully, often unsuccessfully, to 'tough' or 'hard-boiled' ideals of masculinity, that these ideals include an ability to resist the temptations of desire, especially when offered or aroused by openly sexual – and often powerful, independent and treacherous – female characters, and that in general the principal female characters in *noir* tend to divide neatly into two basic types: alluring – and dangerous – *femmes fatales* on the one hand, and dependable, respectable, safe and undemanding partners, wives and girlfriends on the other. However, there are a number of important differences of emphasis among and between these different writers. Kaplan and Harvey, for instance, stress the extent to which *noir's femmes fatales* constitute a departure from convention, and hence their centrality to the difference of *noir* itself. While for Kaplan there are limits to the *femme fatale's* capacity to disturb the patriarchal order – 'often the work of the film is the attempted restoration of order through the exposure and then destruction of the sexual manipulating woman' (1978b: 3) – for Harvey *noir* retains its 'subversive significance' (1978: 33) because its films are persistently marked by failed or doomed romances, and absent or distorted families and family relations.

Meanwhile, in attempting to outline a structural model of *noir*, Damico highlights the extent to which the *femme fatale* is attached to another man, and hence the extent to which she can be read in terms of male rivalry. Damico's emphasis on the male characters in *noir* is echoed by Krutnik and Thomas, for whom masculinity is central. Both see *noir* as dramatizing what Thomas calls 'a particular crisis in male identity' (1992: 59), and both therefore emphasize the extent to which *noir*'s female characters can be viewed as a function of male dilemmas and male anxieties. For Thomas, the 'redemptive' or 'domesticating' woman is as threatening for the male protagonist as the *femme fatale*. Where the latter represents the temptations and dangers of sexual transgression, the former represents the temptations and dangers of 'the hero's domestication' (ibid.), 'women . . . may [thus] represent not only the projected dangers of rejecting "normality" but the oppressiveness of embracing it as well. Generally, the two functions are assigned to separate women, but more than one *femme fatale* turns out to be a would-be wife' (ibid.: 64).

For Krutnik, as for Thomas, the *femme fatale* tends to represent 'conflicting elements within male identity' (1991: 63). However for him the problems faced by *noir*'s male protagonists 'are not solely or even predominantly bound up with their relations with women' (ibid.: 164). Women are only one source or index of more general 'disturbances in or threats to the regimentation of masculine identity and social/cultural authority' (ibid. 164). Krutnik here echoes Dyer, who argues that 'film noir is characterised by a certain anxiety over the existence and definition of masculinity and normality' (1978: 91), and Jacobowitz, who argues that *noir* is a 'genre wherein compulsory masculinity is presented as a nightmare' (1992: 153). For Krutnik, a major hallmark of this nightmare is the fact that 'the conventionalized figuration of "tough", controlled and unified masculinity is invoked not so much as a model of worthwhile or realistic achievement but more as a worrying mark of what precisely is lacking' (1991: 88). Overall, he argues, *films noirs* 'reveal an obsession with male figures who are both internally divided and alienated from the culturally permissible (or ideal) parameters of masculine identity, desire and achievement' (ibid.: xiii).

These writers are all united in their insistence on the centrality of issues of sexuality and gender in *noir*, and on the troubled aspects of the ways these issues are handled. They all also cite the same social and cultural factors in accounting for these aspects of *noir*, and in explaining their historical significance. These factors include the outbreak of the Second World War, the mobilization not just of men but also of women, and the consequent disruption of domesticity, marriage and family life and of the roles which women, in particular, were expected to play. They also include the economic, social and psychological reintegration of returning veterans, 'the post-war drive to get women out of the workforce and return them to the domestic sphere' (Gledhill 1978: 19), and the difficulties, struggles, resentments and suspicions these processes often entailed. However, there are clearly differences between these writers as well, and hence perhaps questions still to be asked about sexuality and gender in *noir*, and about *noir*'s relationship both to the factors cited above and to Hollywood's output as a whole in the wartime and post-war periods.

A crucial factor here, once again, is the imprecise nature of the *noir* canon, and the extent to which it can warrant selectivity, omission, and partial emphasis. Harvey (1978), for instance, is able to ignore the presence and importance of marriage and the family in films like *Kiss of Death* and *Desperate* (1947), and the positive and successful romances in *The Big Sleep*, *Dark Passage* (1947) and *Deadline at Dawn* (1946). Those who stress the centrality of *femmes fatales* are able either to ignore films which lack *femmes fatales*, like *Shadow of a Doubt* (1943), *The Lost Weekend*, *Sorry, Wrong Number* (1948) and *Touch of Evil* (1958), or to treat some, like *The Blue Gardenia* (1952), as occasional exceptions (Kaplan 1978c; Thomas 1992: 61). A similar point has been made by Cowie (1993), who also draws attention to the frequent roles played by women as source novelists and scriptwriters for *noirs*, and to the extent to which films like *Raw Deal* (1948) and *Secret Beyond the Door* (1948) are 'woman's stories'. One of her central arguments is that while the issue of sexual difference in *noir* is always crucial, the gender of its originators and protagonists, together with the gender orientation and appeal of its films, is much more variable – and the category of *noir* in this respect at least much more heterogeneous – than most commentators have hitherto acknowledged.

A similar challenge to the homogeneity of *noir* and its treatment of sexuality and gender emerges from another perspective. Adherents of *noir* are often led to claim it as a unique, particular or privileged site for the expression of those socio-cultural factors listed above (Krutnik 1991: 64; Place 1978: 37). This is a logical position to take, given their commitment to *noir* as a distinct and particular phenomenon. However, evidence can be found both among those who have studied sexuality and gender in other kinds of 1940s films, and among contemporary commentators, that these factors impinged on an array of Hollywood's genres, cycles and films, and that a number of the situations, preoccupations and character-types often associated exclusively with *noir* can be found in genres and films usually seen either as marginal to *noir* or else as totally separate.

Kaja Silverman, for instance, has discussed a range of 1940s films in terms of the 'historical trauma' of war and post-war readjustment and its effects on 'male subjectivity' (1992: 52–121). She cites a number of contemporary left-liberal commentators on Hollywood's output at this time, highlighting the extent to which they were preoccupied not just with male 'toughness,' but also with male protagonists who were apathetic, weary, tempted by the comforts of passivity. In a number of ways, this is consonant with the analyses of Krutnik, Jakobowitz and others. However, alongside such *noirs* as *Gilda* (1946), *Spellbound* (1945) and *The Lost Weekend*, Silverman also discusses comedies, musicals and social problem films like *Hail the Conquering Hero* (1944), *State Fair* (1945), *Pride of the Marines* and *The Best Years of Our Lives* (1946).

Femmes fatales, meanwhile, are identified and labelled in various ways in contemporary reviews of 1940s films, in at least one contemporary study of Hollywood's output, and in several subsequent studies of the representation of women in 1940s Hollywood films. However, these sources all indicate that *femmes fatales* were by no means restricted to *noirs*. In *Movies: A Psychological Study*, Martha Wolfstein and Nathan Leites refer to a character-type they label 'the bitch' ([1950] 1977: 84). However, while 'the bitch' is exemplified by Kitty (Joan Bennett) in *Scarlet Street*, often considered an archetypal *noir*, she is also exemplified by Mrs Macomber (Joan Bennett again) in *The Macomber Affair* (1947), a mix of triangle drama and adventure which has never appeared on anyone's list of *noirs*. Similarly, in *Hollywood's Wartime Women* (1988), Michael Renov identifies a range of female types recurrent in Hollywood's output at this time, among them 'The Inscrutable Female' and 'The Evil Woman'. The former he describes as 'female personae whose origins, intentions and activities are imperfectly understood by the male protagonists' (ibid.: 167); the latter he describes as 'characteristically malevolent' (ibid.: 174). While films like *Laura* and *Gilda* (1946) are listed under the former heading, so too are comedies and westerns like *Ball of Fire* (1941) and *The Ox-Bow Incident* (1943). And while films like *The Dark Mirror* (1946) and *Scarlet Street* are listed under the latter, so too are films like *Manpower* (1941), *Orchestra Wives* (1942) and *The Razor's Edge* (1946).[3]

Among contemporary reviews, *femmes fatales* – and their prevalence – were recognized and labelled in various ways. In its review of *The Locket* (1946), *Time* magazine noted that 'one of Hollywood's hardest worn current themes' was 'vicious womanhood' (3 March 1947), and *Variety* described *Ivy* (1947) as 'another entry in the murderous ladies cycle' (11 June 1947: 8). However, while *The Locket* and *Ivy* figure in most lists of *noirs*, *Ivy*'s position, as part of a cycle of gothic thrillers and woman's films, has, like other films in this cycle, always been ambiguous or marginal as far as proponents of *noir* have been concerned. By contrast, the cycle as a whole has been seen by Doane (1987), Waldman (1983), Walsh (1984), and others as absolutely central to the way Hollywood addressed and represented women in the 1940s. For these commentators, films like *Rebecca* (1940), *Gaslight* (1944), *Jane Eyre* (1944), *Experiment Perilous* (1944), *Undercurrent* (1946), *Dragonwyck* (1946) and *Sleep, My Love* (1948) are characterized by the paranoia, fear and suspicion inherent in scenarios in which, typically, 'the heroine experiences a series of bizarre and uncanny incidents, open to ambiguous interpretation, revolving around the question of whether or not the Gothic male really loves her' (Waldman 1983: 30) – and often, in addition, whether or not he really intends to kill her.

These commentators all ascribe these characteristics to what Walsh calls the 'culture of distrust' generated by events and conditions during the war and post-war period – precisely the same events and conditions used to account for *film noir*. In fact, both Walsh and Doane see these films as combinations of *noir* and the gothic woman's film, while some like Smith have argued that the two trends are parallel, that the investigation and fear of the *femme fatale* in *film noir* is mirrored in the investigation and fear of the fatal male in the gothic woman's film (1988: 64). However, as Cowie has pointed out, things are not quite so simple (1993: 129–30). Many of the gothic films are excluded from the *noir* canon on account of their period settings, and one or two of these films, notably *Undercurrent* and *Sleep, My Love* have been seen by some as unequivocal *noirs*. Both of these films centre on female protagonists, and both of them feature fatal men. On the other hand, there exist period gothic films with *femmes fatales* – like *Ivy* – and period gothics like *My Cousin Rachel* (1952), which centre on the investigation of an equivocal woman by a man.

It would therefore seem as though any absolute division between *noir* and the gothic woman's film is unsustainable, as though they have, in fact, a great deal in common: they frequently centre on an element of potentially fatal sexual attraction; they stress the risks, emotional and physical, this may entail for the central protagonist; they lay a great deal of emphasis on the protagonist's perceptions, feelings, thoughts and subjective experiences; and they share the context of a culture of distrust. One of the reasons these similarities have been obscured – and why the gothic film in particular has been relegated to the margins of the *noir* canon – is that a great deal of writing on *film noir* has stressed its affiliation with the hardboiled novel rather than with the stage thriller or the gothic romance. This affiliation has been stressed by those concerned with its treatment of sexual themes, by those concerned with its mood, its milieu, its language and its character-types, and by those concerned with its structural features and modes of narration.

HARDBOILED FICTION

As indicated earlier, references to hardboiled fiction have been a feature of writing on *film noir* since Nino Frank's article on *Laura, Double Indemnity, The Maltese Falcon* and *Murder, My Sweet*. Some, like Krutnik, have sought not only to explore the hardboiled connection with *noir* in some detail but also to use it as the basis for establishing a canon of films. Tracing its roots in the pulp fiction magazines of the 1910s, and in particular in *Black Mask* in the 1920s, most of those who stress the hardboiled connection tend to characterize the hardboiled style by contrasting it with the style of 'classical' or 'Golden Age' detective fiction. Krutnik sums the contrast up as follows:

> In the 'hard-boiled' mode, ratiocination – the power of deductive reasoning – is replaced by action, and the mystery element is displaced in favour of suspense. Gunplay, illicit or exotic sexuality, the corruption of the social forces of law, and personal danger to the hero are placed to the fore . . . [In addition] . . . Whereas the classical detective is often at one remove from the milieu which gives rise to the socially disruptive act of murder, the 'hard-boiled' investigator immerses himself in this milieu, and is tested by it in a more physical and life-threatening manner. Crucially, the private eye – the most archetypal 'hard-boiled' hero – operates as a mediator between the criminal

underworld and respectable society. He can move freely between these
two worlds, without really being a part of either.

(Krutnik 1991: 39)

Krutnik goes on to note the extent to which the hardboiled idiom 'is "tough",
cynical, epigrammatic, controlled' (ibid.: 43) and the extent to which the
hardboiled style 'involved not merely an Americanisation of the classical crime
or detective story, but also an emphatic process of masculinisation' (ibid.: 42).

A central thesis of most of those who have written on the hardboiled
connection with *noir* is that these elements and aspects of the hardboiled style
all found their way into Hollywood during the course of the 1940s. Through
the increasing adaptation of hardboiled novels and stories, through the
increasing employments of hardboiled authors as script and scenario writers,
and because of the contemporary resonance of – and vogue for – the hardboiled style not just in commercial publishing but also in radio, the *noir*
thriller came into being, transforming and eventually dominating the
Hollywood crime film for over a decade. The key film here is *The Maltese
Falcon*, an adaptation of a novel by Dashiell Hammett. Later instances include
The Big Sleep, Murder, My Sweet, The Lady in the Lake (1946), and other
adaptations of novels and stories by Raymond Chandler, *Double Indemnity*
and *The Postman Always Rings Twice* (1946), adaptations of novels by James M.
Cain, and *Phantom Lady* (1944), *Deadline at Dawn, Fear in the Night* (1947) and
other adaptations of novels and stories by Cornell Woolrich. The work and
the adaptations of Cain and of Woolrich exemplify a strand of hardboiled
fiction and of Hollywood thrillers that centre not on detectives and private-
eyes, but on criminals or victims, or those whose everyday lives are suddenly
put at risk. Hence Crowther's distinction between 'tough-guy heroes', 'men
forced by circumstances to try and survive difficult situations', and 'hardboiled heroes', who 'are usually involved in difficult situations because it is
their work, perhaps as private detectives' (1988: 14). And hence Walker's
distinction between 'seeker heroes' and 'victim heroes' (1992: 10–13). These,
though, are usually seen as variants within the same basic trend or tradition.

Marc Vernet has questioned this thesis on historical grounds. He points in
particular to the existence of a chronological gap between the emergence of
hardboiled fiction in the 1920s and the putative emergence of *noir* itself in the
1940s (1993: 14). This gap, he argues, marks the suppression of such 1930s
films as the 1931 version of *Maltese Falcon*, the 1936 version (*Satan Met a
Lady*), the 1935 version of *The Glass Key*, and *Private Detective 62* (a.k.a. *Man
Killer*) (1933). It might be added that it also suppresses a number of 1930s
films scripted by hardboiled writers like William Burnett, whom Vernet
mentions in passing, and Horace McCoy, Peter Ruric (George Sims) and
Eric Taylor, whose work is discussed by Wilt (1991). It might also be added
that commentators like Bradbury (1988: 88–9) and Porter (1981: 197) cite
the Depression in the 1930s as a key influence on hardboiled writers and

writing, while others like Brown (1991: 372), Hamilton (1993: 325) and Sampson (1987: 183) stress the importance of the 1920s. Either way, it is clear that the fundamental features of hardboiled fiction preceded the 1940s. In so far as these features include *femmes fatales*, fatal passion, social alienation, and a preoccupation with the masculine, attempts to account for their appearance in 1940s films in terms of 1940s socio-cultural conditions are thus rendered even more problematic than they are already.

It is worth pointing out that some have questioned the exclusivity of *noir*'s connections with hardboiled writing. Arthur, for instance, argues that 'it is not the detective or "hard-boiled" novels and stories that bear closest relation to *noir* narrativity; rather, it is precisely those works that elude simple genre classification, combining facets of the traditional psychological novel with the hermeneutics of detection and/or criminal activity' (1990: 90–1). He goes on to cite such novels as Kenneth Fearing's *The Big Clock*, J. H. Wallis's *Once Off Guard* (the source for *The Woman in the Window*), and Jay Dratler's *Pitfall*. This is partly a matter of definition, both of *noir* and of hardboiled writing. The point is worth making though, particularly if novels like Graham Greene's *This Gun for Hire* and plays like Somerset Maugham's *Christmas Holiday* are added to the list, and particularly if such sources of the 1940s gothic thriller as the novels of Daphne Du Maurier and the plays of Patrick Hamilton – each equally 'psychological,' and each equally preoccupied with the hermeneutics of detection and criminal activity – are borne in mind as well. The issue of the relationship between the gothic thriller and *film noir* has been raised already. It arises again when considering aspects of the putative style of *film noir*, notably its modes and forms of narration and narrative, its aural and visual rhetoric, and its use in general of 'expressionist' devices.

NARRATION AND NARRATIVE

The narratives of *films noirs* are usually characterized as complex – often confusing – and as frequently entailing the use of flashback, and first-person voice-over narration. In these respects films like *Double Indemnity, Laura, The Killers* (1946), *The Locket* and *Out of the Past* (1947) are often considered exemplary. However, questions are often begged here as to precisely what constitutes narrative complexity, as to the frequency of flashback and voice-over within the *noir* canon as a whole, and as to the function or functions these devices character- istically perform.

A particular type of complexity is built into most stories of detection. As Ponder – following Todorov (1977) – explains:

> The detective formula requires a particular kind of plot structure. The forward moving plot is separate from the underlying crime. Works which conform to the detective formula have, as a formal character- istic, a double plot structure. The activity of detection is the action of

the forward moving plot. The detective is engaged in finding out the
identity of the perpetrator and the scope of his crime. The perpetrator
and his criminal activities establish the second, previous plot. The previous, past plot is complete, or nearly so, when the present, forward
moving plot begins. The climax of the past plot is the commission of an
irrevocable crime, which provokes the motivating force of the present
plot, which is the uncovering and exposing of the completed, past plot.

(Ponder 1988: 51)

Many *films noirs* are marked by this kind of structure. But then so are many
gothic thrillers and most other kinds of mystery and detective film – any film,
in fact, with a crime and an investigating agent. Picking up Borde and
Chaumeton's comments on the disorienting nature of *noir*'s narratives,
Porfirio argues that the confusing complexity of films like *The Big Sleep*,
The Blue Dahlia (1946), *The Lady from Shanghai* (1948) and *Kiss Me Deadly*
(1955) derives from the 'causal disorders' in the plot, 'from a breakdown in
the logic of its successive action' (1985: 144). He continues:

> When the discourse of either the character or the text is unreliable . . .
> this problem is further compounded. As the discourse opens holes in
> the narrative . . ., the typical *noir* plot leaves many of these gaps
> unchecked by refusing to bring the action to completion. This in
> turn results in numerous false closures or in the sort of unsuccessful,
> last minute summation engaged in by Marlowe (Humphrey Bogart) at
> the end of *The Big Sleep* . . .

(Porfirio 1985: 144–5)

I am not sure myself that the causal disorders to which Porfirio refers are all
that widespread. *The Big Sleep* is a particular case. Raymond Chandler always
had problems plotting his novels, and in attempting a combination of two
different short stories the novel upon which the film was based is especially
marked by these problems. These were merely compounded by the censorable nature of much of the novel's content. Certainly there are few causal
disorders in films like *The Killers* – or even in other Chandler adaptations like
Murder, My Sweet, or in adaptations of equally censorable novels like *Double
Indemnity*. It is true that some *noirs* give the impression of causal disorder.
Although in most cases this is due to the informational overload that often
accompanies detective plots and mysteries, it can also be due to the 'chronological disorders' (Porfirio 1985: 39) and the – actual or potential – discursive
unreliability to which Porfirio also refers. It is here that flashback and voice-
over often play a crucial part.

Both flashback and voice-over were used in Hollywood prior to the 1940s
(Kozloff 1988: 23–40; Turim 1989: 21–59). However, their use became more
frequent at this time, and *film noir* is often seen as a privileged site of this use.

It is important, first of all, to reiterate the extent to which 1940s films other than *noirs* used these particular devices. Biopics like *Yankee Doodle Dandy* (1942) and *The Adventures of Mark Twain* (1944), for example, used voice-over and flashback extensively, as did films like *Citizen Kane* (1941),[4] *How Green Was My Valley* (1941), *Random Harvest* (1942), *The Uninvited* (1943), and *All About Eve* (1950). On the other hand, while flashback and voice-over are certainly common in *films noirs*, the number of films that deploy them is in any list or version of the canon always outweighed by those that do not. It is simply inaccurate to claim that the narratives in *noirs* are 'typically' presented 'in a non-chronological order' (Hirsch 1981: 72). What matters, however, is not the extent to which these particular devices are employed but the uses to which they are typically put, the effects they typically produce, and the extent to which other devices are put to these uses as well.

For Porfirio, flashback and voice-over in *noir* disturb the 'objectivity' and the 'smooth discursive flow' of the average Hollywood film (1985: 153). In addition, they foreground the subjectivity and 'interiority' of *noir*'s principal characters (ibid.: 154). And because they are often deployed in enigmatic narrative contexts, in narratives of actual or potential criminal conspiracy, they highlight the issues of reliability, duplicity and deception. This particular characterization of *noir* seems to me to have considerable merit. Flashback and voice-over, when they are used in *noirs*, are normally used both to focus attention on one or more of the characters, and to produce an intense awareness of – and an intense curiosity about – their mental and emotional states. Sometimes, as in *Detour* (1945), the focus is on the narrator, sometimes, as in *The Killers*, on the characters various narrators describe, and sometimes, as in *Double Indemnity*, on the narrator's transparent thoughts and feelings, stated in retrospect, on the one hand, and the opaque thoughts, feelings and motives of the character with whom he or she is emotionally involved on the other. At times, as in *Laura*, we may come to realize that an internal narrator has been lying – or has at least been economical with the truth – and on occasion, as in *Possessed* (1947), we may be invited to speculate on an internal narrator's mental sanity. What matters is that there is a sustained focus on the thoughts and feelings of at least one major character.[5]

What matters, too, is that the characters focused on are mentally and emotionally vulnerable. More often than not, they are – or they imagine themselves to be – physically vulnerable as well. Their existence, their very being is at stake. Detectives risk danger and death. Amnesiacs risk losing their identity. Ordinary people find themselves stalked by gangsters or unknown assailants, or lured or tricked into a world of crime. They may risk losing their sanity. They may become hooked or addicted. They may imagine or find themselves endangered by those they most love, those they most desire, those with whom they are emotionally obsessed. These, I would argue, are elements characteristic of most *films noirs*. However, they are not confined to *noirs*. They can also be found in the gothic woman's film, the period thriller, and in what Maureen Turim calls 'psychological melodrama' (1989: 143). 'Interiority' – or 'vulnerable interiority' – is, in other words, a 1940s trend, a trend by no means restricted to films within the category or canon of *film noir*.

This trend was marked in contemporary reviews of all these kinds of film. The terms used most regularly to mark it were terms like 'psychological drama', 'psychological melodrama' and 'psychological thriller'. Attention was drawn both to the extent to which 'psychology' had become a feature of genres traditionally geared to action and suspense, and to the increasing popularity of psychiatry and psychoanalysis as frameworks within which to explore, describe and motivate extreme psychological states. Thus on the one hand the *Spectator* notes in its preview of *I Walk Alone* (1948) that 'we have now got so used to the psychological thriller that a plain common or garden gangster film with people shooting each other without first laying bare their souls seems extraordinarily old-fashioned' (2 December 1947), the press book for *Ministry of Fear* (1945) highlights the extent to which 'Director Fritz Lang puts the emphasis on the psychological drama contained in the story of a man whose life is continually on the threshold of fear, dread and death', and *Variety* observes that in *Cat People* (1942), suspense is 'confined to psychology and mental reactions, rather than to transformations to grotesque and marauding characters for visual impact' (18 November 1942: 8). On the other hand, the *New York Times* refers in its review of *The Locket* to 'the fad for so-called psychological drama' (20 March 1947) and in its review of *The Dark Past* (1948) to 'the mating of Freud and films' (25 December 1948), while the *Motion Picture Herald* describes *The Dark Mirror* as 'another in the cycle of psychiatric pictures' (5 October 1946: 3257) and *Variety* reports complaints from regional exhibitors and a professional psychiatrist about the plethora of 'psychiatric pictures' ('Theatre Owners List 3 B. O. "Poisons"', 29 December 1948: 3, 55; 'Allied Raps "Sophisticated" Pix', 16 February 1949: 8; and 'Medico Slams Show Biz For Psychiatry Mania', 4 May 1949: 2).

The emphasis in 1940s films on psychology, psychiatry and psychoanalysis – and the ideological uses to which they were put – has been discussed at length by Doane (1987: 38–69), Krutnik (1991: 45–55) and Walker (1992). What I want to stress here is the extent to which it transcended the generic and canonic boundaries drawn up by proponents of *noir*. Doane refers to *Johnny Belinda* (1948) and *Guest in the House* (1944) in addition to *Possessed*, *The Dark Mirror* and *Shock* (1946). Walker refers to *The Snake Pit* (1948) and *Spellbound* in addition to *Whirlpool* (1949) and *The Locket*. And the review press refers to *Cat People* as well as to *Ministry of Fear* and *I Walk Alone*. The same might be said both of the elements of vulnerability, danger and risk discussed above, which can be found in *Dragonwyck* as well as in *Double Indemnity*, in *Suspicion* as well as in *Out of the Past*, in *Jane Eyre* as well as in *The Woman in the Window*, and of the visual and aural rhetoric – the use of extreme chiaroscuro, discordant sounds and music, and other expressive and 'expressionist' devices – often used to mark all these elements in all these films, and often hailed, like them, not only as exclusive to *noir*, but as one of its principal hallmarks.

VISUAL AND AURAL EXPRESSIONISM

In their highly influential article, 'Some Visual Motifs of Film Noir', Janey Place and Lowell Peterson argue that 'Nearly every attempt to define *film noir* has agreed that visual style is the consistent thread that united the very diverse films that together comprise this phenomenon' ([1974] 1996: 65). As we have seen already, this is not strictly true. Other features and other factors have been cited as definitive of *noir*. Moreover, among the original proponents of *noir*, neither Frank nor Rey nor Chartier even mention visual style. Nevertheless, Place and Peterson go on to discuss such visual motifs as portraits and mirror reflection, choker close-ups, the use of wide-angle lenses and visual distortion, cutting from extreme close-up to high-angle long shot, and what they call the 'archetypal' *noir* composition: 'the extreme high-angle long shot, an oppressive and fatalistic angle that looks down on its helpless victim to make it look like a rat in a maze' (ibid.: 68). Most of their attention, though, is devoted to lighting:

> Noir lighting is 'low-key.' The ratio of key to fill light is great, creating rich, black shadows. Unlike the even illumination of high-key lighting which seeks to display attractively all areas of the frame, the low-key *noir* style opposes light and dark, hiding faces, rooms, urban landscapes – and, by extension, motivations and true character – in shadow and darkness which carry connotations of the mysterious and the unknown.
>
> (Place and Peterson [1974] 1996: 66)

Noting that the 'harsh lighting of the low-key *noir* style was even employed on the photography of leading actresses' (ibid.), they go on to argue that

> it is the constant opposition of areas of light and dark that characterizes *film noir* photography. Small areas of light seem on the verge of being completely overwhelmed by the darkness that threatens them from all sides. Thus faces are shot low-key, interior sets are always dark, with foreboding shadow patterns lacing the walls, and exteriors are shot 'night-for-night.'
>
> (Place and Peterson [1974] 1996: 67)

This is probably the dominant conception of *noir*'s visual style. Nevertheless, a number of subsequent commentators have qualified or questioned Place and Peterson's descriptions. Hirsch, for instance, sees these and other elements of *noir*'s style as restricted to 'splashy set pieces' and 'italicised moments', moments which stand out from an otherwise 'flattened . . . almost zombie-like verbal and visual mode' (1981: 86). And Krutnik maintains that

> It is doubtful that one could convincingly show that *film noir* is actually characterised by a unified body of stylistics – rather, it seems to be the case that what is referred to as the *'noir* style' tends to be a more disparate series of stylistic markings which can be seen as *noir* when they occur in conjunction with sets of narrative and thematic conventions and narratological processes. In isolation or even when combined together, the elements identified by such critics as Paul Schrader and Place and Peterson . . . are not specific to the *film noir*, nor to the crime film, nor even to 1940s cinema.
>
> (Krutnik 1991: 19)

There are clearly a number of discrepancies among and between these different positions, and at least two different issues at stake. The first concerns the extent to which the visual elements discussed by Place and Peterson – or the set-pieces discussed by Hirsch – are present or prevalent in *noir*. The second concerns the extent to which they are exclusive to it. In dealing with either issue, the imprecise nature of the *noir* canon is, once again, a major factor. Nevertheless, it can be pointed out that such 'quintessential' *noirs* as *The Big Sleep*, *The Maltese Falcon*, *Laura* and *The Woman in the Window* all lack cuts from extreme close-up to high-angle long shot, the 'archetypal' high-angle composition, and, for that matter, the *noir* set-piece. *Laura*, *The Maltese Falcon* and *The Woman in the Window* contain very little low-key lighting, and lack choker close-ups. And with the possible exception of the scene in which Debby (Gloria Graeme) is shot, and of the scene in which Cody Jarrett (James Cagney) is blown to bits, *The Big Heat* (1953) and *White Heat* respectively lack chiaroscuro effects of any kind – and the same is true of more marginal *noirs* like *They Won't Believe Me* (1947), *Boomerang!* (1947) and *Whirlpool* (1949).

In considering the second issue, it should be pointed out first of all that in his autobiography, Edward Dmytryk – director of such *'noir* classics' as *Crossfire*, *Cornered* and *Murder, My Sweet* – notes that the term '"low-key lighting" is a misnomer; what it really means is high contrast' (1978: 90). He goes on to add that this is 'the generally accepted style of lighting mystery, suspense and heavy mood films' (ibid.: 90),[6] and in this he is supported by cinematographer John Alton. Alton, often hailed as 'The Master of the Film Noir Mood' (Gach 1996), refers in his book, *Painting with Light* ([1949] 1995), both to 'mystery lighting' and to 'criminal lighting'. In neither case is there any indication that the techniques and effects he describes are anything other than traditional. Moreover, in his discussion of criminal lighting, he explicitly refers to earlier films:

Years ago, when in pictures we showed Jimmy Valentine cracking a
safe, he usually carried a typical flashlight in one hand . . . In some
scenes the flashlight was placed on the floor. In either case the light
source was established as a low one. To create an authentic effect, the
cameraman lit the character from a low light which illuminated the
face from an unusual angle. It distorted the countenance, threw
shadows seldom seen in everyday life across the face. This light, which
exaggerates features, became so popular that even in our films today,
when we want to call the attention of the audience to a criminal
character, we use this type of illumination.

(Alton [1949] 1995: 54–5)[7]

The implication here, that low-key or high contrast lighting was standard
in 'mystery, suspense and heavy mood films' in the 1940s, is amply borne out
by sequences, scenes and sometimes lengthy passages not only in marginal
noirs like *Sleep, My Love, Hangover Square* (1945) and *Rebecca* (which are all
gothic thrillers), or like *Cat People, I Walked with a Zombie* (1943) and *The
Ghost Ship* (1943) (which are all horror films), but also in 'heavy mood'
westerns like *Blood on the Moon* (1948), Shakespearean adaptations like
Macbeth (1948), wartime espionage dramas like *Joan of Paris* (1942), 'standard'
crime thrillers and detective films like *Quiet Please, Murder* (1942) and *One
Dangerous Night* (1943), and even in musicals like *Blues in the Night* (1941).[8] It
might be noted in addition that versions of the achetypal *noir* composition
occur in *Rebecca* and *Jane Eyre*, and that, to quote Barry Salt, 'one finds that by
the end of the 'forties even in romantic melodramas like *Letter from an
Unknown Woman* (Max Ophuls, 1948), there is little use of lens diffusion,
even on female Close Ups, so that this phenomenon certainly cannot be
associated with the vague category of so-called *film noir*, as some have tried to
do' ([1983] 1992: 233). And it might be noted, too, that nearly all these films
have 'splashy set pieces' of one kind or another: the denouement in the fog at
the end of *Rebecca*, for instance, or the first appearance of Mr Rochester
(Orson Welles) in *Jane Eyre*.[9]

Several similar points have been made by Vernet. His own argument,
though, tends to highlight pre-1940s films, and to centre on the putative
provenance of *noir*'s visual style in the German Expressionist cinema of the
late 1910s and the 1920s. He begins by noting the presence of heavy
chiaroscuro effects in the gothic horror films of the 1930s, in the Tod
Browning–Lon Chaney thrillers of the 1920s, and in such 1930s crime films
as *City Streets* (1931). In addition, he notes that the cinematographers
associated with *film noir*

are not callow youths seeking to impose a new style: on the contrary
they are usually veterans who got their start in the 1910s and 20s. Tony
Gaudio (*High Sierra*) began working in 1911, John F. Seitz (*The Big*

Clock, Double Indemnity, This Gun for Hire) in 1916, Sol Polito (*Sorry, Wrong Number*) in 1918, [Nicholas] Musuraca (*Stranger on the Third Floor, Out of the Past* and *Where Danger Lives*) in 1923, Joseph LaShelle (*Laura, Fallen Angel, Where the Sidewalk Ends*) in 1925, John Alton (*The Big Combo, He Walked by Night, The People Against O'Hara, The Crooked Way*), in 1928.

(Vernet 1993: 10)

His principal point, however, is that 'Expressionist' lighting preceded not only *noir* but Expressionism too. Noting the systematic use of chiaroscuro effects in the films of Alvin Wickoff and Cecil B. DeMille (films like *Kindling* and *The Cheat*, made in 1915, and *The Heart of Nora Flynn*, made in 1916), he argues that expressionist lighting is a tradition in Hollywood cinema, a tradition which has its origins in 'the experiments carried out by the team of Griffith and Bitzer' in and around 1909 (ibid.: 9).

Vernet's arguments do not constitute proof that Expressionism had no impact either on *noir* or on American cinema as a whole in the 1940s. They do, though, cast doubt on simplistic accounts of a *noir* style – of a *noir* 'look' – whose status is in any case open to question. Similar doubts arise when considering *noir*'s use of music and sound, a topic discussed in some detail by Robert Porfirio.

Porfirio argues that sound and music in *noir* are often used not just to heighten atmosphere and mood, but also to accentuate the subjective and psychological focus of *noir*'s systems and modes of narration. He refers here to the 'subjective effect' of the voices heard in the male protagonist's head in *A Double Life* (1948) and the use of a 'dead' track and silence in *The Big Combo* to mark the aural perspective of a mobster deprived of his hearing aid. He also refers to Miklos Rosza's musical scores, and the extent to which, in films like *Brute Force* (1947), *Kiss the Blood Off My Hands* (1948), *The Spiral Staircase* (1946) and *Spellbound*, music is used 'to compliment [*sic*] the psychological states of the characters rather than to reinforce the action on the screen' (1985: 229). He makes similar points about Bernard Herrmann's score for *Hangover Square* (1945). However, he himself argues that *Spellbound* is 'outside the cycle' he identifies as *noir* (ibid.: 228). The same might be said of *The Spiral Staircase* and *Hangover Square*, both of which are normally classed as gothic thrillers, and of *The Leopard Man* (1943) and *Gaslight* (1944), to which Porfirio also refers. Once again, then, the imprecise nature of the *noir* canon, and the possibility that features associated exclusively with *noir* may be part of a more general trend, arises as a problem and an issue which adherents of *noir* rarely acknowledge and rarely confront.

FILM NOIR, NEO-NOIR AND GENRE

As a single phenomenon, *noir*, in my view, never existed. That is why no one has been able to define it, and why the contours of the larger *noir* canon in particular are so imprecise. Many of the features associated with *noir* – the use of voice-over and flashback, the use of high contrast lighting and other 'expressionist' devices, the focus on mentally, emotionally and physically vulnerable characters, the interest in psychology, the culture of distrust marking relations between male and female characters, and the downbeat emphasis on violence, anxiety, death, crime and compromised morality – were certainly real ones, but they were separable features belonging to separable tendencies and trends which traversed a wide variety of genres and cycles in the 1940s and early 1950s. These tendencies and trends were distributed unevenly and are susceptible, as we have seen, to a number of different – sometimes diametrically opposed – interpretations. They were concentrated most heavily in detective films and crime thrillers. But they can be also found in the gothic woman's film, in a number of horror films, and in a number of westerns and post-war social problem films. Sometimes, as with *Double Indemnity, Murder, My Sweet* and *Out of the Past* (and, I would argue, as with *Cat People, Crossfire, Rebecca, The Lost Weekend, The Snake Pit* and *Hangover Square*), several of these tendencies and trends coincide in a single film. But almost by definition, it is impossible for any one film, or any one group of films, to encompass or embody them all, just as it is impossible to claim that any one genre – even the crime or detective film – was ever at any point totally pervaded by their presence. Any attempt to treat these tendencies and trends as a single phenomenon, to homogenize them under a single heading, *'film noir,'* is therefore bound to lead to incoherence, imprecision and inconsistency – in the provision of criteria, in the construction of a corpus, or in almost any interpretation of their contemporary socio-cultural significance. It is also bound to wrench the films themselves from their immediate cyclic and generic contexts, thus treating a hardboiled detective film like *The Maltese Falcon*, a post-war social problem film like *Crossfire*, a psychological melodrama like *Possessed* (1947) and a 1950s rogue cop film like *Touch of Evil* as part of the same general production trend, and thus rendering any historical account of that trend and the films it comprises even more difficult. However, and somewhat ironically, if in Cowie's words *noir* is a 'fantasy', or if an attachment to the term can in Naremore's words mark 'a nostalgia for something that never existed' (1995/6: 25), the phenomenon of neo-*noir* – itself vehicle for this fantasy – is much more real, not only as a phenomenon but also as a genre.

Neo-*noir* is now the most widely accepted term for those films which, from the mid-1960s on, relate to or draw upon the notion, the image and the putative conventions of *film noir*, and, directly or indirectly, on some of the films featuring centrally within most versions of the basic *noir* canon. (For general accounts and overviews, see Erickson 1996, Grist 1992 and Silver and Ward 1992: 398–443. 'Neo-*noir*' seems to have replaced the more awkward *'film après noir'*, a term coined by Larry Gross in 1976.) Films of the 1960s like *Harper* (1966), *Point Blank* (1967) and *Marlowe* (1969), adaptations of hardboiled novels by Ross MacDonald, Donald Westlake (Richard Stark) and

Raymond Chandler respectively, are often cited as the first neo-*noirs*, to be followed in the 1970s by films like *The Long Goodbye, Chinatown, Farewell, My Lovely* (1975) and *Night Moves* (1975), and in the 1980s and 1990s by films like *Body Heat, The Postman Always Rings Twice* (1981), *Against All Odds* (1984), *House of Games* (1987), *The Grifters* (1990), *The Hot Spot* (1990) and *L.A. Confidential* (1997).

A number of differences and distinctions among and between these films should be noted. While the 1960s films draw on the hardboiled novel as source material, they are markedly different from the hardboiled films of the 1940s in their use of colour and sunlight, and in their insistent deployment of other 'signifiers of modernity' such as updated settings and greater sexual frankness (Grist 1992: 267). And as Grist in particular has argued, while most of the early 1970s films use the idea and the image of *noir* as a basis for ideological interrogation, critical parody and a markedly ironic treatment of the figure of the lone private eye, most of the 1980s and 1990s films use them as a basis for uncritical pastiche, thus enabling them to draw on the aura of stylish subversion associated with *noir*, and thus placing them within the trend towards allusion discussed by Carroll (1982) and others.

It should be noted, too, that the idea of *noir* drawn on in these films tends to exclude the gothic thriller – despite updated traces in films like *Jagged Edge* (1985) – as well as the psychologically oriented social problem film. The main point to make here, though, is that what was once an esoteric critical term has now, as Naremore points out, become 'ubiquitous', 'a major signifier of sleekly commodified ambition' (1995/6: 14), and that as a consequence the generic status of *noir* itself has shifted and changed. Aided by the phenomenon of neo-*noir*, promulgated both by film-makers like Walter Hill, David Mamet, Paul Schrader and Martin Scorsese and by reviewers and critics who have either received a formal education in film or who have read the canonic books and articles, '*film noir*' as a term is now freely used in reviews and in listings magazines to describe more or less any new crime film on the one hand,[10] and more or less any crime film made in the 1940s and 1950s on the other. As a result, '*noir*' is now an established generic term; thus, films like *Double Indemnity, Detour* (1945) and *Out of the Past* are now viewed generically as *noirs* in a way they never were when initially released.

For all these reasons, *noir* remains an important focus for genre theory, an important topic for research and debate. For the self-same reasons, though, it is all too easy to forget that the contemporary term used to describe nearly all the films subsequently labelled as *noirs*, whether they were detective films, gangster films, gothic thrillers or psychological horror films, has also figured prominently in accounts of genre in the cinema. That term was melodrama.

NOTES

1 As evidence, consider the following passage from Spencer Selby's book, *Dark City: The Film Noir:*

> I believe that film noir must be and shall always remain something of an enigma. The classification of films has always been a tenuous business and with film noir, which is perhaps the most slippery of all categories, complications of this type reach a level of almost baffling complexity. Still there is something very important about the idea of film noir, whether or not we are able to pin it down.
>
> (1984: 3)

2 Chartier also refers in passing to what he calls 'the French school of films noirs' (1946: 70), by which he means films like *Le Quai des Brumes* (1938) and *L'Hotel du Nord* (1938), and which suggests that the term was in use in France prior to 1946. For discussion of the French school of *films noirs* and their influence on Hollywood, see Vincendeau (1992).

3 Writing in 1953, Sylvia Jarrico also uses the term 'evil' to label what she identifies as a post-war trend in the depiction of women. Linking the trend to 'the Tough Cycle' and to 'the Psychological Cycle', she mentions *Dark Mirror, Leave Her to Heaven* (1945) and *Angel Face* (1953). However, she also mentions *Ruby Gentry* (1952), *Remains to be Seen* (1953) and *The Girl Who Had Everything* (1953).

4 John Belton, among others, argues that *Kane* was an important influence on *film noir* (1994: 190). However, since *Kane* itself is not usually considered to be an example of *noir*, as Belton himself points out, this particular argument seems to me to pose more problems than it solves.

5 The instances of flashback and voice-over I am referring to here are linked to internal narrators or to characters who at some point appear on screen. They are therefore 'homodiegetic', and as such should be distinguished from instances of flashback unrelated to character narration or recollection, and from 'third person' – or 'heterodiegetic' – voice-over narration. Heterodiegetic voice-over narration is common in 'semi-documentary' *films noirs*, in films like *The Naked City* (1948) and *Call Northside 777* (1948). Here its purposes can be quite distinct, and any focus there may be on the interior lives of the principal characters is often achieved by other means. For discussion of these categories, and of heterodiegetic voice-over and the semi-documentary, see Kozloff (1988: 42–101).

6 Certainly this is true of a number of Dmytryk's own earlier films. *The Devil Commands* (1941) for example, a Boris Karloff horror film, contains a dark, rain-washed street scene, interior sequences with patterns of shadow cast by slatted blinds, and a 'splashy set-piece' involving a laboratory experiment and a candlelit conversation in Karloff's house. The extent to which such lighting was standard in the 1940s may explain why, as Walker points out (1992: 27), it received very little comment in the *American Cinematographer* until 1948, and why when it did, the films discussed were by no means always central or canonic *films noirs*. See for instance 'Low Key and Lively Action' (December 1948: 411, 424–6), on *Blood on the Moon*, and 'The Story of Filming *Berlin Express*' (July 1948: 232–3, 250).

7 Jimmy Valentine was a fictional safecracker who initially appeared on film in *Alias Jimmy Valentine* in 1915. This film was remade in 1920 and 1928, and followed by several sequels in the 1930s and early 1940s. It is unclear as to whether Alton here has any particular version in mind.

8 *Blues in the Night* contains both a lengthy subjective montage sequence marking

the central male character's nervous breakdown and a lengthy sequence in the rain which culminates in the shooting of a secondary male character by a trenchcoated *femme fatale.*

9 It is worth noting here that *Variety*'s review of *Jane Eyre* drew attention to 'some excellent photography by George Barnes, practically all in light and shade to emphasize the eeriness of the story' (2 February 1944: 18).

10 This is true of the trade press as well. By 1980, *Variety* was using the term to describe such films as *Union City* (1980) (10 September 1980: 34).

5

MELODRAMA AND THE
WOMAN'S FILM

At one point in *The Locket*, Nancy Blair (Laraine Day) tells her husband Harry (Brian Aherne) that she has been to the movies to see a melodrama. 'A melodrama?' he says. 'Yes', she replies. 'It was ghastly. You ought to see it, Harry. It was about a schizophrenic who kills his wife and doesn't know it.' About half-way through *Shockproof* (1949), Harry Wesson (John Baragrey) picks up the telephone in front of parolee and ex-girlfriend Jenny Marsh (Patricia Knight), threatening that unless she returns to him and to her former life of crime he will inform the authorities that she has secretly married her parole officer, Griff Morant (Cornell Wilde), thus breaking the terms of Morant's employment. Jenny pulls out a gun. 'Stop that!', she exclaims. 'Put down that phone!' 'You're being melodramatic', he retorts. He continues with his call, and she shoots him. Towards the end of *Cornered*, Laurence Gerard (Dick Powell) attempts to kill a man he thinks is Jarnac, an ex-Vichy official reponsible for the death of Gerard's fiancée. It turns out that the man is in fact a member of a secret organization dedicated to tracking down former Nazis, and that the members of this organization are looking for Jarnac themselves. 'Mr. Gerard,' they tell him, 'it would be interesting and daring if Jarnac were some jolly, apparently harmless fellow under our very nose. But we don't think so. Our opponents are not writing cheap melodrama.'

These lines clearly function as self-aware, self-referential comments on the generic status and provenance of the events, scenes and films in whose context they appear. That is, they both avow and disavow their status as melodrama. They thus also give a clear indication as to what the terms 'melodrama' and 'melodramatic' meant at the time the films were made: they meant crime, guns and violence; they meant heroines in peril; they meant action, tension and suspense; and they meant villains, villains who in 'cheap melodrama,' at any rate, could masquerade as 'apparently harmless' fellows, thus thwarting the hero, evading justice, and sustaining suspense until the last minute.

These meanings are supported, sometimes implicitly, sometimes explicitly, by the use of the term 'melodrama' in the reviews and publicity surrounding the films themselves. The *New York Times* (26 December 1945) called

Cornered 'a tough-fibred melodrama': 'Edward Dmytryk, the director, has squeezed every ounce of suspense and excitement out of the material at hand.' And *Variety* described *The Locket* as 'well-made psycho melodrama' (18 December 1946: 14), and *Shockproof* as a 'melodrama of parolees and officers who work with them' (26 January 1949: 11). Meanwhile producer Adrian Scott, writing in *New Theatre* in 1948, referred not only to *Cornered*, but also to *Farewell, My Lovely* and his new film, *Crossfire*, as melodrama. By substituting 'a search for an anti-Semite, instead of a jade necklace', he wrote, he hoped 'to add dimension and meaning to melodrama' (February 1948: 17). Writing in the *New York Times*, Bosley Crowther, at least thought he had succeeded: 'An unqualified "A" for effort', he wrote, 'bringing to the screen a frank and immediate demonstration of the brutality of religious bigotry . . . And an equally high mark for lacing this exceedingly thoughtful theme through a grimly absorbing melodrama' (23 July 1947).

The Locket, Cornered and *Shockproof* – and, for that matter, *Farewell, My Lovely* and *Crossfire* – have, as we have seen, all been categorized or labelled as *films noirs*. As such, their description as melodrama by contemporary publicists, reviewers and production personnel is typical: 'melodrama' – and the shortened and slangier 'meller' – were by far the commonest terms used to describe what are often now called *noirs*, whether they were hard-boiled detective films, gangster films, gothic thrillers and woman's films, paranoid thrillers, psychological thrillers, police films or semi-documentaries.[1] However, if these terms were co-extensive with *noir*, they were by no means bound by its contours (however defined). For as Singer (1990) has pointed out, the term 'melodrama' was used and defined in ways parallel with those already mentioned – parallel, in other words, with terms like 'thriller', 'chiller' and even 'action-adventure' – in the 1900s, the 1910s and the 1920s. Singer cites 'The Taint of Melodrama', an essay written in 1906, as follows: 'Ask the next person you meet casually how he defines a melodramatic story, and he will probably tell you that it is a hodge-podge of extravagant adventures, full of blood and thunder, clashing swords and hair's breadth escapes' (ibid.: 95). This is echoed almost word-for-word in a review of *The Unholy Three* (1925) in *Life* nearly twenty years later: 'melodrama, on the screen,' writes the film's reviewer, 'is identified almost entirely with fast physical action: cowboys or sheiks or cavalrymen riding madly across the country, men hanging by their teeth from the ledges of skyscrapers, railroad wrecks, duels, heroines floating on cakes of ice toward waterfalls, and every known form of autmobile chase' (27 August 1925: 26). (For other examples from this period, see Singer 1990: 94–8 and Neale 1993a: 69–70.)

These definitions and meanings did not change, as Singer himself assumes. Instead they remained remarkably consistent through the 1930s, the 1940s, the 1950s and the 1960s. Hence 'melodrama of international intrigue . . . Naturally the story promises to be thrilling and suspenseful' (*Motion Picture Herald* on *Jesse James*, 14 January 1939: 43); 'well-made thriller, packed with suspense, for the deep-dyed meller fans' (*Film Daily* on *The Threat* (1949), 26 August 1949: 12); 'Alfred Hitchcock formula: shock meller with a couple of particularly lurid scenes' (*Variety* on *Psycho* (1960), 22 June 1960: 6); and 'an old-fashioned gangster melodrama, super-saturated with gunfire and fear' (*Variety* on *The Rise and Fall of Legs Diamond* (1960), 27 August 1960: 6). (For other examples, see Neale 1993a: 70–2.) The term was still used, less frequently, but with precisely the same connotations, in journals like *Variety* in the 1970s and 1980s. *Chato's Land* (1972) was described as 'a violence-drenched meller' (17 May 1972: 28), *They're Playing with Fire* (1984) as a 'horror-suspense meller' (2 May 1984: 18) and *Missing in Action* (1984) as 'a Vietnam action meller' (18 November 1984: 19). Meanwhile, in his book *The Elements of Screenwriting*, Irwin Blacker writes that 'If the plot is all action and little emotion, it is melodrama' (1986: 20).

One of the striking things about all these definitions, uses and meanings is the extent to which they differ from those on offer in Film Studies, where, as Singer points out, '"Melodrama" . . . is all but synonymous with a set of sub-genres that remain close to the hearth and emphasize a register of heightened emotionalism and sentimentality: the family melodrama, the woman's film, the weepie, the soap opera, etc.' (1990: 94). A lineage, a provenance, an aesthetic, an institutional and critical status, a generic – or sub-generic – field of application, and a putatively gender-specific appeal or address to woman have all, since the mid-1970s, been attributed to melodrama in the cinema on this basis, thus helping to comprise both the framework and the substance of what might be termed the 'standard' or 'orthodox' Film Studies account. If only because there is such a discrepancy between the ways the term has been used and defined, it is clear that on the one hand the widespread use of 'melodrama' as a synonym for 'thriller' or 'action-adventure' needs to be explained, and on the other that the tenets of the standard account need to be scrutinized much more closely. In both cases, the history of melodrama in the theatre needs to be addressed, as does the history of 'melodrama' in Film Studies since the early 1970s.

MELODRAMA AND FILM STUDIES

A major point of reference for nearly all academic writing on melodrama and the cinema to have appeared since the mid-1970s has been Thomas Elsaesser's article, 'Tales of Sound and Fury, Observations on the Family Melodrama,' which was first published in *Monogram* in 1972 and which has been anthologized on a number of occasions since then (1987). Elsaesser's article touches upon an array of topics and themes: German ballads, French Romantic drama, the novels of Dostoevsky and Dickens, the Gothic thriller, *film noir*, the role of the voice in American films, the influence of Freud in Hollywood in the late 1940s and 1950s, and the extent to which Freudian theory can provide a vocabulary for describing the dynamics of Hollywood's films. Its principal focus, though, is on films like *Written on the Wind* (1956), *Imitation of Life* (1959), *Rebel Without a Cause, Bigger than Life* (1956), *Some Came Running* (1958) and *Home from the Hill* (1960), and on directors like Nicholas Ray, Douglas Sirk and Vincente Minnelli. Its principal argument is twofold. It is on the one hand that certain tendencies, genres and directors in Hollywood – in particular the Hollywood of the late studio era, and in particular the directors and films mentioned above – deployed form, style and rhythm, camera movement, colour and *mise-en-scène* not only to elaborate themes and issues specific to the films themselves but also to address contemporary social and ideological issues, and in doing so to expose the inadequacies of the affirmative liberal culture, of the corporate, consumerist and domestically oriented cultural ethos, prevalent at the time the films were made ([1972] 1987: 53, 61–2). It is on the other that in doing so, they draw on and parallel a number of the tendencies, genres and authors at work in the novel and on stage in the late eighteenth and nineteenth centuries in Europe. Then, in an era of massive social change, social conflict and social injustice, forms and structures marked above all by arbitrariness and improbability served 'as the literary equivalent of a particular, historically and socially conditioned, *mode of experience*' (ibid.: 49; emphasis in original). 'Melodrama' is the term Elsaesser uses to describe both the plays, novels and films to which he refers, and the forms and structures with which they are marked.

It should be said, first of all, that there is both a context and a subtext to Elsaesser's article. Written in the early 1970s, it was conditioned in part by a renewed interest in Sirk and his films, evident in the seasons held at the Edinburgh Film Festival and at the National Film Theatre in London, in the collection of essays that accompanied these seasons (Halliday and Mulvey 1972), in a special issue of *Screen* (1971, vol. 12, no. 2), in Halliday's interview book, *Sirk on Sirk* (1971), and in subsequent essays in *Screen*, notably Willemen's 'Towards an Analysis of the Sirkian System' (1972–3). It was also conditioned by the nature of that interest, and by the developments within film criticism and film theory of which it was symptomatic. These developments included an attention to ideology and politics, an attention to modernist aesthetics, and an interest in particular in the ideas and the practices of Bertolt Brecht. All of these are discernible in Elsaesser's article. However, Elsaesser's article is also quite specific in its views and positions. As Barbara Klinger has pointed out, film criticism and film theory had not as yet settled into what she calls 'a single dominant paradigm' (1994a: 10). Sirk's work was at this time the focus of an array of methods and concerns – she herself notes the extent to which 'traditional auteurism' played an important role in these discussions (ibid.: 10–18). However, Elsaesser – and *Monogram* – offered a view of Sirk, of Hollywood aesthetics, of ideology and of modernist concerns that was in many ways unique, and in many ways distinct from – and opposed to – the paradigm that was beginning to emerge in *Screen*. An interest in modernism and ideology was by no means eschewed. Elsaesser's article is evidence of that, and it is one of the elements that distinguishes Elsaesser's – and *Monogram*'s – position from that of traditional auteurism. However, Elsaesser and *Monogram* were sceptical about at least two of the elements of what was to become the dominant paradigm: semiotics and an avant-garde Brechtianism. For them, spectacle and the emotional power of Hollywood's films were a fundamental part of the cinematic experience. Abstract thought and learning and linguistics-based theories were therefore things for which and to which the cinema was inherently unsuited.

While by no means overt in Elsaesser's article (semiotics is not even mentioned), the stress laid on *mise-en-scène*, on emotion, on traditional aesthetic categories like irony and pathos, on the critical potential of mainstream Hollywood films and on a mode – or modes – of 'experience' all functioned as implicit challenges to these particular tenets of the paradigm at *Screen*. Indeed, the same can even be said of Elsaesser's use of melodrama as a term, and of the ways in which at least one of its meanings is used to support this implicit agenda. 'In the dictionary sense,' Elsaesser writes, 'melodrama is a dramatic narrative in which musical accompaniment marks the emotional effects.' 'This is', he continues, 'still perhaps the most useful definition, because it allows melodramatic elements to be seen as constituents of a system of punctuation, giving expressive colour and chromatic contrast to the storyline, by orchestrating the emotional ups and downs of the intrigue' ([1972] 1987: 50).

If the dictionary is one source for the definition Elsaesser is using, another is Sirk himself, who in his interview with Halliday also refers to the importance of music: 'the word "melodrama" has rather lost its meaning nowadays', he says, 'people tend to lose the "melos" in it, the music' (1971: 93). He continues:

> at Ufa, I made several pictures which could be called melodramas: *Schlussakkord* was one kind of melodrama; and *Zu Neuen Ufern* and *La Habanera* were another kind of melodrama. But all three were melodramas in the sense of music + drama. Melodrama in the American sense is rather the archetype of a kind of cinema which connects with drama. Most great plays are based on melodramatic situations, or have melodramatic endings: *Richard III*, for example, is practically a melodrama. Aeschylus and Sophocles wrote plenty of melodramas, as well . . . *The Oresteia* is really a melodrama, I think. But what used to take place in the world of kings and princes has been transposed into the world of the bourgeoisie. Yet plots remain profoundly similar.
>
> (Halliday 1971: 93–5)

What is striking about this is that it combines an historical definition of melodrama ('music + drama') with a definition which is both theoretical and personal to Sirk (*Richard III* and the plays of Aeschylus and Sophocles were written long before melodrama as a term even existed). Sirk hints in passing that there is – or was – something called melodrama 'in the American sense', but what it is remains unclear and unexplained. Elsaesser's approach is somewhat similar. The novels and plays to which he refers were written during the era of melodrama proper, and he is careful to sketch in their historical contexts. But he too ranges widely in his choice of examples. And at times he too deploys elements of an historical definition for purposes of his own – as is apparent in *his* discussion of music and drama.

In other words, neither Sirk nor Elsaesser were solely or even principally concerned with the provision of an historically precise account of melodrama. And this is important, for Elsaesser and Sirk played a key role not just in establishing melodrama as a topic of investigation, discussion and debate, but also in establishing a basic set of terms, concerns and definitions and an initial canon or corpus of films. They thus also played a key role in establishing some of the tenets of the standard account. Hence on the one hand a number of subsequent articles – by Nowell-Smith ([1977] 1987a), by Kleinhans (1978) and by Rodowick ([1982] 1987) among others – which used Elsaesser's term 'family melodrama' and the canon of films on which he focused as a basis for discussions about ideology, class, and Oedipal conflict. And hence on the other two articles by Laura Mulvey ([1977/8] 1987, 1986) which used Sirk's films, the 1950s canon, and the identification of melodrama with the family and domesticity in order not only to pose and to insist upon the importance of issues of gender, but also to identify melodrama with women and the woman's film.

This has proved a decisive step. As explored and elaborated by Cook (1983), Doane (1987), Gledhill (1985c, 1987b), Linda Williams ([1984] 1987) and others, it has come to constitute a cornerstone of the standard account, especially when extended, as it has been by Modleski (1982), Ang (1985), Kuhn ([1984] 1987), Kaplan (1992) and Gledhill (1992), to popular fiction and to radio and television soap opera. (For an extensive bibliography, see Gledhill 1987a.) Debate here has usually focused on issues of audience and audience-address, on the extent to which these genres and forms allow for the articulation of a female point of view, and on the extent to which that point of view – and the fate of female protagonists – may be channelled, distorted, recuperated or dictated by patriarchal contexts of production, circulation and reception. But Gledhill in particular has also sought to relate the woman's film, soap opera, and popular woman's fiction to historical accounts of melodrama both inside and outside the cinema. She has also sought to argue that the status of the woman's film was a low one, and that this can be related both to the lowly status of melodrama as a form, and to the lowly status of women, female discourse, and female concerns. And she has sought to argue too that melodrama and the woman's film were marked by an absence of 'realism' – a term, a category, and an (historically varying) set of aesthetic modes and practices valued much more highly by 'elite' – and usually male – critics and theorists (1987b: 10–13, 26–7, 31–6). She has thus articulated two further tenets of the standard account. A final tenet, implicit in her point about realism, and related in turn to arguments made by Merritt (1983), has perhaps best been summed up by Scott Simmon. 'From the time of Griffith's Biographs onwards,' he writes, 'the film industry has understood and promoted melodramas as everything *but* melodrama, a word they (and the audience) shunned as meaning "failed drama" or, at best, old-fashioned drama' (1990: 45).

As to some extent we have seen already, all of these tenets are open to question. To begin with, it is worth saying something about realism, and about the extent to which the film industry may – or may not – have 'shunned' melodrama as a term.

MELODRAMA, REALISM, AND THE DISCOURSE OF THE FILM INDUSTRY

As is evident from some of the reviews cited above, far from shunning or avoiding them, all of the industry's journals – *Variety, Motion Picture Herald, Film Daily, Moving Picture World* and the like – frequently used the terms 'melodrama', 'meller' and 'melodramatic' in their reviews and discussions of films. (In *Variety*'s case, in reviews of over 1,500 films in the 1930s, the 1940s and the 1950s alone.) In addition, the studios themselves also used them in press releases, publicity sheets and advertisements: an advertisement for *Alias Jimmy Valentine* (1920) claimed the film 'as the most sensational melodrama of the decade' (*Variety*, 16 April 1920: 37); an advertisement for *The Suspect* (1945) begins with the statement that 'Universal believes *The Suspect* is a fine motion picture in the tradition of exciting melodrama' (*Motion Picture Herald*, 13 January 1945: n.p.); and a publicity sheet for *The Street with No Name* (1948) held on microfiche in the BFI library in London contains the following phrases and terms: 'gripping action, spine tingling suspense, stark realism! A melodrama paced for sensational success'.

Although there are occasions on which terms like melodrama are used in a pejorative sense (as in 'baldly stated, the story is only so much melodrama' in *Moving Picture World*'s review of *The Whispering Chorus* (1918), 6 April 1918: 128), it is in fact much more common to find it used neutrally, as a term of generic description. Thus a melodrama could be good, bad, indifferent or standard, depending upon the nature of the films and, of course, the judgement of its reviewer. If *Terror on a Train* (1953) was 'Poor melodrama' (*Motion Picture Herald*, 'Product Digest' 3 September 1953: 577), and if *Somewhere in the Night* (1946) was 'Choice Melodrama' (*Variety*, 12 June 1946: 6), *Son of Frankenstein* (1939) was simply 'Melodrama' (*Motion Picture Herald*, 21 January 1939: 40). In addition, while Poverty Row companies like Freuler Film Associates set up Monarch Melodramas to make action films and mysteries (Turner and Price 1979: 50), and while Consolidated Pictures made *Captured in Chinatown, A Police Melodrama* in 1935, MGM, one of the industry's most prestigious and conservative studios – of all studios the least likely to use a term the industry as a whole had shunned – advertised *Gaslight* as 'MGMelodrama' (*Motion Picture Herald*, 6 May 1944, n.p.), and made two films with the word 'melodrama' in the title: *Manhattan Melodrama* in 1934, and *Washington Melodrama* in 1941. And in 1956, the *Motion Picture Herald* advised exhibitors to use the following copy in publicizing Alfred Hitchcock's US remake of *The Man Who Knew Too Much* (1955): 'suspense beyond *Rear Window* and *To Catch a Thief*. The master of melodrama, who does hair-raising thrillers for everybody's entertainment, has topped his own record for excitement on the screen' (16 June 1956: 39).[2]

In contrast to 'melodrama', 'realism' is a term that the industry and its press actually did tend to avoid. There are occasions on which 'melodrama', when used in a pejorative sense, is taken to imply a failure of plausibility – hence of verisimilitude rather than realism – as in 'an illogical story, trickling over with melodrama' (*Variety* on *Forbidden Trails* (1920), 21 May 1920: 34) and as in 'it's a film for the bloodthirstier and more credulous type of melodrama addict' (*Motion Picture Herald* on *Secrets of a Nurse* (1938), 19 November 1938: 40). But there are also occasions on which 'realism' and 'realistic' are used in tandem with 'melodrama' – as we have already seen in the case of *The Street with No Name* – and these are particularly interesting. In most instances, they imply either that the film in question is marked by a particularly powerful, intense, or convincing set of appropriate generic effects, or else – and this is especially interesting from an historical point of view – that it involves sordid, sensational or low-life events, characters and settings, and thus perhaps draws on elements of Naturalism.[3] Hence, 'powerful melodrama . . . Down to earth and highly realistic' (*Film Daily* on *The Postman Always Rings Twice*, 15 March 1946: 16); 'punchy action, realistic melodrama and sustained audience interest' (*Variety* on *Bataan*, 26 May 1943: 8); 'Ultra-realistic melodrama dealing with various and sordid aspects of a backwash of modern life' (*Motion Picture Herald* 'Product Digest' on *The Man with the Golden Arm* (1955), 17 December 1955: 706); and 'virile realist melodrama' (*Variety* on *The Big House* (1930), 2 July 1930: 25).

MELODRAMA, GENDER, DOMESTICITY AND ROMANCE

The mere occurrence of this last phrase in particular would be unthinkable within the framework of the standard account, which has not just associated melodrama with women and femininity, it has also seen melodrama as one of the few generic areas in Hollywood in which masculinity in general, and 'virile' masculinity in particular, has been consistently qualified, questioned, impaired or castrated – unable to realize or express itself in action (Elsaesser [1972] 1987: 35–7; Lang 1989: 104, 119–32, 209–33; Nowell-Smith [1977]

1987a: 71–4; Rodowick [1982] 1987: 278–9; Modleski [1984] 1987: 332–4). However, *Variety*'s review of *The Big House* is by no means unique. Indeed, it represents the norm. Hence, 'virile melodrama . . . The narration centres about the regeneration of a young man in the great north woods' (*Exhibitors Herald and Motography* on *Virtuous Men* (1919), 19 April 1919: 38). And hence 'he-man melodrama' (*Variety* on *The Storm* (1938), 2 November 1938: 15), 'Penal melodrama' with a 'Mainly masculine story' (*Motion Picture Herald* on *6,000 Enemies* (1939), 27 May 1939: 32) and 'cactus country meller with an all-male cast' (*Variety* on *Bad Lands* (1939), 16 August 1939: 14).

Within this context, female-centred narratives, sentiment, romance and domesticity are seen – and marked out – either as anomalies, or else as separate and optionally additional generic components. Hence the following: 'vigorous melodramatic picture with an all-male cast and no semblance of romantic interest' (*Variety* on *The Fighting 69th* (1939), 10 January 1940: 14); 'it's an all-male cast, but absence of romance is not missed in the rapid-fire unfolding of vivid melodrama' (*Variety* on *Sahara* (1943), 29 September 1943: 8); and '*Undercover Girl*, by its very title, suggests a conventional melodrama with a twist that the girl is the gangster's foil' (*Variety* on *Undercover Girl* (1950), 11 January 1950: 6).

All this may help explain why the occurrence of terms like 'romantic melodrama' or 'domestic melodrama' is in fact relatively rare. I have come across only two examples of the latter, both of them perfectly consonant with the notions of melodrama prevalent elsewhere in the industry's relay. Hence, 'domestic melodrama . . . With the picture nearing the two-hour mark it suddenly turns into a murder mystery' (*Motion Picture Herald* 'Product Digest' on *East Side, West Side* (1949), 17 December 1949: 122), and 'interesting domestic melodrama about a psychopathic killer' (*Variety* on *The House on Telegraph Hill* (1951), 7 March 1951: 6). Some of the canonic 1950s 'family melodramas' (a term I have not encountered at all) *were* called melodramas, but for similar or parallel reasons. *Written on the Wind* was described as a melodrama by the *Film Daily* because it was 'fraught with a variety of sensational themes' (19 December 1956: 47). *Home from the Hill* was described by *Variety* as 'full-blooded melodrama' because it contained 'high-octane situations and characters' (10 February 1960: 6). And *Rebel Without a Cause* was called a 'juvenile delinquency melodrama' by the *Film Daily* because it contained 'some startling, if luridly theatrical, scenes (a knife fight, a "chicken" race with stolen cars) which will offer the full quota of thrills to seekers after the sensational' (27 October 1955: 10). (For discussion of the labelling of these and other 1950s films as 'sensational' and 'adult', see Klinger 1994a: 36–68 and 1994b.)

The term 'romantic melodrama,' meanwhile, is slightly more common, but also more complex. Mostly it is a hybrid term used to indicate a hybrid film, a film which mixes elements of the thriller with an element of romance, as in 'Romantic Melodrama – For the melodrama die-hards there are a number of moments of unadulterated viciousness that should win their whole-hearted approval' (*Film Daily* on *Two Smart People* (1946), 6 June 1946: 8), and 'romantic melodrama of sex and murder at the beach' (*Variety* on *Female at the Beach* (1956), 13 July 1955: 6). However, there does seem to be at least one ambiguous instance, *All That Heaven Allows* (1955), which the *Film Daily* describes as a 'Romantic Melodrama Slated for High Grosses' (25 October 1955: 10). A clue here may be offered by the subsequent description, which talks of 'all the ups-and-downs suffered by Miss Wyman and [Rock] Hudson during their relationship', and more particularly by a review of the film in the *Hollywood Reporter*, which speaks of the extent to which 'Douglas Sirk's direction develops emotional tension' (25 October 1955: 3). What motivates the use of the term 'melodrama' here, then, may not be the element of romance itself but a particular – perhaps 'feminine' – version of the tensions and thrills putatively offered men by thrillers and action films. The same might be said of *Motion Picture Herald*'s review of *Paid in Full* (1949), which refers to 'a melodramatic story line that twists and turns in many directions' (24 December 1949: 130), and also of its review of *Autumn Leaves* (1956), which claims that the film's director, Robert Aldrich, 'punches every dramatic scene for all its worth' (18 April 1956: 6).

All That Heaven Allows, *Paid in Full* and *Autumn Leaves* were all also described as 'woman's films' (or marked in one way or another as of particular interest to women). As such, though, they were very much in a minority. Aside from instances such as *Leave Her to Heaven* (1945), *Mildred Pierce* (1945), *Nora Prentiss* (1947), *The Reckless Moment* (1949), *The File on Thelma Jordan* (1949) and *No Man of Her Own* (1950), which were all thrillers of one kind or another and which hence corresponded to the dominant conception of melodrama, *Stella Dallas* (1937), *The Toy Wife* (1938), *Forgotten Women* (1949), *A Life of Her Own* (1950), *Hilda Crane* (1956) and *Another Time, Another Place* (1958) are the only other examples I have come across.[4] How, then, was the woman's film predominantly labelled? What was its industrial and critical status? And what were its sources and antecedents? Is the standard account in need of revision here as well?

THE WOMAN'S FILM

The first thing to say in this context is that a great deal of important and highly sophisticated work has been done on various phases and cycles of the woman's film in the 1930s, the 1940s and the 1950s, and on individual films like *Stella Dallas* and *Now, Voyager* (1942), *Mildred Pierce* and *The Reckless Moment*. (Aside from those cited already, see Allen 1984; Cook 1983; Cowie 1984; Fischer 1983; Jacobs 1981, 1991; Palmer 1986; Viviani [1979] 1987; Waldman 1983; Walsh 1984.) However, very little work has been done on the woman's film prior to the 1930s, and there as yet exists no general historical overview. The nearest thing to the former – and to an account, in particular, of the origins of the woman's film – is the chapter on 'The Origins of the Woman's Film at Biograph' in Simmon's book on D. W. Griffith (1993: 68–103). The nearest thing to the latter is Basinger's book, *A Woman's View* (1993).

Basinger offers the following 'working definition' of the woman's film: 'A woman's film is a movie that places at the center of its universe a female who is trying to deal with emotional, social, and psychological problems that are specifically connected to the fact that she is a woman' (1993: 20). Using this definition as a basis, she goes on to argue that the woman's film extended generically beyond the confines of melodrama (as defined and understood within Film Studies). Equating the former with the latter would, she writes, 'eliminate more than half of the films that are concerned with women and their fates, among them Rosalind Russell's career comedies, musical biographies of real-life women, combat films featuring brave nurses on Bataan, and westerns in which women drive cattle west and men over the brink' (ibid.: 7). She continues:

> there are huge differences among such titles as the screwball comedy *Unfinished Business* (1941), the murder story *Sudden Fear* (1952), the western *Johnny Guitar* (1954), the musical *Love Me or Leave Me* (1955), the film noir *The Locket* (1946), or the biographical *Madame Curie* (1943), yet each can be defined as a woman's film. In women's films, the fixed conventions, while they *do* exist, do not exist in quite the same way as in other genres. The woman's film isn't set in any one time or place, and its locale can be real or imaginary. It can be contemporary or historical. It can easily be a biography of a real person, and just as easily be a totally fictional account of a tomboy, a princess, a space explorer, or an ordinary shop girl. It may be purely a generic type of woman's film of the type most people envision when they think of women's films (a melodrama with a big-name female movie star), but it may also be a female version of some other, presumably more 'masculine' genre, such as a western or a gangster movie.
>
> (Basinger 1993: 9)

Simmon also notes that 'the woman's film has remained elusive' (1993: 68). 'One might suspect', he writes, 'that something of its elusiveness arises from its being an oppositional genre, as it were, definable only in opposition to genres tracing the ambitions of male heroes' (ibid.). However, he argues that 'such an explanation clearly won't do in Griffith's era: The woman's film found its mature form before the genres centering on goal-driven males. (Earlier Westerns had yet to rely on the lone cowboy hero, significantly only gradually after 1909 with the first "Broncho Billy" films.)' (ibid.). He defines this 'mature form' in terms of what he calls an 'overplot' – 'a woman's ordeal and suffering, and occasionally her triumph, within domestic confines' (ibid.: 69) – and in terms of its variations, 'subgenres loosely defined by whether the suffering woman is seen as a daughter (e.g. *Now, Voyager*; *Johnny Belinda*), a wife (*Rebecca*; *A Letter to Three Wives*), a mother (*Stella Dallas*; *Imitation of Life*), or a "fallen woman" (loose in morals and thus initially loose in family definition – *Ladies of Leisure*; *Back Street*)' (ibid.). He might well have added at least one other variation, that of lover or fiancée or would-be wife (*Kitty Foyle* (1940), *All That Heaven Allows*). And he might have stressed the extent to which, in any one film, these categories and roles overlap or come into conflict, hence helping to generate dramatic and ideological tension (*All That Heaven Allows*, *Letter from an Unknown Woman* and *Now, Voyager* are particularly good examples).

As others have done, Basinger and Simmon stress the extent to which the woman's film 'carries with it certain "resistances" to its overt arguments' (Simmon 1993: 71). For Simmon, 'The repressive narratives are regularly questioned and even undercut, partly via mise-en-scène and acting but also by conflicts within the narratives themselves' (ibid.). Hence 'even the purest examples of the genre, such as King Vidor's 1937 version of *Stella Dallas*, with its story line ending in the social "eradication" of the mother, also holds a counterstory of Stella's personal triumph over the patriarchal world around her, or at least her refusal to submit to it' (ibid.). Similarly, for Basinger, 'The woman's film was successful because it worked out of a paradox. It both held women in social bondage and released them into a dream of potency and freedom' (1993: 6):

> If it is true, as many suggest, that Hollywood films repressed women and sought to teach them what they ought to do, then it is equally clear that, in order to achieve this, the movies first had to bring to life the opposite of their own morality. To convince women that marriage and motherhood were the right path, movies had to show women making the mistake of doing something else. By making the Other live on the screen, movies made it real. By making it real, they made it desirable. By making it desirable, they made it possible. They gave the Other substance, and thus gave it credibility. In asking the question, What should a woman do with her life? they created the possibility of an answer different from the one they intended to provide at the end of the movie.
>
> Thus, what emerges on close examination of hundreds of women's movies is how strange and ambivalent they really are. Stereotypes are presented, then undermined, and then reinforced. Contradictions abound, which at first sight seem to be merely the result of carelessness, the products of commercial nonsense. But they are more than plot confusion. They exist as an integral and even necessary aspect of what drives the movies and gives them their appeal. These movies

were a way of recognizing the problems of women, of addressing their desire to have things be better than they are offscreen.

(Basinger 1993: 6–7)

However, although Basinger and Simmon both successfully demonstrate the complexities and contradictions at work in the woman's film, although they both offer useful and pertinent definitions, and although Simmon, in particular, makes reference to the industry, and to 'a shift in nickelodeon audience demographics, as working-class wives and mothers discovered a permissible, affordable mode of commercialized leisure' (1993: 68), neither trace the history of the woman's film as a product, a term or a category. Nor do they discuss the industrial factors that continued to govern its existence at the end of the nickelodeon era, or, to any great extent, the aesthetic and cultural strands and traditions upon which it drew.

With the changes in audience demographics and the emergence of the type of film discussed by Simmon, it seems likely that the term 'woman's film' was first used in the 1910s. However, a complicating factor here is the emergence in the 1910s of the serial queen adventure films, thrillers and mysteries of the kind discussed by Singer alongside the more domestically and familially oriented of films of the kind discussed by Simmon. As Singer (1990) and as Bowser (1990: 185–8) have both pointed out, the serial queen films – films, series and serials like *The Woman Who Dared* (1910), *The Exploits of Elaine* (1914–15), *The American Girl* (1917) and *Ruth of the Rockies* (1920) – appear to draw on the ideology and the image of the 'New Woman'. With its emphasis on modernity, activity and independence, and its connections with suffragism and the struggle for women's rights, New Womanhood was at least in some respects directly opposed to the sentimental Victorian familialism that, however troubled, lay at the heart of Griffith's films. Its influence came to be felt in the flapper films and comedies of the 1920s, as well as in domestic dramas and the serial queen films (Higashi 1994: 87–116, 147–75; Staiger 1995: 181–2). The serial queen films were called melodramas. Whether they were also ever called – or thought of – as woman's films is as yet unknown.

By the early 1920s, indications that a certain type of film may appeal in particular to women began to appear regularly in the industry's journals. *Wid's Daily's* review of *The Foolish Matrons* (1921) argues that the film 'Will Please Women Audiences' (3 July 1921: 12). There are similar examples in its reviews of *Devotion* (1921) (3 July 1921: 19), *Footlights* (1921) (9 October 1921: 4) and *Jane Eyre* (1921) (16 October 1921: 10), and in an advertisement for *The Child Thou Gavest Me* (1921) (26 August 1921: 3). The first instance I have come across of the use of the term 'woman's film' occurs three years later, in a review of *Christine of the Hungry Heart* (1924) in the *Film Daily*, *Wid's Daily's* successor (26 October 1924: 6).

Christine of the Hungry Heart is typical of the woman's film in a number of ways. According to the *Film Daily*, it tells the story of a woman who, having

191

cast off 'a worthless husband, marries an important surgeon only to leave him because his work keeps him from her too often. She elopes with a writer to Brazil but when the authorities take her child away she returns and in the end is re-united with her surgeon-husband who discovers her as she is looking after her first husband as he is about to die.' It 'places at the center of its universe a female who is trying to deal withe emotional, social, and psychological problems'. Its protagonist suffers, as a wife, as a mother and as a lover. It clearly seeks to 'teach' women 'what they ought to do.' (*Film Daily*'s review says that the film 'is rather more preachment than entertainment'). And it clearly emphasizes the importance of choice (an element that Basinger (1993: 19–23) discusses at some length). It is clear, too, that *Christine of the Hungry Heart* 'brings to life the opposite of its own morality', that it creates 'the possibility of an answer different from the one . . . intended', and that it does so by 'making the Other live on the screen'. Interestingly, the review argues not only that the film 'will cause discussion among women who have advanced ideas and who rebel at the old formula of "a woman's place"', but also that it is 'really a preachment as to what a married woman should expect of her husband' – a statement that can be read in two quite distinct, and opposite, ways.

The film – and its review – are typical in other ways too. Firstly, *Christine of the Hungry Heart* is neither a career comedy nor a biography, combat film or western. These kinds of films, even when centred on female characters, were rarely if ever called 'woman's films'. Thus although Basinger's argument here is logical (as well as polemical), it ignores the fact that the industry itself tended to define – and to confine – the woman's film in particular ways. As Simmon points out, the woman's film as such was above all about women whose roles and whose lives were defined in domestic or familial terms. This was the definition the industry presumed and perpetuated in its address to women and to female audiences, even as a number of the films it made also questioned or undermined it in the ways Simmon and Basinger indicate.

Secondly, *Christine of the Hungry Heart* was adapted from a best-selling novel by a woman, Kathleen Norris. Although woman's films were frequently adapted from novels, stories and plays written by men (*Kitty Foyle*, for instance, from a novel by Christopher Morley, and *Waterloo Bridge* (1940) from Robert Sherwood's play), a significant number were adapted from novels, stories and plays written by women: *The Reckless Moment* (1949) from a story by Elizabeth Sanxay Holding, *Rebecca* and *My Cousin Rachel* from novels by Daphne Du Maurier, *Love is a Many-Splendored Thing* (1955) from a novel by Han Suyin, and both versions of *Humoresque* (1920 and 1946), both versions of *Imitation of Life* (1934 and 1959), and all three versions of *Back Street* (1932, 1941 and 1961) from novels and stories by Fannie Hurst. (In addition, as Lizzie Francke has shown, female writers like Catherine Turney, Zoe Atkins, Lenore Coffee and Silvia Richards often worked on scenarios, scripts and adaptations for woman's films (1994: 45–54). Meanwhile the tradition of what might be called the 'woman's novel', a tradition that has its roots in the late eighteenth century, is discussed by Ardis 1990; Armstrong 1987; Baym 1978; Brown 1975, 1990; Douglas 1977; Kelley 1984; Matthews 1987; and Papashvily 1956.)

Thirdly and finally, *Christine of the Hungry Heart* is described not as melodrama, but as drama – 'another of those heart-tugging teary dramas that women "love"'. 'Drama', along with 'romance', 'love story', 'mother love story', 'comedy drama' and 'soap opera', was by far the most common term used to describe woman's films (Neale 1993a: 74), and drama, whose provenance may lie in the theatrical genre of *drame* as defined and described by Diderot ([1758] 1965) and by subsequent theatre historians like Hartnoll ([1972] 1987: 143) and Roberts ([1972] 1974: 274), was certainly distinguished from melodrama in the industry's press. The anonymous reviewer of *Bobbie the Coward* (1911) in the *Moving Picture World* wrote that 'melodrama takes place after true drama because it aims to give a thrill rather than an edifying emotion' (29 July 1911: 209). And in an article entitled 'Techniques of the Photoplay' in the same magazine, Epes Winthrop Sargent distinguishes between tragedy, drama, melodrama and comedy drama: 'Most cowboy stories are melodramatic because they are elemental and violent . . . Comedy drama is merely melodrama with the comedy element made superior to the dramatic action . . . Simple drama occupies a place between melodrama and tragedy in that it lacks the violence of the one and the loftiness of the other' (1911: 613).[5]

Ironically, the only thing not really typical about *Film Daily's* review is its somewhat dismissive and condescending tone – '*just* another of those heart-tugging teary dramas that women "love"'' (my emphasis). For although, like individual melodramas, individual woman's films could be judged good, bad or indifferent, the genre as a whole occupied not a lowly or humble or despised position within the film industry but, rather, a lofty one. Indeed, what were adjudged to be the finest woman's films were also consistently regarded – along with what were adjudged to be the finest social problem films, biopics, epics and literary adaptations – as exemplifying Hollywood and its product at their best. Hence phrases such as 'a credit to the industry as a whole' and 'tastefully mounted, high quality production that ranks as a work of art' in *Variety's* review of *Magnificent Obsession* (1936) (8 January 1936: 12) and in the *Hollywood Reporter's* review of *Harriet Craig* (1950) (27 October 1950: 3), respectively. Hence the persistent association with the woman's film of producers – like Samuel Goldwyn – who craved respectability and prestige. (Goldwyn produced both versions of *Stella Dallas*. It might be noted that in discussing the success of the 1925 version, Frances Marion, who worked on the script, wrote that 'Everyone was surprised that Sam chose a simple story like "Stella Dallas" at a time when the public seemed to be clamoring for spectacles and lurid melodrama' (Marion 1972: 122).) And hence the fact that very few woman's films were made either by Hollywood's Poverty Row studios – Monogram, PRC, Republic and the like – or by B units at the majors. These units and studios largely specialized instead in adventure serials, crime thrillers, action films and westerns – i.e. in melodramas of one kind or another.

One reason for this was the industry's presumption, sometimes in the face of statistical evidence to the contrary, that women constituted an important, even dominant, sector of the viewing population, providing the bulk of the audience at matinees and playing a decisive role in choosing the films heterosexual couples went to see in the evening ('"Men Top Pic Fans" – Gallup' and 'Pollock Challenges Gallup Findings, Sez Women Sway Men's Pic Choices', *Variety*, 5 August 1942: 3 and 19 August 1942: 12). Another – related – reason was that since the 1910s the film industry had, like vaudeville before it, sought to attract female patrons, not just to increase its ticket sales and profits but also to provide itself with an aura of respectability (Merritt 1976).

Clearly, a particular conception of women, women's interests, and women's social status is at stake here. The roots of this conception lie firmly in the middle-class Cult of True Womanhood, an ideology whose own roots lay in the late eighteenth and nineteenth centuries. According to this ideology, women, when defined in domestic and familial terms, when occupying domestic and familial roles, and when defined or figured in particular as wives and as mothers, represented the height of 'civilized' sensibility, virtue and feeling (Welter 1966). The Cult of True Womanhood was modified, adapted and updated during the course of the nineteenth and early twentieth centuries. It was challenged by the advent of the New Woman in the 1890s and the rearticulation of New Womanhood in the 1920s (Banta 1987; Dumenil 1995: 98–144; Filene [1974] 1986: 6–112; Freedman 1974; Higashi 1994: 87–116; McGovern 1968; Ryan 1982; Smith-Rosenberg 1985; Staiger 1995: 35–53; Yellis 1969). And it was challenged by the reaction against what Betty Friedan called 'The Feminine Mystique' in the early 1960s (Friedan 1963). (See also Chafe 1972: 226–44, and Matthews 1987: 208–22.) In its pure form the Cult of True Womanhood was in decline by the end of the nineteenth century. But in modified form, and in conjunction with modified forms of New Womanhood (and modified ideologies of heterosexual relations, courtship, marriage and family life), it clearly influenced society in general and the film industry and its producers in particular through to the late 1950s and early 1960s.

Evidence of this can be found in the tenets of the Production Code, with its strictures about adultery and 'illicit sex', 'scenes of passion' and prostitution, and its requirement that the 'sanctity of marriage and the home' be upheld in Hollywood's films. Evidence can also be found in the nature and type of the films themselves, with their focus on the romantic, the familial and the domestic, on women as actual or potential wives and mothers, in the regimes of poetic justice and compensating values that the Production Code prescribes for them, and sometimes also in the vocabulary of the industry's reviews. The recurrence of the word 'human' as a synonym for the humane and sympathetic sensibilities with which women were associated is particularly striking. *Variety* described the 1932 version of *Back Street* as 'a human document faithfully translated into celluloid and sound' (30 August 1932: 14) and the 1954 version of *Magnificent Obsession* as 'a moving human drama' (12 May 1954: 5). The *Film Daily* described *Claudia* (1943) as 'a production with heart and soul, with emotional strength, tenderness and humanity far beyond one's fondest expectations. Women especially will find it one of the most memorable theater-going experiences of the year' (19 August 1943: 6).

It is undoubtedly the case that woman's films themselves were frequently marked by the complexities and contradictions, the undercurrents and countercurrents, to which Basinger, Simmon and others have drawn attention. It is undoubtedly also the case that both in general terms and in specific instances such as the 'fallen woman' films of the early 1930s the Production Code functioned as a framework for negotiation rather than as a mechanically applied or inscribed set of precepts (Inglis 1985; Jacobs 1991; Maltby 1993a; Vasey 1995). My point would be, though, that just as the Production Code also functioned, nevertheless, as a public statement of the ideological principles Hollywood claimed to uphold, so the Cult of True Womanhood remained, in modified form, a point of reference for Hollywood and the woman's film a major site of and for its exploration. (Tellingly, the chapter on *Susan Lennox: Her Fall and Rise* (1932) in Gabriel Miller's book *Screening the Novel* (1980: 19–45) is entitled 'The New Woman Gets the Old Treatment'.) It may thus be no accident that although Hollywood continued to make films marked by some of the features and concerns of the traditional woman's film in the 1970s, the 1980s and the 1990s, the term itself disappeared in the 1960s, at the same time as the Production Code, and at the same time as 1960s feminism mounted a series of challenges to 'the feminine mystique'. Henceforth the films made within this tradition would take account of these challenges and changes if only in the guise, in many cases, of an anti-feminist backlash. Henceforth plot resolutions would be less rigidly governed by precepts of the kind embodied in the Code. And henceforth too, women would on occasion play more varied roles in other kinds of films, some of them, like the roles in some of the action films of the 1980s and 1990s, reminiscent not so much of the traditional woman's film as of serial queen melodrama. (For discussion of some or all of these developments, see Cook 1998; Ehrenstein 1978; Geraghty 1980/1; Haskell [1974] 1987: 323–402; Islam 1995; Kaplan 1992: 180–219; Mellen 1973; Tasker 1993: 14–34, 132–66; Traube 1992: 97–169; Vlasopolos 1988; Walters 1992: 106–235; White 1989; Willis 1997: 60–128; Williamson 1993: 39–41, 52–4, 58–60, 249–51, 261.)

Does this mean, though, that there are no connections at all between melodrama, drama and the woman's film? After all, the suffering and virtuous heroine was a standard figure in nineteenth-century melodrama, an often pure incarnation of the Cult of True Womanhood. Domestic and familial relations and values were a key feature of many nineteenth-century melodramas, and what Michael R. Booth has termed 'domestic melodrama' an identifiable sub-genre or form (Booth 1965: 118–41, and 1991: 153). 'Drama' as well as 'melodrama' was used as a term to describe the plays themselves. (*Black Ey'd Susan*, *The Corsican Brothers* and *Under the Gaslight* were all billed as 'drama'.) And *drame* has often been cited as either a precursor or an early form of melodrama (Brooks 1976: 13; Rahill 1967: xiv; Vincent-Buffault [1986] 1991: 226–40). If on the other hand there are clear but hitherto largely unexplored connections between nineteenth-century melodrama and genres like the thriller, the horror film, the western and action-adventure, what is the nature of these connections? How can they be accounted for? In order to answer at least some of these questions we need finally to take a look at stage melodrama and its history in a little more detail.

MELODRAMA AND HOLLYWOOD'S GENRES

As a theatrical genre, melodrama came into existence in the late eighteenth century in France and Germany. During the course of the following century it spread and developed from there to Britain, to America, to the rest of Europe, and to a number of European colonies. Its initial definition was both formal and specific: melodrama was a dramatic passage, scene or play in which at first spoken dialogue, then later mute action, was accompanied – and often underlined – by music (Branscombe 1980; Neumeyer 1995: 61–73). During the course of its subsequent development music remained a key ingredient. But its use became more generalized, more varied, and less specific in kind than it had been at first. Whole plays and all sorts of actions – including, sometimes, singing and dancing – were accompanied by music (Cross 1977: 155–67; Mayer 1980; Neumeyer 1995: 73–5).

By then, a set of further basic features and conventions had become firmly established. These included: (1) an unequivocal dramatic conflict between good and evil; (2) the eventual triumph of the former over the latter; (3) three principal character-types or functions: hero, heroine and villain; (4) a demonstrative and often hyperbolic aesthetic by means of which characters were typed, dramatic conflict was established and developed, and motive, emotion and passion were laid bare; (5) an often highly episodic, formulaic and action-packed plot, normally initiated and often driven by the villain, dependent for its initiation, development and resolution on fate, chance and coincidence, and characterized throughout by 'an overabundance . . . of reversals and recognitions' (Jacobs 1993: 126); and (6) the generation of what were called 'situations'.[6] (A situation is defined in the *Oxford English Dictionary* as 'a particular conjunction of circumstances (esp. of a striking or exciting nature) under which the characters are presented in the course of a novel or play'. On the stage, situations sometimes took the form of tableaux. But they were always in any case 'pictorial' in nature. And they existed for the purposes of dramatic display, and the revelation of dramatic developments, reversals, recognitions and confrontations and of the reactions of the characters to them. See Meisel 1983: 39–51.)

Before proceeding further, it is worth emphasizing the extent to which these features are much more obviously characteristic of the genres labelled as melodrama by the industry's relay than they are of the woman's film. As Murray Smith has pointed out, melodrama's Manichaean moral structure is 'the exception rather than the rule' in the woman's film: 'If the Manichaean structure is evident anywhere within Hollywood cinema, then it is within genres other than those we now recognize as "melodramatic": the gangster film, the Western, the horror movie, the thriller, the adventure film, and the war picture' (1995: 206). The same might be said not just of the figure of the villain and of the villain's key role both as representative of evil and as the 'active principle' (Booth 1991: 160) in the development of melodrama's plots – 'If you have villains, you have melodrama', as King Vidor is reported as saying in Brownlow (1990: 298) – but also of the violent nature of the villain's activities, and indeed of 'The violence necessary' to unveil melodrama's 'hidden moral order' (Cox 1987: 49). And it might be added that while domestic and familial values are part of that order, they neither define nor exhaust its parameters – such values can be found in most nineteenth-century art.

The kinship between nineteenth-century melodrama and Hollywood's genres of action and suspense is also apparent in their actions and situations, and in the passions and emotions they help generate and bring to the fore. Whether characterized in terms of 'a deadlock, a temporary suspension of the action' or 'a point of equilibrium' in the action, most situations, as Lea Jacobs has noted, tend to block or halt the progress of the narrative (1993: 131). As such they tend to render the characters involved powerless, passive or vulnerable, and the same is true, she argues, of the subordination of character to plot in melodrama, and of melodrama's reliance on chance and coincidence in setting up and enchaining situations, incidents and actions. She then goes on to draw a number of parallels between the powerless and passive protagonists of melodrama and the powerless and passive protagonists of the woman's film and of a number of canonic 1950s family dramas (ibid.: 138–42).

Jacobs' argument is important. But, in drawing the parallels she draws, she fails to consider some of the differences in nature between the situations, plots and actions involved. And in discussing powerlessness and passivity, she fails to consider the figure of the villain. As is well known, melodrama's actions and situations include 'Bodies roped to railway lines, heroes in cellars where tidewater is rising, circular saws or steam hammers threatening the lives of helpless victims, early Christians about to be thrown to the lions, sinking ships . . . earthquakes, volcanoes, tempest, fire and flood' (Disher 1954: 1), all of which are much more reminiscent of thrillers and action films, of disaster films, and even of biblical epics – of films like *No Man's Gold* (1926), *The Towering Inferno*, *Quo Vadis*, *Star Wars* and *Speed* (1994) – than they are of woman's films and films like *Written on the Wind* and *Home from the Hill*. And while melodrama's villains are by no means omnipotent – they are foiled on a regular basis and of course always defeated in the end – they are never characterized as passive or powerless.

Three further points are worth making here. Firstly, as Jacobs herself points out, melodramatic situations always involve suspense, and suspense is as much a property of thrillers and action films as it is of romantic or domestic dramas. Secondly, as Jacobs also points out, it is perfectly possible for the heroes and heroines of melodrama to overcome the situations with which they are confronted and thus to counteract any impression of powerlessness and passivity their regular embroilment in situations may otherwise create. In this respect they bring to mind serial queens and action heroes like Rambo and John McClane. And thirdly, there is no inherent correlation between powerlessness, passivity and gender. The heroes of *Objective, Burma!*, *Rear Window* and *Ben-Hur* (1959) are often as powerless as Rosa Moline (Bette Davis) in *Beyond the Forest* (1949), the example Jacobs uses to explore this particular issue.

Of course from a Formalist point of view, all fictional characters are functions of the plots in which they appear. In summarizing Sergei Balukhatyi's *Poetics of Melodrama* (1926), it is therefore hardly surprising that Daniel Gerould stresses this particular point:

> In a certain sense, melodrama is devoid of 'heroes' possessing free activity who make their destinies for themselves. The dramatic spring is not the character, but the plot with its emotional bases; the characters are only its 'tools,' and are defined in their character traits only as much as is necessary for motivating the progression of the plot.
>
> (Gerould 1978: 161)

The key phrase here, though, is 'emotional bases,' for according to Gerould it is Balukhatyi's thesis that 'All elements of melodrama – its themes, technical principles, construction, and style – are subordinate to one overriding aesthetic goal: the calling forth of "pure," "vivid" emotions. Plot, character, and dialogue, working in unison, serve to elicit from the spectator the greatest possible intensity of feeling' (ibid.: 154). Intensity of feeling, however, is by no means confined to the spectator, for 'The fundamental task of the melodramatist is "baring the passions" which constitute the motive force of the characters' actions' (ibid.: 155).

Gerould's account of Balukhatyi's book stresses the importance of pathos and sentiment, of love and of 'maternal feelings' (ibid.: 156). But he also cites 'envy,' 'self-seeking' and 'vengeance.' And in giving examples of the 'usual material' used as a basis for melodrama's stories, events and situations, he cites, among others, 'murders, large-scale thefts and forgeries, confrontations with a murdered victim, trial, sentencing, preparation for the execution, hard labor, beggary,' and 'futile efforts to earn a living' (ibid.: 155). Other writers on melodrama have argued that its dominant emotion is fear (Mason 1993: 17; Sharratt 1980: 279). Nearly all, though, have stressed its dedication to breathtaking thrills.

Thrills and fear were certainly among the elements laid bare in the earliest melodramas, whose varieties included 'gothic melodrama', 'equestrian melodrama', 'nautical' and 'martial' melodrama, 'cape-and-sword melodrama' and, in America, 'frontier melodrama' too (Bank 1990; Booth 1965: 67–117; Grimstead 1968: 16–17, 101–3, 143, 190, 200, 215–20, 227; Rahill 1967: 75–84, 106–13, 129–33, 140–1, 152–60, 225–6, 230–9; Smith 1976: xvi–xvii). They were also laid bare in such later varieties as 'crook plays' (Quinn [1927] 1936, II: 110), 'crime plays' (Smith 1973: ix), 'Civil War melodrama' (Toll 1976: 168), 'toga plays' (Mayer 1994a), Grand Guignol (Gordon [1988] 1997; Gunning 1991b) and 'sensation drama' (Booth 1965: 145–75). Even domestic melodrama, in its various forms and guises the most persistent site of pathos, romance and mother-love, is characterized by Booth in terms of criminals, crime and villainy (ibid.: 139).

However, a series of additional developments serve to complicate this picture. Some may help pinpoint more precisely the theatrical antecedents of the woman's film and of Hollywood's other dramas. Others may help account for the varied aesthetic character of Hollywood's melodramas during the studio era and the period preceeding it. Accounts vary in detail, in emphasis, and in terminology, but it is clear that between the middle of the nineteenth century and the 1870s and 1880s there developed what Rahill calls 'modified melodrama' (1967: xv), Smith 'bourgeois drama' (1973: xxi), Brooks 'drawing room drama' (1976: xii), and McConachie (1992: 225–7) 'well-made melodrama.' Rahill's account runs as follows:

> melodrama did not confine itself to the popular theatre, and from this circumstance arises much of the confusion . . . as to what melodrama is and what it isn't. It spilled over into the theatre of the middle classes. Here, reacting to audiences of greater sophistication, it underwent a gradual change as the nineteenth century moved into its second half. The 'heart' became the target of playwrights rather than the nervous system, and firearms and the representation of convulsions of nature yielded the center of the stage to high-voltage emotionalism, examination of soul-states, and the observation of manners. The employment of music was curtailed and the more extravagant embellishments in the field of scenic display were discarded. Something like subtlety was attempted here and there in characterization, with the result that stock types lost some of their rigidity. Increasingly as the century wore on heroines were to be discovered who were less than blameless,

especially in love, villains who were more to be pitied than censured when all the evidence was in, and even heroes who refused to fight!

(Rahill 1967: xv)

La Dame aux camelias serves as an example, an example that is echoed by Smith (1973: xxi) and by Lewis (1973: 156). Rahill also mentions *East Lynne*, *Way Down East*, 'the famous "Adelphi dramas" associated with the professional career of Celine Celeste,' 'the Henry Irving repertoire at the Lyceum,' 'the plays of Bartley Campbell and James A. Herne' and 'French drawing-room melodrama' (1967: xv). There are clear connections here between modified melodrama, *drame* and the woman's film on the one hand, and other Hollywood dramas on the other. 'Popular' or 'classical' melodrama, meanwhile, melodrama cut to the pattern of blood, thunder and thrills established earlier on in the nineteenth century, found its home initially in the cheaper theatres patronized by poorer, working-class audiences, 'Drury Lane in England' (ibid.: xv) and the 'ten–twenty–thirty' cent houses in America (ibid.: xv, 272–83), then in the store-front theatres and nickelodeons, in the celluloid melodramas, that eventually displaced them:

> the movies, which specialized in the very type of show that was the standby of 'ten, twent' thirt,' did a far better job. The millions who thrilled to *The Great Train Robbery* on the screen were able to compare it with the stage play, and its superiority was obvious. The old theatres were transformed into nickelodeons, and on their bellying sheets were to be seen such soul-stirring matters as Pearl White thrown from cliffs by the villainous Paul Panzer in *The Perils of Pauline*; Grace Cunard hounded and harried week after week in *The Broken Coin*; and Broncho Billy Anderson riding to the rescue of imperiled damsels on the payroll of the Essanay Company.
>
> (Rahill 1967: 283)

Rahill's account is, I think, substantially correct. Certainly it is supported by those who have written about the divisions in melodrama, about ten–twenty–thirty cent theatre, and about the immediate theatrical provenance of many early genres and films.[7] However, one or two points of modification need to be made before the picture of melodrama on the stage in the late nineteenth and early twentieth centuries is complete, and before the range of dramatic and melodramatic influences on early film and on Hollywood's later genres can be outlined in more detail.

Theatre historians like Butsch (1994) and McConachie (1992) stress the 'feminized' as well as the middle-class nature of modified melodrama, a stress clearly consonant with the account I have given so far of the theatrical antecedents of the woman's film. They also argue that a major site of and for this feminization was 'sensation melodrama'. Sensation melodrama is a rather loose category, encompassing as it does plays like *Lady Audley's Secret* and *East Lynne*, which are essentially domestic and familial in character and setting, and plays like *Under the Gaslight*, which were marked by the spectacular staging of spectacular events – avalanches, chariot races, train wrecks and the like. One of the things that united them, though, was what Butsch calls 'an assertive model of femininity' (1994: 390). This model could take a number of forms. One was that of complex female 'villains' like Lady Audley in *Lady Audley's Secret*. Another was that of 'vigorous heroines' like Laura Courtland in *Under the Gaslight* (ibid.). What this suggests is that certain strands of sensation melodrama fed into the woman's film while others fed into the serial queen films of the kind discussed by Singer (1990).

McConachie also argues that sensation melodrama was a major site of and for the incorporation of 'well-made' aesthetic values and techniques, i.e. those techniques and values associated with the plays of Eugene Scribe and others – compositional unity, causal coherence, and so on (1992: 226). Dion Boucicault and Augustin Daly are cited as among those adopting these values and techniques, which McConachie clearly regards as much more compatible with contemporary middle-class taste than those of what he calls 'traditional melodrama' (ibid.: 226–7). On the one hand they were used to tone down, to complicate or to motivate more fully the twists and turns of melodrama's narratives and the stereotypical traits of its characters. On the other, they were used to motivate the staging of 'everyday' settings and scenes (Booth 1981: 1–29; Gillette 1971: 185–92). Meanwhile, the more spectacular and extraordinary aspects of sensation melodrama were rendered acceptable to middle-class values and tastes by their well-made aesthetic framework and by the extent to which they embodied and displayed what the film industry would later call 'high production values' – values which were largely absent from melodrama of the ten–twenty–thirty cent variety, if only for reasons of cost. Much has been made by Fell ([1974] 1986), Vardac (1949) and others of film's ability to reproduce and to amplify these values. But a distinction still needs to be made between those films which did so cheaply and unconvincingly – and which were often compared as a consequence with ten–twenty–thirty cent theatre (Neale 1993a: 71) – and those which did so expensively and plausibly, within the economic and aesthetic frameworks provided by modified melodrama, sensation melodrama, and also by what around the turn of the century was being called 'new melodrama', which was associated in particular with David Belasco and William Gillette, and which was essentially a further step in the well-made direction (Gerould 1983: 24–7; Marker 1975).[8]

It is clear by the turn of the century that melodrama had become what Singer calls a 'cluster concept' (1992: 1). It is also clear that it had become what might be called a cluster form, a form marked by a number of distinct aesthetic features and traditions, all of which found their way into the cinema and many of which continue to be drawn on today.[9] Instances of 'the melodramatic' run the gamut from the villainy perpetrated by Dracula, Darth

Vader and the Terminator, to Marylee Hadlee's dionysiac dance in *Written on the Wind*, Indiana Jones's hair's breadth escapes, the tableau-like situation caused by the (melodramatic) train crash in *The Greatest Show on Earth* (1952), the chariot race in *Ben-Hur*, the pathos of Lisa's fate in *Letter from an Unknown Woman*, the horror of Marion Crane's fate in *Psycho*, and the excitement caused by John McClane's actions in *Die Hard*. Instances of 'melodrama' run the gamut from horror films to thrillers to westerns, from woman's films to war films to action-adventure in general.

Many of these points were made some time ago by Michael Walker (1982), though they seem to have been lost as the standard account has taken hold. The genealogical aspects of Walker's account are similar to the account I have given here. As far as genre is concerned, Walker distinguishes between two basic categories, 'Action melodramas – swashbucklers, war stories, westerns, crime thrillers, adventure stories – in which the basic story is concerned with the hero or heroes in conflict with the villains/the enemy/the bad guys/a hostile environment . . . and in which the "love interest" is to a greater or lesser extent peripheral' (ibid.: 16), and 'Melodramas of passion, in which the concern is not with the external dynamic of action but with the internal traumas of passion' (ibid.: 17), and which are exemplified, among others, by the woman's film.[10] I have no real quarrel with this. All I would emphasize is that the film industry and most contemporary reviewers tended to equate melodrama with the genres of action rather than passion, probably because they contain more of melodrama's traditional – and 'popular' – ingredients. All I would add is that while lip service has from time to time been paid within Film Studies to the multi-generic nature of nineteenth-century melodrama and to the multi-generic nature of its cinematic heritage, the standard account has tended to founder on the assumption that the woman's film embodies their quintessence. Walker's is one of the few accounts to have taken on board the nature of some of melodrama's basic conventions – its Manichaean structures, for instance, and its dedication to thrills and suspense. It is therefore one of the few accounts to have acknowledged the extent to which the woman's film – and other melodramas of passion – are related to modified and secondary rather than basic and primary nineteenth-century conventions and forms. Most important of all, it is one of the few accounts to have acknowledged the extent to which nineteenth-century melodrama, in all its guises, was both a fundamental progenitor of nearly all of Hollywood's non-comic genres, and a fundamental source of many of its cross-generic features, devices and conventions.

NOTES

1 Other instances include: 'Suspenseful and intriguing mystery melodrama . . . a strongly melodramatic tale concocted in Dashiel Hammett's best style' (*Variety* on *The Maltese Falcon*, 1 October 1941: 9); 'skillfully blended blood-and-thunder

melodrama with psychological overtones' (*Motion Picture Herald* 'Product Digest' on *This Gun for Hire*, 21 May 1942: 563); 'murder meller' (*Variety* on *Double Indemnity*, 26 April 1944: 12); 'psychological melodrama' (*Rob Wagner's Script* on *Gaslight*, 15 July 1944: 24); 'eerie murder melodrama of the London gaslight era' (*Variety* on *Hangover Square*, 17 January 1945: 13); 'socko melodrama loaded with suspense and tension' (*Variety* on *The Killers*, 7 August 1946: 15); 'prison meller' (*Variety* on *Brute Force*, 18 June 1947: 8); 'gangster melodrama' (*Variety* on *Key Largo*, 7 July 1948: 6); 'class melodrama' (*Variety* on *The Snake Pit*, 3 November 1948: 11); 'documentary melodrama' (*Motion Picture Herald* 'Product Digest' on *He Walked by Night* (1948), 13 November 1948: 4381); 'Brutally taut melodrama, dripping with blood, decorated with corpses, gunplay, slugging matches and psychiatry' (*Film Daily* on *White Heat*, 26 August 1949: 12); 'crime melodrama' (*New York Times* on *The Big Heat*, 15 October 1953); and 'Hardboiled private eye meller' (*Variety* on *Kiss Me Deadly*, 20 April 1955: 6). For further examples, see Neale (1993a: 70, 71, 78 n. 28, and 79 n. 38 and n. 41).

2 It is worth pointing out that Hitchcock himself used the term in this way. In his 'Lecture at Columbia University', which was originally delivered in 1939 and which has subsequently been published in Sidney Gottlieb's book *Hitchcock and Hitchcock*, he is recorded as saying that 'melodrama was the original mainstay of motion picture material, on account of its obvious physical action and physical situation. After all, the words "motion picture" mean action and movement' (1995: 268–9). This is consonant with the way he uses the term elsewhere in Gottlieb's book (ibid.: 124, 130, 135, 197, 217, 259). It is also consonant with the way other Hollywood directors used the term. In an interview in McCarthy and Flynn's book *Kings of the Bs*, Phil Karlson refers to the 'melodramas' he made in the early 1950s (1975: 337). And in an interview in *The Velvet Light Trap* with McGilligan, Weiner and Bruce (1975), Raoul Walsh was asked what kinds of stories he liked to direct. 'Adventure and melodramas', he replied. 'Why melodrama?' 'I think you have got to do something like that to keep the people in the theater interested – mystery, violence, chase.' When asked if he ever wanted to direct love stories, he replied, 'Love Stories? No' (ibid.: 18).

3 Within this context, it is worth drawing attention to a specific brand of American Naturalism, a brand which combined a Naturalist version of Neo-Darwinism with the conventions of contemporary melodrama, and which is perhaps best exemplified by the novels and stories of Jack London, Rex Beach and James Oliver Curwood. All three provided source material for a cycle of 'Northwest melodramas' (adventure films set in the Klondike and the Yukon) in the late 1910s and 1920s. London and Curwood also provided source material for an overlapping cycle of 'dog melodramas', adventure films centred on the likes of Rin-Tin-Tin, Silverstreak and Braveheart, whose origins lay in London's *White Fang*. Examples of the former include *North Wind's Malice* (1920), *The Golden Snare* (1921), *The Barrier* (1926) and *The Wolf Hunters* (1926). Examples of the latter include *Where the North Begins* (1923), *White Fang* (1923), *Baree, Son of Kazan* (1927) and *The Snarl of Hate* (1927). 'Melodrama', 'Northwest melodrama', 'Northwoods melodrama' and 'dog melodrama' were the contemporary terms used most often to describe these films.

4 *Stella Dallas* is described by the *Motion Picture Herald* as 'undiluted melodrama aimed straight at the lachrymal glands' (31 July 1937: 36), *The Toy Wife* by *Variety* as 'an old-fashioned melo' (25 May 1938: 17), *Forgotten Women* by *Film Daily* as 'a little over-melodramatic' (11 June 1949: 6), *A Life of Her Own* by the *Motion Picture Herald* 'Product Digest' as 'a melodrama aimed straight at the tear-ducts' (12 August 1950: 433), *Hilda Crane* by *Variety* as 'a repeat on a long line of melodramas' (2 May 1956:

11), and *Another Time, Another Place* by *Variety* as 'A Triangle melodrama set in wartime Britain' (23 April 1958: 6).

5 These definitions and distinctions are shared not just by contemporary reviewers, but also by early historians of the cinema like Hampton ([1931] 1970: 31, 41–2, 104, 342), and by those writing on film from a non- or pre-Film Studies point of view, like Hurst (1979: 2, 16, 22), Mast (1973: 5) and Mordden (1988: 251), and by historians of the theatre and early film like Fell ([1974] 1986) and Vardac (1949).

6 It is worth comparing this with the list of elements provided in Michael Allen's forthcoming book on D. W. Griffith. These elements are 'antithesis' (the division of characters, moral values, forms of behaviour and thematic material into bipolar opposites); 'hyperbole' (the maximizing of antitheses, emotions and forms of stylistic and dramatic expression); 'stereotype' (the repetitive permutation of a rigid, limited and absolute set of roles and characteristics); 'coincidence' (which can often give rise to forms of surprise); 'mystery' (the extent to which patterns of events and coincidence create the impression of hidden forces at work in the fictional world); and 'poetic justice' (the providential working out of events). For Allen, the features marked by antithesis, in particular, are susceptible to complication if not outright reversal; and for him, the device that binds many of these elements together in Griffith's films, at least, is recognition.

7 In addition to those already cited, see James (1980) and Kendrick (1991: 126–7) on the first of these topics, Fell ([1974] 1986: 15–16), Moses ([1925] 1964: 292–305) and Nasaw (1993: 36–7) on the second, and Booth (1965: 182), Fell ([1974] 1986: 17), Moses ([1925] 1964: 305–8) and Singer (1990: 95–6) on the third. Moses, a source for Booth and a precursor of Rahill in this regard, wrote that 'by outdoing melodrama the moving picture has been one of the agents to kill melodrama of the violent kind' in the theatre ([1925] 1964: 213).

8 As Sumiko Higashi (1990, 1991) has pointed out, when the DeMilles, Belasco and the Jesse L. Lasky Feature Play Company wished to 'legitimate the Feature Film as Art', they turned among other things to the 'reformulated' melodramas of the DeMilles and Belasco themselves. As John C. Tibbetts (1985: 53–110) has pointed out, they were by no means alone. It is worth in this context citing an advertisement placed in the *Moving Picture World* for Monopol's *Temptations of the Great City* (1911) (15 July 1911: 47). The advertisement claims that the film is 'A High Class Melodrama': 'No Suicides, No Murders, No Hold-Ups, No Kidnapping, but still a good strong Melodrama.' It also worth citing director Frank Borzage, who in 1922 was willing and able to write as follows:

> As for melodrama, it is a vastly belittled type of entertainment. Of course the old melodrama, the type disparagingly referred to as 'ten, twenty, thirty,' contained little merit beside its ability to thrill. There was no characterisation except for that which arose from the situations themselves. Situations created character, true to the rule of melodrama. But today in the pictures we have the old melodramatic situations fitted out with true characterisations.
>
> (Milne 1922: 116)

9 Aside from obvious instances like *Die Hard* and *Speed*, it is worth drawing attention here to a number of recent films – like *Blue Velvet* (1986) and *Fargo* (1996) – which combine a highly traditional Manichaean structure with a modern deadpan tone and a modern, or 'postmodern', sense of irony and possible pastiche.

10 For discussions of passion and pathos in the woman's film and in melodramas of passion in general, see Affron (1982) and Neale (1986).

Part III

HOLLYWOOD'S GENRES
Theory, industry and history

6

GENRE THEORY

During the course of previous chapters, theories about a number of individual genres have been identified, outlined and discussed. 'Genre theory', however, is by no means confined to the analysis of individual genres, nor is it restricted to the consideration of these genres in isolation one from another. Just as Hollywood has always produced an array of genres, so genre theory has always concerned itself with ideas applicable, at least in principle, to all Hollywood's genres or to its generic array as a whole. The extent to which the range of genres actually focused on in theories of this kind remains partial and selective, hence the extent to which the theories themselves provide an accurate picture of Hollywood's output will be discussed at greater length in Chapter 7. Here, I want to consider these theories in more detail. They tend to fall into two basic groups – those which deal with the aesthetic components and characteristics of genres, and those which deal with their social and cultural significance.

AESTHETIC THEORIES

Most aesthetic theories of genre take as their starting point the issues of repetition and variation, similarity and difference, and the extent to which the elements repeated and varied are simple or complex. As noted in Chapter 1, most modern conceptions of genre derive from Romanticism, and Romantic attitudes to genre were largely hostile. This hostility was directed not just at the putatively routine, formulaic and impersonal nature of genres, but also, as a corollary, at their putative lack of creativity, originality and individuality. In consequence, the element of repetition inherent in all genres was stressed, along with the allegedly simple – or simple-minded – nature of the conventions, meanings, structures and characters they were held to embody or contain. While genre texts were more or less 'all the same', conventions were thought of as clichés, meanings as transparent and impoverished, structures as formulae, and characters as one-dimensional stereotypes. As also noted in Chapter 1, the conceptions of genre underlying these attitudes were shared by most of the critics and theorists who later wished to contest them. As a result, those who wrote in praise of Hollywood's genres often found themselves using the same epithets and concepts as those who did not. For example, Schatz's proposition that 'a genre film . . . involves familiar, essentially one-dimensional characters acting out a predictable story pattern within a familiar setting' (Schatz 1981: 6) is little different from Sutherland's critical description of 'genre fiction' cited in Chapter 1.

Schatz goes on to argue that the world of the genre film 'is predetermined and essentially intact. The narrative components of a non-genre film – the characters, setting, plot, techniques, etc. – assume their significance as they are integrated into the individual film itself. In a genre film, however, these components have prior significance as elements of some generic formula' (1981: 10). This formula is established by repetition. Generic elements are repeated. So too are the 'formal, narrative, and thematic' contexts in which they conventionally occur (ibid.). Repetition also helps generate audience knowledge, allowing viewers to weigh a 'film's variations against the genre's preordained, value-laden narrative system' (ibid.).

These propositions are standard, and some of them clearly shed light on important aspects of Hollywood's genres. Schatz is right to stress the prior significance of elements and their contexts in westerns, musicals, gangster films and the other genres with which he is concerned. He is right to stress the importance of audience knowledge. And he is right to stress the possibility of 'variations', a point I shall return to in a moment. However, in addition to recalling the points made earlier in this book regarding genre and non-genre films, I would wish to dispute the idea that characters in genre films as Schatz defines them are always one-dimensional, story patterns always predictable, and settings always familiar. I would also wish to question the degree of emphasis he places on the 'predetermined' nature of genres and their worlds, and in general to temper the emphasis he places on repetition and sameness as opposed to variation and change.

In maintaining that characters in genre films are one-dimensional, Schatz tends to conflate characters with their generic roles, and to underestimate the extent to which these roles permit or even necessitate more than one set of traits and dimensions. For instance even if, as he himself is at pains to argue, most westerns require a protagonist capable of 'mediating' between 'the community and the wilderness' (1981: 51), 'savagery and civilization' (ibid.: 47), and the other oppositions that are said to constitute the genre's basic thematic and dramatic material, that protagonist must possess at least two sets of traits, and these traits must exist in actual or potential conflict with one another. If in addition this role is embodied in characters who, like Yellowleg (Brian Keith) in *The Deadly Companions* (1961) and Howie Kemp (James Stewart) in *The Naked Spur* (1952), possess obsessive or neurotic personalities, these traits are augmented by others which may be generically inessential, but which can nevertheless be found in at least some of the genre's films. Similarly, if biopics require protagonists who possess talent and ambition on the one hand and humility or hubris on the other, two sets of traits are as likely as one. If, as well, as in *Nixon* and *Funny Girl*, success in the protagonist's principal field of endeavour is counterpointed with ultimate failure either in that same field or in another, a further set of traits – a further dimension of character – is clearly possible. Moreover, if the western and the biopic combine, as they do in *Custer of the West* and *The Lawless Breed* (1952), the number of generically requisite traits and the number of dimensional possibilities increase still further.

Another way of thinking about this issue is in terms of what Cawelti calls 'stereotype vitalization' (1976: 11). As far as character is concerned, Cawelti argues that stereotype vitalization tends to take two basic forms. 'The first is the stereotypical character who also embodies qualities that seem contrary to the stereotypical traits' (ibid.). As examples he cites Sherlock Holmes, and the characters played in westerns by Gary Cooper. Just as Holmes combines the traits of 'the supreme man of reason' with those of the 'dreamy romantic poet', so Cooper 'is typically a man of violence, enormously skilled with guns and fists and faster on the draw than anyone else; yet he also plays a character of great shyness and gentleness' (ibid.). In this respect, as Cawelti points out, Cooper's characters are similar to the protagonists in western novels like *Destry Rides Again*, *Shane*, and *The Virginian*, all of whom could be said to exemplify the point about potentially contradictory sets of generically determined traits made above. The second form of vitalization is 'the addition of significant touches of human complexity or frailty to a stereotypical figure' (ibid.: 11–12). Cawelti cites the traits of comic ageing assigned the characters played by Joel McCrea and Randolph Scott in *Ride the High Country*. The traits of neurotic obsession assigned Yellowleg and Howie Kemp clearly serve as examples as well.

The degree to which story patterns in genres are predictable, meanwhile, depends in part on what is meant by story pattern and in part on what is meant by predictable. If 'story pattern' is taken to refer to the shape of the story in its broadest sense, it is clear that the violent climaxes of war films and westerns and the happy resolutions of romantic comedies are generically requisite and therefore predictable. However, the paths to these climaxes and resolutions vary considerably. Whatever the degree of adherence to pre-established formulae, the unfolding of any individual war film or any individual romantic comedy is therefore always far less predictable at the moment by moment level. Moreover, the story patterns of the war film or the western permit death or defeat as well as victory and survival, and some genres, like romantic drama, can appropriately end either happily, with the central protagonists united, or unhappily, with the protagonists separated from one another in some way. So even at the broader narrative level, predictability is rarely total. In addition, although specific cycles have their predictable characteristics, the story patterns of genres like the social problem film and science fiction have been historically less fixed than those of the western, the war film, romantic comedy, or even romantic drama. And in the case of the western and the war film, as we have seen in Chapter 3, these patterns are in any case less fixed than critics and theorists have tended to argue. As we have also seen in Chapter 3, the predictable rise and fall pattern of the gangster film has been subject to historically distinct forms of motivation. As a result, the ways in which the pattern has been presented have varied too, depending on the extent to which the gangster's fall has been preceded by scenes of remorse, regret and redemption or by scenes of unrepentant defiance. In all these ways, predictability is as varied and as multi-dimensional as genres themselves, not an absolute quality, but a matter of degree.

Meanwhile, it is clearly the case that genres like the social problem film, the musical, the biopic, and most forms of comedy do not require particular physical settings. It is therefore also clearly the case that settings in genres can only be characterized as familiar if a number of genres are ignored or if the term 'setting' is redefined. Before insisting himself on a distinction between genres that entail specific settings and those that do not, and before using this distinction to found a socio-cultural theory of Hollywood's genres (see pp. 221–2), this is precisely what Schatz proceeds to do. 'Each genre film', he writes

> incorporates a specific cultural context . . . in the guise of a familiar *social community*. This generic context is more than the physical setting, which some genre critics have argued defines the genre as such. The American frontier or the urban underworld is more than a physical locale which identifies the Western or the gangster film; it is a cultural milieu where inherent thematic conflicts are animated, intensified, and resolved by familiar characters and patterns of action. Although all drama establishes a community that is disturbed by conflict, in the genre film both the community and the conflict have been conventionalized. Ultimately, our familiarity with any genre seems to depend less on recognizing a specific setting than on recognizing certain dramatic conflicts that we associate with specific patterns of action and character relationships.
>
> (Shatz 1981: 21; emphasis in original)

Aside from highlighting the extent to which Schatz here contradicts his earlier comments on settings, two points are worth noting, one local and specific, the other more general. The first is that the gangster film is by no means always set in the 'urban underworld'. As noted in Chapter 3, there have been several cycles of rural gangster films too. The second is that although the notion of generically specific cultural milieux is a useful one, it cannot simply substitute for the concept of setting as such. The cultural milieu of rural gangster films is similar in a number of ways to that of urban gangster films: both feature professional criminals and professional representatives of law and order; both feature physical forms of dramatic conflict; and both entail the representation of illegal activity. But their physical settings are different, and this difference inflects the ways in which the cultural milieu is represented. From the 1920s on, urban gangster films tend to focus on racketeering and on what Walter Lippmann ([1931] 1967) called 'service crime' – bootlegging, gambling, the provision of drugs and the like. Their criminal protagonists tend to acquire a great deal of wealth and power and this is displayed in ways which draw on contemporary iconographies of urban luxury. Rural gangster films tend to focus on armed robbery. Their criminal protagonists acquire money, but rarely wealth or power. Although on occasion sporting fashionable clothes, they are rarely seen as living in luxury or as moving in powerful or fashionable social circles. As a result, the cultural milieux differ in detail in a number of ways, and these differences have been associated with distinct generic attitudes and meanings. While urban and rural gangsters share the same basic status as outlaws and as social outsiders, the former are often shown acquiring the trappings, and sometimes also the status, of an insider in ways which persistently contrast with what happens to the latter. In consequence, although depicting crimes of personal enrichment rather than any form of service crime, rural gangster film has always been able to draw more consistently and unequivocally on the image of what Hobsbawm (1969) called the 'social bandit' – the outlaw who represents or fights for the aspirations of the poor, the oppressed, and the socially disenfranchised – than its urban counterpart.

For Schatz, the world of each and every Hollywood genre and of each and every genre film is 'predetermined' by convention. Narrative patterns, character types and cultural milieux are for each genre film fixed in advance. Thus although he seems to acknowledge the possibility of variation and change, these are only ever treated as additional extras, inessential options. Genres for Schatz are closed and continuous rather open and intermittent systems. That is why he rarely acknowledges the existence of hybrids. That is why the array of genres he discusses rarely appear to interact with one another. That is why rates of production appear rarely, if ever, to fluctuate. And that is why external events and industrial changes only impinge on genres in catastrophic and exceptional ways (as in the demise of the 'classical' gangster film, discussed in Chapter 3, or the demise of the studio system, discussed in Chapter 7).

All this is evident in Schatz's theory of 'generic development'. Citing film theorist Christian Metz (1974: 148–61) and art historian Henri Focillon ([1934] 1942), Schatz puts forward the view that genres pass through a number of 'stages'. At its earliest stage 'a genre tends to exploit the cinematic medium *as a medium* . . . At this stage, genre films transmit a certain idealized cultural self-image with as little "formal interference" as possible.' Next, 'Once a genre has passed through its experimental stage where its conventions have been established, it enters into its classical stage. We might consider this stage as one of *formal transparency.* Both the narrative formula and the film medium work together to transmit and reinforce that genre's social message.' Finally, once 'the genre's straightforward message has "saturated" the audience . . . the genre evolves into what Focillon terms the age of refinement. As a genre's classic conventions are refined and eventually parodied and subverted, its transparency gradually gives way to *opacity*: we no longer look *through* the form . . . rather we look *at* the *form itself* to examine and appreciate its structure and its cultural appeal.' In this way, genres progress from 'transparency to opacity – from straightforward storytelling to self-conscious formalism' (1981: 38; emphasis in original).

There are a number of problems with this theory. As Alan Williams has pointed out, 'Schatz locates this shift to opacity *within individual genres*, such that a "new" genre in the 1980s would have to go through a "classical" stage before evolving into self-conscious formalism' (1984: 123; emphasis in original). There is little evidence that this is the case. If anything, new 1980s genres like the sword-and-sorcery film (and new 1970s genres like the Vietnam war film) are highly self-conscious. The same is true, as Williams goes on to point out, of many 1910s and 1920s genres too: 'One can find self-conscious Westerns, such as Fairbanks' *Wild and Woolly*, as early as the late teens. In fact, the entire mid-to-late silent cinema seems remarkably "formalistic"' (ibid.: 123–4). A similar point has been made by Gallagher, who argues that a feature of the early western was its 'Hyperconsciousness' (1986: 205), and in general that

> 'Self-consciousness' is too readily assumed to have come to movies only in reaction against Hollywood's so-called 'classic codes' . . . It is perhaps natural that people today, attuned to contemporary film styles and only vaguely acquainted with the past, should feel they are on to something new when in an ostentatiously revisionist film by Robert Altman (*McCabe and Mrs Miller*, 1971, or *Buffalo Bill and the Indians*, 1976) they perceive references to motifs and conventions from other westerns made twenty or thirty years earlier and thus cast forcibly into a 'straight man's' role for the revisionist's lampoon. But they forget that even such putatively naive classics as *Stagecoach* were similarly perceived by audiences in 1939; indeed *Stagecoach* in particular is a virtual anthology of gags, motifs, conventions, scenes, situations, tricks and characters drawn from past westerns, thus consciously revisiting not only the old West but old westerns as well, and reinterpreting at the same time these elements for modern minds.
>
> (Gallagher 1986: 208)

If anything, he concludes, a 'superficial glance at film history suggests cyclicism rather than evolution' as a more accurate theory of generic development (ibid.).

Another point made by Williams is that Schatz's theory locates change and the causes of change within genres themselves rather than within 'the film-making system or the social context' (1984: 59). In fact, despite the points Schatz himself makes regarding the role of the Second World War in the inhibition of self-consciousness in the 1940s war film and the role of independent production in the development of a general generic self-consciousness in the early 1970s, the role of the 'real world' in the development of genres is explicitly argued to diminish once the genre itself is established: 'The subject matter of any film story is derived from certain "real-world" characters, conflicts, settings, and so on. But once the story is repeated and refined into a formula, its basis in experience gradually gives way to its own internal narrative logic' (Schatz 1981: 36). I would make two responses to this. The first is that the impact of the 'real world' is necessarily continuous. Its influence can be detected even where genres themselves are at their most self-consciously self-referential. Schatz cites as examples of formalistic opacity a number of 'self-reflexive' post-war musicals – *The Barkleys of Broadway* (1949), *An American in Paris* (1951), *Singin' in the Rain* (1952) and *It's Always Fair Weather*. He also cites a number of 1950s westerns. What he does not do is to link these instances of formal and thematic 'sophistication' to Hollywood's – self-conscious – cultivation of an 'adult' image in the wake of a series of post-war crises (declining audiences, government investigations, the demise of vertical integration, competition from television and other leisure pursuits, and so on) (Klinger 1994b). My second response, though, is to argue that this impact is always mediated through existing institutions, conventions and forms, and that there is never a point – even at the beginning – at which real-world characters, conflicts and settings find their way directly onto the screen. There are always genres. There are always aesthetic forms. And they always possess their own logic. Even when films were new, they deployed generic and aesthetic conventions from photography, from the theatre, from popular stories, and from numerous other forms of art, entertainment and representation.[1]

This is a theoretical as well as an historical point. It relates to arguments put forward by the Russian Formalists, who maintained that artistic forms and conventions possessed their own irreducible characteristics, and who themselves put forward a theory of generic development. Here, individual genres are placed within wider generic and aesthetic formations. Dominant genres – and dominant devices within these genres – are perpetually changed and displaced in a process of contestation and change (Eikenbaum [1927] 1978; Erlich 1981; Tynyanov [1927] 1978). According to Viktor Shklovsky, such displacements occur according to a principle known as 'the canonization of the junior branch': 'When the "canonized" art form reaches an impasse, the way is paved for the infiltration of the elements of non-canonized art, which by this time have managed to evolve new artistic devices' (Erlich 1981: 260).

A different concept of generic evolution is clearly at stake here. It is a concept which seeks to emphasize discontinuities and breaks rather than

213

smooth, organic development. And it is a concept which insists on the interplay between canonic and non-canonic genres and forms, which takes account of the transience of generic hierarchies, which stresses the role of hybridization in the formation and dissolution of genres, and which refuses to prescribe the conditions for generic impasse, or to specify the mechanisms by which non-canonic genres find a place within generic formations or a position of dominance within them. However, although I have tried elsewhere to apply some of these ideas to Hollywood genres (Neale 1990a: 60–1), it is clear that a number of problems remain. One is that 'dominance' is hard to measure: numerical dominance is clearly different from box-office dominance, and box-office dominance is clearly different from critical approbation, as the B western and the post-1960s blockbuster both make plain. Another is that traces of a notion of stages can still be detected, as is readily apparent in Jauss's summary of Formalist theory:

> the historical alternation of the dominating genre manifests itself in the three steps of canonization, automation, and reshuffling. Successful genres . . . gradually lose their effective power through continual reproduction; they are forced to the periphery by new genres often arising from a 'vulgar' stratum if they cannot be reanimated through a restructuring (be it through the playing up of previously suppressed themes or methods, or through the taking up of materials or the taking-over of the functions of other genres).
>
> (Jauss 1982: 106)

While one can see how this theory might apply to the reanimation of the A western in the late 1930s, its restructuring in the 1950s and 1960s, and its eventual displacement by space opera and other forms of action-adventure in the 1980s and 1990s, it can account neither for the demise of the traditional woman's film (which had nothing to do with 'continual reproduction', and everything to do with the demise of the 'feminine mystique', the advent of the 1960s women's movement, and Hollywood's changing perception of its audience), nor for the revival of the biopic in the late 1930s (a genre which was neither new nor vulgar, but which helped Hollywood generate an aura of respectability at a time when, as Muscio points out (1997: 129–37, 141–72), it was under intense government scrutiny). More importantly, the 'three steps' to which Jauss refers are in the end all too reminiscent of 'the evolutionary model of growth, flowering and decay' which he himself rightly rejects as teleological (1982: 88).

In recognition of some of these problems, Rick Altman has offered a different view of genre formation and genre development. Taking his cue from Jameson (1975), he argues in a series of different publications ([1984] 1986, 1987, 1996a: 283–5) that one can distinguish between 'semantic' and 'syntactic' approaches to genre and genres:

214

While there is anything but general agreement on the exact frontier separating semantic from syntactic views, we can as a whole distinguish between generic definitions which depend on a list of common traits, attitudes, characters, shots, locations, sets, and the like – thus stressing the semantic elements which make up the genre – and definitions which play up instead certain constitutive relationships between unde-signated placeholders – relationships which might be called the genre's fundamental syntax. The semantic approach thus stresses the genre's building blocks, while the syntactic view privileges the structures into which they are arranged.

(Altman 1987: 95)

He then goes on to suggest that these two approaches are complementary, not mutually exclusive, to argue that every genre possesses both semantic traits and syntactic characteristics, and to propose in addition that

When genres are redefined in terms of their semantic and syntactic dimensions, new life is breathed into the notion of genre history. Instead of simply enumerating the minor variations developed by various studios or directors within a general, fundamentally stable generic framework, genre history based on a semantic/syntactic hypothesis would take as its object three interrelated concerns: 1) the introduction and disappearance of basic semantic elements (e.g. the musical's deployment of a succession of styles – from operetta and chansonnier crooning and opera to swing and folk to rock and nos-talgia); 2) the development and abandoning of specific syntactic solu-tions (e.g., the move from the early sound period identification of music with sadness, usually in three-person plots assuring a sad, solitary odd-man-out, to the post-1932 emphasis on music as a celebration of a joyous union of opposites, in the culture as well as the couple); 3) the ever-changing relationship between semantic and syntactic aspects of the genre (e.g., the way in which diegetic music, the musical's semantic element *par excellence*, is transformed from a flashy but unin-tegrated element of spectacle into a signifier of success and a device for reversal of the traditional image-over-sound hierarchy).

(Altman 1987: 97–8)

It is clear that the approach that Altman takes here possesses considerable heuristic value, as the examples cited above and as the following passage from an earlier text make plain:

When we analyze the large variety of wartime films that portray the Japanese or Germans as villains, we tend to have recourse to extra-filmic events in order to explain particular characterizations. We thus miss the extent to which films like *All Through the Night* (Vincent Sherman, 1942), *Sherlock Holmes and the Voice of Terror* (John Rawlins, 1942), or the serial *The Winslow Boy* (Anthony Asquith, 1948) simply transfer to a new set of semantic elements the righteous cops-punish-criminals syntax that the gangster genre of the early thirties had turned to starting with *G-Men* (William Keighley, 1935) . . . Or take the development of the science fiction film. At first defined only by a relatively stable science fiction semantics, the genre began borrowing the syntactic relationships previously established by the horror film, only to move in recent years toward the syntax of the western.

(Altman [1984] 1986: 34–5)

However, as Altman himself acknowledges, questions remain. To what extent, for example, is music in the musical (by no means all of which, incidentally, is diegetic, as a glance at any number of dance sequences in 1940s and 1950s musicals will confirm) a semantic rather than a syntactic building-block? There is no doubt that music and different styles of music possess their own semantic charge. There is no doubt that music can function, usually in combination with other elements, as a meaningful mark of the genre. And there is no doubt that most musicals position their music within broader syntactic structures. However, music itself possesses its own syntactical features, and passages of music in musical films constitute syntactic building-blocks too. Indeed, one of the features of the genre's syntactic history is the extent to which Busby Berkeley's experiments in the stacking of musical numbers towards the end of many of his 1930s films were abandoned when Berkeley left Warners to work at MGM in 1939 (see Rubin 1993).

Similar issues are raised by gags in comedies and shoot-outs in westerns. Are these to be regarded as semantic units, syntactic units, or both? At first sight, as 'constitutive elements', they appear to be the former. However, a number of the earliest comedies consisted, simply, of gags. Does this mean that the genre lacked a syntax? Or does it mean that the syntax of the gag – a structure of escalating destruction, disorder or discomfiture – provided the genre's syntax as well? Meanwhile, while it is plausible to suggest that a shoot-out lacking any kind of syntactic context might be regarded as an autonomous semantic unit, it is also plausible to suggest that a western lacking a shoot-out (or at least some kind of violent contest) might be considered syntactically deficient.

As Altman suggests, then, the 'frontier' between semantics and syntax is by no means always clear-cut, and this can be a problem when seeking to use the concepts he proposes. Another problem – a problem with the exposition of these concepts, if not with the concepts themselves – is that the range of genres Altman uses to explain them tends to be rather narrow: the western and the musical predominate; the biblical epic, the teenpic, romantic drama and the social problem film are all conspicuous by their absence. However, it should be recognized that the boundary between semantics and syntax is acknowledged to be blurred in linguistics itself (Crystal 1971: 234–9; Leech 1974: 178–201; Lyons 1977, I: 114–19). And Altman is at least willing to refer to the disaster film and the caper film, if only to contrast them with the western and the musical ([1984] 1986: 38). Ultimately, the strengths and weaknesses of the 'semantic/syntactic approach' can only be discovered by trying to use it more widely. (See Grant 1998 for an example.) What is valuable about it as an hypothesis is that it is premissed on the importance of history, on the recognition of heterogeneity, and on the possibility of difference, variation, and change. To that extent, it shares a number of features with ideas put forward by Jauss (1982), by Neale (1980, 1999) and by Cohen (1986), for all of whom genres, literary or cinematic, are best conceived of as processes.

As Jauss has pointed out, 'as soon as one is prepared to desubstantiate the classical concept of genre', as soon as one is prepared to recognize the transience of genres, to deprive them of eternal or essential features, and to conceive these features instead as both historically provisional and empirically diverse, they begin to take on a 'processlike appearance' (1982: 79). This point is echoed by Cohen, who argues that 'since each genre is composed of texts that accrue, the grouping is a process, not a determinate category. Genres are open categories. Each member alters the genre by adding, contradicting, or changing constituents, especially those of members most closely related to it' (1986: 204). In fact, as Jauss makes clear, this process is manifest not just in the way texts and their constitutents are grouped, but also in the way extra-textual norms and expectations shift and change, in the way labels and names are altered and redefined, and in the way each of these aspects of genre interact with one another over time:

> the relationship between the individual text and the series of texts formative of a genre presents itself as a process of the continual founding and altering of horizons. The new text evokes for the reader (listener) the horizon of expectations and 'rules of the game' familiar to him from earlier texts, which as such can then be varied, extended, corrected, but also transformed, crossed out, or simply reproduced.
>
> (Jauss 1982: 88)

In addition to changes in the meaning of generic terms like 'war film' (as noted in Chapter 3), and to those changes in the syntactic features of the early musical referred to in Altman above, one might cite here the extent to which the 1930s social problem film was more often about (and thus, in terms of horizons of expectation, more likely to be about) criminality, urban deprivation, legal injustice and political corruption than racial prejudice, and that in the 1950s the reverse was the case. At a more specific level, at the level of the individual text, one might cite the extent to which *Titanic* (1998) seeks to abolish the hitherto established hierarachy between the contemporary block-buster's romance and action/disaster plots, or the extent to which *Halloween* in the late 1970s sought to combine in a single figure the horror film's hitherto separate forms of psychological and supernatural monstrosity.

There can be a danger in citing specific examples like these of overemphasizing unusually innovative or influential features and texts, hence of underestimating the elements of variation and difference present in every text. While influential innovations are historically important, they can give a misleading picture of Hollywood's output. Routine differences, 'minor' variations and uninfluential innovations are important too, if only because they always actualize (and thus exhaust) one particular set of generic possibilities, and if only because they always contribute in some way to the generic corpus, and to the available repertoire of generic constituents and generic expectations. Thus *Before I Hang* (1940) and *The Man with Nine Lives* (1940) are very similar to *The Man They Could Not Hang* (1939), and *The Man They Could Not Hang* is very similar to *The Walking Dead* (1936). All four star Boris Karloff, and in all four the Karloff character is bent on some form of serial revenge. However, in *The Walking Dead* and *The Man They Could Not Hang* he is brought back to life by another character (rather than created by one, as in *Frankenstein*), whereas in *Before I Hang* and *The Man with Nine Lives* his personality is changed by other means. In *The Walking Dead* he is brought back to life by a scientist, whereas in *Before I Hang*, *The Man With Nine Lives* and *The Man They Could Not Hang* he plays a (medical) scientist himself. The medical activities in which he is involved, and which in the case of *The Man With Nine Lives* and *Before I Hang* help motivate his extreme behaviour, are slightly different. In *Before I Hang* he is maddened by a rejuvenation serum, in *The Man With Nine Lives* he is involved in cryogenics, and in *The Man They Could Not Hang* he is working on restoring life to the dead. Moreover, although the serial acts of aggression and murder in all of these films are themselves repetitive, each killing is differently staged and every victim, of course, is unique. In addition, while the array of horror and science fiction on offer was limited both in scope and in numbers when *Before I Hang*, *The Man With Nine Lives* and *The Man They Could Not Hang* were first released, these films were generically contextualized not only by similar mad-scientist films like *The Return of Dr X* (1939) but also by a number of different trends: straightforwardly supernatural horror films like *The Mummy's Hand* (1940), old–dark–house horror-comedies like *The Ghost Breakers* (1940), science fiction adventure serials like *Buck Rogers* (1939) and science fiction spy films like *Television Spy* (1939) (itself part of a short-lived 'television' cycle). And of course they were contextualized in a different way by numerous detective films, musicals, dramas (domestic, romantic and social), comedies (slapstick, romantic, domestic and occasionally satirical) and westerns (A and B, singing

218

and otherwise), a number of historical adventure films, and several war films and biopics, among others, as well.

These examples serve to illustrate the points made by Jauss and by Cohen. They also help make a number of others. The first is that the repertoire of generic conventions available at any one point in time is always *in* play rather than simply being *re*-played, even in the most repetitive of films, genres and cycles (the term 'repertoire' here is derived from Fowler 1982). That is why it is so difficult to define genres in anything other than basic terms (a war film is a film about the waging of war; a detective film is a film about the investigative activities of a detective; a musical is a film with numerous passages of singing and dancing). More elaborate definitions always seem to throw up exceptions. The second point is that any generic repertoire always exceeds, and thus can never be exhausted by, any single film. This is in part because the norms, conventions, and traditions of which each repertoire consists are multiple, and in part because some of them are mutually incompatible: as science fiction, mad-doctor films are fundamentally different from serial adventure films, just as cavalry westerns are different from westerns centred on sheriffs and towns.

The third point, on the other hand, is that generic repertoires themselves can be at least partly compatible: mad-doctor films combine some of the elements of horror and some of the elements of science fiction, just as old-dark-house films combine some of the elements of horror and some of the elements of comedy. In this way, hybrid films, cycles and genres are formed, and in this way not only do 'the members of a generic classification have multiple relational possibilities with each other' (Cohen 1986: 210), they also have multiple relational possibilities with members of other classifications as well. This in turn is possible, as a final point, both because, as Cohen points out, genres are not necessarily defined by a single trait, and because, as Bordwell and Thompson ([1979] 1986) have pointed out, generic traits are heterogeneous in kind, which means that traits can be combined simultaneously (as well as sequentially) and that genres can therefore 'cross-breed':[2]

> There is no single principle by which genres can be defined. Some genres are distinguished chiefly by shared subject matter. A science-fiction film is usually about advanced technology, a Western is usually about life on some frontier. Other genres are distinguished by certain objects or settings: a samurai film includes swords, a gangster film usually requires a city. Comedies and disaster films seem to be defined chiefly by a type of story situation. Musicals share only a style of performance, singing and/or dancing. The detective film . . . is partly defined by the plot pattern of an investigation that brings mysterious early causes to light at the climax. The flexibility of genre definitions is shown by the ability of genres to cross-breed freely. You can have a musical Western (*Cat Ballou*) or gangster film (*Bugsy Malone*), a

219

melodrama that is also a mystery (*The Spiral Staircase*), a combination of science-fiction and horror (*Alien*), a science-fiction detective tale (*Blade Runner*), even a horror Western (*Billy the Kid Meets Dracula* [*sic*]).

(Bordwell and Thompson [1979] 1986: 97. For detailed discussion
of specific examples, see Petlewski 1979 and Knee 1994.)

These points necessarily qualify another Russian Formalist idea – the idea that each genre is governed by a single 'dominant' device (Tynyanov [1927] 1978). (Aside from a few remarks in Neale (1990a: 65–6), and Mellencamp's proposal that 'music is the dominant code' in the musical (1990: 195), attempts to apply this idea to Hollywood's genres are few and far between.) They also render the interplay between repetition and difference within and across generic repertoires and corpuses much more complex than many aesthetic theories of genre are willing to recognize. This same complexity can complicate – and sometimes undermine – the tasks set themselves by many socio-cultural theories of genre as well.

SOCIO-CULTURAL THEORIES

Partly, perhaps, because Hollywood's genres have so often been regarded as aesthetically impoverished, genre theory has frequently concerned itself instead with their socio-cultural significance. Basing their claims on the perceived ubiquity, longevity and popularity of genres and of 'genre films', theorists of all kinds have consistently argued that genres are important socio-cultural phenomena and that they perform important socio-cultural functions. Where they differ is in the stances they have taken, stances which can be broadly divided into what Altman (1987) has called 'the ritual approach' and 'the ideological approach'.

The ritual approach was pioneered by Cawelti and is also exemplified by the work of Braudy (1976), McConnell (1976), Sobchack (1982), Wood (1975), Wright (1975) and Schatz (1981, 1983). The term 'ritual' itself derives, in this context, from Henry Nash Smith ([1950] 1971). It was first explicitly used by Schatz, who argued that genres should be seen 'as a form of collective cultural expression' (1981: 13) and hence as vehicles of and for the exploration of ideas, ideals, cultural values and ideological dilemmas central to American society. As Altman points out, these are the principal hallmarks of the ritual approach. They are premissed on the commercial nature of genres and 'formula stories', to use Cawelti's term, and hence on what Cawelti himself was one of the first to formulate as a particular form of 'audience response':

Formulas enable the members of a group to share the same fantasies
. . . [Patterns] that do not perform this function do not become

formulas. When a group's attitudes undergo some change, new formulas arise and existing formulas develop new themes and symbols, because formula stories are created and distributed almost entirely in terms of commercial exploitation. Therefore, allowing for a certain degree of inertia in the process, the production of formulas is largely dependent on audience response. Existing formulas commonly evolve in response to new audience interests.

(Cawelti 1976: 34)

The extent to which Cawelti here elides any distinction between 'fantasies', 'attitudes' and 'interests' will, together with other problems associated with the ritual approach, be discussed in more detail in a moment. In the meantime, Cawelti himself exemplifies his argument by referring to the then-recent 'black-oriented, action-adventure film', a version of 'traditional formulas like the western, the hard-boiled detective story, and the gangster saga' which enabled 'the new black self-consciousness to find expression in conventional forms of fantasy not significantly different in their assumptions and value structures from the sort of adventure stories . . . enjoyed by American audiences for decades' (1976: 35). He concludes by putting forward a number of hypotheses about the relationship between formulas and culture, at least two of which were to become additional cornerstones of the ritual approach. The first is that 'Formula stories affirm existing interests and attitudes' (ibid.: 35), the second that 'Formulas resolve tensions and ambiguities resulting from the conflicting interests of different groups within a culture or from ambiguous attitudes toward particular values. The action of a formula story will tend to move from an expression of tension of this sort to a harmonization of these conflicts' (ibid.).

These hypotheses are adopted and expanded on by Schatz, who links them to his thesis about generic communities and hence to Hollywood's generic array. Each genre, he argues, tends to deal with its own set of socio-cultural issues, ambiguities and conflicts:

> What emerges as a social problem (or dramatic conflict) in one genre is not necessarily a problem in another. Law and order is a problem in the gangster and detective genres, but not in the musical. Conversely, courtship and marriage are problems in the musical but not in the gangster and detective genres. Individualism is celebrated in the detective genre (through the hero's occupation and world view) and in the gangster film (through the hero's career and eventual death), while the principal characters in the musical compromise their individuality in their eventual romantic embrace and thus demonstrate their willingness to be integrated into the social community.
>
> (Schatz 1981: 25)

In this way, genres possess their own individual identity while at the same time belonging to a larger generic – and cultural – system. This generic system is divisible into genres of two basic kinds, genres of 'determinate space' and genres of 'indeterminate space':

In a genre of determinate space (Western, gangster, detective, et al.), we have a symbolic arena of action. It represents a cultural realm in which fundamental values are in a state of sustained conflict. In these genres . . . the contest itself and its necessary arena are 'determinate' – a specific social conflict is violently enacted within a familar locale according to a prescribed system of rules and behavioral codes.

(Schatz 1981: 27)

Because the conflict centres on the nature and control of this arena, space, the setting itself, tends to figure as part of an iconographical system. By contrast,

genres of indeterminate space generally involve a doubled . . . hero in the guise of a romantic couple who inhabit a 'civilized' setting, as in the musical, screwball comedy, and social melodrama. The physical and ideological 'contest' which determines the arena of action in the Western, gangster, and detective genres is not an issue here. Instead, genres of indeterminate space incorporate a civilized, ideologically stable milieu, which depends less upon a heavily coded place than on a highly conventionalized value system. Here conflicts derive not from a struggle for control of the environment, but rather from the struggle of the principal characters to bring their own views into line either with one another's or, more often, in line with that of the larger community.

(Schatz 1981: 27–9)

In addition,

these genres use iconographic conventions to establish a social setting – the proscenium or theater stage with its familiar performers in some musicals, for example, or the repressive small-town community and family home in the melodrama. But because the generic conflicts arise from attitudinal, (generally male–female) oppositions rather than from a physical conflict, the coding in these films tends to be less visual and more ideological and abstract.

(Schatz 1981: 29)

These are suggestive terms and concepts. But there are specific problems with their application as well as more general problems with the ritual approach as a whole. Firstly, it should be noted in passing that Virginia

Wright Wexman has argued that marriage (if not courtship) is 'central' to the western, because dynastic (rather than companionate) marriage is central to the nexus of land, property, patrimony and ethnic dominance that for her lies at the heart of the western's ideology (1993: 67–129). This does not mean that marriage is dramatically central to the western, or that the western is really a genre of indeterminate space. It does mean, though, that elements within it are susceptible to indeterminate generic treatment and the genre as a whole to indeterminate generic hybridity, as we have seen in Chapter 3 and as we shall further see below.

Secondly and more importantly, and even allowing for the fact that he explicitly confines himself to the studio era – he argues in a later book that since then the genre system and its ritual functions have come to an end (1983: 20–28) – the range of genres to which Schatz refers is extremely limited. There is no mention, for example, of the social problem film, comedian comedy, epics and spectacles, horror films or biopics, let alone anything as amorphous as the crime thriller or as protean as action-adventure. While some of these genres can be slotted into the categories Schatz proposes, others cannot, either because hybridization and overlap take place on a regular basis, or simply because the genres themselves do not fit. The biopic and the social problem film, for example, might initially be thought of as genres of indeterminate space. They do not have particular arenas of action; they are not marked by a consistent iconography; and they tend to deal with attitudinal oppositions rather than physical struggles for control of an environment. This is certainly true of biopics like *Dr Erlich's Magic Bullet* (1940) and of social problem films like *Gentleman's Agreement*. But what about biopics like *They Died With Their Boots On* (1941), which features numerous battles, fights and wars, and which culminates in Custer's Last Stand? And what about social problem films like *Dead End* and *Riot in Cell Block 11*, which feature struggles for the control of urban slums and of prison respectively? The categories Schatz has proposed simply cannot be applied here with any consistency.

They Died With Their Boots On is a western as well as a biopic. It is thus an example of generic hybridity. Musical westerns like *Calamity Jane* (1953), *Seven Brides for Seven Brothers* (1954) and *Oklahoma!* (1955) are examples of hybridity too. Given that Schatz himself argues that the western is a genre of determinate space and the musical a genre of indeterminate space, what happens in instances like this? These particular examples suggest that the physical struggles associated with the former give way to the reconcilable oppositions associated with the latter. Musical westerns are therefore perhaps more musical than western. But the settings and the iconography of the western remain, as do a number of its typical antinomies. And in these films especially, the indeterminate aspects of the western, the aspects that centre on marriage and on the differences between dynastic and companionate marriage in particular, come to the fore. Moreover, in most singing westerns, as distinct, perhaps, from most musical westerns, physical conflict remains as well. To suggest for the sake of conceptual consistency that the latter should be excluded from the corpus of westerns and the former from the corpus of musicals would be to ignore important aspects of the genres concerned and, to adopt a quote from Maltby, 'to use generic classification in a very reductive fashion' (1995: 108).

There are other problems too. One is the implication that socio-cultural issues can be neatly parcelled out among and between different genres. Another is the implication that these issues remain the same, and that the production of the genres that deal with them is smoothly continuous. The presence of frontier mythology in a number of war films, adventure films and science fiction films, and its absence from a number of westerns, is an obvious counter to the first. The intermittent production of spectacles and epics in the 1930s and 1940s is an obvious counter to the second. Further examples can be found in the period of America's participation in the Second World War. The cultural issues associated with America's involvement in the war found articulation in an enormous array of Hollywood's genres, from war films, spy films and musicals to Tarzan films, westerns and horror films. At the same time, the war gave rise to at least three new genres, the occupation/resistance film, the home front drama, and the home front comedy. It also saw the temporary demise of the gangster film and the social problem film, and the permanent demise of screwball comedy. And it witnessed the revival of service comedy, the modification of the war film and the biopic along the lines discussed in Chapter 3, the removal of some of the western's more blatant racist trappings – and their wholesale transference to films about the war with Japan.[3]

Because of the involvement of government agencies like the OWI in the setting of generic and cultural agendas, it might be argued that the period between 1942 and 1945 was a special case. However, on the one hand reference might be made to similar shifts and changes in less obviously exceptional periods like the mid-1930s, which among other things witnessed the birth of screwball comedy, the revival of the historical adventure film and the establishment of the singing western alongside modifications to the gangster film, the short-lived revival of the romantic western, and the total disappearance of films with ancient settings. (For more on the mid-1930s, see Chapter 7.) On the other it might be argued that this particular case, precisely because it is special, at least has the merit of posing questions as to how audiences' 'interests' and 'attitudes' and socio-cultural dilemmas and values normally find their way into Hollywood's genres.

The standard answer to this, from a ritual point of view, is that in a market economy, generic formulas which engage these interests and deal with these dilemmas become popular and, hence, commercially successful. Formulas are promulgated by the agencies of cultural production. Successful formulas are repeated because they make money, and it is in this way, through the box-office or the cash till, that audiences are able to influence their establishment and subsequent development. It is in this way, too, that they are able to engage in a form of 'cultural expression', that their interests, beliefs and values are able to find widespread, if indirect, articulation. The theoretical equation, therefore, is one in which profitability is an index of popularity, popularity an index of significance, and significance a matter of socio-cultural values and dilemmas.

There are a number of problems with this position, and a number of problems, too, with this equation. Firstly, while the idea that box-office success is an index of popularity seems obvious to the point of tautology, the assumption that all those who pay to see films always like or approve of them is not. There are all kinds of reasons why people pay to see films. And there are all kinds of reactions to them. Despite the current interest in Film Studies in audiences and in what audiences do with their experiences of films, we know very little about either. Secondly, while it seems more than likely that the sustained commercial success of a particular formula is indeed an index of approval, there are no grounds for assuming that that approval is ideologically based. It may be based on aesthetic preference or, as Cawelti (1976) points out, on a liking for particular patterns of fantasy. While aesthetic forms and fantasies always draw on and interact with ideological material, they also always possess their own specificity. There would otherwise be no need or grounds for the existence of at least three different genres dealing with the ideological issues of courtship, coupledom and community: the musical, romantic drama, and romantic comedy. There would be no grounds for preferring the style or the manner of any particular generic or cyclic treatment of the same basic ideological material over any others. And there would be no grounds either for the struggles between generic preference and ideological commitment documented by Pinedo (1997), among others.

Thirdly, at least one of the factors in the equation is open to challenge on empirical grounds. On the one hand, as Powdermaker points out, 'Year after year, the list of top box-office hits indicates great diversity in audience tastes' despite the industry's attachment to formulas and cycles' (1951: 41). On the other, evidence from contemporary audience surveys suggests that westerns were produced in large numbers during the studio era despite the fact that they were popular only with rural audiences and young adolescent boys and despite the fact that they were actively disliked by a majority of the viewing population as a whole (Jowett 1985). While this does not mean that westerns were unprofitable, it does mean that profitability – and popularity – was and is always relative. The westerns at stake in these surveys were mostly B films and hence for the most part cheap to produce. Profits were small but they were guaranteed, not least because the companies making these films could rely on a small but regular audience.

Fourthly and finally, as this particular example helps make clear, there are problems with equating audiences, societies, cultures and populations. Ritual theory is heavily dependent on the assumption that audiences are or were American, that American audiences are representative of the American population, and that the American population as a whole is always preoccupied in the same way with the same cultural issues and dilemmas. However, Hollywood has always attempted to appeal to international audiences, and its formulas and films have sometimes been adjusted as a result (Guback 1969; Jarvie 1992; Nowell-Smith 1998; Saunders 1994; Thompson 1985; Vasey 1997).[4] Most of its genres have proved popular abroad, and versions of at least one 'quintessential' American genre, the western, have been produced at various times in a number of different European countries (Feilitzsch 1993; Frayling 1981; Schneider 1998). During the studio era, Hollywood addressed its films first and foremost to the white populations of America. Partly in consequence, America's non-white populations often complained about its formulas or simpy did not bother to see its films. Moreover, whites of various backgrounds, beliefs and political persuasions sometimes complained about formulas as well, mounting censorship campaigns and boycotts around particular cycles and genres. The best documented cases are those of the gangster and the 'fallen woman' films of the early 1930s (Black 1994: 107–32; Maltby 1993b; Jacobs 1991). But they are not the only ones. And as we have seen, the tastes of America's white populations were in any event far from homogeneous. (In addition to the surveys referred to above, evidence is available in Jenkins' discussions (1992: 157–84) of regional resistence to 'Broadway-centred comedy' in the era of early sound.)

This particular point overlaps with another. There is an assumption built into nearly all genre theory that audiences and readers not only consume some or all of the genres on offer in exactly the same way, but also that they consume nothing else. However, as Roberts points out in *An Aesthetics of Junk Fiction*, things are not quite so simple. He suggests that there are a number of 'reader-to-genre relationships' (1990: 12) and hence a number of types of reader, ranging from the 'exclusivist' and the 'fan' to the 'occasional reader' and the 'allergic'.[5] Moreover, within every reader 'there lies an intricate pattern of addictions, preferences, random interests, avoidances, and allergies which is never quite the same as the pattern in any other reader' (ibid.: 85). In addition, the 'preference hierarchies' which every reader possesses extend beyond the boundaries of any particular genre and indeed any particular medium to incorporate all kinds of cultural forms and all kinds of socio-cultural activity (ibid.: 99). Thus while it is likely that most sectors of America's population and many sectors of the world's population were and are aware of the cultural issues dealt with on a regular basis in Hollywood's genres, it is also likely that their understanding of those issues and their relationship to them varied and continues to vary enormously.

Nearly all these points can be made in response to the ideological approach to genre as well. For while the ritual approach tends to downplay the contentious and coercive aspects of Hollywood and its genres, the ideological approach tends to downplay the heterogeneity of Hollywood's output, of Hollywood's audiences, and of the uses those audiences make of Hollywood's films. Altman sums up the differences between the two approaches as follows. Where the former attributes 'authorship to the audience, with the studios simply serving, for a price, the national will', the latter is concerned to show 'how audiences are manipulated by the business and political interests of Hollywood'; where the former 'sees Hollywood as responding to societal pressure and thus expressing audience desires', the latter 'claims that Hollywood takes advantage of spectator energy and psychic investment in order to lure the audience into Hollywood's own positions' (1987: 94).

As examples of the ideological approach, Altman cites the work of *Cahiers du Cinéma*, *Jump Cut* and *Screen*. Judith Hess Wright's 'Genre Films and the Status Quo' ([1974] 1986) was initially published in *Jump Cut*. She argues that genre films

came into being and were financially successful because they temporarily relieved the fears aroused by a recognition of social and political conflicts; they helped to discourage any action that might otherwise follow upon the pressure generated by living with these conflicts. Genre films produce satisfaction rather than action, pity and fear rather than revolt. They serve the interests of the ruling class by assisting in the maintenance of the status quo, and they throw a sop to oppressed groups who, because they are unorganized and therefore afraid to act, eagerly accept the genre film's absurd solutions to economic and social conflicts. When we return to the complexities of the society in which we live, the same conflicts assert themselves, so we return to genre films for easy comfort and solace – hence their popularity.

(Wright [1974] 1986: 41)

Different genres possess their own individual characteristics, their own settings, their own conflicts, and their own ways of resolving the ideological issues with which they deal. The science fiction film is set in the future and deals with the intrusion of 'others'; the gangster film is set in the present and deals with the contradictions that stem from striving for social and financial success; and the western is set in the past and deals with the ethics of violence. But they all ultimately serve the same purposes, hence they all ultimately function in identical ways.

My own earlier book, *Genre* (1980), derives from the work of *Screen*. It attempts to place more emphasis on difference, in particular on the different pleasures different genres provide. Thus the musical is contrasted with the detective film. Where the former involves the pleasures of spectacle, the latter is marked much more by the pleasures of narration; where the former emphasizes the pleasures of looking and listening, the latter is much more marked by the pleasures involved in confronting and resolving enigmas. However, differences like these are in the end seen solely as variants on the Hollywood feature film, the pleasures themselves solely as a means by which the spectator is subject to Hollywood's 'machine'. Thus as Collins points out, 'Neale has argued for a less monolithic notion of genre as a way of coming to terms with the diversity of the Hollywood film, but a master system that coordinates all apparent differences remains firmly in place' (1989: 99).

The social role of Hollywood and the pleasures of its genres are important issues. But theories like these tend to close them off in a self-confirming circuit of conclusion and premiss. Functionalist, reductive, and profoundly pessimistic, they are more or less immune to empirical argument, political nuance, and the actualities of socio-cultural change. The capitalist character of Hollywood is not in dispute. But in an era in which nearly all cultural artefacts circulate as commodities, 'stressing the capitalist character of modern cultural production is itself neither optimistic nor pessimistic' (Nowell-Smith 1987b: 88). Meanwhile for all their insistence on Hollywood's power, ideological theories pay little attention to its policies, its practices, its structures and the nature of its output. And for all their insistence on the importance of change, they pay little attention to its history.

Shorn of their pessimism, most ideological theories are in all these respects not that different from ritual ones. Aware of their strengths as well as their weaknesses, Altman argues for a recognition of the ideological and ritual aspects of all Hollywood's genres, and for an approach which combines or alternates the theories themselves (1987: 94). The extent to which this is feasible remains to be seen. In the meantime, and in conclusion, it is worth drawing attention to an article by Kapsis (1991), and in the process both to another approach and to the only detailed study I know of the relationship between generic production, box-office success, audience preference and industrial practice at a specific and particular point in time.

Critical of theories which ignore the role of the industry, Kapsis draws on 'the production of culture perspective', a perspective which focuses on 'the interorganizational network of production companies, distributors, mass media gatekeepers, and retailers' and on the conflicts among and between them, as well as on 'the market, pressure groups and censorship, statute law and governments, technology', and all the other factors that play a part in generic and cyclic production (1991: 70). He argues that in Hollywood, there is 'a complex network of interorganizational relationships which mediates between the movie production company and the consumer. Which genres finally get made depends on how organizational gatekeepers at various stages of the film production process assess the product in relation to their perception of audiences' future tastes' (ibid.: 71). By way of example, he takes a close look at the cycle of horror films produced in the late 1970s and early 1980s.

Noting that in its earliest phase horror films not only proved popular at the box-office but also often received favourable reviews and mass-media publicity, Kapsis observes that by late 1980 production executives began to worry about market saturation and to cut down on new productions. Their worries were augmented by increasingly adverse reviews, increasingly adverse publicity, and the consequent concerns and interventions of CARA (the Classification and Ratings Administration of the MPAA). However, and despite the fact that domestic rentals for the horror films released in 1982 reached an all-time high, their worries and decisions were conditioned mainly by the importance of the foreign market, and founded for the most part on a perception that the market for horror films abroad had been in decline for over a year. In consequence, the number of films produced continued to diminish. The lack of fresh projects meant a decline in the quality and quantity of horror films released in 1983 and a consequent decline in box-office income. As a result, the cycle came to an end.

Neither the end of the cycle nor the ensuing long-term decline in horror production were due to any observable decline in the popularity of horror films among audiences in America, or to any identifiable change in the basic nature of the films themselves. Although their cultural significance changed with their increasing notoriety, it is unclear how – or whether – that notoriety altered the perceptions of the audiences who saw them or any putative social, cultural or ideological role the films themselves may have had. What *is* clear is that economic factors and industrial decisions played a crucial part. Along with the attention it seeks to give to an array of other factors and its refusal to provide answers to the questions it raises in advance of empirical analysis, it is for this reason that the production of culture perspective is much more likely than ritual or ideological theories to provide convincing accounts of the socio-cultural significance of genres and cycles. Given that this is the case, and given that so many definitions and theories of genre found themselves, as we have seen, on the commercial and industrial nature of Hollywood, it is to important to take a more sustained look at Hollywood's practices, at Hollywood's output, and at some of the accounts put forward to describe them from a generic point of view. In this way, a number of conclusions can be drawn, and a number of questions and topics for further research raised and proposed.

NOTES

1 See among others, Barber (1993), Barnouw (1981), Crafton (1982: 9–135), Fell ([1974] 1986, 1987), Gunning (1989), Hollyman ([1977] 1983), Horak (1985: 97–100), Kovacs ([1976] 1983), Musser (1990c: 15–54) and Trachtenberg (1987).
2 This paragraph draws on and extends points made by Fowler (1982: 54–74), who in turn draws on Wittgenstein's discussion of 'family resemblances' (1953: 31–6). Wittgenstein argues that language games resemble one another not because they each possess a common defining trait, but because, like families, they share a group of traits and because, like family members, some games possess traits which others do not. In this particular context, the family metaphor might well be

extended: if family members marry compatible members of other families, any children they may have are likely to combine the traits of the families to which they belong in different ways and to different degrees.

3 For some or all of these points, see Cripps (1997: 187–205), Dick ([1985] 1996), Doherty (1993a), Dower (1986), Fyne ([1994] 1997), Koppes and Black (1987), Maltby (1995: 374–5), Neale and Krutnick (1990: 169), Polan (1986: 45–99), Roberts and Olson (1995: 244–7), Schindler (1979), Slotkin (1992: 313–43) and Worland (1997).

4 Saunders notes the surprised perception among German critics in the early 1920s that Hollywood's 'society dramas' 'showed competence, even excellence, in a genre allegedly more suitable to German capabilities' (1994: 107).

5 The role of fandom and allergy in the production, circulation and reception of genres in the cinema remains relatively unexplored, as does the extent to which taste and allegiance play a part in the construction of generic identities. Simon Frith has noted the extent to which popular musical genres 'flourish on a sense of exclusivity; they are as much (if not more) concerned to keep people out as in' (1996: 88). Except among relatively small groups of fans, exclusivity seems much less central to popular cinema, perhaps because films are much more expensive to make than musical recordings and therefore because Hollywood has always tended to attempt to sell most of its films to as many taste groups and markets as it can. However, exclusivity clearly plays a part in wider generic distinctions, in distinctions between 'art', 'independent' and 'commercial' films, for instance.

7

GENRE AND HOLLYWOOD

Numerous references have been made during the course of previous chapters to the industrial practices and structures of Hollywood. As we have seen, the commercial and industrial nature of Hollywood has been viewed as responsible not just for the formulaic nature of its genres, but also for the existence of genres as such. Reference has been made to the activities of particular companies. And the role of Hollywood's inter-textual relay, a relay which involves each of its industrial sectors, have been stressed throughout this book. The status of Hollywood as an industry and the status of its films as commodities have also been stressed in accounts of genre which seek to emphasize the importance of variety and difference as well as the importance of repetition (Belton 1994: 62–3, 115–16; Neale 1980: 52–3). These accounts underline the extent to which all industries in capitalist economies produce products for a market and, in the long term at least, for profit. Hollywood produces artistic products. Artistic products, unlike cars or tables, are 'one-of-a-kind items' (Belton 1994: 63). 'Henry Ford could manufacture thousands of cars exactly alike; here sameness was a virtue. But every movie had to be different; otherwise the movie audiences would not appear at the theatres again and again' (Jacobs 1939: 162). Thus in the film industry, as in many other industries, multiple copies are made of each item, but the items copied are all unique, all to a greater or lesser degree distinct one from another. The car industry and the table-manufacturing industry generate lines, models and fashions in order to open up new markets and in order to ensure a constant flow of demand. But the individual items within each range are as identical to one another as they can be made to be. In the film industry the items within as well as across different ranges have to be different. For Hollywood, genres provide a cost-effective equivalent to lines and ranges, producing a demand for similarities within the variety of product on offer and therefore minimizing the degrees of difference involved. Within and across the array of its output, Hollywood's product is therefore always diverse – each of its films are always new, each of its genres always different from one another. But within its ranges and models, within its genres, its films are also always similar. Genres thus perform a number of economic functions. They enable the industry to meet the obligations of variety and difference inherent in its product. But they also enable it to manufacture its product in a cost-effective manner, and to regulate demand and the nature of its output in such a way as to minimize the risks inherent in difference and to maximize the possibility of profit on its overall investment.

Propositions such as these have provided the basis for numerous accounts of genre and Hollywood, especially those focused on Hollywood's studio era and on the companies (often also called studios) which developed what has sometimes been called the 'the studio system'. The periodization of Hollywood's history has recently become a contentious issue, in particular for those who wish to label the studio era and its output as 'classical' (Bordwell, Staiger and Thompson 1985; Cowie 1998; Maltby 1998; M. Smith 1998). Broadly speaking however, the studio era refers to the period between the mid-to-late 1920s and the late 1940s, with some overspill into the mid-to-late 1950s. This was a period in which the American film industry came to be dominated by a small group (or 'oligopoly') of eight 'major' companies. Three companies, Universal Pictures, Columbia Pictures and United Artists (who financed and distributed independent projects) produced and distributed films. The remaining five, Loews-MGM, Paramount Publix, the Fox Film Corporation (20th Century-Fox after 1935), Warner Bros and RKO (after 1928), were 'vertically integrated'. They both produced and distributed films and also owned and operated first-run cinemas and cinema chains. These eight companies were supplemented by a group of 'Poverty Row' companies, Monogram, Republic, Mascot and the like, who specialized in serials and B films, independents such as Goldwyn and Selznick, and specialists in animation such as Fleischer and Disney. The key to this system was exhibition. Collusion between the 'Big Five' and the 'Little Three' ensured that the films they produced and the films they distributed were guaranteed first-run exhibition in the cinemas owned by the Big Five themselves. In addition, by means of practices such as block-booking (the renting of films in groups), independent cinemas and cinema chains were forced to show nearly all these films if they wished to show any at all. Until compelled by government legislation to abandon block-booking and to begin 'divorcement' of their exhibition interests from their interests in production and distribution in 1948, these companies and their clients were secure in the knowledge that there was a built-in long-term demand for their product and that all the films they released would be shown. They were therefore able to employ in-house staff on long-term contracts and to invest in in-house facilities. And they were therefore able to develop routinized production plans and practices along lines similar to those used in other industries engaged in the mass production of goods – to develop what has sometimes been called a 'factory system' (Balio [1976] 1985: 195–400; Belton 1994: 61–80; Bordwell, Staiger and Thompson 1985: 134–141, 311–29; Gomery 1986; Schatz 1988a, 1996).

According to conventional wisdom, genre and genres were a key component in this system. The routines and formulas of genre complemented the routines and formulas of factory production. They enabled the studios to plan, to produce and to market their films in predictable ways and to dovetail their output with the expertise of their production staff (particularly screen-writers, producers, directors, and stars) and with the plant, the costumes, the props and the other facilities in which they had each invested. This in turn enabled each of the studios to specialize, to contribute their own generic expertise to an overall output of films that was generically varied, but also generically fixed and generically consistent, for over thirty years. Thus while for Phillips 'an efficient and quality production system was able to turn out films which conformed unproblematically to formulae' (1996: 133–4), for Ryall Hollywood's cinema was and is 'a cinema of genres, a cinema of westerns, gangster films, musicals, melodramas, and thrillers' (1998: 327). (See also Hayward 1996: 164–5, 356.)

I have no intention here of standing conventional wisdom on its head. But I do wish to question some of its tenets, especially those which overemphasize specialization, those which assume that genres as traditionally defined were the sole or even the principal units of production planning and practice, and those which underestimate the intermittent, mixed, generically heteroge-neous and sometimes even generically indeterminate nature of Hollywood's output in the studio era as measured in traditional terms. This in turn will lead to some questions about accounts of Hollywood genres and Hollywood's output in the post-studio era as well.

THE STUDIO ERA

Like any other system, the studio system was subject to development, to change, to interaction with other systems, events and institutions, and hence to the vagaries of history. It is usually argued that it was at its height in the mid-1930s, after the wave of theatre acquisitions and mergers in the late 1910s and the 1920s, after the coming of sound, just after the worst years of the Depression, and just prior to the Second World War. The studios had been forced to economize. The introduction of double bills had increased the demand for low budget features and B films. Most of the studios had adopted the 'producer-unit' system – a system which enabled a relatively large group of managers to supervise a relatively small groups of films each year. (The producer-unit system replaced the 'central producer', which as the term suggests entailed centralized supervision of a larger group of films.) Newly amended procedures for administering the newly amended Production Code were in place. And the passing of the National Recovery Act by President Roosevelt's administration had assured the studios that their oligopolistic practices would be tolerated for the time being at least as a means of stabilizing the industry and of helping the studios themselves, many of which had gone into the red in the early 1930s, back on their feet (Balio 1993;

Belton 1994: 63–70; Gomery 1986: 3–25; Schatz 1988a: 159–294, and 1996). For all these reasons, conditions at this time were as ripe as they were ever going to be for the practices of the studios and of the system as a whole to conform to the tenets of conventional wisdom. It is therefore worth taking a closer look at the films that were made, at the companies that made them, at their planning and production practices, at some of the personnel involved, and at the way the films were categorized and described in the industry's relay.

Over 95 feature films were released in the US in the first three months of 1934 and reviewed in *Variety*. Among them were a 'light programmer' called *If I Were Free* (9 January: 16), *Above the Clouds,* 'one of the first of the newsreel cameraman cycle' (9 January: 16), an 'entertaining western of "Black Beauty" type' called *Smoky* (9 January: 16), *Olsen's Big Moment,* a 'Comedy feature best suited to the nabes' (9 January: 16), '*By Candlelight,* a 'class romance with slight farcical variations' (9 January: 16), an 'Igloo drama' called *Man of Two Worlds* (16 January: 15), *The Fighting Code,* a 'western' (16 January: 15), *Miss Fane's Baby is Stolen,* a 'Kidnap yarn' (23 January: 13), a 'Puppet show fantasy' called *I Am Suzanne* (23 January: 13), a 'Drawing room comedy drama' called *As Husbands Go* (30 January: 12), and *Women in His Life,* the 'story of an attorney and his troubles, plus gangsters' (30 January: 30). Also among them were *All of Me,* a 'drama' (6 February: 14), *Hi Nelli!,* 'Paul Muni as a news-paperman' (6 February: 14), *I've Got Your Number,* 'Another in the Warner comedy series' (6 February: 14), *Moulin Rouge,* a 'musical' with a 'backstage story' (13 February: 14), an 'Animal thriller' called *Devil Tiger* (13 February: 14), *Curtain at Eight* a 'backstage murder mystery' (13 February: 14), a 'Sex propaganda' film called *The Road to Ruin* (20 February: 14), a 'costume picture' called *Catherine the Great* (20 February: 14), and *It Happened One Night,* which 'starts off to be another long distance bus story' (27 February: 17). Among them too were *Wonder Bar,* a 'musical' which is also 'a "Grand Hotel" of a Paris boite-de-nuit' (6 March: 14), *Palooka,* a 'comedy . . . prizefight film' (6 March: 14), *No More Women,* 'Quirt and Flagg under the Hays morality code' (6 March: 14), *Spitfire,* 'Katharine Hepburn . . . with a picture built around her' (13 March: 16), a 'racetrack yarn' called *The Big Race* (6 March: 27), *House of Rothschild,* a contribution to 'the biographical cycle' (20 March: 16), and *Jimmy the Gent,* a 'Very funny Cagney picture' (27 March: 12).

Immediately striking is the variety of films released and the variety of terms used to describe them. Immediately striking also is the relative paucity of canonic genres and 'genre films'. Terms like 'comedy', 'western' and 'musical' can be found, as can films which correspond to them. But they exist alongside broader or more indeterminate ones like 'drama' and 'costume picture' (which rarely if ever features in genre theory, but which according to *Variety* ('Drama As All-Time Top B.O.', 18 January 1950: 5, 18) were among the top three categories of box-office hits), more unfamiliar ones like 'racetrack yarn', and more specific ones like 'western of the "Black Beauty" type'. They also exist alongside hybrids like 'comedy drama' and 'comedy. . . prizefight film', terms indicative of production and exhibition categories like 'programmer' and 'nabes' (neighbourhood theatres), terms indicative of series or cycles like 'Quirt and Flagg' and 'another long distance bus story', and the use of stars and star names alongside or in lieu of traditional generic indices, as in 'Very funny Cagney picture' and 'Katharine Hepburn . . . with a picture built around her'. It is clear that some of these examples can be subsumed into canonic generic groupings or considered under canonic generic headings. But it is equally clear that they are by no means the only groupings and headings in play.

In all these respects, the first three months of 1934 are no different from the first three months of 1935 or 1936, or indeed from any or all of these years as a whole. Thus the remainder of 1934 saw the release of *Trumpet Blows*, 'Paramount's addition to the fast-moving cycle of Mexican pictures' (17 April: 18), *Ferocious Pal*, a 'Dog story neatly planned for the family houses' (1 May: 14), *The Black Cat*, a 'Combination of Karloff and Lugosi, the two horror specialists' (22 May: 15), *Murder at the Vanities*, 'Herein they mix up the elements of musical show and a murder mystery, with effective comedy to flavor' (22 May: 15), *Let's Be Ritzy*, a 'Domestic comedy drama' (10 July: 13), *The Notorious Sophie Lang*, a 'Synthetic thriller of the comedy genre' (24 July: 14), *The Count of Monte Cristo*, a 'Costume film' (2 October: 37), *We Live Again*, a 'Remake of Tolstoy's "Resurrection"' (6 November: 16), a 'War drama' called *Shock* (20 November: 15), *College Rhythm*, an 'Entertaining semi-musical' (27 November: 15), and a 'Football picture' called *The Band Plays On* (25 December: 12). The year 1935 saw the release of *Forsaking All Others*, a 'romantic comedy' (1 January: 18), *Inside Information*, a 'Police dog story' (1 January: 18), *The County Chairman*, a 'Will Rogers feature in the familiar American idiom' (22 January: 14), *Clive of India*, 'another in 20th Century's . . . cycle of historical cinematography' (22 January: 14), *Charlie Chan in Paris*, a 'Typical Chan story' (29 January: 14), and *In Old Santa Fe*, a 'Ken Maynard dude ranch western' (20 March: 17). It also saw the release of *Les Miserables*, a 'prestige picture' (24 April: 12), a 'Baseball picture' called *Swell Head* (8 May 1935: 16), an 'aviation thriller' called *Air Hawks* (12 June: 12), *The Headline Woman*, a 'time-worn newspaper story' (26 June: 23), *The Crusades*, an 'Elaborate spectacle' (28 August: 12), a 'woman's picture' called *Dark Angel* (11 September: 17), *O'Shaughnessey's Boy*, the 'Usual Beery–Cooper father and son theme' (9 October: 14), *The Payoff*, a 'Sports and newspaper story, garnished with gangsterism and romance' (13 November: 16), *Mutiny on the Bounty*, a 'Powerful picturization of the well-circulated sea novel' (13 November: 16), and *The Littlest Rebel*, a 'Shirley Temple picture' (25 December: 15). Finally, 1936 saw the release of *Magnificent Obsession*, a 'Capital romance' (8 January: 12), *Two in the Dark*, 'a powerful contribution to the murder mystery cycle' (5 February: 33), a 'George O'Brien action picture' called *Whispering Smith Speaks* (19 February: 12), *Brides Are Like*

That, a 'Lightweight comedy romance' (25 March: 15), *Special Investigator*, a 'Western with G–Man switch' (29 April: 15), *Country Beyond*, 'an experiment to see how the "Thin Man" formula works on a mountie story' (6 May: 18), *Till We Meet Again*, a 'Routine spy story' (13 May: 14), *Revolt of the Zombies*, 'horror' (10 June: 18), and 'Another Racetrack pic' called *Down the Stretch* (11 November: 14).

The examples cited above are not intended to reflect in any precise sense the range of films made in the mid-1930s or the balance among and between them. But the nature of Hollywood's output as exemplified here, and the terms used by a journal like *Variety* to describe it, is perfectly consonant with the accounts provided by Balio (1993), Dooley ([1979] 1981), Maltby (1995), Schatz (1988a, 1996) and others of Hollywood's studios, practices and films in the 1930s. For instance Balio notes that Hollywood's output was planned on an annual seasonal basis. As Maltby points out, this necessarily placed a great deal of emphasis on cycles as units of calculation and on cyclic formulas (such as those associated with long distance bus films) as templates for films (1995: 111). He goes on to point out that the 'classical' gangster film, far from being an all–pervasive genre in the early 1930s, was in fact the cyclic product of a single annual season.

Balio notes too that the nature of Hollywood's annual output was deter-mined in outline, and sometimes also in detail, at company headquarters (for the most part in New York), that the fundamental divisions in planning and output were budgetary divisions, and that these divisions overlapped with categories of distribution and exhibition. The majors 'rationalized production first of all', he writes, 'by dividing output into A and B groups and then by allocating a specified amount of the total production budget to each group' (1993: 98). In addition, 'the class A output . . . was . . . divided into three tiers – superspecials, specials and programmers. Superspecials typically consisted of prestige pictures and big-budget musicals with top stars. Costing $1 million and more to produce, only a handful of such pictures would be produced by a studio in any given year' (ibid.). Superspecials were often road-shown. (See the section on epics and spectacles in Chapter 3.) Like specials, they tended to be produced by independents like Selznick and Goldwyn – Selznick's *Gone with the Wind* (1939) was a superspecial – as well as by the majors themselves. Specials 'constituted the bulk of the class-A line. Like superspecials, they were based on presold properties and contained popular stars, but they followed the principal production trends, conformed to regular running times, and had lower production budgets' (ibid.). Specials usually opened on a first-run basis in metropolitan theatres owned by the Big Five. That is to say, they would be shown as the only or the principal feature in these theatres before being shown either singly or in double bills in smaller rural or neighbourhood areas. Programmers, finally, 'had the lowest budgets of the group. They were typically based on original stories and contained minor stars and running times as short as fifty minutes. Such films were called programmers because they could fill either the top or bottom of the bill' (ibid.). If shown at the bottom of a double bill, programmers functioned as B films. Like A films, programmers and B films were produced by specialized units within each of the major companies by the mid-1930s. Along with serials, they were the only films made by the companies on Poverty Row. (Other small-scale independents like Willis Kent Productions made exploitation and 'sex propaganda' films like *The Road to Ruin* for exhibition in independent theatres outside the spheres of circulation normally associated with Hollywood's companies and Hollywood's films.) As we have seen, terms associated with all these divisions often feature in *Variety*'s reviews.

Balio goes on to detail the additional ways in which the majors planned and categorized the films that they made – the additional ways and means by which they sought not only to spend their money, but also 'to protect their investment by reducing risks' (1993: 101). One way was to make films in series: 'Once successfully launched, a series creates loyal and eager fans who form a core audience. By keeping production costs in line with this ready-made demand, series are almost guaranteed a profit' (ibid.). Series were built around characters, performers and formats, some of them generic in a traditional sense (like the Charlie Chan detective films), others based on ingredients derived in the first instance from particular films (like the 'Quirt and Flagg' films, which were based on characters played by Victor McClaglen and Edmund Lowe in *What Price Glory?* (1926). *What Price Glory?* is normally considered a war film. But most of the films in the series were knockabout action-comedies). Series tend to be associated with the Little Three and with Poverty Row, but Balio points in addition to the *Thin Man* series at MGM (which gave rise to a cycle of wisecracking comedy-whodunnit romances like *The Princess Comes Across* (1936) and *Country Beyond*) and the *Gold Diggers* series at Warners (which fed off a cycle of films about gold digging that included *The Easiest Way* (1931) and *The Greeks Had a Word for Them* (1932)) (ibid.).

Another way was to contribute not just to cycles, but also to 'production trends'. The distinction between the two is not entirely clear-cut. Judging by the way Balio uses it as a means of charting Hollywood's output across the decade as a whole (1993: 179–312), the latter seems for him to imply greater stability and hence greater longevity than the former. However, while production trends could be long term – like the trend towards 'prestige pictures', a category that for Balio dominates the 1930s – they were as subject to annual planning and production regimes, and hence to short-term fluctuations, as cycles themselves. As the example of the prestige picture makes clear, production trends are not necessarily synonymous with genres as traditionally defined and conceived. (Prestige pictures included biopics and literary classics – like *Les Miserables* – as well as a number of woman's films, musicals, costume adventure films and costume dramas.) The same is true of cycles. For as Balio points out, 'studios did more than imitate picture types' (ibid.: 101). Sometimes they reworked or transposed the ingredients of specific films, as *Country Beyond* and *Special Investigator* both make clear. Sometimes 'they even mimicked narrative structure' (ibid.). Thus 'the so-called "one locale" setting of MGM's *Grand Hotel*, which provided the basis for interweaving several unrelated narrative threads, inspired such pictures as Columbia's *American Madness*, which is set in a bank . . . and Paramount's *Big Broadcast*, which is set in a radio station' (ibid.), as well as *Wonder Bar*, set as it is in 'a Paris boite-de-nuit'. (For further discussion of *Grand Hotel* and its influence, see Dooley [1979] 1981: 83–98.) Cycles could also be 'started by a topical event' ('Prison-Break Film Cycle Current, Schoolboy Bums Next Big Theme', *Variety*, 16 March 1955: 2). *Miss Fane's Baby is Stolen*, for instance, was one of a number of 'kidnap yarns' made in the wake of the abduction of Charles Lindbergh's son.[1]

As *Wonder Bar*, *Special Investigator* and *Country Beyond* all illustrate, cycles could and did generate hybrids. Although Balio does not discuss them, the regular production of hybrids was another means by which the studios tried to hedge their bets. (According to Dick 1993: 118, Harry Cohn at Columbia instituted a long-term policy of 'making melange movies', of 'defining the Columbia product as a blend of different strains'.) Appealing to fans of the various 'picture types', formulas and cycles that might be involved, hybrids also enabled individual films to offer a variety of different aesthetic ingredients. This was crucial. For as Barry and Sargent pointed out:

> Photoplays cannot be made with only type of audience in mind. Nor can they be made for any particular community . . . Every photoplay possesses something which can be selected around which to build an an advertising campaign. In fact, in every photoplay there are different highlights which when brought to the attention of different groups or classes of the community will build attention.
>
> (Barry and Sargent 1927: 90)

As a result, and as *Variety's* reviews make clear, hybrids were common. Hollywood's feature films had always tended to alternate comedy and drama, excitement and pathos, reflection and action, as Barry Salt has pointed out ([1983] 1992: 111–13). Long-standing hybrids like comedy drama therefore merely rendered more systematic the more localized or *ad hoc* procedures of a film like *The Payoff*. They also exemplified Hollywood and its product in ways which have barely begun to be explored (and which genre criticism and 'post-modern theory' alike have served to obscure rather than illuminate, as we shall see further below).

'The most common way' of planning production and of attempting to minimize risk, according to Balio, 'was to rely on stars' (1993: 101). This point is reinforced by the use of star names as descriptive terms in *Variety's* reviews, and by the extent to which stars and 'featured players' function as the principal categories in *Variety*'s surveys of each year's output. ('Leading Film Names of '33', 2 January 1934: 1, 27', 'Leading Film Names of '34', 1 January: 1, 36–8, 'Leading Film Names of 1935', 1 January 1936: 4–5.) It is also reinforced by Schatz's account of studios like Warners, MGM and Universal (1988a). Schatz makes clear that along with budgetary categories like superspecials, specials and programmers, the names of stars and featured players were the principal headings under which company executives in New York conceived, planned and classified each year's annual output. He also makes clear that the balance among and between budgetary and player-oriented categories varied from studio to studio and from period to period. MGM laid more emphasis on stars than some other companies. (Schatz at one point (ibid.: 361) cites a production agenda that consists simply of a list of star names.) But all studios, even minor ones, tried to create stars. And all studios, including minor ones, used stars and featured plays as an organizing principle – hence the phrase 'Ken Maynard dude ranch western' to describe a Poverty Row western like *In Old Santa Fe.*

Writing about MGM in the late 1920s, Schatz makes clear as well that 'star vehicles were perceived differently by . . . executives, depending on their particular vantage point in the system' (1988a: 40). When executives in New York 'translated one season's box-office receipts into the next season's budget, they conceived it in terms of "star units" – so many Lon Chaneys or Norma Shearers or Lillian Gishes' (ibid.). But while 'New York saw a "Lon Chaney" as a marketable commodity to be moved through the distribution–exhibition process', production executives in Hollywood 'saw it is as a certain type of story that demanded a certain mobilization of MGM's resources' (ibid.). It is partly for this reason that Schatz tends to use terms like 'star-genre formulations' and 'star-formula combinations' rather than 'genre' or 'genres' as such. However, it is apparent throughout Schatz's book that the types of stories in which stars appeared were by no means always identical, hence that star-genre formulations were by no means always fixed. (Maltby suggests that 'The star system provided one of the principal means by which Hollywood offered audiences guarantees of predictability, while the plots in which the star persona was embedded offered a balancing experience of novelty' (1995: 92). This would vary from star to star. The plots in which 'horror specialists' like Bela Lugosi and Boris Karloff appeared would vary less than the plots of such 'Cagney pictures' as *Jimmy the Gent* and *G-Men*.) It is also apparent that some stars (like Katharine Hepburn) were not associated with any particular story type, and that the story types associated with others were by no means always equivalent to those with which genre critics and theorists have traditionally dealt. (Will Rogers, for instance, specialized in rural and small-town comedy dramas like *The County Chairman*.) Even where they were, the formulas associated with some stars were often much more specific than traditional genre terms are able to suggest. Deanna Durbin, for instance, appeared in musicals. But the musicals she appeared in tended to combine 'romantic comedy and family melodrama' (Schatz 1988a: 238) while affording her 'the chance to display not only her captivating innocence but also a remarkable vocal range that allowed her to sing popular ballads and opera' (ibid.: 239). In nearly all her films 'Durbin was depicted as a victim of a broken home and fragmented family who sought somehow to restore the traditional order' (ibid.: 242). In that respect, she was similar to Shirley Temple and to a number of non-musical child stars and juvenile performers in the 1930s (ibid.: 243). In that respect too, her musicals were very different from those of Fred Astaire, Ginger Rogers and other contemporary adult musical stars. 'Star-genre formulations' and 'star-formula combinations' are therefore by no means as synonymous as Schatz sometimes appears to suggest.

Deanna Durbin's films were made at Universal in the mid-to-late 1930s and early 1940s. They were produced by Joe Pasternak and variously directed by Henry Koster, Norman Taurog and Edward Ludwig. But they were not the only films, or even the only kinds of films, in which Universal, Pasternak, Koster, Taurog and Ludwig were involved. Universal, of course, tends to be associated with horror films. But at the point at which the first of the Durbin musicals was released in 1936, Universal had made and released only five horror films in three years, fewer than the number of its murder mysteries, comedies and musicals, and fewer still than the number of its woman's films. Like other studios, Universal had adjusted the nature of its output a number of times during the course of the decade. As one of the Little Three, it tended to concentrate on programmers. However, when Junior Laemmle became production head in the late 1920s he attempted to upgrade its product. Although by the mid-1930s this policy had had to be tempered, Universal still produced the occasional prestige costume film like *Show Boat* (1936) and the occasional prestige drama like *Magnificent Obsession* (Schatz 1988a: 82–7; Dick 1997: 73–94).

Pasternak joined Universal in 1936. Although nearly all the films he produced in the late 1930s were Durbin musicals, he also produced *Destry Rides Again* in 1939 and *Seven Sinners*, which Hirschhorn describes as 'a sultry tropical romance' ([1983] 1986: 119), in 1940. Koster also joined Universal in 1936. In the 1930s and 1940s he directed comedies like *The Rage of Paris* (1938) as well as Durbin musicals. Taurog, meanwhile, directed a range of films, from *Mrs. Wiggs of the Cabbage Patch* (1934) to *Rhythm of the Range* (1937) to *Young Tom Edison*, for a number of different studios. Most of these films were light in tone and were often aimed at children, though *Young Tom Edison* can also be seen as a contribution to the cycle of biopics about famous Americans that traversed the late 1930s and the 1940s. Edward Ludwig, finally, 'worked for several studios in various genres' (Katz [1979] 1994: 851). These included musicals like Durbin's *That Certain Age* (1938). But they also included 'action pictures' like *The Barrier* (1937), *Coast Guard* (1939) and *They Came to Blow Up America* (1943) (ibid.).

These points all raise questions about genre specialization. Universal was not unique in offering a diversity of films each year. Edward Ludwig was not unique in working in various genres. And while it is clear that some performers, like Deanna Durbin, were associated with a very particular type of film, it is also clear that others (like James Cagney) possessed a range of skills and a persona that were compatible with a number of different ones. Studios required flexibility as well as expertise. They needed to adjust to new cycles and trends as well to find suitable vehicles for their employees (Balio 1993: 81). That is one reason why a number of actors, directors, producers and screenwriters moved from studio to studio or became temporarily or permanently unemployed in the 1930s. It is also why studio lots, props and costumes were diverse in nature. One of the virtues of shooting in studios was that studio stages could accommodate all kinds of sets and that sets could be temporary rather than permanent. Wardrobe and prop departments were permanent. But they were permanent not just because old props and old costumes had to be looked after but also because new ones were always being made. Arguably the only companies and units to specialize in a narrow range of films for any length of time in the 1930s were the musical units and some of the units producing B films, comedy shorts and newsreels at the majors, Fleischer, Disney and the in-house animation units at Warners, Universal, Columbia and MGM, and some of the companies on Poverty Row. According to Fernett, Poverty Row specialized in 'action, intrigue, adventure and mystery' (1973: 115). However as Taves points out, Poverty Row made musicals, comedies and dramas as well (1993b: 332). Even Willis Kent productions made westerns and action films as well as sex propaganda.[2]

As Balio concludes, 'Studios reduced risk by providing a variety of pictures every season' (1993: 310).

> Although each studio is said to have had a 'house style' based on a 'speciality genre,' this survey indicates that the Big Five specialized in several trends at once and that these specialities changed in response to the market. For example, MGM started the decade concentrating on sentimental comedies and prestige pictures based on sophisticated Broadway plays and ended the decade concentrating on family films and musicals. Warners branched out from 'topicals' during the Depression to biopics, woman's pictures, and swashbucklers. Universal made its mark with horror pictures during the first half of the decade and with Deanna Durbin musicals during the last half.
>
> (Balio 1993: 311)

Once the Little Three, Poverty Row and the cycles in which they were all involved are factored into the equation, the picture is one in which – as Dooley's ([1979] 1981) survey of Hollywood's output in the 1930s makes clear – murder mysteries rub shoulders with long distance bus films, prestige costume films rub shoulders with singing westerns, comedies and woman's films rub shoulders with horror films and musicals, kidnap yarns rub shoulders with racetrack pics, comedy dramas rub shoulders with boxing films, spy films rub shoulders with aviation thrillers, and action melodramas about government employees rub shoulders with football, college and military films of all kinds. It is therefore hardly surprising that the 'Genre Index' in the AFI Catalogue of 1930s feature films consists not of fourteen categories (the number discussed in Chapter 3), but of 61 (Hanson 1993: 1073).[3]

THE POST-STUDIO ERA

By the mid-1980s, fifty years later, the structures and practices of Hollywood and of the American film industry as a whole were in many ways very different. Vertical integration had been declared illegal in 1948, and during the course of the following decade the Big Five had been forced to sell off their theatres. At the same time, against a background of changes in the location, the demographic profile and the lifestyles of the American population, the beginnings of a lengthy period of decline in cinema attendances, a decline augmented in the 1950s and 1960s by the rapid diffusion of television, meant that the making of films became fraught with greater financial risks than ever before. Deprived of guaranteed exhibition and operating in a shrinking national and international market, the routine in-house production of relatively large numbers of films and the employment of production staff on long-term contracts no longer made economic sense. Staff were laid off in large numbers, RKO collapsed, and by the 1960s the studio system was at an end.

With the Little Three now on a par with the others (and with Disney moving into distribution as well as production), the remaining majors sought to retain their power and to lower the ever-increasing risks inherent in production by making fewer films, by making more expensive films, by abandoning B films, serials, newsreels and shorts, by introducing widescreen, big-screen and other new technologies, by making blockbusters which could be road-shown at premium prices, by engaging in co-productions, by drawing more extensively on pre-sold properties and relying more on international markets, by attempting to target audiences (especially teenage and adult audiences) more precisely, by producing television programmes, by deriving income from the screening of films on television, and by acting as distributors, facility houses and as sources of finance for independent projects. The ranks of the independents had been augmented in the 1940s by stars, directors and producers attracted by lower tax-rates and the possibility of greater control over the films they made. They had been further augmented by the laying-off of in-house production staff, many of whom now became freelance. One of the consequences was an increasingly prominent role for talent agents. Another was a substantial change in the mode of production. Studio and independent projects alike were increasingly put together on a one-off basis or on the basis of plans for much smaller groups of films than had been the case in the studio era. 'Package production', the assembly of financing, personnel and the means of production around individual projects became the norm.

Despite these and other changes (notably the spread of drive-in theatres, the introduction of multiplex theatres, and the modification and eventual abandonment of the Production Code in 1968), conditions in Hollywood and in the industry as a whole remained unstable for over two decades. Audiences continued to decline. Theatres continued to close. A number of companies underwent changes in ownership as well as in organization. Some were taken over (sometimes several times) by large-scale conglomerates with diverse business interests or with interests in a variety of forms of leisure and entertainment. Some diversified themselves. Some sold off their studio facilities. It was only in the mid-1970s, in the wake of a period of overproduction, a series of spectacular box-office failures and a sudden decline in the revenues derived from the rental of films to television, that a 'new', more stable, and more consistently profitable Hollywood began to emerge.[4]

What is now usually called 'the New Hollywood' was essentially a combination of the structures and practices that emerged during the course of the 1950s and 1960s, one or two subsequent modifications, and a more propitious set of social and industrial conditions.[5] Package and independent production remained in place, as did the mixed role of the remaining majors (and an increasing number of 'mini-majors' like Orion and Tri-Star and later New Line and Miramax) as distributors of independent productions and as producers or co-producers of films of their own. (According to Pryluck (1986: 131), 'About a third of the films released by the majors in 1983 were "in-house" productions'.) With the exception of a number of senior producers and some of the technicians employed in facility houses, production personnel worked on a freelance basis, nearly all of them represented by agents.

The production each year of one or two heavily pre-publicized blockbusters, now not road-shown or stagger-released but 'blanket-released' (released simultaneously in large numbers of cinemas) formed the economic cornerstone of Hollywood's output, all of them financed and most of them produced or co-produced by the majors. Most of these blockbusters (indeed most of Hollywood's films) were made with audiences in their teens and their twenties in mind. They were thus increasingly different in character from the blockbusters of the 1950s and 1960s, though like earlier blockbusters they served to pioneer a number of technological innovations, notably in the fields of special effects and sound. The income from cinema screenings of these and other films was augmented by income from screenings on broadcast, cable and satellite television, by income from spin-offs and tie-ins (soundtrack albums, comic strips, books, toys and games and the like),[6] and by income from video rentals and sales. The advent of cable, satellite and video served to expand the media environment into which feature films were released, to increase the number of 'windows' through which films could be viewed and consumed and to multiply the dimensions of the inter-textual relay. Together with favourable legislation and a halting of the decline in cinema attendances, it also encouraged a new wave of conglomerate mergers and takeovers, an increasing exploitation of the 'synergies' within and between the products these conglomerates produced and the media channels and outlets they owned and controlled, and even the return of vertical integration.

By the mid-1980s, then, the ownership, structure and practices of the US film industry and the cultural environment in which it was now located had changed a number of times and in many ways since the 1930s. They were to change again in the 1990s, as conglomeration and synergy tended to accelerate on a national and international scale, as some of the mini-majors disappeared and as others were absorbed by the majors, and as the costs of making blockbusters and routine features alike continued to rise.[7] However, while the mid-1980s were marked by an increase in the number of films produced, in the number of films distributed, in the number of cinemas and cinema screens and in profits (Brown 1995: 363, 367, 368; Finler 1988: 287), what had not changed were the risks inherent in film production. Just as they had been reduced in the studio era by vertical integration and oligopoly control, these risks may have been tempered by conglomeration, by the number of industries in which conglomerates were involved, by the scale and the range of products they produced, by the synergies among and between these products, and by the number of windows, markets and advertising channels available for films in a global, multi-media environment. But there remained no cast-iron formulas for success, for the simple reason that films remained one-of-a-kind items; there remained no guarantees that films would make money, for the simple reason that a feature film remains 'a product that consumers must pay for before they know how much enjoyment they will receive' (Hoskins, McFadyen and Finn 1997: 56). It is therefore not surprising to find that there are similarities as well as differences between the generic range and nature of Hollywood's output in the mid-1980s and its nature and range in the mid-1930s, similarities as well as differences in the strategies used to alleviate risks and protect investments despite the changes in structure, in environment, and in the process of film production.

Among the films released in the first quarter of 1984 and reviewed by *Variety* were *Hot Dog . . . The Movie*, which 'attempts to be a party pic on skis aimed directly at the teen audience' (18 January: 22), *Deathstalker*, 'another low budget sword and sorcery item' (18 January: 26), a 'sophisticated comedy' called *Scandalous* (25 January: 21), a 'romantic comedy' called *The Buddy System* (25 January: 21), 'a youth-oriented rock picture' called *Footloose* (15 February: 24), *Against All Odds*, 'a well-engineered second try at 1947's "Out of the Past"' (15 February: 24), *Preppies*, an 'exploitation comedy aimed at both the teenage drive-in movie audience and the somewhat older crowd for subsequent cable-tv exposure' (15 February: 26), *Lassiter*, a 'formula picture designed to exploit the charm of Tom Selleck' (22 February: 18), and a 'father and son drama' called *Misunderstood* (29 February: 15). Also among them were an 'action picture' called *Running Hot* (7 March: 209), an 'old-fashioned gothic horror film' called *The House Where Death Lives* (7 March: 320), an 'adventure drama with doses of comedy' called *Tank* (14 March: 20), *Greystoke: The Legend of Tarzan, Lord of the Apes*, an 'epic adventure' (21 March: 16), and a 'Western' called *Triumphs of a Man Called Horse* (28 March: 28).

Among the films released later that year were *The Bounty*, a 'superior remake' (25 April: 18), a 'women's prison film' called *10 Violent Women* (9 May: 526), 'a run of the mill sci-fi thriller' called *Dreamscape* (16 May: 26), *Indiana Jones and the Temple of Doom*, a 'surefire commercial attraction' (16 May: 26), *The Karate Kid*, '"Rocky" for kids' (23 May: 12), *Star Trek III, The Search for Spock*, 'an emotionally satisfying science fiction adventure' (30 May: 12), *Hollywood High Part II*, 'Abysmal drive-in fare' (6 June: 21), *The Evil That Men Do*, an 'Assembly-line Charles Bronson pic' (13 June: 18), *Girls Night Out*, a 'standard slasher pic' (20 June: 17), *The Muppets Take Manhattan*, a 'Charming family pic' (11 July: 16), *Places in the Heart*, the 'first of a trio of rural dramas' (19 September: 20), a 'horror thriller' called *Impulse*, a 'romance' called *Falling in Love* (21 November: 16), 'a Chuck Norris actioner' called *Missing in Action* (21 November: 16), a 'farce' called *Micki and Maude* (5 December: 16), a 'sci-fi epic' called *Dune* (5 December: 16) and a 'baseball picture' called *Tiger Town* (19 December: 19).

Once again, then, we find generic variety. We also find star vehicles like *Lassiter*, star-formula combinations like *The Evil That Men Do* and *Missing in Action*, hybrids like *Tank*, contributions to cycles like *Places in the Heart*, and contributions to longer-term trends like *Star Trek III* and *Dune*. We find transposed formulas derived from individual films like *Karate Kid*. We find contributions to series. We find remakes. We find films categorized by audience and exhibition site like *Preppies*, *The Muppets Take Manhattan* and *Hollywood High Part II*. We find action films and comedies, romances and dramas, even a father and son film, a Tarzan film, a version of *Mutiny on the Bounty* and a baseball picture. There are numerous differences of course. Horror films, teenpics and science fiction films of all kinds are far more prevalent than musicals and westerns. (Indeed the term 'musical' does not appear at all.) Unlike the 1930s, there are a number of sword-and-sorcery and slasher films; unlike the 1930s there are no G-man films, no racetrack pics and no newspaper stories. These differences, though, are differences in generic fashion and in the nature of the series, cycles, trends and target exhibition sites and audiences involved rather than in the strategies used to minimize risk – even blockbusters like *Indiana Jones and the Temple of Doom* and *Star Trek III* are analogous in some respects to the superspecials of the 1930s.

These points are borne out further if we glance briefly at the films released in 1985 and 1986. Those released in 1985 included *The Party Animal*, a 'sexploitation pic' (23 January 1985: 16), *Heavenly Bodies*, a 'film trying to cash in on the aerobic dance craze' (30 January: 18), *The Slugger's Wife*, a 'Baseball pic set to rock music' (30 March: 12), and a 'family film' called *Sylvester* (30 March: 12). They also included *Silverado*, an 'attempt to revive the Western genre' (3 July: 16), *Day of the Dead*, 'third edition of the zombie series' (3 July: 16), *My Science Project*, 'Funniest of the current crop of science pics' (14 August: 16), *Back to the Future*, 'Summertime comedy hit' (26 June: 18), *Jagged Edge*, 'a suspenseful variation on what used to be called neighborhood programmers' (11 September: 14), a 'drama' called *Plenty* (11 September: 14), a 'familiar political drama' called *Marie* (25 September: 14), a 'biopic' called *Sweet Dreams* (2 October: 9), a 'Schwarzenegger action fantasy' called *Commando* (9 October: 23), a 'spy thriller' called *Target* (6 November: 26), *Once Bitten*, a 'combo of teen sex comedy and vampire genre' (6 November: 28), *King Solomon's Mines*, a 'remake . . . imitative of Indiana Jones' (27 November: 15), *Out of Africa*, a 'period romance' (11 December: 17) and *The Jewel of the Nile*, 'a sequel to "Romancing the Stone"' (11 December: 17).

The films released in 1986 included an 'Action film' called *Black Moon Rising* (15 January: 23), *Hannah and Her Sisters*, a 'comedy-drama' (22 January: 18), *My Chauffeur*, a 'screwball comedy aimed at young women' (29 January: 14), a 'teen comedy' called *Seven Minutes to Heaven* (29 January: 15), a 'black comedy' called *The Imagemaker* (29 January: 14), 'an entry in the ever-expanding half-man, half-robot genre' called *Eliminators* (5 February: 32) and *Wildcats*, a 'Formula football pic' (12 February: 22). They also included *Quicksilver*, an 'attempt to followup "Footloose" on bikes' (12 February: 24), a 'teen pic' called *Lucas* (2 April: 16), a 'romantic drama' called *Fire With Fire* (7 May: 9), *Big Trouble in Little China*, 'action-adventure along the lines of "Indiana Jones and the Temple of Doom"' (2 July: 13), a 'Formula slasher picture' called *Shadows Run Black* (16 July: 16), a 'mixture of comedy and drama' called *Nothing in Common* (23 July: 16), a 'drama' called *The Boy Who Could Fly*, *Radioactive Dreams*, 'Raymond Chandler meets Mad Max' (24 September: 13), a 'service comedy' called *Weekend Warriors* (29 October: 11), a 'carbon of *Police Academy*' called *Recruits* (29 October: 14), a 'Rustic romance' called *Nobody's Fool* (5 November: 12), *Heartbreak Ridge*, a 'contemporary war pic' (3 December: 19), *Billy Galvin*, a 'Family drama which will play well on television and videocassette' (3 December: 19) and *No Mercy*, a contribution to the 'blooming genre of lone-cop-turned vigilante stories' (17 December: 18).

Once again these examples are not designed to be precisely representative. But both in and of themselves and in tandem with the examples from the mid-1930s, they serve to qualify the tenets of a number of accounts of New Hollywood and genre. These accounts tend to stress the differences between the New and the old, and to do so on two distinct grounds. Firstly, writers like Hoberman (1985), Monaco (1979) and Silverman (1978) have argued that the New Hollywood is characterized by what Hoberman calls 'sequelitis'

(1985: 38) and is thus more reliant than the old on sequels, series, remakes. Whether taken as a sign of creative atrophy, conglomerate domination, commercial timidity or all three at once, the recycling of established stories, characters, ideas and performers has been seen as a distinctive feature of Hollywood's output in the late 1970s and 1980s. However, as Simonet has shown (and as our discussion of Hollywood's output in the 1930s helps to illustrate), 'far more recycled-script films appeared before the conglomerate takeovers than before' (1987: 157). Reviewing a sample of 3,490 films released between 1940 and 1979, categorizing each of them as new films, series films, remakes or sequels, and grouping series films, remakes and sequels together as 'recycled-scripts', Simonet points out that

> there were approximately six times as many recycled-script films in the 1940s as in the 1970s. Recycled-script films accounted for approximately one-quarter of U.S. feature, fictional film production in the 1940s and approximately one-tenth in the 1970s. Series films accounted for the bulk of the difference between the two decades. Sequels were slightly more numerous in the 1970s.
>
> The turning point was the mid-1950s. Recycled-script films dropped from 20 percent of the total in 1952 to 10 percent in 1955 and to just 4 percent in 1958. Percentages remained single-digit during the 1960s before a slight rise in the 1970s, peaking (for the years studied) at 12 percent in 1976.
>
> (Simonet 1987: 157–9. For a detailed study of one particular studio-era series, see Budner 1990.)

Perceptions of sequelitis in the 1970s may therefore have been governed by comparisons with the previous decade. As Simonet points out, they may have been governed too by the emerging fashion for prequels like *Butch and Sundance* (1979) and for recycled-script films with numbers or years in their titles (*Rocky II* (1979), *The Concorde – Airport 79* (1979) and the like), though the actual incidence of such films 'was not high' (1987: 161). As he goes on to point out, 'recycled scripts remained "relatively few in number" in the early 1980s' (ibid.). (Simonet here is quoting from 'Hollywood More Original Than Supposed: Lucrative Re-do Wave Still Minor', *Variety*, 7 December 1983: 5.) Perceptions at this time may have been influenced by 'a small number of high-visibility sequels' like *Return of the Jedi*, which 'alone collected 9 percent of all domestic rentals in 1983' (Simonet 1987: 161). 'Bonanzas like that, accompanied by merchandising and ancillary versions in other media, brought the "sequel trend" to journalistic attention', he argues, 'but they obscured the act [*sic*] that Hollywood has recycled scripts throughout history' (ibid.). *Indiana Jones and the Temple of Doom*, *Hollywood High Part II* and *Day of the Dead* thus represent a strand in Hollywood's output no different in essence, in prevalence or in purpose from *Gold Diggers of 1935* (1935), *Charlie Chan in Paris* or *After the Thin Man* (1936).[8]

Often bolstered by the tenets of post-modern theory, a second strand of writing on New Hollywood and genre has been marked by its stress on hybridity. Collins (1995: 125–56), Hill (1998: 101), Phillips (1996: 134–7), Sartelle (1996: 516) and a number of others have all argued that the output of the New Hollywood can be distinguished from the old by the hybridity of its genres and films. Most argue in addition that this hybridity is governed by the multi-media synergies characteristic of the New Hollywood, by the mixing and recycling of new and old and low art and high art media products in the modern (or post-modern) world, and by the propensity for allusion and pastiche that is said to characterize contemporary artistic production. For some it is also governed by the education in film theory and history received by many modern film-makers, and by the logic of package production.

There can be no doubt that many New Hollywood films are marked not only by what Thompson and Bordwell call 'movie consciousness' (1994: 714), but also by 'popular culture consciousness' too. And there can be no doubt that allusion, pastiche and hybridity are characteristic of a number of New Hollywood's films. However, allusion, pastiche and hybridity are not the same thing, nor are they as extensive or as exclusive to New Hollywood as is sometimes implied. As such oft-cited films as *Silverado* and *Body Heat* both make clear, allusion and pastiche may entail generic self-consciousness, but they need not entail generic hybridity. In fact, pastiche and allusion function in both these films as means of attempting to secure (or to 'revive') an imaginary form of generic purity, a single and stable generic identity as a western and as a neo-*noir* thriller respectively.[9]

Silverado and *Body Heat* were directed by Lawrence Kasdan, and it is Kasdan's films, along with those directed by John Carpenter, Robert Zemeckis, Joe Dante, Brian Da Palma and the Coen brothers, which tend to be cited as examples of New Hollywood's propensity for allusion and pastiche (Belton 1994: 306–7; Carroll 1982; Collins 1995: 127–40; Hill 1998: 101; Phillips 1996: 136). Quite how representative these films are is a matter for debate and empirical research. But it is clear that *Falling in Love*, *Target* and *Misunderstood* are no more marked by pastiche and allusion than such studio-era equivalents as *Magnificent Obsession*, *Till We Meet Again* and *O'Shaughnessy's Boy*. It is also clear that the allusive dimensions of many studio-era films are often invisible to contemporary scholars. Aside from referring again to the comments made on *Stagecoach* and the western by Gallagher (1986: 208), one might cite as an example here the extent to which the exchange of 'Oh yeah's' between the Clark Gable character and the long distance bus driver (Ward Bond) in *It Happened One Night* is an allusion to similar exchanges between the Gable character and the gangster played by Wallace Beery in *The Secret Six*. One might point too to Barker and Sabin's discussion of the allusions to James Fenimore Cooper's novel *The Last of Mohicans* in *The Birth of a Nation* and of the allusions to *The Birth of a Nation* in the 1920 Hollywood version of Cooper's novel (1995: 72–4). Finally, one might note as well that there was a multi-media environment in the 1930s, an environment that included vaudeville and popular theatre, radio and comic books, pulp magazines, newspapers and the music of Tin Pan Alley and Broadway. This was not the same environment as that of the 1980s or 1990s, nor was it as extensively cross-owned by media corporations. But it was one in which a number of the majors had a stake (Hilmes 1990: 7–115; Jewell 1982: 9–10, and 1984; McLaughlin 1988: 69–97, 121–33, 143–9; Millard 1995: 158–62, 176– 88; Sanjek [1988] 1996: 147–58; Shepherd 1982: 82–6; J. Smith 1998: 27–32). And it did constitute an extensive field of multi-media consciousness, institutional crossover and inter-textual cross-reference, as a glance at any comedian comedy and almost any revue, musical comedy or low budget action film or serial will verify. (For some examples, see Aylesworth 1985: 29–103; Balio 1993: 161–4; Barbour 1970: 27–9, 71–2; Cline 1984: 10–27; Gehring 1994; Gifford 1984: 62–5, 72–3, 92–3, 224–7; Jenkins 1992; Malone [1985] 1987: 142–52; Schoell 1991: 194–200; Seidman 1981; Toll 1982: 82–5, 109–12, 136–43, 169–71, 222–33; Weales 1985.)

Hybridity itself, meanwhile, is not confined to New Hollywood either. As has been made clear a number of times during the course this book, generic hybridity is as common in old Hollywood as it is in the New Hollywood. As Richard Maltby has pointed out, 'most movies use categorical elements in combination' (1995: 108). Aside from the examples given in this chapter and elsewhere in this book, it is worth citing Basinger's comments on *Tripoli* (1950):

If you sit down to watch a movie in which Maureen O'Hara plays an ambitious young woman trying to marry her way upward into financial security, would you inevitably label it a woman's picture? Suppose it is set in a desert, and O'Hara wears harem pants. Could it be a woman's picture anyway? What if it is called *Tripoli*, and it stars John Payne as a United States Marine. Is it a combat movie? But how about if it has Howard DaSilva as a pirate? Maybe it's a swashbuckler. And it's set in 1805, so it must be a costume film . . . or maybe a historical drama.

Tripoli exists, and it does star Payne and O'Hara. Watching it, one can recognize elements from many types of films – musicals, Westerns, service films, traditional war films, and even the woman's film. It's a story about the marines fighting the Barbary pirates. It contains within its running time traditional events that have come to be associated with all the genres named above, and probably more. It's a grab bag of plots, a crazy quilt.

(Basinger 1986: 1)

As Basinger goes on to point out, '*Tripoli* is not the only film that mixes generic components' (ibid.: 2). That does not make it representative of old or transitional Hollywood. But it does serve to qualify the stress laid on hybridity as a distinguishing feature of the New Hollywood. So too do the generic precursors of the films that tend to be cited as examples of New Hollywood's hybridity. The citing of examples is in fact rather rare. Detailed discussion is even rarer. Phillips (1996) cites *Raising Arizona* (1986). Collins (1995) cites *Blade Runner, Who Framed Roger Rabbit?* (1988), *Wild at Heart* (1990) and *Back to the Future III*. And Sartelle (1996) cites *Terminator 2, Star Wars, Jurassic Park* (1993) and *Back to the Future*. *Raising Arizona, Who Framed Roger Rabbit?, Back to the Future* and *Back to the Future III* are comedies. As such they can accommodate the generic allusions and the additional generic paradigms upon which they draw in the same way and to precisely the same degree as virtually any Marx Brothers comedy, any Hope and Crosby *Road* film, or any of the early sound comedies discussed by Henry Jenkins (1992). It is true, as it is true of most Coen brothers films, that *Raising Arizona* is characterized by the tonal shifts and uncertainties that help mark its generic allusions; it is true, as it is true of many of the examples given here, that the *Back to the Future* films use and allude to the paradigms of science fiction to an extent that is rare in studio-era Hollywood; and it is true that *Who Framed Roger Rabbit?* combines animation and live-action in ways which were also rare (though not entirely unknown) in the studio era. These are distinctive features. They help to characterize these and other New Hollywood films. Some of them also help to exemplify New Hollywood's movie consciousness. But that does not make the films themselves any more generically hybrid than *Tripoli*, or any of the other studio-era examples cited above.

Wild at Heart is a road movie and *Blade Runner* science fiction. I see no evidence of unusual hybridity in these films at all. The same is true of *Star Wars, Terminator 2* and the other blockbusters cited by Sartelle (1996). These are science fiction films with an accent on those elements of action-adventure that have comprised part of the genre's repertoire since the turn of the century. Like many other New Hollywood blockbusters – *Raiders of the Lost Ark* (1981), *Superman* (1978), *Alien, Dick Tracy* (1990), *Independence Day* (1996) and the like – they derive from and allude, as is well known, to the B adventure, sci-fi and action films, serials and low budget features of the 1930s, the 1940s and the 1950s. As such, while their budgets and their status in the industry have changed, they are no more hybrid than *Flash Gordon, Dick Tracy* (1937), *The Perils of Nyoka* (1942), *Superman* (1948), *The War of the Worlds* (1953), *It! The Terror from Beyond Space* (1958) and the other serials and films which preceded them, or the radio serials, comic strips and pulp magazine stories on which these serials and films were often based. Indeed it could be argued that we have yet to see any New Hollywood blockbuster equivalent in hybridity to the *The Phantom Empire* (1935), an old Hollywood serial about a singing cowboy in outer space.

It is hard to know why the confusions and the misconceptions here have arisen. It is possible that allusion and hybridity have become confused. It is possible that orthodox accounts of old Hollywood and genre have had a misleading impact on accounts of New Hollywood. It is also possible that accounts of New Hollywood and genre have been influenced by accounts of 'high concept' film-making, a practice which seeks to construct packages and films around ideas, components and taglines that lend themselves to easy encapsulation – and hence to easy marketing – and that often entail combinations of the 'Raymond Chandler meets Mad Max' variety (Wyatt 1991, 1994). But whatever the specificities of circumstance and style high concept films entail, however linked they may be to the industrial conditions of New Hollywood, combinations like this are arguably no different in kind or in purpose from those to be found in old Hollywood films like *Wonder Bar* (*Grand Hotel* meets the musical?) or *Country Beyond* (*The Thin Man* meets the Mounties?). Moreover, it should be noted that in defining high concept, Wyatt himself stresses the extent to which high concept films work 'within genre' (1991: 91).

All-in-all, whatever the reasons, accounts of New Hollywood and genre tend to overemphasize hybridity. According to Dominick, the highest percentage of films released between 1979 and 1983 fall into the category of 'General Drama' (1987: 147). According to Harwood, 'Most of the top box-office films' in the 1980s 'were comedies', which 'represented a significantly greater proportion than the next most popular, action/adventure movies. These were followed by science-fiction films, dramas (including domestic melodrama), thrillers and fantasy films' (1997: 33–4). While there are plenty of examples of hybridity in the sample cited above, these categories are all represented in relatively straightforward ways as well. All-in-all, whatever the reasons, the confusions and misconceptions surrounding the output of New Hollywood and old Hollywood alike tend to focus on notions of genre. This is nowhere more apparent than in the way the term is deployed in Gomery's and in Sartelle's contributions to *The Oxford History of World Cinema* (Nowell-Smith 1996). Where for Sartelle 'The period of which *Terminator 2* is representative . . . is "post-generic"' (1996: 516), for Gomery, 'the very basis of the success of the success of "New" Hollywood was the regular production of genre films' (1996c: 480). This is therefore an appropriate point to review the issues at stake in the concept of genre, to draw some conclusions, and to pose some questions for further research.

ISSUES, CONCLUSIONS AND QUESTIONS

It is clear that in their descriptions of New Hollywood cinema, Gomery and Sartelle are using the terms 'genre' and 'generic' in different ways. For Sartelle they suggest the categories associated with Hollywood's output in the studio era and the extent to which the films themselves conformed to them. (New Hollywood 'is "post-generic", he writes (1996: 516), 'in the sense that, while films belonging to the traditional Hollywood genres were still being made, they coexisted with an explosion of emerging new categories'). For Gomery, they indicate films 'that could be most easily packaged, and sold on a mass scale to audiences around the world' (1996c: 480). If we add to these meanings some of the others discussed earlier on in this book, it becomes apparent once again that 'genre' and 'generic' are multifaceted concepts and terms: if genre can mean 'category', generic can mean 'constructed or marked for commercial consumption'; if genre can mean 'corpus', generic can mean 'conventionally comprehensible'; if genre can mean 'formula', generic can mean 'those aspects of representation that entail the generation of expectations'; and so on.

It is the multiple nature of these facets and meanings that have helped generate the variety of uses to which these concepts have been put. As we have seen, these uses have focused overwhelmingly on Hollywood and its films. They have varied from the provision of means by which to analyse the aesthetic workings and the industrial and mass-produced nature of Hollywood's films to the provision of means by which to theorize their socio-cultural significance. They have included the provision of aesthetic and ideological contexts for the discussion of individual films and auteurs (John Ford and the western, Douglas Sirk and melodrama, and so on). And they have included the provision of means by which to analyse the nature of Hollywood's output at specific points in time. Books and articles on genre have ranged from detailed studies of specific genres and generic traditions to studies which use these traditions as a way of discussing particular groups or collections of films. They have ranged as well from theoretical discussions of genre to discussions of its role in Hollywood's commercial and industrial practices and structures.

As I hope I have made apparent, much of this work is extremely valuable. However, as I hope I have also made apparent, some of its tenets, some of its practices and some of its presuppositions are open to question. Genre critics and theorists have repeatedly argued for the importance of genre as a means of conceptualizing the links between Hollywood's films and US society, between Hollywood's industry and Hollywood's art, between Hollywood's producers and Hollywood's consumers, and between Hollywood's present and Hollywood's past. However as Richard Maltby has argued (Maltby and Bowles 1994: 128–34; Maltby 1995: 107–43), most critics and theorists have in practice nearly always used the concept of genre as a way of avoiding detailed study of anything other than selective samples of Hollywood's art. As we have seen in the case of melodrama and *film noir*, 'Genre criticism has understood genre in Hollywood quite differently from the industry itself, ignoring most of the industry's own categories and introducing alternatives of its own' (1995: 116). As we have seen in Chapter 6, it has also constructed structural models and evolutionary schemas as a way of avoiding rather than conducting socio–cultural and historical analysis. Where structural models

have substituted generically internal thematic antinomies for detailed contextual research, the 'imposition of an internal historical structure in which
texts influence each other', a characteristic of all evolutionary schemas and
most genre histories, has tended to 'eliminate the need to consider external
questions of industry, economics and audience in favor of a search for
recurrent textual structures' (ibid.). Finally, as we have repeatedly seen, rather
than looking in full at the nature of Hollywood's output either in general or
at any particular point in time, genre criticism has tended to concern itself
with exemplary films and with canons of excellence (whether defined in
terms of artistic merit, ideological subversiveness, or conformity to a particular theoretical model). In addition it has tended to assume throughout that
Hollywood has always organized the production and distribution of its films
in ways which dovetail not just with the genres it has identified but also with
genre itself as a category. Genre criticism has thus not just constructed a series
of misleading pictures of Hollywood's output, it has also, according to Maltby,
constructed a misleading picture of 'the industry itself, which categorizes its
product by production size and by the audience sector to whom it is primarily
appealing, organizing its production schedules around cycles and sequels
rather than genres as such' (1995: 130).

I myself would qualify this last point. While the evidence discussed in this
chapter suggests that cycles and sequels were and are important as factors in
the planning of productions, it also suggests that star-genre formulations, star-
formula combinations, production trends, cyclic formulae, generic formulae,
generic hybrids and traditionally defined genres were and are important as
well. Thus while I endorse Maltby's insistence on the importance of industrial
factors and of thorough historical and socio-cultural analysis, and while I
share many of his views on the limitations of genre criticism and genre theory,
I would myself maintain that the latter still have a role to play in understanding Hollywood, its history and its films. At least some of the definitions
discussed in Chapter 3 make sense; and at least some of the terms and
descriptions used by the industry coincide with those used by critics and
theorists.

The limitations of existing genre criticism and theory need, nevertheless, to
be acknowledged, and an agenda of the kind implicit in Maltby's comments
needs to be set. In doing so, there are a number of examples to follow. Among
them are Doherty's work on the 1950s teenpic (1988), Jacobs' work on the
fallen woman films of the late 1920s, the 1930s and early 1940s (1991),
Jenkins' work on early sound comedy (1992), Kapsis' work on the early
1980s horror film (1991), Klinger's work on 'local genres' (1994b), Leutrat's
work on the 1920s western (1985), Maltby's work on the gangster films of the
early 1930s (1993b), Riblet's work on Keystone comedy (1995), Singer's
work of serial-queen melodrama (1990), Stanfield's work on the 1930s
western (1999) and Tudor's work on the horror film (1989). In various
ways and to varying degrees, this work is characterized by painstaking

industrial, socio-cultural and historical research, by a thorough viewing of more than a handful of canonic films, and by willingness to question and abandon orthodox views. For the most part, however, it is confined to single well-recognized genres or to single intra-generic cycles. Studies are needed of unrecognized genres like racetrack pics, of semi-recognized genres like drama, of cross-generic cycles and production trends like overland bus and prestige films, and of hybrids and combinations of all kinds.[10]

In tandem with studies of well-recognized genres, studies like this are more likely to provide an accurate picture both of the industry and its output and of the socio-cultural significance and role of its films, particularly if focused on particular periods. As I hope I have shown, our picture of the 1980s and even of the 1930s is partial at best. The same is even more true of the 1910s, the 1920s and the 1990s. If we glance briefly at the 1950s, whose output and whose industrial and socio-cultural conditions and contexts are relatively well-explored, it soon becomes apparent that the role of circus films like *The Greatest Show on Earth*, *Trapeze* (1956) and *The Big Circus* (1959) in the move toward road shows, in the promotion of an upgraded version of the cinematic experience and in the promotion of a traditional image of old-fashioned entertainment (a role it shares with show-business biopics in particular) has been all but ignored. It soon becomes apparent that the paranoid scenarios associated with 1950s science fiction, scenarios in which outsiders invade or infiltrate US communities, families and homes, are shared by crime films like *The Desperate Hours* (1955) and *Suddenly* (1954) and by westerns like *Day of the Outlaw* (1959), and are mirrored, doubled or reversed by heist films in western and gangster guise like *The Raid* and *Violent Saturday* (1955) and by numerous imperial adventure films, numerous cavalry westerns, numerous spy films, and numerous science fiction films about the exploration of outer space. And it soon becomes apparent that a preoccupation with race relations and ethnic identity can be found in virtually every area and in virtually every type of Hollywood production (Neale 1998). Studies of well-recognized genres in isolation are unlikely to shed further light on tendencies and trends such as these. A cross-generic and multi-cyclic approach, an approach which pays heed to 'local' and 'minor' genres and trends, and which in addition takes on board the factors involved in the 'production of culture perspective' adopted by Kapsis, is, to repeat, much more likely to produce reliable results.

Such an approach is also likely to dovetail with the more extensive conceptions of genre discussed towards the end of Chapter 1. For in addition to opening up other areas of the cinema to generic analysis, conceptions such as these permit a more inclusive and flexible approach to Hollywood's output, one which can encompass minor trends, local and non-canonic genres, cyclic contributions, star-formula combinations and hybrids. They also necessitate an attention to the industry, its relay and its audiences in ways which are likely to generate much more knowledge than we possess at the moment about the array of generic calculations at stake in film production, distribution and exhibition, about the construction of generic images in and through the industry's relay, and about the generic expectations and terms in circulation in the process of reception. To that extent they are likely, too, to support, to qualify and to promote debate around the statement which opens the chapter on genre in Maltby's book on Hollywood cinema and with which I would like to conclude. 'Hollywood', Maltby writes, 'is a generic cinema, which is not quite the same as saying that it is a cinema of genres' (1995: 107).

NOTES

1 In 'Reusable Packaging, Generic Products and the Recycling Process', Altman argues that cycles are studio-specific (1998: 11–16, 36). This is simply not true. The overland bus cycle included *Fugitive Lovers* (1934), which was produced at MGM, and *Cross Country Cruise* (1934), which was produced at Universal. And as *Variety*'s review makes clear, *Trumpet Blows* was Paramount's 'contribution' to a cycle that encompassed films made by other studios too.

2 This remained the case throughout the studio era and into the era of transition discussed below. Thus in 1954 the *Motion Picture Herald* reported that 'Content-wise', Columbia's 'properties run the gamut. There are frothy musicals, Biblical epics, stark dramas, domestic comedies and domestic tragedies as well as the ever-popular Westerns' ('Columbia Big Guns Loaded with Star and Story Power', 24 July 1954: 41). As far as I have been able to determine, genre specialization was more widespread in the 1900s and the 1910s (in some cases, then, prior to the establishment of 'Hollywood' as such). Keystone's specialization in comedy would clearly be an example, as would the Albuquerque Film Manufacturing Company's specialization in three-reel westerns, the Bostock Jungle and Film Company's specialization in animal pictures, and the Submarine Film Company's specialization in underwater dramas. However, most of these companies were short-lived and small, and even in the 1900s and 1910s most companies, however small, produced different lines, brands and genres. Whether determined by investment in locations, facilities or performers, specialization was more often either line- or brand-related or cyclic – confined to small groups of films made during specific and limited periods – than generic in the traditional sense of the term. See the entries on individual companies in Fernett (1988) and Slide ([1986] 1990), the references to the 'film subjects' indexed by company in Musser (1990c), the references to the genres and topics indexed by company in Bowser (1990), and the references to specific instances in Lahue (1971: 46, 132, and 1973: 80); Lyons (1974: 10–13); Musser (1994: 163); Slide (1970: 50–7, 1978: 87–96, and 1980: 70–1) and Staiger (1980: 21). For brief year-by-year surveys, see Tarbox (1983). For the differences between genres and generic terminology in the earliest years of the cinema and in later ones, see Neale (1990a: 55–6).

3 These terms are: Adventure, Allegory, Animal, Automobile racing, Aviation, Biography, Black, Boxing, Children's works, College, Comedy, Comedy-drama, Compilation, Crime, Detective, Disaster, Documentary, Domestic, Drama, Educational/cultural, Elderly, Espionage, Exploitation, Fantasy, Football, Gambling, Gangster, Historical, Horror, Horse race, Island, Jungle, Legal, Medical, Melodrama, Military, Musical, Musical comedy, Mystery, Newspaper, Northwest, Police, Political, Prison, Religious, Road, Romance, Romantic comedy, Rural, Science fiction, Screwball comedy, Social, Society, Sports, Teenage, Travelogue, War, Western, with songs, Yiddish, Youth. In use, these terms in turn tend to

generate hybrids and combinations. *Hi Nelli!*, for instance, is categorized as 'Newspaper, comedy-drama' (Hanson 1993: 911), *Devil Tiger* as 'Jungle, Animal, Documentary, Drama' (ibid.: 497), and *The Road to Ruin* as 'Exploitation, Teen-age, Drama, with songs' (ibid.: 1809). It is worth noting in this context that the headings used to identify the 'Types of Subject' in the section on 'The New Season Product' in the *Motion Picture Herald* on 3 June 1939 were similarly numerous. They were Western, Human Interest, Comedy, Adventure, Domestic Comedy, Aviation, Newspaper Story, Biography, Personal History, Political, City Life, Small Town Life, Family Life, Domestic Problems, Psychological, War, Emotional Drama, Father and Son, Sports, Crime, Sea Adventure, Romance, Society, Chain Gang, Medical, Domestic Comedy, Fantasy, Action-Adventure, Musical, Railroad, Mystery, Juvenile Comedy, Comedy, with Music, and Marital Comedy (pp. 15–17). (See also the categories used by Jones (1946: 334) in her 'breakdown of the types and kinds of feature-length motion pictures submitted to and approved by the Production Code Administration during the year 1945'.)

4 For some or all of these developments, see Alvey (1997); Anderson (1994); Balio ([1976] 1985: 401–573, and 1990a: 3–256); Belton (1992: 69–228, and 1994: 69–228, 257–73); Boddy ([1990] 1993: 132–54); Bordwell, Staiger and Thompson (1985: 330–7); Davis (1997: 1–90); Edgerton (1983); Finler (1988: 25–9, 33–5); Gomery (1992: 89–99, 230–53, and 1996); Hillier (1992: 7–15); Hilmes (1990: 140–70); Izod (1988: 122–77); Laskos (1981: 18–27); Maltby (1995: 71–4); Pirie (1981b: 40–5); Reddick (1988); Rose (1995: 52–331); Schatz (1988a: 411–92); Segrave (1992, and 1997: 140–235) and Vianello (1984).

5 As Peter Kramer has explained, the term 'New Hollywood' was initially asso-ciated with what has also been called the 'Hollywood Renaissance', with the stylistic and thematic innovations introduced into Hollywood in the late 1960s and early 1970s by film-makers like Robert Altman, Hal Ashby, Monte Hellman, Arthur Penn and Bob Rafelson (1998). Since the mid-1970s, however, it has been associated much more with the industrial and contextual changes detailed here. (See also M. Smith 1998.)

6 It should be noted that spin-offs and tie-ins are not new. Sheet music sales of film scores and theme songs and fiction tie-ins of all kinds date back to the 1910s. See J. Smith (1998: 28–9) and Singer (1993).

7 For some or all of the developments, changes and practices in the New Hollywood since the mid-1970s, see Allen (1998); Balio ([1976] 1985: 574–630, 1990a: 259–415, and 1996, 1998); Dale (1997: 1–115); Davis (1997: 90–5, 113–47, 172–5); Finler (1988: 17, 35); Hillier (1992: 15–37); Hilmes (1990: 171–99); Hoskins, McFadyen and Finn (1997); Gomery (1992: 263–99, and 1996c); Izod (1988: 181–98); Kleinhans (1998); Lees and Berkowitz ([1978] 1981); Lewis (1998b); Litwak (1986); Maltby (1995: 74–8); Phillips ([1975] 1982); Rose (1995: 355–93); Schatz (1993); Segrave (1997: 236–82); Sergi (1998); Thompson and Bordwell (1994: 699–703); Wasko (1994) and Wyatt (1994, 1998a, 1998b).

8 In *A Cinema Without Walls*, Timothy Corrigan argues that 'In the last twenty years especially, the sequel and the series film have been industrial and media cousins, the first being the theatrical descendant from the television family of the second . . . and both being extended versions of the repetitions inherent in the remake' (1991: 168). He continues, suggesting that 'In the neutralization of the former competition between media they once promoted, the sequel, remake, and series now can be commonly defined as the valorization of repetition beyond narrative differences. What they now promote is the consumption of a technology and images that can reconcile the differentiating competition between television and the movies' (ibid.). Finally, he argues that 'Today, the sequel, the series, and the

remake presume and respond to . . . a distracted and interrupted viewing that, to put it simply, remembers moments and images but not their motivations . . . In all three, narrative repetitions do not serve primarily to organize and anchor time but to make temporal repetition itself a technological distraction. If narratives once used repetitions to anchor and highlight differences, repetition now supports distraction' (ibid.: 168–9). There is no space here to question or counter these theses in detail. However, it is worth pointing out that serials, sequels and even 'remakes' predate the cinema. They are all common on the stage and/or in written fiction in the nineteenth century. In the cinema, as we have seen, they all predate television, which in any case was only a competitor to Hollywood in the strict sense in the early-to-mid-1950s. They also predate radio, which provided the same kind of (qualified) competition in the 1930s and 1940s, as well as a number of the serials and serial formats used not just on television but in Hollywood films as well. While the extent to which series and sequels of the kind discussed in this Chapter used repetition to anchor differences rather than the other way round is open to question, the attenuation of narrative and motivation in New Hollywood's blockbusters has, as Buckland points out (1998), both been somewhat overstated and in any case corresponds, to the extent that it is true, to similar degrees of attenuation in the studio-era B films and serials from which they derive. Finally, it is not my experience that contemporary audiences watch films in cinemas in a distracted or interrupted way. Certainly there is no modern equivalent to the practice common when I was a child of entering and leaving the cinema in the middle of programmes and films.

9 Such purity, of course, is 'inauthentic', dependent on artifice, self-consciousness and on what Phillips calls 'knowingness', 'a complicity between film-maker and spectator as they produce meaning in the deployment and reading respectively of . . . generic signifiers' (1996: 136). According to Phillips, 'Both film-maker and audience are aware of their revisiting of generically constructed worlds which increasingly are perceived as having their own history, their own independent reality' (ibid.). This awareness and this perception are for Phillips among the hallmarks of 'postmodern Hollywood and . . . of postmodern cultural production in general' (ibid.: 137). However, he provides no evidence that they exist, or conversely that they did not exist earlier on in Hollywood's history. His argument depends almost entirely on a presumption that audiences, film-makers and genres alike were once aesthetically naive, pure and innocent. As such it appears to share the fantasies that animate Kasdan's films and is in my view at least highly suspect.

10 For discussion of at least some minor, local or non-canonic genres, cycles and trends, see Cohan and Hark (1997); Doherty (1993b); Grindon (1996); Morey (1995); Rubin (1994) and Schaefer (1992).

APPENDIX

Chronological Index of 'Principal' *Noirs* from Borde and Chaumeton (1955)

FILMS NOIRS

1941 *The Maltese Falcon*
1942 *This Gun for Hire*
1943 *Journey Into Fear*
1944 *Murder, My Sweet*
      Ministry of Fear
      Phantom Lady
      The Mask of Dimitrios
1946 *Lady in the Lake*
      Notorious
      Gilda
      The Big Sleep
      Somewhere in the Night
1947 *The Lady from Shanghai*
      Dead Reckoning
      Ride the Pink Horse
      Out of the Past
      Dark Passage
1948 *Sorry, Wrong Number*
      The Big Clock
      Chicago Deadline
1949 *The Window*
1951 *Macao*

CRIMINAL PSYCHOLOGY

1940 *Rebecca*
1941 *Suspicion*
1942 *Shadow of a Doubt*
      King's Row

1944 *Double Indemnity*
The Woman in the Window
Laura
1945 *Hangover Square*
The Spiral Staircase
Conflict
Leave Her to Heaven
Love Letters
Fallen Angel
1946 *The Strange Love of Martha Ivers*
The Postman Always Rings Twice
The Locket
1947 *The Paradine Case*
Born to Kill
The Two Mrs Carrolls
1948 *Sleep, My Love*
Rope
1949 *Under Capricorn*
Whirlpool
House of Strangers
1950 *Night and the City*
Gun Crazy
1951 *Strangers on a Train*
1952 *The Sniper*
Angel Face

COSTUME CRIME FILMS

1941 *Doctor Jekyll and Mr Hyde*
1944 *Experiment Perilous*
Gaslight
The Suspect
1946 *Dragonwyck*
1947 *Ivy*
1948 *So Evil, My Love*

GANGSTERS

1946 *The Killers*
1949 *White Heat*
Criss-Cross
1950 *The Enforcer*
The Asphalt Jungle
1952 *The Big Heat*

DOCUMENTARY POLICE THRILLERS

1947 *Kiss of Death*
  Crossfire
1948 *He Walked by Night*
  Street With No Name
  The Naked City
1949 *Port of New York*
1950 *Where the Sidewalk Ends*
  Panic in the Streets
  The Enforcer
1952 *The Big Heat*

SOCIAL TRENDS

1945 *The Lost Weekend*
1947 *Nightmare Alley*
  Crossfire
1949 *Border Incident*
  Thieves' Highway
  The Set-Up
1950 *Breaking Point*
  The Lawless
1951 *The Big Carnival*
1953 *The Wild One*

BIBLIOGRAPHY

(Most references to newspapers, magazines and trade journals are given in full in the text or the notes.)

Abel, R. (1998) '"Our Country"/Whose Country? The "Americanisation" Project in Early Westerns', in Buscombe and Pearson 1998, 77–95.

Adair, G. (1989) *Hollywood's Vietnam, From The Green Berets to Full Metal Jacket*, London: Heinemann.

Adamson, J. ([1973] 1974) *Groucho, Harpo, and Chico and Sometimes Zeppo: A History of the Marx Brothers and a Satire on the Rest of the World*, London: Coronet.

Affron, C. (1982) *Cinema and Sentiment*, Chicago: Chicago University Press.

Agee, J. ([1949] 1967) 'Comedy's Greatest Era', *Agee on Film* [1958], vol. 2, London: Peter Owen, 2–19.

Albini, J. L. (1971) *The American Mafia: Genesis of a Legend*, New York: Appleton-Century-Crofts.

Aleiss, A. (1991) '*The Vanishing American*: Hollywood's Compromise to Indian Reform', *Journal of American Studies* 25, 3: 467–72.

—— (1995) 'Native Americans: The Surprising Silents', *Cineaste* 21, 3: 34–5.

Alewyn, R. ([1974] 1983) 'The Origin of the Detective Novel', trans. G. W. Stowe, in Most and Stowe 1983, 62–78.

Allen, J. (1984) 'Introduction: *Now, Voyager* as a Woman's Film: Coming of Age Hollywood Style', in J. Allen (ed.), *Now, Voyager*, Madison: University of Wisconsin Press, 9–39.

Allen, J. S. (1981) *Popular French Romanticism: Authors, Readers and Books in the 19th Century*, Syracuse: Syracuse University Press.

Allen, M. (1998) 'From *Bwana Devil* to *Batman Forever*, Technology in Contemporary Hollywood Cinema', in Neale and Smith 1998, 109–29.

—— (forthcoming) *Family Secrets: The Films of D. W. Griffith*, London: British Film Institute.

Allen, R. C. (1980) *Vaudeville and Film, 1895–1915: A Study in Media Interaction*, New York: Arno Press.

Alloway, L. (1963) 'On the Iconography of the Movies', *Movie* 7: 4–6.

—— (1971) *Violent America: The Movies 1946–1964*, New York: Museum of Modern Art.

Altick, R. (1957) *A Social History of the Mass Reading Public*, Chicago: Chicago University Press.

Altman, R. (ed.) (1981a) *Genre: The Musical*, London: RKP/British Film Institute.

([1978] 1981b) 'The American Film Musical: Paradigmatic Structure and Mediatory Function', in Altman 1981a, 197–207.

—— ([1984] 1986) 'A Semantic/Syntactic Approach to Film Genre', in Grant 1986a, 26–39.

—— (1987) *The American Film Musical*, Bloomington: Indiana University Press.

—— (1996a) 'Cinema and Genre', in Nowell-Smith 1996, 276–85.

—— (1996b) 'The Musical', in Nowell-Smith 1996, 294–303.

—— (1998) 'Reusable Packaging: Generic Products and the Recycling Process', in N. Browne (ed.), *Refiguring American Film Genres*, Berkeley: University of California Press, 1–41.

—— ([1949] 1999) *Film/Genre*, London: British Film Institute.

Alton, J. [1949] (1995) *Painting with Light*, Berkeley: University of California Press.

Alvey, M. (1997) 'The Independents: Rethinking the Television Studio System', in L. Spigel and M. Curtin (eds), *The Revolution Wasn't Televised: Sixties Television and Social Conflict*, New York: Routledge, 139–58.

Ambrose, S. E. (1994) '*The Longest Day* (1962): "blockbuster" history', *Historical Journal of Film, Radio and Television* 14, 4: 421–31.

Andersen, C. (1988) 'Biographical Film', in Gehring 1988, 331–51.

—— (1994) *Hollywood TV: The Studio System in the Fifties*, Austin: University of Texas Press.

Andersen, R. (1979) 'The Role of the Western Film Genre in Industry Competition, 1907–1911', *Journal of the University Film Association* 31, 2: 19–27.

Andersen, T. (1985) 'Red Hollywood', in S. Ferguson and B. Groseclose (eds), *Literature and the Visual Arts in Contemporary Society*, Columbus: Ohio University Press, 183–9.

Ang, I. (1985) *Watching Dallas, Soap Opera and the Melodramatic Imagination*, London: Methuen.

Aquila, R. (ed.) (1996) *Wanted Dead or Alive: The American West in Popular Culture*, Urbana: University of Illinois Press.

Aranda, F. (1975) *Luis Buñuel: A Critical Biography*, London: Secker and Warburg.

Ardis, A. L. (1990) *New Women, New Novels: Feminism and Early Modernism*, New Brunswick: Rutgers University Press.

Armitage, S. (1981) 'Rawhide Heroines: The Evolution of the Cowgirl and the Myth of America', in S. Girgus (ed.), *The American Self, Myth, Ideology, and Popular Culture*, Albuquerque: University of New Mexico Press, 166–81.

Armstrong, N. (1987) *Desire and Domestic Fiction: A Political History of the Novel*, New York: Oxford University Press.

Arnzen, M. A. (1994) 'Who's Laughing Now? The Postmodern Splatter Film', *Journal of Popular Film and Television* 21, 4: 176–84.

Arthur, P. S. (1990) *Shadows on the Mirror: Film Noir and Cold War America, 1945–1957*, New York University Ph.D. thesis, 1985, Ann Arbor: UMI Dissertation Information Service.

Asbury, H. (1927) *The Gangs of New York: An Informal History of the Underworld*, New York: Knopf.

Asheim, L. (1947) 'The Film and the Zeitgeist', *Hollywood Quarterly* 2, 4: 414–16.

Athearn, R. G. (1986) *The Mythic West in Twentieth-Century America*, Lawrence: University Press of Kansas.

Aumont, J., Bergala, A., Marie, M. and Vernet, M. (1992) *Aesthetics of Film*, trans. R. Neupert, Austin: University of Texas Press.

Auster, A. and Quart, L. (1988) *How the War Was Remembered: Hollywood and Vietnam*, New York: Praeger.

Aylesworth, T. G. (1985) *Broadway to Hollywood: Musicals from Stage to Screen*, London: Bison Books.

Babington, B. and Evans, P. W. (1985) *Blue Skies and Silver Linings: Aspects of the Hollywood Musical*, Manchester: Manchester University Press.

—— (1989) *Affairs to Remember: The Hollywood Comedy of the Sexes*, Manchester: Manchester University Press.

—— (1993) *Biblical Epics: Sacred Narrative in the Hollywood Cinema*, Manchester: Manchester University Press.

Bakhtin, M. (1965) *Rabelais and His World*, trans. H. Iswolsky, Bloomington: University of Indiana Press.

Balint, M. (1959) *Thrills and Regressions*, London: Hogarth Press.

Balio, T. (ed.) ([1976] 1985) *The American Film Industry*, Madison: University of Wisconsin Press.

—— (ed.) (1990a) *Hollywood in the Age of Television*, Boston: Unwin Hyman.

—— (1990b) 'Introduction to Part 1', in Balio 1990a, 3–40.

—— (1993) *Grand Design: Hollywood as a Modern Business Enterprise, 1930–1939*, New York: Scribner's.

—— (1996) 'Adjusting to the New Global Economy: Hollywood in the 1990s', in A. Moran (ed.), *Film Policy: International, National and Regional Perspectives*, London: Routledge, 23–38.

—— (1998) '"A Major Presence in All of the World's Important Markets": Globalization of Hollywood in the 1990s', in Neale and Smith 1998, 58–73.

Bank, R. K. (1990) 'Frontier Melodrama', in D. H. Ogden, with D. McDermott and R. K. Sarlos (eds), *Theatre West: Image and Impact*, Amsterdam: Rodopi, 151–60.

Banta, M. (1987) *Imagining American Women: Ideas and Ideals in Cultural History*, New York: Columbia University Press.

Baral, R. ([1962] 1970) *Revue: The Great Broadway Period*, New York: Fleet Press Corporation.

Barber, X. T. (1993) 'The Roots of Travel Cinema: John L. Stoddard, E. Burton Holmes and the Nineteenth-Century Illustrated Travel Lecture', *Film History* 5, 1: 68–84.

Barbour, A. (1970) *Days of Thrills and Adventure*, London: Collier Books.

Barker, M. and Sabin, R. (1995) *The Lasting of the Mohicans: History of an American Myth*, Jackson: University of Mississippi Press.

Barnouw, E. (1974) *Documentary: A History of the Non-Fiction Film*, Oxford: Oxford University Press.

—— (1981) *The Magician and the Cinema*, New York: Oxford University Press.

Barnouw, E. and Krishnaswarmy, S. (1980) *Indian Film*, Oxford: Oxford University Press.

Barr, C. (1967) *Laurel and Hardy*, London: Studio Vista.

Barra, A. (1989) 'The Incredible Shrinking Epic', *American Film* 14, 5: 40–5, 60.

Barrios, R. (1995) *A Song in the Dark: The Birth of the Musical Film*, New York: Oxford University Press.

Barry, J. F. and Sargent, E. W. (1927) *Building Theatre Patronage: Management and Merchandising*, New York: Chalmers.

Barth, G. (1980) *City People: The Rise of Modern City Culture in Nineteenth Century America*, Oxford: Oxford University Press.

Basinger, J. (1986) *The World War II Combat Film: Anatomy of a Genre*, New York: Columbia University Press.

—— (1993) *A Woman's View: How Hollywood Spoke to Women, 1930–1960*, London: Chatto and Windus.

—— (1994) *American Cinema: One Hundred Years of Filmmaking*, New York: Rizzoli.

Baudrillard, J. (1990) *Fatal Strategies*, trans. P. Beichtmn and W. G. Niesluchowski, New York: Semiotext(e).

Baxter, J. (1970) *Science Fiction in the Cinema*, London: Zwemmer.

Baym, N. (1978) *Women's Fiction: A Guide to Novels By and About Women in America, 1820–1870*, Ithaca, N.Y.: Cornell University Press.

Bazin, A. (1971a) 'The Western, or the American Film par excellence', in *What is Cinema?*, vol. 2, trans. and ed. H. Gray, Berkeley: University of California Press, 140–8.

—— (1971b) 'The Evolution of the Western', in *What is Cinema?*, vol. 2, 149–57.

Bederman, G. (1995) *Manliness and Civilization: A Cultural History of Gender and Race in the United States, 1880–1917*, Chicago: Chicago University Press.

Beer, G. (1970) *The Romance*, London: Methuen.

Behlmer, R. (1979) 'Introduction: From Legend to Film', in R. Behlmer (ed.), *The Adventures of Robin Hood*, Wisconsin: Wisconsin University Press, 11–41.

Bell, D. (1962) *The End of Ideology*, New York: The Free Press.

Belton, J. (1990) *Widescreen Cinema*, Cambridge, Mass.: Harvard University Press.

—— (1994) *American Cinema, American Culture*, New York: McGraw-Hill.

Ben-Amos, D. (1976) 'Analytical Categories and Ethnic Genres', in D. Ben-Amos (ed.), *Folklore Genres*, Austin: University of Texas Press, 215–42.

Bennett, T. (1981) 'Popular Culture and Hegemony in Post-War Britain', in *Politics, Ideology and Popular Culture*, Milton Keynes: Open University.

Benshoff, H. M. (1997) *Monsters in the Closet: Homosexuality and the Horror Film*, Manchester: Manchester University Press.

Berenstein, R. J. (1996) *Attack of the Leading Ladies: Gender, Sexuality and Spectatorship in Classic Horror Cinema*, New York: Columbia University Press.

Berg, C. R. (1989) 'Immigrants, Aliens, and Extraterrestrials: Science Fiction's Alien "Other" as (among Other Things) New Hispanic Imagery', *CineAction!* 18: 3–17.

Berg, R. (1990) 'Losing Vietnam: Covering the War in an Age of Technology', in Dittmar and Michaud 1990, 41–68.

Bergala, A. (1978) '*Dora et la Lanterne Magique*', *Cahiers du Cinéma* 287: 52–3.

Bergen, R. (1983) 'Whatever Happened to the Biopic?', *Films and Filming* 346: 21–2.

Bergman, A. (1971) *We're in the Money: Depression America and Its Films*, New York: Harper and Row.

Bergson, H. ([1900] 1911) *Laughter: An Essay on the Meaning of the Comic*, trans. C. Brereton and F. Rothwell, London: Macmillan.

Berkhofer Jr., R. E. ([1978] 1979) *The White Man's Indian: Images of the American Indian from Columbus to the Present*, New York: Vintage Books.

—— (1995) *Beyond the Great Story: History as Text and Discourse*, Cambridge, Mass.: Harvard/Belknap.

Bernstein, J. (1997) *Pretty in Pink: The Golden Age of Teenage Movies*, New York: St. Martin's Griffin.

Bernstein, M. (1994) *Walter Wanger: Hollywood Independent*, Berkeley: University of California Press.

Betrock, A. (1986) *The I Was a Teenage Juvenile Delinquent Rock 'n' Roll Horror Beach Party Book*, London: Plexus.

Bianchi, A. (1986) 'Le Roman Feuilleton en Italie', in R. Guise and H.-J. Neuschafer (eds), *Richesses du Roman Populaire*, Nancy: Centre de Recherches sur le Roman Populaire, 389–97.

Billington, R. A. ([1981] 1985) *Land of Savagery, Land of Promise: The European Image of the American Frontier in the Nineteenth Century*, Norman: University of Oklahoma Press.

Bingham, D. (1994) *Acting Male: Masculinities in the Films of James Stewart, Jack Nicholson, and Clint Eastwood*, New Brunswick: Rutgers University Press.

Birch, M. J. (1987) 'The Popular Fiction Industry: Market, Formula, Ideology', *Journal of Popular Culture* 21, 3: 79–102.

Bird, C. G. (1976) *The Role of Family in Melodrama, 1797–1827*, California: Josten's Publications.

Biskind, P. (1983) *Seeing is Believing: How Hollywood Taught Us to Stop Worrying and Love the Fifties*, London: Pluto.

Black, G. D. (1994) *Hollywood Censored: Morality Codes, Catholics, and the Movies*, Cambridge: Cambridge University Press.

Blacker, I. R. (1986) *The Elements of Screenwriting: A Guide for Film and Television Writers*, London: Collier Macmillan.

Blakemore, D. (1992) *Understanding Utterances: An Introduction to Pragmatics*, Oxford: Blackwell.

Bloom, C. (1996) *Cult Fiction: Popular Reading and Pulp Theory*, Houndmills: Macmillan.

Boddy, W. ([1990] 1993) *Fifties Television: The Industry and Its Critics*, Urbana: University of Illinois Press.

—— (1998) '"Sixty Million Viewers Can't Be Wrong": The Rise and Fall of the Television Western', in Buscombe and Pearson 1998, 119–40.

Bogle, D. ([1979] 1991) *Toms, Coons, Mulattoes, Mammies and Bucks: An Interpretive History of Blacks in American Films*, New York: Continuum.

Bold, C. (1987) *Selling the Wild West: Popular Western Fiction, 1860–1960*, Bloomington: Indiana University Press.

—— (1991) 'Popular Forms 1', in Elliott 1991, 285–305.

Booth, M. R. (1965) *English Melodrama*, London: Herbert Jenkins.

—— (1981) *Victorian Spectacular Theatre, 1850–1910*, London: Routledge and Kegan Paul.

—— (1991) *Theatre in the Victorian Age*, Cambridge: Cambridge University Press.

Borde, R. and Chaumeton, E. (1955) *Panorama du Film Noir Américain (1941–1953)*, Paris: Editions de Minuit.

Bordman, G. (1981) *American Operetta: From HMS Pinafore to Sweeney Todd*, New York: Oxford University Press.

—— (1982) *American Musical Comedy: From Adonis to Dreamgirls*, New York: Oxford University Press.

—— (1985) *American Musical Revue: From The Passing Show to Sugar Babies*, New York: Oxford University Press.

Bordwell, D. (1979) 'Art Cinema as a Mode of Film Practice', *Film Criticism* 4, 1: 56–64.

—— (1985) *Narration and the Fiction Film*, London: Methuen.

Bordwell, D., Staiger, J. and Thompson, K. (1985) *The Classical Hollywood Cinema: Film Style and Mode of Production to 1960*, London: Routledge.

Bordwell, D. and Thompson, K. ([1979] 1986) *Film Art: An Introduction*, New York: Knopf.

Botting, F. (1996) *Gothic*, London: Routledge.

Bowen, K. (1990) '"Strange Hells": Hollywood in Search of America's Lost War', in Dittmar and Michaud 1990, 226–35.

Bowser, E. (1990) *The Transformation of Cinema, 1907–1915*, New York: Scribner's.

Bradbury, R. (1988) 'Sexuality, Guilt and Detection: Tension between History and Suspense', in B. Doherty (ed.), *American Crime Fiction: Studies in the Genre*, London: Macmillan, 88–99.

Bradby, D., James, L. and Sharratt, B. (eds) (1980) *Performance and Politics in Popular*

Drama: Aspects of Entertainment in Theatre, Film and Television, 1800–1976, Cambridge: Cambridge University Press.

Brahms, C. and Sherrin, N. (1984) *Song by Song: The Lives and Work of 14 Great Lyric Writers*, Bolton: Ross Anderson.

Branscombe, P. (1980) 'Melodrama', in S. Sadie (ed.), *The New Grove Dictionary of Music and Musicians*, vol. 12, London: Macmillan, 116–18.

Braudy, L. (1976) *The World in a Frame: What We See in Films*, Garden City: Anchor Doubleday.

Brewster, B. (1987) 'Film', in D. Cohn-Sherbok and M. Irwin (eds), *Exploring Reality*, London: Allen and Unwin, 145–67.

—— ([1982] 1990 'A Scene at the "Movies"', in Elsaesser 1990, 318–25.

—— (1991) '*Traffic in Souls*: An Experiment in Feature-Length Narrative Construction', *Cinema Journal* 31, 1: 37–56.

Bristow, J. (1991) *Empire Boys: Adventures in a Man's World*, London: HarperCollins.

Britton, A. (1983) *Cary Grant: Comedy and Male Desire*, Newcastle upon Tyne: Tyneside Cinema.

—— (1984) *Katharine Hepburn: The Thirties and After*, Newcastle upon Tyne: Tyneside Cinema.

—— (1986) 'Blissing Out: The Politics of Reaganite Entertainment', *Movie* 31/2: 1–42.

Brooks, P. (1976) *The Melodramatic Imagination: Balzac, Henry James, Melodrama, and the Mode of Excess*, New Haven, Conn.: Yale University Press.

Brophy, P. ([1983] 1986) 'Horrality – the Textuality of Modern Horror', *Screen* 27, 1: 2–13.

Brosnan, J. (1974) *Movie Magic: The Story of Special Effects in the Cinema*, London: MacDonald.

—— (1978) *Future Tense: The Cinema of Science Fiction*, London: MacDonald and James.

Brown, B. (1991) 'Popular Forms II', in Elliott 1991, 357–79.

Brown, G. (1990) *Domestic Individualism: Imagining Self in Nineteenth-Century America*, Berkeley: University of California Press.

Brown, G. (1995) *Movie Time: A Chronology of Hollywood and the Movie Industry from Its Beginnings to the Present*, New York: Macmillan.

Brown, H. R. (1975) *The Sentimental Novel in America, 1789–1860*, New York: Octagon Books.

Brown, J. A. (1996) 'Gender and the Action Heroine: Hardbodies and *The Point of No Return*', *Cinema Journal* 35, 3: 52–71.

Brownlow, K. (1979) *The War, the West and the Wilderness*, London: Secker and Warburg.

—— (1990) *Behind the Mask of Innocence: Sex, Violence, Prejudice, Crime: Films of Social Conscience in the Silent Era*, London: Jonathan Cape.

Brunette, P. (1991) 'The Three Stooges and the (Anti-)Narrative of Violence: De(con)structive Comedy', in Horton 1991a, 174–87.

Bruno, G. ([1987] 1990) 'Ramble City: Postmodernism and *Blade Runner*', in Kuhn 1990a, 183–95.

Buchsbaum, J. (1986) 'Tame Wolves and Phoney Claims: Paranoia and Film Noir', *Persistence of Vision* 3, 4: 35–47.

Buckland, W. (1998) 'A Close Encounter with *Raiders of the Lost Ark*: Notes on Narrative Aspects of the New Hollywood Blockbuster', in Neale and Smith 1998, 166–77.

Budner, L. (1990) *From Social Realism to Burlesque: A History of One Hollywood Film*

Series, New York University Ph.D. thesis, 1982, Ann Arbor: UMI Dissertation Information Service.

Bukataman, S. (1991) 'Paralysis in Motion: Jerry Lewis's Life as a Man', in Horton 1991a, 188–205.

Burke, W. L. (1988) *The Presentation of the American Negro in Hollywood Films, 1946–1961: An Analysis of a Selected Sample of Feature Films*, Northwestern University Ph.D. thesis, 1965, Ann Arbor: UMI Dissertation Information Service.

Buscombe, E. (1970) 'The Idea of Genre in the American Cinema', *Screen* 11/2: 33–45.

—— (ed.) (1988a) *The BFI Companion to the Western*, London: André Deutsch/British Film Institute.

—— (1988b) 'The Western: A Short History', in Buscombe 1988a, 15–54.

—— (1995a) 'Inventing Monument Valley, Nineteenth-Century Landscape Photography and the Western Film', in P. Petro (ed.), *Fugitive Images: From Photography to Video*, Bloomington: Indiana University Press, 87–108.

—— (1995b) Book review in *Journal of Film and Video* 47/1–3: 124–30.

—— (1996) 'The Western', in Nowell-Smith 1996, 286–94.

Buscombe, E. and Pearson, R. (1998) *Back in the Saddle Again: New Essays on the Western*, London: British Film Institute.

Bush, C. (1988) 'Landscape', in Buscombe 1988a, 167–70.

Butler, A. M. (1994) 'Selling the Popular Myth', in Milner, O'Connor and Sandweiss 1994, 771–801.

Butler, I. (1970) *Horror in the Cinema*, London: Zwemmer.

Butsch, R. (1994) 'Bowery B'hoys and Matinee Ladies: The Re-Gendering of Nineteenth Century American Audiences', *American Quarterly* 46, 3: 374–405.

Byars, J. (1991) *All that Hollywood Allows: Re-Reading Gender in 1950s Melodrama*, London: Routledge.

Byers, T. B. (1989) 'Kissing Becky: Masculine Fears and Misogynist Moments in Science Fiction Films', *Arizona Quarterly* 45, 3: 77–95.

Byrge, S. (1987) 'Screwball Comedy', *East–West Film Journal* 2, 1: 17–25.

Cadogan, M. (1992) *Women with Wings: Female Flyers in Fact and Fiction*, Houndmills: Macmillan.

Cameron, I. (1975) *A Pictorial History of Crime Films*, London: Hamlyn.

—— (ed.) (1992) *The Movie Book of Film Noir*, London: Studio Vista.

—— (ed.) (1996a) *The Movie Book of the Western*, London: Studio Vista.

Cameron, I. and Pye, D. (1996) *The Movie Book of the Western*, London: Studio Vista.

Campbell, R. (1978) 'The Ideology of the Social Consciousness Movie: Three Films of Darryl F. Zanuck', *Quarterly Review of Film Studies* 3, 1: 49–71.

Carnes, M. C. (ed.) (1996) *Past Imperfect: History According to the Movies*, London: Cassell.

Carroll N. (1981) 'Nightmare and the Horror Film: The Symbolic Biology of Fantastic Beings', *Film Quarterly* 34, 3: 16–25.

—— (1982) 'The Future of an Allusion: Hollywood in the Seventies (and Beyond)', *October* 20: 51–81.

—— (1984) '*King Kong*: Ape and Essence', in Grant 1984, 215–44.

—— (1990) *The Philosophy of Horror, or Paradoxes of the Heart*, New York: Routledge.

—— (1991) 'Notes on the Sight Gag', in Horton 1991a, 25–42.

—— (1998) 'The Professional Western: South of the Border', in Buscombe and Pearson 1998, 46–62.

Caughie, J. (ed.) (1981) *Theories of Authorship*, London: Routledge.

Cavell, S. (1981) *Pursuits of Happiness: The Hollywood Comedy of Remarriage*, Cambridge, Mass.: Harvard University Press.

Cawelti, J. (1970) *The Six-Gun Mystique*, Bowling Green: Bowling Green University Press.

—— ([1973] 1974) 'Reflections on the New Western Films', in Nachbar 1974a, 113–17.

—— (1976) *Adventure, Mystery and Romance: Formula Stories as Art and Popular Culture*, Chicago: Chicago University Press.

Chabrol, C. ([1955] 1985) 'The Evolution of the Thriller', trans. L. Heron, in Hillier 1985a, 158–64.

Chafe, W. H. (1972) *The American Woman: Her Changing Social, Economic, and Political Roles, 1920–1970*, New York: Oxford University Press.

—— ([1986] 1991) *The Unfinished Journey: America Since World War II*, New York: Oxford University Press.

Chambers, J. W. (1994) '*All Quiet on the Western Front* (1930): The Antiwar Film and the Image of the First World War', *Historical Journal of Film, Radio and Television* 14, 4: 377–411.

Chan, K. (1998) 'The Construction of Black Male Identity in Black Action Films of the Nineties', *Cinema Journal* 37, 2: 35–48.

Chandler, R. (1945) Letter dated 7 January 1945, quoted in J. C. Oates, 'The Simple Art of Murder', *The New York Review of Books* 42, 20: 40.

Charness, C. (1990) *Hollywood Cine-Dance: A Description of the Interrelationship of Camerawork and Choreography in Films by Stanley Donen and Gene Kelly*, University of New York Ph.D. thesis, 1977, Ann Arbor: UMI Dissertation Information Service.

Chartier, J.-P. (1946) 'Les Américains aussie font des films "noirs"', *La Revue du Cinema* 1, 2: 67–70.

Cheatwood, D. (1982) 'The Tarzan Films: An Analysis of Determinants of Maintenance and Change in Conventions', *Journal of Popular Culture* 16, 2: 127–42.

Cheyfitz, E. (1989) '*Tarzan of the Apes*: US Foreign Policy in the Twentieth Century', *American Literary History* 1, 2: 339–60.

Christopher, N. (1997) *Somewhere in the Night: Film Noir and the American City*, New York: The Free Press.

Churchill, W. (1992) *Fantasies of the Master Race: Literature, Cinema and the Colonization of Native Americans in the Movies*, Monroe: Common Courage Press.

Clarens, C. (1968) *Horror Movies: An Illustrated History*, London: Secker and Warburg.

—— (1980) *Crime Movies: An Illustrated History*, London: W. W. Norton.

Clark, J., Merck, M. and Simmons, D. (eds) (1981) *Move Over Misconceptions: Doris Day Reappraised*, London: British Film Institute.

Clery, E. J. (1995) *The Rise of Supernatural Fiction, 1762–1800*, Cambridge: Cambridge University Press.

Cline, W. C. (1984) *In the Nick of Time: Motion Picture Sound Serials*, Jefferson: McFarland.

Clover, C. J. (1992) *Men, Women and Chainsaws: Gender in the Modern Horror Film*, London: British Film Institute.

Cohan, S. (1993) '"Feminizing" the Song-and-Dance Man. Fred Astaire and the Spectacle of Masculinity in the Hollywood Musical', in Cohan and Hark 1993, 46–69.

—— (1997) *Masked Men: Masculinity and the Movies in the Fifties*, Bloomington: Indiana University Press.

Cohan, S. and Hark. I. R. (1993) *Screening the Male: Exploring Masculinities in Hollywood Cinema*, London: Routledge.

—— (1997) *The Road Movie Book*, London: Routledge.

Cohen, R. (1986) 'History and Genre', *New Literary History* 17, 2: 203–18.

Cohen, S. S. (ed.) (1996a) *Monster Theory: Reading Culture*, Minneapolis: University of Minnesota Press.

—— (1996b) 'Preface: In a Time of Monsters', in Cohen 1996a, vii–xiii.

—— (1996c) 'Monster Culture (Seven Theses)', in Cohen 1996a, 3–25.

Collins, J. (1989) *Uncommon Cultures: Popular Culture and Post-Modernism*, New York: Routledge.

—— (1995) *Architectures of Excess: Cultural Life in the Information Age*, New York: Routledge.

Collins, J. M. (1988) 'The Musical', in Gehring 1988, 269–84.

Conger, S. M. and Welsch, J. R. (1984) 'The Comic and the Grotesque in James Whale's Frankenstein Films', in Grant 1984, 290–306.

Considine, D. M. (1981) 'The Cinema of Adolescence', *Journal of Popular Film and Television* 9, 3: 123–36.

Cook, P. (1978) 'Duplicity in *Mildred Pierce*', in Kaplan 1978a, 68–82.

—— (1983) 'Melodrama and the Woman's Picture', in S. Aspinall and R. Murphy (eds), *Gainsborough Melodrama*, London: British Film Institute, 14–28.

—— (ed.) (1985) *The Cinema Book*, London: British Film Institute.

—— (1998) 'No Fixed Address: the Woman's Picture from *Outrage* to *Blue Steel*', in Neale and Smith 1998, 229–46.

Copjec, J. (ed.) (1993) *Shades of Noir: A Reader*, London: Verso.

Corn, J. J. (1979) 'Making Flying "Thinkable": Women Pilots and the Selling of Aviation, 1927–1940', *American Quarterly* 32, 4: 556–71.

Corner, J. (1996) *The Art of Record: A Critical Introduction to Documentary*, Manchester: Manchester University Press.

Corrigan, T. (1991) *A Cinema Without Walls: Movies and Culture After Vietnam*, London: Routledge.

Cosandey, R., Gaudreault, A. and Gunning, T. (1992) *Un Invention du Diable? Cinema des Premiers Temps et Religion*, Sainte-Foy: Les Presses de l'Université Laval.

Countryman, E. (1988) 'Frontier', in Buscombe 1988a, 124–5.

Coursodon, J.-P. (1964) *Keaton et Cie*, Paris: Seghers.

—— (1986) *Buster Keaton*, Paris: Atlas L'Hermier.

Cowie, E. (1984) 'Fantasia', *m/f* 9: 71–105.

—— (1993) '*Film Noir* and Women', in Copjec 1993, 121–65.

—— (1998) 'Storytelling: Classical Hollywood Cinema and Classical Narrative', in Neale and Smith 1998, 178–90.

Cox, J. N. (1987) *In the Shadows of Romance: Romantic Tragic Drama in Germany, England and France*, Athens, O.: Ohio University Press.

Coyne, M. (1997) *The Crowded Prairie: American National Identity in the Hollywood Western*, London: I. B. Tauris.

Cozarinsky, E. (1980) 'American Film Noir', in R. Roud (ed.), *Cinema – A Critical Dictionary*, London: Secker and Warburg, 57–64.

Crafton, D. (1982) *Before Mickey: The Animated Film 1898–1928*, Cambridge, Mass.: MIT Press.

—— (1993) 'The View from Termite Terrace: Caricature and Parody in Warner Bros Animation', *Film History* 5: 204–30.

—— ([1988] 1995) 'Pie and Chase: Gags, Spectacle and Narrative in Slapstick Comedy', in Karnick and Jenkins 1995, 106–19.

Crane, J. L. (1994) *Terror and Everyday Life: Singular Moments in the History of the Horror Film*, Thousand Oaks: Sage Publications.

Creed, B. (1993) *The Monstrous-Feminine: Film, Feminism, Psychoanalysis*, London: Routledge.

Cripps, T. (1979) *Black Film as Genre*, Bloomington: Indiana University Press.

—— (1993) *Making Movies Black: The Hollywood Message Movie from World War II to the Civil Rights Era*, New York: Oxford University Press.

—— (1997) *Hollywood's High Noon: Moviemaking and Society before Television*, Baltimore: Johns Hopkins University Press.

Cross, G. B. (1977) *New Week – East Lynne: Domestic Drama in Performance, 1820–1874*, London: Associated University Presses.

Crowther, B. (1988) *Film Noir: Reflections in a Dark Mirror*, London: Virgin.

Crystal, D. (1971) *Linguistics*, Harmondsworth: Penguin.

Culler, J. (1975) *Structuralist Poetics. Structuralism, Linguistics and the Study of Literature*, London: Routledge.

Curry, R. (1995) '*'Goin' to Town* and Beyond: Mae West, Film Censorship and the Comedy of Unmarriage', in Karnick and Jenkins 1995, 211–37.

Custen, G. F. (1992) *Bio/Pics: How Hollywood Constructed Public History*, New Brunswick: Rutgers University Press.

—— (1997) *Twentieth Century's Fox: Darryl F. Zanuck and the Culture of Hollywood*, New York: Basic Books.

Dadoun, R. ([1970] 1989) 'Fetishism in the Horror Film', trans. A. Williams, in Donald 1989, 39–61.

Dale, M. (1997) *The Movie Game: The Film Business in Britain, Europe and America*, London: Cassell.

Dall'Asta, M. (1992) *Un Cinéma Musclé: Le Surhomme dans le Cinéma Muet Italien (1913–1926)*, trans. from the Italian by F. Arno and C. Tatum Jr., Belgium: Editions Yellow Now.

—— (1995) 'Exploiting the War: Preparedness Serials and Patriotic Women', Unpublished paper.

Damico, J. ([1978] 1996) 'Film Noir: A Modest Proposal', in Silver and Ursini 1996, 95–105.

Dardis, T. (1979) *Keaton: The Man Who Wouldn't Lie Down*, London: André Deutsch.

—— (1983) *Harold Lloyd: The Man on the Clock*, New York: Viking Press.

Davis, B. (1973) *The Thriller*, New York: Dutton.

Davis, M. (1990) *City of Quartz*, London: Verso.

Davis, R. L. (1997) *Celluloid Mirrors: Hollywood and American Society Since 1945*, Fort Worth: Harcourt Brace.

Davis, S. (ed.) (1991) *Pragmatics: A Reader*, Oxford: Oxford University Press.

Dawson, G. (1994) *Soldier Heroes: British Adventure, Empire and the Imaginary of Masculinities*, London: Routledge.

DeBauche, L. M. (1997) *Reel Patriotism: The Movies and World War I*, Madison: University of Wisconsin Press.

Delameter, J. (1974) 'Performing Arts: The Musical', in Kaminsky 1974, 120–40.

—— (1981) *Dance in the Hollywood Musical*, Ann Arbor: UMI Research Press.

—— (1996) 'Warner Bros.' *Yellowstone Kelly*, A Case Study in the Interaction of Film and Television', *Film History* 8: 176–85.

Deloria, P. J. (1998) *Playing Indian*, New Haven: Yale University Press.

Denisoff, R. S. and Plasketes, G. (1990) 'Synergy in 1980s Film and Music', *Film History* 1: 257–76.

Denning, M. (1987) *Mechanic Accents: Dime Novels and Working-Class Culture in America*, New York: Verso.

Denvir, J. (ed.) (1996) *Legal Reelism: Movies as Legal Texts*, Urbana: University of Illinois Press.

Denzin, N. K. (1989) *Interpretive Biography*, London: Sage.

Derrida, J. (1992) 'The Law of Genre', in *Acts of Literature*, ed. D. Attridge, New York: Routledge, 221–52.

Derry, C. (1987) 'More Dark Dreams: Some Notes on the Recent Horror Film', in Waller 1987a, 162–74.

—— (1988) *The Suspense Thriller: Films in the Shadow of Alfred Hitchcock*, Jefferson: MacFarland.

Diawara, M. (ed.) (1993) *Black American Cinema*, New York: Routledge.

Dick, B. F. (1993) *The Merchant Prince of Poverty Row: Harry Cohn of Columbia Pictures*, Lexington: University Press of Kentucky.

—— ([1985] 1996) *The Star-Spangled Screen: The American World War II Film*, Lexington: University Press of Kentucky.

—— (1997) *City of Dreams: The Making and Remaking of Universal Pictures*, Lexington: University Press of Kentucky.

Diderot, D. ([1758] 1965) 'On Dramatic Poetry', trans. B. H. Clarke in B. H. Clarke (ed.) [1918] 1965, *European Theories of the Drama*, New York: Crown, 238–52.

Dika, V. (1990) *Games of Terror: Halloween, Friday the Thirteenth and the Films of the Stalker Cycle*, London: Associated University Presses.

Dippie, B. (1982) *The Vanishing American: White Attitudes and U.S. Indian Policy*, Lawrence: University of Kansas Press.

Disher, M. W. (1954) *Melodrama: Plots That Thrilled*, London: Rockliff.

Dittmar, L. and Michaud, G. (eds) (1990) *From Hanoi to Hollywood: The Vietnam War in American Film*, New Brunswick: Rutgers University Press.

Dixon, J. K. (1913) *The Vanishing Race: The Last Great Indian Council*, Garden City: Doubleday, Page.

Dmytryk, E. (1978) *It's A Hell of A Life But Not A Bad Living*, New York: New York Times Books.

Doane, M.-A. (1987) *The Desire to Desire: The Woman's Film of the 1940s*, Basingstoke: Macmillan.

Doherty, T. (1988) *Teenagers and Teenpics: The Juvenilization of American Movies in the 1950s*, Boston: Unwin Hyman.

—— (1988/9) 'Full Metal Genre: Stanley Kubrick's Vietnam Combat Movie', *Film Quarterly* 42, 2: 25–30.

—— (1993a) *Projections of War: Hollywood, American Culture and World War II*, New York: Columbia University Press.

—— (1993b) 'The Age of Exploration: The Hollywood Travelogue Film', *Cineaste* 20, 2: 38–40.

Dominick, J. R. (1987) 'Film Economics and Film Content: 1964–1983', in B. A. Austin (ed.), *Current Research in Film: Audiences, Economics and Law*, vol. 3, Norwood: Ablex, 136–53.

Donald, J. (ed.) (1989) *Fantasy and the Cinema*, London: British Film Institute.

Donnelly, W. (1971/2) 'A Theory of the Comedy of The Marx Brothers', *The Velvet Light Trap* 3: 8–15.

Dooley, R. ([1979] 1981) *From Scarface to Scarlett: American Films in the 1930s*, New York: Harcourt Brace Jovanovich.

Doty, A. (1988) 'Music Sells Movies: (Re)New(ed) Conservatism in Film Marketing', *Wide Angle* 10, 2: 70–9.

Douglas, A. (1977) *The Feminization of American Culture*, New York: Knopf.

Douglas, M. (1968) 'The Social Control of Cognition: Some Factors in Joke Perception', *Man* 3: 361–76.

Dove, G. N. (1989) *Suspense in the Formula Story*, Bowling Green: Bowling Green University Popular Press.

Dowell, P. (1995) 'The Mythology of the Western: Hollywood Perspectives on Race and Gender in the Nineties', *Cineaste* 21, 1–2: 6–10.

Dower, J. W. (1986) *War Without Mercy: Race and Power in the Pacific War*, New York: Pantheon Books.

Drinnon, R. M. (1981) *Facing West: The Metaphysics of Indian-Hating and Empire Building*, Minneapolis: University of Minnesota Press.

Ducrot, O. and Todorov, T. (1979) *Encyclopedic Dictionary of the Sciences of Language*, trans. C. Porter, Baltimore: Johns Hopkins University Press.

Duhamel, M. (1955) 'Preface' to Borde and Chaumeton 1955: vii–x.

Dumenil, L. (1995) *The Modern Empire: American Culture and Society in the 1920s*, New York: Hill and Wang.

Durgnat, R. ([1970] 1996) 'Paint it Black: The Family Tree of the *Film Noir*', in Silver and Ursini 1996, 37–51.

Dyer, R. (1977) 'Homosexuality and Film Noir', *Jump Cut* 16: 18–21.

—— (1978) 'Resistance through Charisma: Rita Hayworth and *Gilda*', in Kaplan 1978a, 91–9.

—— ([1977] 1981) 'Entertainment and Utopia', in Altman 1981a, 175–89.

—— (1993) 'Is *Car Wash* a Musical?', in Diawara 1993, 93–106.

—— (1997) *White*, London: Routledge.

Dyson, J. (1997) *Bright Darkness: The Lost Art of the Supernatural Horror Film*, London: Cassell.

Easthope, A. (1986) *What a Man's Gotta Do: The Masculine Myth in Popular Culture*, London: Paladin.

Eaton, M (1981) 'Laughter in the Dark', *Screen* 22, 2: 21–5.

Edgerton, G. R. (1983) *American Film Exhibition and an Analysis of the Motion Picture Industry's Market Structure, 1963–1980*, New York: Garland.

Edmonds, A. (1991) *Fatty: The Untold Story of Fatty Arbuckle*, London: McDonald.

Edmonds, I. G. (1997) *Big U: Universal in the Silent Days*, South Brunswick: A. S. Barnes.

Edwards, E. (1984) 'The Relationship Between Sensation-Seeking and Horror Movie Interest and Attendance', Unpublished Ph.D. thesis, University of Tennessee.

Ehrenreich, B. (1983) *The Hearts of Men: American Dreams and the Flight from Commitment*, London: Pluto Press.

Ehrenstein, D. (1978) 'Melodrama and the New Woman', *Film Comment* 14, 5: 59–62.

Eikenbaum, B. M. ([1927] 1978) 'The Theory of the Formal Method', trans. I. R. Titunik, in Matejka and Pomorska 1978, 3–37.

Elley, D. (1984) *The Epic Film: Myth and History*, London: Routledge and Kegan Paul.

Elliott, E. (ed.) (1991) *The Columbia History of the American Novel*, New York: Columbia University Press.

Ellis, J. (1981) *Visible Fictions: Cinema: Television: Video*, London: Routledge.

Ellwood, R. S. (1997) *The Fifties Spiritual Marketplace: American Religion in a Decade of Conflict*, New Brunswick: Rutgers University Press.

Elsaesser, T. (1971) 'The American Cinema 2. Why Hollywood', *Monogram* 1: 4–10.

—— (1975) 'The Pathos of Failure', *Monogram* 6: 11–13.

—— ([1969] 1981) 'Vincente Minnelli', in Altman 1981a, 8–27.

—— ([1972] 1987) 'Tales of Sound and Fury: Observations on the Family Melodrama', in Gledhill 1987a, 43–69.

—— (with Adam Barker) (ed.) (1990) *Early Cinema: Space, Frame, Narrative*, London: British Film Institute.

Englehardt, T. (1995) *The End of Victory Culture: Cold War America and the Disillusion of a Generation*, New York: Basic Books.

Erens, P. (1984) *The Jew in American Cinema*, Bloomington: Indiana University Press.

Erickson, T. (1996) 'Kill Me Again: Movement Becomes Genre', in Silver and Ursini 1996, 307–29.

Erlich, V. (1981) *Russian Formalism: History–Doctrine*, New Haven: Yale University Press.

Essoe, G. (1979) *Tarzan of the Movies*, Syracuse: Citadel Press.

Etulain, R. W. (1973) 'The Historical Development of the Western', *Journal of Popular Culture* 7, 3: 75–84.

Evans, P. W. (1996) '*Westward the Women: Feminising the Wilderness*', in Cameron and Pye 1996, 206–13.

Evans, P. W. and Deleyto, C. (eds) (1998), *Terms of Endearment: Gender and Sexuality in Hollyood Romantic Comedy of the Eighties and Nineties*, Edinburgh: Edinburgh University Press.

Everson, W. K. (1978) *American Silent Film*, New York: Oxford University Press.

—— ([1969] 1992) *The Hollywood Western: 90 Years of Cowboys, Indians, Trainrobbers, Sheriffs and Gunslingers, and Assorted Heroes and Desperados*, New York: Citadel.

Faller, G. S. (1992) *The Function of Star-Image and Performance in the Hollywood Musical: Sonja Henie, Esther Williams, and Eleanor Powell*, Northwestern University Ph.D. thesis, 1987, Ann Arbor: UMI Dissertation Information Service.

Feilitzsch, H. F. v. (1993) 'Karl May: The "Wild West" as Seen in Germany', *Journal of Popular Culture* 17, 3: 179–89.

Fell, J. L. (ed.) (1983) *Film Before Griffith*, Berkeley: University of California Press.

—— ([1974] 1986) *Film and the Narrative Tradition*, Berkeley: University of California Press.

—— (1987) 'Cellulose Nitrate Roots: Popular Entertainments and the Birth of Film Narrative', in *Before Hollywood: Turn-of-the Century American Film*, New York: Hudson Hills, 39–44.

Fenin, G. and Everson, W. K. (1962) *The Western: From Silents to Cinemera*, New York: Orion Press.

Fernett, G. (1973) *Hollywood's Poverty Row, 1930–1950*, Satellite Beach: Coral Reef Publications.

—— (1988) *American Film Studios: An Historical Encyclopedia*, Jefferson: McFarland.

Ferraro, T. J. (1989) 'Blood in the Marketplace: The Business of Family in the *Godfather* Narratives', in W. Sollers (ed.), *The Invention of Ethnicity*, New York: Oxford University Press. 176–286.

Feuer, J. ([1982] 1993) *The Hollywood Musical*, Houndmills: Macmillan/British Film Institute.

Fiedler, L. (1968) *The Return of the Vanishing American*, New York: Stein and Day.

Fielding, R. (1972) *The American Newsreel, 1911–1967*, Norman: University of Oklahoma Press.

Filene, P. G. ([1974] 1986) *Him/Her/Self: Sex Roles in Modern America*, Baltimore: Johns Hopkins University Press.

Finch, C. (1984) *Special Effects: Creating Movie Magic*, New York: Abbeville.

Finler, J. (1988) *The Hollywood Story*, London: Octopus.

Fischer, L. ([1976] 1981) 'The Image of Woman as Image: The Optical Politics of *Dames*', in Altman 1981a, 70–84.

—— (1983) 'Two-Faced Women: The "Double" in Women's Melodrama of the 1940s', *Cinema Journal* 23, 1: 24–43.

—— (1991) 'Sometimes I Feel Like a Motherless Child: Comedy and Matricide', in Horton 1991a, 60–78.

Fischer, L. and Landy, M. ([1982] 1987) '*Eyes of Laura Mars*: A Binocular Critique', in Waller 1987a, 62–78.

Focillon, H. ([1934] 1942) *Life of Forms in Art*, trans. C. B. Hogan and G. Kubler, New Haven: Yale University Press.

Foil, S. L. (1991) *An Examination of the Conceptual Approach to Film Genre with a Specific Application to the Definition of the Apocalyptic*, Northwestern University Ph.D. thesis, 1989, Ann Arbor: UMI Dissertation Information Service.

Fordin, H. (1975) *The Movies' Greatest Musicals, Produced in Hollywood USA by the Freed Unit*, New York: Ungar.

Fore, S. (1991) 'The Same Old Others: The Western, *Lonesome Dove* and the Lingering Difficulty of Difference', *The Velvet Light Trap* 27: 49–62.

Forshey, G. E. (1992) *American Religious and Biblical Spectaculars*, Westport: Praeger.

Foucault, M. ([1975] 1977) *Discipline and Punish*, trans. A. Sheridan, London: Allen Lane.

Fowler, A. (1982) *Kinds of Literature: An Introduction to the Theory of Genres and Modes*, Oxford: Clarendon Press.

Francke, L. (1994) *Script Girls: Women Screenwriters in Hollywood*, London: British Film Institute.

Frank, N. (1946) 'Un Nouveau Genre "Policièr", L'Aventure Criminelle', *L'Écran Français* 61: 8–9, 14.

Franklin, H. B. ([1985] 1990) 'Visions of the Future in Science Fiction Films, 1970–1982', in Kuhn 1990a, 19–31.

Frayling, C. (1981) *Spaghetti Westerns: Cowboys and Europeans from Karl May to Sergio Leone*, London: Routledge.

Freadman, A. (1988) 'Untitled (On Genre)', *Cultural Studies* 2, 1: 67–99.

Freedman, E. B. (1974) 'The New Woman: Changing Views of Women in the 1920s', *Journal of American History* 56: 372–93.

French, P. (1973) *Westerns*, London: Secker and Warburg.

Freud, S. ([1905] 1976) *Jokes and their Relation to the Unconscious*, trans. J. Strachey, The Pelican Freud Library, vol. 6, Harmondsworth: Penguin.

—— ([1910] 1977) 'A Special Type of Choice of Object Made by Men (Contributions to the Psychology of Love 1)', trans. J. Strachey, in *On Sexuality: Three Essays on Sexuality and Other Works*, The Pelican Freud Library, vol. 7, Harmondsworth: Penguin, 231–42.

—— ([1908] 1985a) 'Creative Writers and Day-Dreaming', trans. J. Strachey, in *Art and Literature*, The Pelican Freud Library, vol. 14, Harmondsworth: Penguin, 129–41.

—— ([1927] 1985b) 'Humour', trans. J. Strachey, in *Art and Literature*, The Pelican Freud Library, vol. 14, Harmondsworth: Penguin, 425–33.

Friar, R. E. and Friar, N. A. (1972) *The Only Good Indian . . . The Hollywood Gospel*, New York: Drama Book Specialists.

Fried, A. ([1980] 1993) *The Rise and Fall of the Jewish Gangster in America*, New York: Columbia University Press.

Friedan, B. (1963) *The Feminine Mystique*, New York: W. W. Norton.

Friedman, L. (1984) '"Canyons of Nightmare": The Jewish Horror Film', in Grant 1984, 126–52.

Friedman, L. M. (1993) *Crime and Punishment in American History*, New York: Basic Books.

Frith, S. (1996) *Performing Rites: On the Value of Popular Music*, Oxford: Oxford University Press.

Frye, N. (1957) *Anatomy of Criticism: Four Essays*, Princeton: Princeton University Press.

Fuchs, C. J. (1990) 'Vietnam and Sexual Violence', in O. Gilman Jr. and L. Smith (eds), *America Rediscovered: Critical Essays on Literature and Films of the Vietnam War*, Hamden: Garland, 120–33.

Fullerton, R. (1979) 'Creating a Mass Book Market in Germany: The Story of the "Colporteur Novel"', 1870–1890', *Journal of Social History* 2, 4: 489–511.

Furia, P. (1990) *The Poets of Tin Pan Alley: A History of America's Greatest Lyricists*, New York: Oxford University Press.

Fyne, R. (1992) *Hollywood Fights a War: A Comparison of the Images of the Fighting Man of World War II Combatants in Selected Hollywood Films Produced Between September 1, 1939 and December 7, 1941 With Those Produced Between December 8, 1941 and August 15, 1945*, New York University Ph.D. thesis, 1976, Ann Arbor: UMI Dissertation Information Service.

—— ([1994] 1997) *The Hollywood Propaganda of World War II*, Lanham: Scarecrow Press.

Gabbard, K. (1996) *Jammin' at the Margins: Jazz and the American Cinema*, Chicago: Chicago University Press.

Gach, G. (1996) 'John Alton: Master of the Film Noir Mood', *American Cinematographer* 77, 9: 87–92.

Gallafent, E. (1994) *Clint Eastwood, Filmmaker and Star*, New York: Continuum.

Gallagher, T. (1986) 'Shoot-Out at the Genre Corral: Problems in the "Evolution" of the Western', in Grant 1986a, 202–16.

Garcia, R. and Eisenschitz, B. (eds) (1994) *Frank Tashlin*, Locarno: Editions du Festival.

Gartenberg, J. (1988) 'Vitagraph Comedy Production', in E. Bowser (ed.), *The Slapstick Symposium*, Brussels: Federation Internationale des Archives du Film, 45–8.

Gaudreault, A. (1992) 'La Passion du Christ: Une Forme, Un Genre, Un Discours', in Cosandey, Gaudreault and Gunning 1992, 91–101.

Gedin, P. (1977) *Literature in the Marketplace*, London: Faber.

Gehring, W. D. (1983) *Charlie Chaplin: A Bio-Bibliography*, Westport: Greenwood Press.

—— (1984) *W. C. Fields: A Bio-Bibliography*, Westport: Greenwood Press.

—— (1986) *Screwball Comedy: A Genre of Madcap Romance*, Westport: Greenwood Press.

—— (1987) *The Marx Brothers: A Bio-Bibliography*, Westport: Greenwood Press.

—— (1988) *Handbook of American Film Genres*, Westport: Greenwood Press.

—— (1990) *Laurel and Hardy: A Bio-Bibliography*, Westport: Greenwood Press.

—— (1994) *Groucho and W. C. Fields, Huckster Comedians*, Jackson: University of Mississippi Press.

Genette, G. (1969) 'Vraisemblance et Motivation', in *Figures II*, Paris: Seuil, 71–99.

Genne, B. E. (1992) *The Film Musicals of Vincente Minnelli and the Team of Gene Kelly and Stanley Donen, 1944–1958*, University of Michigan Ph.D. thesis, 1984, Ann Arbor: UMI Dissertation Information Service.

George, R. (1990) 'Some Spatial Characteristics of the Hollywood Cartoon', *Screen* 31, 3: 296–321.

Geraghty, C. (1980/1) 'Three Women's Films', *Movie* 27/8: 85–90.

Gerould, D. (1978) 'Russian Formalist Theories of Melodrama', *Journal of American Culture* 1, 1: 152–67.

—— (1983) 'The Americanization of Melodrama', in D. Gerould (ed.), *American Melodrama*, New York: Performing Arts Journal Publications, 7–29.

Gevinson, A. (1988) 'The Birth of the American Feature Film', in P. C. Usai and L. Cordelli (eds), *Sulla Via di Hollywood*, Pordenone: Edizioni Biblioteca dell' Immagine, 132–55.

Gifford, D. (1984) *The International Book of Comics*, London: W. H. Smith.

Gilbert, J. (1986) *A Cycle of Outrage: America's Reaction to the Juvenile Delinquent in the 1950s*, New York: Oxford University Press.

Gillette, A. S. (1971) 'American Scenography: 1716–1969', in *The American Theatre: A Sum of Its Parts*, New York: Samuel French, 181–96.

Glass, F. (1989) 'The New Bad Future: *Robocop* and 1980s Sci-Fi Films', *Science as Culture* 5: 7–49.

—— (1990) 'Totally Recalling Arnold: Sex and Violence in the New Bad Future', *Film Quarterly* 44, 1: 2–13.

Gledhill (1978) '*Klute* Part I: A Contemporary Film Noir and Feminist Criticism', in Kaplan 1978a, 6–21.

—— (1985a) 'History of Genre Criticism', in Cook 1985, 58–64.

—— (1985b) 'The Horror Film', in Cook 1985, 99–105.

—— (1985c) 'Melodrama', in Cook 1985, 73–81.

—— (ed.) (1987a) *Home is Where The Heart Is: Studies in Melodrama and the Woman's Film*, London: British Film Institute.

—— (1987b) 'The Melodramatic Field: An Investigation', in Gledhill 1987a, 5–39.

—— (1992) 'Speculations on the Relationship between Soap Opera and Melodrama', *Quarterly Review of Film and Video* 14, 1–2: 103–24.

Glover, D. (1989) 'The Stuff that Dreams are Made of: Masculinity, Femininity and the Thriller', in D. Longhurst (ed.), *Gender, Genre and Narrative Pleasure*, London: Unwin Hyman, 67–83.

Goetzmann, W. H. and Goetzmann, W. N. (1986) *The West of the Imagination*, New York: Knopf.

Goldman, E. F. ([1961] 1973) *The Crucial Decade – and After: America 1945–1960*, New York: Knopf.

Gomery, D. (1986) *The Hollywood Studio System*, Houndmills: Macmillan.

—— (1992) *Shared Pleasures: A History of Movie Presentation in the United States*, London: British Film Institute.

—— (1996a) 'The Economics of the Horror Film', in Weaver and Tamborini 1996, 49–62.

—— (1996b) 'Transformation of the Hollywood System', in Nowell-Smith 1996, 443–51.

—— (1996c) 'The New Hollywood', in Nowell-Smith 1996, 475–82.

Gordon, M. ([1988] 1997) *The Grand Guignol: Theater of Fear and Terror*, New York: Da Capo.

Gottlieb, S. (ed.) (1995) *Hitchcock on Hitchcock*, London: Faber and Faber.

Gow, G. (1969) *Suspense in the Cinema*, Cranbury: A. S. Barnes.

Graff, H. G. (1995) *Conflicting Paths: Growing Up in America*, Cambridge, Mass.: Harvard University Press.

Grant, B. K. (ed.) (1984) *Planks of Reason: Essays on the Horror Film*, Metuchen: Scarecrow Press.

—— (ed.) (1986a) *Film Genre Reader*, Austin: University of Texas Press.

—— (1986b) 'Introduction' to Grant 1986a, ix–xvi.

—— (1986c) 'The Classic Hollywood Musical and the "Problem" of Rock 'n' Roll', *Journal of Popular Film and Television* 13, 4: 195–205.

—— (ed.) (1995) *Film Genre Reader II*, Austin: University of Texas Press.

—— (ed.) (1996) *The Dread of Difference: Gender and the Horror Film*, Austin: University of Texas Press.

—— (1998) 'Rich and Strange: The Yuppie Horror Film', in Neale and Smith 1998, 280–93.

Grant, M. (1994) 'James Whale's *Frankenstein*: The Horror Film and the Symbolic

Biology of the Cinematic Monster', in S. Bann (ed.), *Frankenstein: Creation and Monstrosity*, London: Reaktion Books, 113–35.

Green, M. (1979) *Dreams of Adventure, Deeds of Empire*, New York: Basic Books.

—— (1984) *The Great American Adventure*, Boston: Beacon Press.

Gregory, C. (1976) 'Living Life Sideways', *Journal of Popular Film* 5, 3–4: 289–311.

Griffiths, A. (1996) 'Science and Spectacle: Native American Representation in Early Cinema', in S. E. Bird (ed.), *Dressing in Feathers: The Construction of the Indian in American Popular Culture*, Boulder: Westview Press, 79–95.

Grimstead, D. (1968) *Melodrama Unveiled: American Theater and Culture, 1800–1850*, Chicago: Chicago University Press.

Grindon, L. (1996) 'Body and Soul: The Structure of Meaning in the Boxing Film Genre', *Cinema Journal* 35, 4: 54–69.

Grist, L. (1992) 'Moving Targets and Black Widows: Film Noir in Modern Hollywood', in Cameron 1992, 267–85.

—— (1996) '*Unforgiven*', in Cameron and Pye 1996, 294–301.

Grixti, J. (1989) *Terrors of Uncertainty: The Cultural Contexts of Horror Fiction*, London: Routledge.

Gross, L. (1976) 'Film Apres Noir', *Film Comment* 12, 4: 44–9.

Grossman, J. R. (ed.) (1994) *The Frontier in American Culture*, Berkeley: University of California Press.

Guback, T. (1969) *The International Film Industry: Western Europe and America since 1945*, Bloomington: Indiana University Press.

Guerrero, E. (1993) *Framing Blackness: The African American Image in Film*, Philadelphia: Temple University Press.

Gunning, T. (1989) 'An Aesthetic of Astonishment: Early Film and the (In)credulous Spectator', *Art and Text* 34: 31–45.

—— (1991a) *D. W. Griffith and the Origins of the American Narrative Film: The Early Years at Biograph*, Urbana: University of Illinois Press.

—— (1991b) 'Heard Over the Phone: *The Lonely Villa* and the De Lorde Tradition of the Terrors of Technology', *Screen* 32, 2: 184–96.

—— (1995a) 'Crazy Machines in the Garden of Forking Paths: Mischief Gags and the Origins of Film Comedy', in Karnick and Jenkins 1995, 87–105.

—— (1995b) 'Response to "Pie and Chase"', in Karnick and Jenkins 1995, 121–2.

Guynn, W. (1990) *A Cinema of Nonfiction*, London: Associated University Presses.

Haines, H. W. (1990) '"They Were Called and They Went": The Political Rehabilitation of the Vietnam Veteran', in Dittmar and Michaud 1990, 81–97.

Halberstam, J. (1995) *Skin Shows: Gothic Horror and the Technology of Monsters*, Durham: Duke University Press.

Hall, S. (1996) '*How the West Was Won*: History, Spectacle and the American Mountains', in Cameron and Pye 1996, 255–61.

—— (In progress) 'Hard Ticket Giants: Hollywood Blockbusters in the Wide Screen Era', Ph.D. thesis, University of East Anglia.

Hall, S. and Whannel, P. (1964) *The Popular Arts*, London: Hutchinson.

Halliday, J. (1971) *Sirk on Sirk: Interviews with Jon Halliday*, London: Secker and Warburg.

Halliday, J. and Mulvey, L. (eds) (1972) *Douglas Sirk*, London: Edinburgh Film Festival.

Hamand, M. C. (1988) *The Effects of the Adoption of Sound on Narrative and Narration in the American Cinema*, University of Madision-Wisconsin Ph.D. thesis, 1983, Ann Arbor: UMI Dissertation Information Service.

Hamilton, C. (1993) 'American Genre Fiction', in M. Gidley (ed.), *Modern American Culture: An Introduction*, London: Longman, 312–34.

279

Hamilton, M. (1996) *The Queen of Camp: Mae West, Sex and Popular Culture*, London: Pandora.

Hamm, C. ([1979] 1983) *Yesterdays: Popular Song in America*, New York: Norton.

Hammond, P. (1974) *Marvellous Méliès*, London: Gordon Fraser.

—— (1981) 'Georges, This is Charles', *Afterimage* 8/9: 39–48.

Hampton, B. ([1931] 1970) *History of the American Film Industry*, New York: Dover Press.

Hansen, C. A. (1988) 'The Hollywood Musical Biopic and the Regressive Performer', *Wide Angle* 10, 2: 15–23.

Hanson, P. K. (executive ed.) (1993) *The American Film Institute Catalog of Motion Pictures Produced in the United States: Feature Films, 1931–1940* (3 vols.), Berkeley: University of California Press.

Haralovich, M. B. (1979) 'Sherlock Holmes: Genre and Industrial Practice', *Journal of the University Film Association* 31, 2: 53–7.

Haraway, D. (1985) 'A Manifesto for Cyborgs: Science, Technology and Socialist-Feminism in the 1980s', *Socialist Review* 80.

Hardy, P. (ed.) (1984) *The Encyclopedia of Western Movies*, London: Octopus.

—— (ed.) ([1986] 1995a) *The Overlook Film Encyclopedia: Horror*, Woodstock: The Overlook Press.

—— (1995b) 'The Horror Film in Perspective', in Hardy 1995a, ix–xiii.

—— (ed.) ([1984] 1995c) *The Aurum Film Encyclopedia: Science Fiction*, London: Aurum Press.

—— (1996) 'Crime Movies', in Nowell-Smith 1996, 304–12.

Hark, I. R. (1993) 'Animals or Romans: Looking at Masculinity in *Spartacus*', in Cohan and Hark 1993, 151–72.

Hart, J. D. (1963) *The Popular Book: A History of America's Literary Taste*, Berkeley: University of California Press.

Hartnoll, P. (ed.) ([1972] 1987) *The Concise Oxford Companion to the Theatre*, Oxford: Oxford University Press.

Harvey, J. (1987) *Romantic Comedy: Hollywood from Lubitsch to Sturges*, New York: Knopf.

Harvey, S. (1978) 'Woman's Place: The Absent Family in Film Noir', in Kaplan 1978a, 22–34.

Harwood, S. (1997) *Family Fictions: Representations of the Family in 1980s Hollywood*, Houndmills: Macmillan.

Haskell, M. ([1974] 1987) *From Reverence to Rape: The Treatment of Women in the Movies*, Chicago: University of Chicago Press.

Hay, J. (1990) '"You're Tearing Me Apart!": The Primal Scene of Teen Films', *Cultural Studies* 4, 3: 331–8.

Hayward, S. (1996) *Key Concepts in Cinema Studies*, London: Routledge.

Henderson, A. and Bowers, D. B. (1996) *Red, Hot and Blue: A Smithsonian Salute to the American Musical*, Washington: Smithsonian Institution Press.

Henderson, B. (1978) 'Romantic Comedy Today: Semi-Tough or Impossible?', *Film Quarterly* 31, 4: 11–23.

—— (1981/2) 'Musical Comedy of Empire', *Film Quarterly* 35, 2: 2–16.

Higashi, S. (1990) 'Cecil B. DeMille and the Lasky Company: Legitimating Feature Film as Art', *Film History* 4, 3: 181–97.

—— (1991) 'Melodrama as a Middle-Class Sermon: *What's-His-Name*', P. C. Usai and L. Codelli (eds), *L'Eredita DeMille*, Pordenone: Edizione dell'Immagine, 224–49.

—— (1994) *Cecil B. DeMille and American Culture: The Silent Era*, Berkeley: University of California Press.

—— (1996) 'Antimodernism as Historical Representation in a Consumer Culture:

Cecil B. DeMille's *The Ten Commandments*, 1923, 1956, 1993', in V. Sobchack (ed.), *The Persistence of History: Cinema, Television, and the Modern Event*, New York: Routledge, 91–112.

Higham, C. and Greenberg, J. (1968) *Hollywood in the Forties*, Cranbury: A. S. Barnes.

Hilfer, T. (1990) *The Crime Novel: A Deviant Genre*, Austin: University of Texas Press.

Hilger, M. (1986) *The American Indian in Film*, Metuchen: Scarecrow Press.

—— (1995) *From Savage to Nobleman: Images of Native Americans in Film*, Lanham: Scarecrow Press.

Hill, J. (1986) *Sex, Class and Realism: British Cinema 1956–1963*, London: British Film Institute.

—— (1998) 'Film and Postmodernism', in Hill and Church 1998, 96–105.

Hill, J. and Church, P. C. (eds) (1998) *The Oxford Guide to Film Studies*, Oxford: Oxford University Press.

Hillier, J. (ed.) (1985a) *Cahiers du Cinéma, The 1950s: New-Realism, Hollywood, New Wave*, Cambridge, Mass.: Harvard University Press.

—— (1985b) 'Introduction' to Hillier 1985a, 1–27.

—— (1992) *The New Hollywood*, London: Studio Vista.

Hilmes, M. (1990) *Hollywood and Broadcasting: From Radio to Cable*, Urbana: University of Illinois Press.

Hirsh, E. D. (1967) *Validity in Interpretation*, New Haven: Yale University Press.

Hirsch, F. (1978) *The Hollywood Epic*, New York: A. S. Barnes.

—— (1981) *Film Noir: The Dark Side of Hollywood*, New York: Da Capo.

Hirschhorn, C. ([1983] 1986) *The Universal Story*, London: Octopus.

Hoberman, J. (1985) 'Ten Years That Shook the World', *American Film* 10, 8: 34–59.

Hobsbawm, E. (1969) *Bandits*, New York: Dell.

Hodgens, R. (1959) 'A Brief Tragical History of the Science Fiction Film', *Film Quarterly* 13, 2: 30–9.

Hogan, D. J. ([1986] 1988) *Dark Romance: Sex and Death in the Horror Film*, Wellingborough: Equation.

Holland, S. (unpublished) 'The Thrill of the Chase-Film: Gender, Genre and Narrativizing the Spectacular in Early Cinema.'

Hollinger, K. (1996) 'The Monster as Woman: Two Generations of Cat People', in Grant 1996, 296–308.

Hollows, J. and Jancovich, M. (1995) *Approaches to Popular Film*, Manchester: Manchester University Press.

Hollyman, B. S. P. ([1977] 1983) 'Alexander Black's Picture Plays, 1893–1894', in Fell 1983, 236–43.

Holmlund, C. (1993) 'Masculinity as Multiple Masquerade: The "Mature" Stallone and the Stallone Clone', in Cohan and Hark 1993, 213–29.

Hoppenstand, G. (ed.) (1982) *The Dime Novel Detective*, Bowling Green: Bowling Green University Press.

Horak, J. C. (1985) 'The Magic Lanterne Moves: Early Cinema Reappraised', *Film Reader* 6: 93–101.

Horton, A. S. (1991a) *Comedy/Cinema/Theory*, Berkeley: University of California Press.

—— (1991b) 'Introduction' to Horton 1991a, 1–21.

Hoskins, C., McFadyen, S. and Finn, A. (1997) *Global Television and Film: An Introduction to the Economics of the Business*, Oxford: Clarendon Press.

Houseman, J. (1947) 'Today's Hero: A Review', *Hollywood Quarterly* 2, 2: 159–63.

281

Hovet, T. (unpublished) 'Representing the Whole World: Narrative and "Difference" in *Ben-Hur* (1925)'.

Hoxter, J. (1996) '*The Evil Dead*, Die and Chase: From Slapstick to Splatshtick', *Necromicon* 1: 71–83.

Huie, W. O. (1975) *Buster Keaton's Comic Vision: A Critical Analysis of Five Films*, University of Texas, Austin Ph.D. thesis 1975, Ann Arbor: UMI Dissertation Information Service.

Hungerford, M. J. (1951) *Dancing in Commercial Motion Pictures*, New York: Columbia University Press.

Hunt, I. (1993) 'What Are Big Boys Made Of?: *Spartacus*, *El Cid* and the Male Epic', in Kirkham and Thumim 1993, 65–83.

Hunter, I. (1989) 'Providence and Profit: Speculation in the Genre Market', *Southern Review* 22: 211–23.

Hurst, R. M. (1979) *Republic Studios: Between Poverty Row and the Majors*, Metuchen: Scarecrow Press.

Hutcheon, L. (1985) *A Theory of Parody: The Teachings of Twentieth-Century Art Forms*, London: Methuen.

Hutchings, P. (1995) 'Genre Theory and Criticism', in Hollows and Jancovich 1995, 59–77.

—— (1996) 'Tearing Your Soul Apart: Horror's New Monsters', in V. Sage and A. Lloyd-Smith (eds), *Modern Gothic: A Reader*, Manchester: Manchester University Press, 89–103.

Hutchison, D. (1987) *Film Magic: The Art and Science of Special Effects*, New York: Prentice-Hall.

Hutter, A. D. ([1975] 1983) 'Dreams, Transformations, and Literature: The Implications of Detective Fiction', in Most and Stowe 1983, 230–51.

Hyde, A. F. (1990) *An American Vision: Far Western Landscape and National Culture, 1820–1920*, New York: New York University Press.

Inglis, R. A. (1985) 'Self-Regulation in Operation', in Balio [1976] 1985, 377–400.

Isenberg, M. T. (1975) 'An Ambiguous Pacifism: A Retrospective on World War I Films, 1930–1938', *Journal of Popular Film* 4, 2: 98–115.

—— (1981) *War on Film: The American Cinema and World War I*, London: Associated University Presses.

Islam, N. (1995) '"I Want to Shoot People" – Genre, Gender and Action in the Films of Kathryn Bigelow', in L. Jayamanne (ed.), *Kiss Me Deadly: Feminism and Cinema for the Moment*, Sydney: Power Publications, 91–125.

Izod, J. (1988) *Hollywood and the Box Office, 1895–1986*, Houndmills: Macmillan.

Jacobowitz, F. (1992) 'The Man's Melodrama: *The Woman in the Window* and *Scarlet Street*', in Cameron 1992, 152–64.

Jacobs, L. (1939) *The Rise of the American Film: A Critical History*, New York: Harcourt Brace.

Jacobs, L. (1981) '*Now, Voyager*: Some Problems of Enunciation and Sexual Difference', *Camera Obscura* 7: 89–109.

—— (1991) '*The Wages of Sin: Censorship and the Fallen Woman Cycle: 1928–1942*', Madison: University of Wisconsin Press.

—— (1993) 'The Woman's Picture and the Poetics of Melodrama', *Camera Obscura* 31: 121–47.

James, D. (1995) *That's Blaxploitation! Roots of the Baadasssss 'Tude (Rated X by an All-Whyte Jury)*, New York: St. Martin's Griffin.

James, E. (1994) *Science Fiction in the Twentieth Century*, Oxford: Oxford University Press.

James, L. (1980) 'Is Jerrold's Black Eye'd Susan More Important than Wordsworth's

Lucy? Melodrama, the Popular Ballad and the Dramaturgy of Emotion', in Bradby, James and Sharratt 1980, 3–16.

Jameson, F. (1975) 'Magical Narratives: Romance as Genre', *New Literary History* 7: 135–63.

Jancovich, M. (1992a) *Horror*, London: Batsford.

—— (1992b) 'Modernity and Subjectivity in *The Terminator*: The Machine as Monster in Contemporary American Culture', *The Velvet Light Trap* 30: 3–17.

—— (1996) *Rational Fears: American Horror in the 1950s*, Manchester: Manchester University Press.

Jarrico, S. (1953) 'Evil Heroines of 1953', *Hollywood Review* 1, 3: 1, 3–4.

Jarvie, I. (1992) *Hollywood's Overseas Campaign: The North Atlantic Movie Trade, 1920–1950*, Cambridge: Cambridge University Press.

Jauss, H. R. (1982) *Toward an Aesthetic of Reception*, trans. T. Bahti, Brighton: Harvester Press.

Jeffords, S. (1988) 'Masculinity as Excess in Vietnam Film: The Father/Son Dynamic', *Genre* 21: 487–515.

—— (1989) *The Remasculinization of America: Gender and the Vietnam War*, Bloomington: Indiana University Press.

—— (1994) *Hard Bodies: Hollywood Masculinity in the Reagan Era*, New Brunswick: Rutgers University Press.

Jenkins, H. (1986) 'The Amazing Push-Me/Pull-You Text: Cognitive Processing, Narrational Play and the Comic Film', *Wide Angle* 3–4: 35–44.

—— (1992) *What Made Pistachio Nuts? Early Sound Comedy and the Vaudeville Aesthetic*, New York: Columbia Press.

—— (1995) 'Historical Poetics', in Hollows and Jancovich 1995, 99–122.

Jennings, F. (1993) *The Founders of America*, New York: Norton.

Jewell, R. B. (with R. Harbin) (1982) *The RKO Story*, London: Octopus.

—— (1984) 'Hollywood and Radio: Competition and Partnership in the 1930s', *Historical Journal of Film, Radio and Television* 4, 2: 125–41.

Johnston, C. and Willemen, P. (eds) (1973) *Frank Tashlin*, Edinburgh: Edinburgh University Press.

Jones, D. B. (1945) 'The Hollywood War Film: 1942–1944', *Hollywood Quarterly* 1, 1: 1–19.

—— (1946) 'Feature Length Pictures: 1944–1945', *Hollywood Quarterly* 1, 3: 334.

Jones, D. E. (1970) 'Blood 'N Thunder: Virgins, Villains and Violence in the Dime Novel Western', *Journal of Popular Culture* 4, 2: 507–17.

—— (1980) 'The Earliest Western Films', *Journal of Popular Film and Television* 8, 2: 42–6.

Jones, K. (1996) '*Dead Man*', *Cineaste* 22, 2: 45–6.

Jones, P. G. (1976) *War and the Novelist: Appraising the American War Novel*, Columbia: University of Missouri Press.

Jowett, G. S. (1985) 'Giving Them What they Want: Movie Audience Research Before 1950', in B. A. Austin (ed.), *Current Research in Film: Audiences, Economics and Law*, vol. 1, Norwood: Ablex, 19–35.

Kaemmel, E. ([1962] 1983) 'Literature under the Table: The Detective Novel and its Social Mission', trans. G. W. Most, in Most and Stowe 1983, 55–61.

Kagan, N. (1974) *The War Film*, New York: Pyramid.

Kamin, D. (1984) *Charlie Chaplin's One-Man Show*, Metuchen: Scarecrow Press.

Kaminsky, S. M. (1974) *American Film Genres*, New York: Dell.

Kane, K. (1976) *Visions of War: Hollywood Combat Films of World War II*, Ann Arbor: UMI Research Press.

—— (1988) 'The World War II Combat Film', in Gehring 1988, 65–103.

Kaplan, A. (1990) 'Romancing the Empire: The Embodiment of American Masculinity in the Popular Historical Novel of the 1890s', *American Literary History* 2, 3: 659–90.

Kaplan, E. A. (1978a) *Women in Film Noir*, London: British Film Institute.

—— (1978b) 'Introduction' to Kaplan 1978a, 1–5.

—— (1978c) 'The Place of Women in Fritz Lang's *The Blue Gardenia*', in Kaplan 1978a, 83–90.

—— (1992) *Motherhood and Representation: The Mother in Popular Culture and Melodrama*, London: Routledge.

Kapsis, R. E. (1991) 'Hollywood Genres and the Production of Culture Perspective', in B. A. Austin (ed.), *Current Research in Film: Audiences, Economics and the Law*, vol. 5, Norwood: Ablex, 68–85.

Karimi, A. M. (1976) *Toward a Definition of the American Film Noir (1941–1949)*, New York: Arno Press.

Karnick, K. B. (1995) 'Commitment and Reaffirmation in Hollywood Romantic Comedy', in Karnick and Jenkins 1995, 123–46.

Karnick, K. B. and Jenkins, H. (1995a) *Classical Hollywood Comedy*, New York: Routledge.

—— (1995b) 'Introduction: Golden Eras and Blind Spots – Genre, History and Comedy', in Karnick and Jenkins 1995a, 1–13.

—— (1995c) 'Introduction: Funny Stories', in Karnick and Jenkins 1995a, 63–86.

—— (1995d) 'Introduction: Acting Funny', in Karnick and Jenkins 1995a, 149–67.

Karpf, S. (1973) *The Gangster Film: Emergence, Variation and Decay of a Genre, 1930–1940*, New York: Arno Press.

Katz, E. ([1979] 1994) *The Film Encyclopedia*, New York: HarperCollins.

Kay, K. (1977) '*Part-Time Work of a Domestic Slave*, or Putting the Screws in Screwball Comedy', in K. Kay and D. Peary (eds), *Women and the Cinema: A Critical Anthology*, New York: Dutton, 311–23.

Keil, C. (1992) '*From the Manger to the Cross*: The New Testament Narrative and the Question of Stylistic Retardation', in Cosandey, Gaudreault and Gunning 1992, 112–20.

Kelley, M. (1984) *Private Woman, Public Stage: Literary Domesticity in Nineteenth-Century America*, New York: Oxford University Press.

Kelley, S. M. (1995) 'Giggles and Guns: The Phallic Myth in *Unforgiven*', *Journal of Film and Video* 47, 1–3: 98–105.

Kemp, P. (1986) 'From the Nightmare Factory: HUAC and the Politics of Noir', *Sight and Sound* 44, 4: 266–70.

Kendall, E. (1990) *The Runaway Bride: Hollywood Romantic Comedy of the 1930s*, New York: Knopf.

Kendrick, W. (1991) *The Thrill of Fear: 250 Years of Scary Entertainment*, New York: Grove Press.

Kerr, P. (1979) 'Out of What Past? Notes on the B Film Noir', *Screen Education* 32, 3: 45–65.

Kerr, W. (1975) *The Silent Clowns*, New York: Knopf.

Kett, J. F. (1977) *Rites of Passage: Adolescence in America, 1790 to the Present*, New York: Basic Books.

Kinnard, R. (1998) *The Blue and the Gray on the Screen: Eighty Years of Civil War Movies*, New York: Birch Lane Press.

Kirkham, P. and Thumim, J. (1993) *You Tarzan: Masculinity, Movies and Men*, London: Lawrence and Wishart.

Kislan, R. (1980) *The Musical: A Look at the American Musical Theater*, Englewood Cliffs: Prentice-Hall.

—— (1987) *Hoofing on Broadway: A History of Show Dancing*, London: Simon and Schuster.

Kitses, J. (1969) *Horizons West*, London: Thames and Hudson.

Klein, M. (1990) 'Historical Memory, Film and the Vietnam Era', in Dittmar and Michaud 1990, 19–40.

Klein, N. N. (1993) *7 Minutes: The Life and Death of the American Animated Cartoon*, New York: Verso.

Kleinhans, C. (1978) 'Notes on Melodrama and the Family Under Capitalism', *Film Reader* 3: 40–7.

—— (1998) 'Independent Features: Hopes and Dreams', in Lewis 1998a, 307–27.

Klinger, B. (1994a) *Melodrama and Meaning: History, Culture and the Films of Douglas Sirk*, Bloomington: Indiana University Press.

—— (1994b) '"Local" Genres: The Hollywood Adult Film in the 1950s', in J. Bratton, J. Cook and C. Gledhill (eds), *Melodrama: Stage Picture Screen*, London: British Film Institute, 134–46.

Knee, A. (1994) 'The Compound Genre Film: *Billy the Kid versus Dracula* Meets *The Harvey Girls*', in E. D. Cancalon and A. Spacagna (eds), *Intertextuality in Literature and Film*, Gainesville: University of Florida Press.

Knight, A. (1985) 'The Movies Learn to Talk: Ernst Lubitsch, Rene Clair and Rouben Mamoulian', in E. Weis and J. Belton (eds), *Film Sound: Theory and Practice*, New York: Columbia University Press, 213–20.

Knight, S. (1980) *Form and Ideology in Crime Fiction*, Bloomington: Indiana University Press.

Koelb, C. (1975) 'The Problem of Tragedy as a Genre', *Genre* 8, 3: 248–66.

Kolodny, A. (1975) *The Lay of the Land: Metaphor as Experience and History in American Life and Letters*, Chapel Hill: University of North Carolina Press.

—— (1984) *The Land Before Her: Fantasy and Experience of the American Frontiers, 1630–1860*, Chapel Hill: University of North Carolina Press.

Kooistra, P. (1989) *Criminals as Heroes: Structure, Power and Identity*, Bowling Green: Bowling Green State University Popular Press.

Koppes, C. R. and Black, G. D. (1987) *Hollywood Goes to War: How Politics, Profits and Propaganda Shaped World War II Movies*, New York: The Free Press.

Koszarski, R. (1990) *An Evening's Entertainment: The Age of the Silent Feature Picture, 1915–1928*, New York: Scribner's.

Kovacs, K. S. ([1976] 1983) 'George Melies and the *Feerie*', in Fell 1983, 244–57.

Kozloff, S. (1988) *Invisible Storytellers: Voice-Over Narration in American Fiction Film*, Berkeley: University of California Press.

Kramer, P. (1988) 'Vitagraph, Slapstick and Early Cinema', *Screen* 29, 2: 98–104.

—— (1989) 'Derailing the Honeymoon Express: Comicality and Narrative Closure in Buster Keaton's *The Blacksmith*', *The Velvet Light Trap* 23: 101–16.

—— (1995) 'The Making of a Comic Star: Buster Keaton and *The Saphead*', in Karnick and Jenkins 1995, 190–210.

—— (1998a) 'Post-classical Hollywood', in Hill and Church 1998, 289–309.

Kramer, P. (1998b) 'Bad Boy: Notes on a Popular Figure in American Cinema, Culture and Society, 1895–1905', in J. Fullerton (ed.), *Celebrating 1895: The Centenary of Cinema*, London: John Libbey, 117–30.

Kress, G. and Threadgold, T. (1988) 'Towards a Social Theory of Genre', *Southern Review* 21, 3: 215–43.

Kreuger, M. (1977) Show Boat: *The Story of a Classic American Musical*, New York: Oxford University Press.

Krutnik, F. (1984) 'The Clown-Prints of Comedy', *Screen* 25, 4–5: 50–9.

Krutnik, F. (1990) 'The Faint Aroma of Performing Seals: The "Nervous" Romance and the Comedy of the Sexes', *The Velvet Light Trap* 26: 57–72.

—— (1991) *In a Lonely Street: Film Noir, Genre, Masculinity*, London: Routledge.

—— (1994) 'Jerry Lewis: The Deformation of the Comic', *Film Quarterly* 48, 1: 12–26.

—— (1995a) 'A Spanner in the Works? Genre, Narrative and the Hollywood Comedian', in Karnick and Jenkins 1995, 17–38.

—— (1995b) 'The Handsome Man and His Monkey: The Comic Bondage of Dean Martin and Jerry Lewis', *Journal of Popular Film and Television* 23, 1: 16–25.

Kuhn, A. ([1984] 1987) 'Women's Genres: Melodrama, Soap Opera and Theory', in Gledhill 1987a, 339–49.

—— (ed.) (1990a) *Alien Zone: Cultural Theory and Contemporary Science Fiction Cinema*, London: Verso.

—— (1990b) 'Introduction: Cultural Theory and Science Fiction Cinema', in Kuhn 1990a, 1–12.

Lahue, K. C. (1964) *Continued Next Week: A History of the Moving Picture Serial*, Norman: University of Oklahoma Press.

—— (1968) *Bound and Gagged: The Story of the Silent Serials*, New York: Castle Books.

—— (1971) *Dreams for Sale: The Rise and Fall of Triangle Film Corporation*, South Brunswick: A. S. Barnes.

—— (1973) *Motion Picture Pioneer: The Selig Polyscope Company*, South Brunswick: A. S. Barnes

Landy, M. (1991) *British Genres: Cinema and Society, 1930–1960*, Princeton: Princeton University Press.

—— (1996) *Cinematic Uses of the Past*, Minneapolis: University of Minnesota Press.

Landy, M. and Villarejo, A. (1995) *Queen Christina*, London: British Film Institute.

Lang, R. (1989) *American Film Melodrama: Griffith, Vidor, Minnelli*, Princeton: Princeton University Press.

Langer, M. (1994) 'The Exploitation Film', *Film History* 6, 3: 291–2.

Langman, L. (1992) *A Guide to Silent Westerns*, Westport: Greenwood Press.

Langman, L. and Finn, D. (1994) *A Guide to American Silent Crime Films*, Westport: Greenwood Press.

—— (1995a) *A Guide to American Crime Films of the Thirties*, Westport: Greenwood Press.

—— (1995b) *A Guide to American Crime Films of the Forties and Fifties*, Westport: Greenwood Press.

Laskos, A. (1981) 'The Hollywood Majors', in Pirie 1981a, 10–39.

Lawson, J. H. (1953) *Film in the Battle of Ideas*, New York: Masses and Mainstream Press.

Lazarsfield, P. F. (1947) 'Audience Research in the Movie Field', *Annals of the American Academy of Political and Social Science* 254: 160–8.

Leab, D. J. (1975) *From Sambo to Superspade: The Black Experience in Motion Pictures*, London: Secker and Warburg.

—— (1995) 'Viewing the War with the Brothers Warner', in K. Dibbets and B. Hogenkamp (eds), *Film and the First World War*, Amsterdam: Amsterdam University Press, 223–33.

Lears, T. J. J. (1981) *No Place of Grace: Antimodernism and the Transformation of American Culture, 1880–1920*, New York: Pantheon.

Lebel, J.-P. (1967) *Buster Keaton*, London: Zwemmer.

Leech, G. (1974) *Semantics*, Harmondsworh: Penguin.

—— (1983) *The Principles of Pragmatics*, London: Longman.

Lees, D. and Berkowitz, S. ([[1978] 1981) *The Movie Business: A Primer*, New York: Vintage Books.

Lehman, P. (1991) '"What no red-blooded man needs lessons in doing", Gender and Race in *Tarzan of the Apes*', *Griffithiana* 40/1: 124–9.

Lenihan, J. H. (1980) *Showdown: Confronting Modern America in the Western Film*, Urbana: University of Illinois Press.

—— (1992) 'English Classics for Cold War America', *Journal of Popular Film and Television* 20, 3: 42–51.

Lent, T. O. (1995) 'Romance, Love and Friendship: The Redefinition of Gender Relations in Screwball Comedy', in Karnick and Jenkins 1995, 314–31.

Leutrat, J.-L. (1973) *Le Western*, Paris: Armand Colin.

—— (1985) *L'Alliance Brisée: Le Western des Années 1920*, Lyon: Presses Universitaires de Lyon.

—— (1987) *Le Western: Archéologie d'un Genre*, Lyon: Presses Universitaires de Lyon.

Leverenz, D. (1991) 'The Last Real Man in America: From Natty Bumppo to Batman', *American Literary History* 3, 4: 753–81.

Levich, J. (1996) 'Western Auguries: Jim Jarmusch's *Dead Man*', *Film Comment* 32, 3: 39–41.

Levinson, S. C. (1983) *Pragmatics*, Cambridge: Cambridge University Press.

Lévi-Strauss, C. (1967) *Structural Anthropology*, trans. C. Jacobson and B. G. Schoepf, Garden City: Doubleday.

Levy, S. (1997) *King of Comedy: The Life and Art of Jerry Lewis*, New York: St. Martin's Griffin.

Lewis, J. (1992) *The Road to Romance and Ruin: Teen films and Youth Culture*, New York: Routledge.

—— (ed.) (1998a) *The New American Cinema*, Durham: Duke University Press.

—— (1998b) 'Money Matters: Hollywood in the Corporate Era', in Lewis 1998a, 87–121.

Lewis, P. C. (1973) *Trooping: How the Show Came to Town*, New York: Harper and Row.

Lindsey, S. S. (1996) 'Horror, Femininity, and Carrie's Monstrous Puberty', in Grant 1996, 279–95.

Lippmann, W. ([1931] 1967) 'The Underworld as Servant', in G. Taylor (ed.), *Organized Crime in America*, Ann Arbor: University of Michigan Press, 58–69.

Litwak, M. (1986) *Reel Power: The Struggle for Influence and Success in the New Hollywood*, Los Angeles: Silman-James Press.

Louvish, S. (1997) *Man on the Flying Trapeze: The Life and Times of W. C. Fields*, London: Faber and Faber.

Luciano, P. (1987) *Them or Us: Archetypal Interpretations of Fifties Alien Invasion Narratives*, Bloomington: Indiana University Press.

Lukow, G. and Ricci, S. (1984) 'The "Audience" Goes "Public": Inter-Textuality, Genre and the Responsibilities of Film Literacy', *On Film* 12: 29–36.

Lundberg, D. (1984) 'The American Literature of War: The Civil War, World War I and World War II', *American Quarterly* 36, 3: 373–88.

Lusted, D. (1996) 'Social Class and the Western as Male Melodrama', in Cameron and Pye 1996, 63–74.

Lyons, J. (1977) *Semantics*, 2 vols, Cambridge: Cambridge University Press.

—— (1981) *Language, Meaning and Context*, London: Fontana.

Lyons, T. J. (1974) *The Silent Partner: The History of the American Film Manufacturing Company*, New York: Arno Press.

McArthur, C. (1972) *Underworld USA*, London: Secker and Warburg.

—— (1973) 'Iconography and Iconology', unpublished paper.

McArthur, C. (1982) 'War and Anti-War', *The Movie* 45: 881–4.

McCaffrey, D. (1968) *Four Great Comedians*, New York: Barnes.

—— (1976) *Three Classic Silent Screen Comedies Starring Harold Lloyd*, London: Associated University Presses.

McCann, R. D. (ed.) (1993) *The Silent Comedians*, Metuchen: Scarecrow Press.

McCarthy, T. and Flynn, C. (eds) (1975) *Kings of the Bs*, New York: Dutton.

McCarty, J. (1993) *Hollywood Gangland: The Movies' Love Affair with the Mob*, New York: St. Martin's Press.

McConachie, B. A. (1992) *Melodramatic Formations: American Theater and Society, 1820–1870*, Iowa City: University of Iowa Press.

McConachie, B. A. and Freedman, D. (eds) (1988) *Theatre for Working-Class Audiences in the United States, 1830–1980*, Westport: Greenwood Press.

McConnell, F. (1976) *The Spoken Seen: Film and the Romantic Imagination*, Baltimore: Johns Hopkins University Press.

MacDonald, J. K. (1987) *Who Shot the Sheriff? The Rise and Fall of the Television Western*, New York: Praeger.

McGee, M. T. and Robertson, R. J. (1982) *The J. D. Films: Juvenile Delinquency in the Movies*, Jefferson: McFarland Press.

McGilligan, P., Weiner, D. and Bruce, D. (1975) 'Raoul Walsh Remembers', *The Velvet Light Trap* 15: 42–9.

McGovern, J. R. (1968) 'The American Woman's Pre-World War I Freedom in Manners and Morals', *Journal of American History* 60: 315–33.

MacGowan, K. (1965) *Behind the Screen*, New York: Delacorte.

McKee, A. L. (1995) '"L'Affaire Paslin" and *All This and Heaven Too*: Gender, Genre and History in the 1940s Woman's Film', *The Velvet Light Trap* 35: 33–51.

McLaughlin, R. G. (1988) *Broadway and Hollywood: A History of Economic Interaction*, Ph.D. thesis, 1971, Ann Arbor: UMI Dissertation Information Service.

McLean, A. (1997) 'The Thousand Ways There Are to Move: Camp and Oriental Dance in the Hollywood Musicals of Jack Cole', in M. Bernstein and G. Studlar (eds), *Visions of the East: Orientalism in Film*, London: I. B. Tauris, 130–57.

McLean, A. F. (1965) *American Vaudeville as Ritual*, Lexington: University of Kentucky Press.

McMahon, K. (1994) '*Casualties of War*: History, Realism, and Limits of Exclusion', *Journal of Popular Film and Television* 22, 1: 12–21.

Malmgren, C. D. (1980) 'Philip Dick's *Man in the High Castle* and the Nature of Science-Fictional Worlds', in G. E. Slusser, G. R. Guffey and M. Rose (eds), *Bridges to Science Fiction*, Carbondale: Southern Illinois University Press, 125–30.

Malone, B. C. ([1985] 1987) *Country Music, USA*, Wellingborough: Equation.

Maltby, R. (1983) *Harmless Entertainment: Hollywood and the Ideology of Consensus*, Metuchen: Scarecrow Press.

—— (ed.) (1989) *Dreams for Sale: Popular Culture in the 20th Century*, London: Harrap.

—— ([1984] 1992) 'Film Noir: The Politics of the Maladjusted Text', in Cameron 1992, 39–48.

—— (1993a) 'The Production Code and the Hays Office', in Balio 1993, 37–72.

—— (1993b) '"Grief in the Limelight": Al Capone, Howard Hughes, The Hays Code and the Politics of the Unstable Text', in J. Combs (ed.), *Movies and Politics: The Dynamic Relationship*, New York: Garland Publishing, 133–82.

—— (1995) *Hollywood Cinema: An Introduction*, Oxford: Blackwell.

—— [1992] (1996) 'A Better Sense of History: John Ford and the Indians', in Cameron and Pye 1996, 34–49.

—— (1998) '"Nobody Knows Everything": Post-Classical Historiographies and Consolidated Entertainment', in Neale and Smith 1998, 21–44.

Maltby, R. and Bowles, K. (1994) 'Hollywood: The Economics of Utopia', in J. Mitchell and R. Maidment (eds), *The United States in the Twentieth Century: Culture*, Sevenoaks: Hodder and Stoughton/Open University, 99–134.

Maltby, R. and Vasey, R. (1994) 'The International Language Problem: European Reactions to Hollywood's Conversion to Sound', in D. W. Ellwood and R. Kroes (eds), *Hollywood in Europe: Experiences of a Cultural Hegemony*, Amsterdam: VU University Press, 68–93.

Maltin, L. (1972) *Great Movie Shorts*, New York: Bonanza Books.

—— (1982) *The Great Movie Comedians*, New York: Crown.

—— ([1980] 1987) *Of Mice and Magic: A History of American Animated Cartoons*, New York: Plume.

Mandel, E. (1984) *Delightful Murder: A Social History of the Crime Story*, London: Pluto.

Marchetti, G. (1989) 'Action–Adventure as Ideology', in I. Angus and S. Jhally (eds), *Cultural Politics in Contemporary America*, New York: Routledge, 182–97.

—— (1993) *Romance and the 'Yellow Peril': Race, Sex and Discursive Strategies in Hollywood Films*, Berkeley: University of California Press.

Marion, F. (1972) *Off With Their Heads!*, New York: Macmillan.

Marker, L.-L. (1975) *David Belasco: Naturalism in the American Theatre*, Princeton: Princeton University Press.

Martin, A. V. (1990) *Critical Approaches to American Studies: The Vietnam War in History, Literature and Film*, University of Iowa Ph.D. thesis, 1987, Ann Arbor: UMI Dissertation Information Service.

Martin, L. and Segrave, K. ([1988] 1993) *Anti-Rock: The Opposition to Rock 'n' Roll*, New York: Da Capo.

Mars, F. (1964) *Le Gag*, Paris: Editions du Cerf.

Mason, J. D. (1993) *Melodrama and the Myth of America*, Bloomington: Indiana University Press.

Masson, Alain ([1976] 1981) 'George Sidney: Artificial Brilliance/The Brilliance of Artifice', trans. L. Heron, in Altman 1981a, 28–40.

Mast, G. (1976) *The Comic Mind: Comedy and the Movies*, New York: Random House.

—— (1987) *Can't Help Singin': The American Musical on Stage and Screen*, Woodstock: Overlook Press.

Matejka, L. and Pomorska, K. (eds) (1978) *Readings in Russian Poetics: Formalist and Structuralist Views*, Ann Arbor: Michigan Slavic Publications.

Mates, J. (1985) *America's Musical Stage: Two Hundred Years of Musical Theatre*, New York: Praeger.

Matthews, G. (1987) *'Just a Housewife': The Rise and Fall of Domesticity in America*, New York: Oxford University Press.

Mauduy, J. and Henriet, G. (1989) *Géographies du Western*, Paris: Nathan.

Mayer, D. (1980) 'The Music of Melodrama', in Bradby, James and Sharratt 1980, 49–63.

—— (1994a) *Playing Out the Empire: Ben-Hur and Other Toga Plays and Films, 1883–1908. A Critical Anthology*, Oxford Clarendon Press.

—— (1994b) 'Introduction' to Mayer 1994a, 1–20.

Meisel, M. (1983) *Realizations: Narrative, Pictorial and Theatrical Arts in Nineteenth-Century England*, Princeton: Princeton University Press.

Mellen, J. (1973) *Women and Their Sexuality in the New Film*, New York: Dell.

Mellencamp, P. (1990) 'The Sexual Economics of *Golddiggers of 1933*', in P. Lehman (ed.), *Close Viewings: An Anthology of New Film Criticism*, Tallahassee: Florida State University Press.

Merritt, R. (1976) 'Nickelodeon Theaters 1905–1914: Building an Audience for the Movies', in T. Balio (ed.), *The American Film Industry*, Madison: University of Wisconsin Press, 59–79.

—— (1983) 'Melodrama: Post-Mortem for a Phantom Genre', *Wide Angle* 5, 3: 24–31.

Metz, C. (1974) *Language and Cinema*, trans. D. J. Umiker-Sebeok, The Hague: Mouton.

Mey, J. L. (1993) *Pragmatics: An Introduction*, Oxford: Blackwell.

Millard, A. (1995) *America on Record: A History of Recorded Sound*, Cambridge: Cambridge University Press.

Miller, D. (1976) *Hollywood Corral*, New York: Popular Library.

Miller, G. (1980) *Screening the Novel: Rediscovered American Fiction in Film*, New York: Ungar.

Milne, P. (1922) *Motion Picture Directors*, New York: Falk.

Milner, C. A. II, O'Connor, C. A. and Sandweiss, M. A. (eds) (1994) *The Oxford History of the American West*, New York: Oxford University Press.

Minnelli, V (with H. Acre) (1974) *I Remember It Well*, Garden City: Doubleday.

Mitchell, L. C. (1981) *Witness to a Vanishing America: The Nineteenth Century Response*, Princeton: Princeton University Press.

—— (1996) *Westerns: Making the Man in Fiction and Film*, Chicago: Chicago University Press.

Mo–ling, L. (ed.) (1981) *A Study of the Hong Kong Swordplay Film*, Hong Kong: The Fifth Hong Kong International Film Festival.

Modleski, T. (1982) *Loving with a Vengeance: Mass-Produced Fantasies for Women*, Hamden: Archon Books.

—— (1986) 'The Terror of Pleasure: The Contemporary Horror Film and Post-modern Theory', in T. Modleski (ed.), *Studies in Entertainment: Critical Approaches to Mass Culture*, Bloomington: Indiana University Press, 155–66.

—— ([1984] 1987) 'Time and Desire in the Woman's film', in Gledhill 1987a, 326–38.

—— (1988) 'A Father is Being Beaten: Male Feminism and the War Film', *Discourse* 10, 2: 62–77.

—— (1995/6) 'Our Heroes Have Sometimes Been Cowgirls: An Interview with Maggie Greenwald', *Film Quarterly* 49, 2: 2–11.

Moews, D. (1977) *Keaton: The Silent Features Close Up*, Berkeley: University of California Press.

Monaco, J. (1979) *American Film Now*, New York: New American Library.

Mooney, H. F. (1968) 'Popular Music since the 1920s: The Significance of Shifting Taste', *American Quarterly* 20, 1: 67–85.

Moore, W. H. (1974) *The Kefauver Committee and the Politics of Crime, 1950–1952*, Columbia: University of Missouri Press.

Mordden, E. (1988) *The Hollywood Studios: House Style in the Golden Age of the Movies*, New York: Knopf.

Morey, A. (1995) '"The Judge Called Me an Accessory": Women's Prison Films, 1950–1962', *Journal of Popular Film and Television* 23, 2: 80–7.

Morris, G. (1993) 'Beyond the Beach: Social and Formal Aspects of AIP's *Beach Party* Movies', *Journal of Popular Film and Television* 21, 1: 2–11.

Morsberger, R. E. and Morsberger, K. M. (1974) '"Christ and a Horse-Race": *Ben-Hur* on Stage', *Journal of Popular Culture* 8, 3: 489–502.

Morton, W. (1993) 'Tracking the Signs of Tarzan: Trans-media Representation of a Pop-culture Icon', in Kirkham and Thumim 1993, 106–25.

Moses, M. J. ([1925] 1964) *The American Dramatist*, New York: Benjamin Blom.

Most, G. W. and Stowe, W. W. (1983) *The Poetics of Murder: Detective Fiction and Literary Theory*, San Diego: Harcourt Brace Jovanovich.

Mueller, J. (1984) 'Fred Astaire and the Integrated Musical', *Cinema Journal* 24, 1: 28–40.

—— (1985) *Astaire Dancing: The Musical Films*, New York: Wings Books.

Muller, E. and Farris, D. ([1996] 1997) *That's Sexploitation!! The Forbidden World of 'Adults Only' Cinema*, London: Titan Books.

Mulvey, L. (1981) 'Afterthoughts on "Visual Pleasure and Narrative Cinema" Inspired by *Duel in the Sun*', *Framework* 15/16/17: 12–15.

—— (1986) 'Melodrama In and Out of the Home', in C. MacCabe (ed.), *High Theory/Low Culture*, Manchester: Manchester University Press, 80–100.

—— ([1977/8] 1987) 'Notes on Sirk and Melodrama', in Gledhill 1987a, 75–9.

Munby, J. (1999) *Public Enemies, Public Heroes: Screening the Gangster from Little Caesar to Touch of Evil*, Chicago: University of Chicago Press.

Murphy, B. (1972) 'Monster Movies: They Came from Beneath the 1950s', *Journal of Popular Film* 1, 1: 31–44.

Muscio, G. (1997) *Hollywood's New Deal*, Philadelphia: Temple University Press.

Musser, C. (1984) 'The Travel Genre in 1903–1904: Moving Toward Fictional Narratives', *Iris* 2, 1: 47–59.

—— ([1984] 1990a) 'The Nickelodeon Era Begins: Establishing the Framework for Hollywood's Mode of Representation', in Elsaesser 1990, 256–73.

—— ([1988] 1990b) 'Work, Ideology and Chaplin's Tramp', in R. Sklar and C. Musser (eds), *Resisting Images: Essays on Cinema and History*, Philadelphia: Temple University Press, 36–67.

—— (1990c) *The Emergence of Cinema: The American Screen to 1907*, Berkeley: University of California Press.

—— (1991) 'Ethnicity, Role-Playing and American Film Comedy: From *Chinese Laundry* to *Whoopee* (1894–1930)', in L. D. Friedman (ed.), *Unspeakable Images: Ethnicity and the American Cinema*, Urbana: University of Illinois Press, 39–81.

—— (1993) 'Passions and the Passion Play: Theatre, Film and Religion in America, 1880–1900', *Film History* 5: 419–56.

—— (1994) 'On "Extras", Mary Pickford and the Red-light Film: Filmmaking in the United States 1913', *Griffithiana* 50: 149–75.

—— (1995) 'Divorce, DeMille and the Comedy of ReMarriage', in Karnick and Jenkins 1995, 282–313.

Nachbar, J. (ed.) (1974a) *Focus on the Western*, Englewood Cliffs: Prentice-Hall.

—— (1974b) 'Riding Shotgun: The Scattered Formula in Contemporary Western Movies' in Nachbar 1974a, 101–12.

—— (1988) 'Film Noir', in Gehring 1988, 65–84.

Nadel, A. (1995) *Containment Culture: American Narratives, Postmodernism, and the Atomic Age*, Durham: Duke University Press.

Naremore, J. (1995/6) 'American Film Noir: The History of an Idea', *Film Quarterly* 49, 2: 12–25.

—— (1998) *More Than Night: Film Noir in its Contexts*, Berkeley: University of California Press.

Nasaw, D. (1993) *Going Out: The Rise and Fall of Public Amusements*, New York: Basic Books.

Nash, G. (1991) *Creating the West: Historical Interpretations, 1890–1990*, Albuquerque: University of New Mexico Press.

Nash, M. (1976) '*Vampyr* and the Fantastic', *Screen* 17, 3: 29–67.

Nash, R. ([1967] 1982) *Wilderness and the American Mind*, New Haven: Yale University Press.

Neale, S. (1980) *Genre*, London: British Film Institute.

—— (1981a) 'Art Cinema as Institution', *Screen* 22, 1: 11–39.

—— (1981b) 'Psychoanalysis and Comedy', *Screen* 22, 2: 29–42.

—— (1986) 'Melodrama and Tears', *Screen* 27, 6: 6–22.

—— (1989) 'Issues of Difference: *Alien* and *Blade Runner*', in Donald 1989, 213–23.

—— (1990a) 'Questions of Genre', *Screen* 31, 1: 45–66.

—— (1990b) '"You've Got to be Fucking Kidding! Knowledge, Belief and Judgement in Science-Fiction', in Kuhn 1990a, 160–8.

—— (1991) 'Aspects of Ideology and Narrative Form in the American War Film', *Screen* 32, 1: 35–57.

—— (1992) 'The *Big* Romance or *Something Wild*?: Romantic Comedy Today', *Screen* 33, 3: 284–99.

—— (1993a) 'Melo Talk: On the Meaning and Use of the Term "Melodrama" in the American Trade Press', *The Velvet Light Trap* 32: 66–89.

—— ([1983] 1993b) 'Masculinity as Spectacle: Reflections on Men and Mainstream Cinema', in Cohan and Hark 1993, 9–20.

—— (1998) '"Vanishing Americans": Racial and Ethnic Issues in the Interpretation and Context of Post-war "Pro-Indian" Westerns', in Buscombe and Pearson 1998, 8–28.

Neale, S. and Krutnik, F. (1990) *Popular Film and Television Comedy*, London: Routledge.

Neale, S. and Smith, M. (1998) *Contemporary Hollywood Cinema*, London: Routledge.

Nelli, H. (1976) *The Business of Crime*, New York: Oxford University Press.

Nerlich, M. ([1977] 1987) *Ideology of Adventure: Studies in Modern Consciousness, 1100–1750*, 2 vols, trans. R. Crowley, Minneapolis, University of Minnesota Press.

Nesteby, J. R. (1982) *Black Images in American Films, 1896–1954: The Interplay Between Civil Rights and Film Culture*, Lanham: University Press of America.

Neumeyer, D. (1995) 'Melodrama as a Compositional Resource in Early Hollywood Sound Cinema', *Current Musicology* 57: 61–94.

Neve, B. (1992) *Film and Politics in America: A Social Tradition*, London: Routledge.

Nevins, F. M. (1996) 'Through the Great Depression on Horseback: Legal Themes in Western Films of the 1930s', in Denvir 1996, 44–69.

Newman, K. (1988) *Nightmare Movies: A Critical History of the Horror Movie From 1968*, London: Bloomsbury.

Newsinger, J. (1993) '"Do You Walk the Walk?": Aspects of Masculinity in Some Vietnam War Films', in Kirkham and Thumim 1993, 126–36.

Nichols, B. (1991) *Representing Reality: Issues and Concepts in Documentary*, Bloomington: Indiana University Press.

Nobles, G. H. (1997) *American Frontiers: Cultural Encounters and Continental Conquest*, Harmondsworth: Penguin.

Noel, M. (1954) *Villains Galore . . . The Heyday of the Popular Story Weekly*, New York: Macmillan.

Nowell-Smith, G. ([1977] 1987a) 'Minnelli and Melodrama', in Gledhill 1987a, 70–9.

—— (1987b) 'Popular Culture', *New Formations* 2: 79–90.

—— (ed.) (1996) *The Oxford History of World Cinema*, Oxford: Oxford University Press.

—— (1998) 'The Bad and the Beautiful: Notes on Some Actorial Stereotypes', in

G. Nowell-Smith and S. Ricci (eds), *Hollywood and Europe: Economics, Culture, National Identity: 1945–95*, London: British Film Institute, 135–41.

O'Connor, J. (1980) *The Hollywood Indian: Stereotypes of Native Americans in Films*, Paterson: New Jersey State Museum.

Olson, E. (1968) *The Theory of Comedy*, Bloomington: Indiana University Press.

Ottoson, R. (1981) *A Reference Guide to the American Film Noir*, Metuchen: Scarecrow Press.

Ousby, I. (1976) *Bloodhounds of Heaven: The Detective in English Fiction from Godwyn to Doyle*, Cambridge, Mass.: Harvard University Press.

Palmer, J. (1978) *Thrillers: Genesis and Structure of a Popular Genre*, London: Edward Arnold.

—— (1987) *The Logic of the Absurd*, London: British Film Institute.

—— (1995) *Taking Humour Seriously*, London: Routledge.

Palmer, R. B. (1985) 'William S. Hart's *Hell's Hinges*: An Ideological Approach to the Early Western', *Canadian Review of Film Studies* 16, 3: 255–70.

—— (1986) 'The Successful Failure of Therapy in *Now, Voyager*: The Woman's Picture as Unresponsive Symptom', *Wide Angle* 8, 1: 29–38.

—— (1994) *Hollywood's Dark Cinema: The American Film Noir*, New York: Twayne.

Panek, L. L. (1987) *An Introduction to the Detective Story*, Bowling Green: Bowling Green University Press.

— (1990) *Probable Cause: Crime Fiction in America*, Bowling Green: Bowling Green State University Popular Press.

Panofsky, I. (1970) *Meaning in the Visual Arts*, Harmondsworth: Penguin.

—— ([1934] 1974) 'Style and Medium in the Motion Pictures', in G. Mast and M. Cohen (eds), *Film Theory and Criticism: Introductory Readings*, New York: Oxford University Press.

Papashvily, H. (1956) *All the Happy Endings: A Study of the Domestic Novel in America, the Women Who Wrote It, the Women Who Read It, in the Nineteenth Century*, New York: Harper.

Paris, M. (1995) *From the Wright Brothers to* Top Gun: *Aviation, Nationalism and Popular Cinema*, Manchester: Manchester University Press.

Park, W. (1974) 'The Losing of the West', *The Velvet Light Trap* 12: 2–5.

Parks, R. (1982) *The Western Hero in Film and Television: Mass Media Mythology*, Ann Arbor: UMU Research Press.

Parrish, J. R. and Pitts, M. R. (1976) *The Great Gangster Pictures*, Metuchen: Scarecrow Press.

Partridge, E. (1961) *Dictionary of Slang and Unconventional English*, 2 vols, London: Routledge and Kegan Paul.

Pasquier, S. du ([1970] 1973) 'Buster Keaton's Gags', ed. and trans. N. Silverstein, *Journal of Modern Literature* 13, 2: 269–91.

Paul, W. (1991) 'Charles Chaplin and the Annals of Anality', in Horton 1991a, 109–30.

—— (1994) *Laughing Screaming: Modern Hollywood Horror and Comedy*, New York: Columbia University Press.

Peary, D. and Peary, D. (eds) (1980) *The American Animated Cartoon: A Critical Anthology*, New York: Dutton.

Peary, G. (1975) '*The Racket*, A "Lost" Gangster Classic', *The Velvet Light Trap* 14: 6–9.

—— (1976) '*Doorway to Hell*', *The Velvet Light Trap* 16: 1–4.

—— (1981) 'Introduction, *Little Caesar* Takes Over the Screen', in G. Peary (ed.), *Little Caesar*, Madison: University of Wisconsin Press, 9–28.

Pendo, S. (1985) *Aviation in the Cinema*, Metuchen: Scarecrow Press.

Penley, C. ([1986] 1989) 'Time Travel, Primal Scene, and the Critical Dystopia', in Donald 1989, 197–212.

Penley, C., Lyon, E., Spigel, L. and Bergstrom, J. (1991) *Close Encounters: Film, Feminism, and Science Fiction*, Minneapolis: University of Minnesota Press.

Perlmutter, R. (1991) 'Woody Allen's *Zelig*: An American Jewish Parody', in Horton 1991a, 206–21.

Petlewski, P. (1979) 'Complications of Narrative in the Genre Film', *Film Criticism* 4, 1: 18–24.

Pfeil, F. (1995) *White Guys: Studies in Postmodern Domination and Difference*, New York: Verso.

Phillips, J. D. ([1975] 1982) 'Film Conglomerate Blockbusters: International Appeal and Product Homogenization', in G. Kindem (ed.), *The American Movie Industry: The Business of Motion Pictures*, Carbondale: Southern Illinois University Press, 325–35.

Phillips, P. (1996) 'Genre, Star and Auteur: An Approach to Hollywood Cinema', in J. Nelmes (ed.), *An Introduction to Film Studies*, London: Routledge, 121–63.

Phillips, R. (1997) *Mapping Men and Empire: A Geography of Adventure*, London: Routledge.

Pinedo, I. C. (1997) *Recreational Terror: Women and the Pleasures of Horror Film Viewing*, Albany: State University of New York Press.

Pines, J. (1975) *Blacks in Films: A Survey of Racial Themes and Images in the American Film*, London: Studio Vista.

—— (1988) 'Blacks', in Buscombe 1988a, 68–71.

—— (1996) 'The Black Presence in American Cinema', in Nowell-Smith 1996, 497–509.

Pirie, D. (ed.) (1981a) *Anatomy of the Movies*, London: Windward.

—— (1981b) 'The Deal', in Pirie 1981a, 40–61.

Place, J. A. (1978) 'Women in Film Noir', in Kaplan 1978a, 35–67.

Place, J. A. and Peterson, L. S. ([1974] 1996) 'Some Visual Motifs of Film Noir', in Silver and Ursini 1996, 65–76.

Podheiser, L. (1983) 'Pep on the Range or Douglas Fairbanks and the World War I Era Western', *Journal of Popular Film and Television* 11, 3: 122–30.

Polan, D. ([1982] 1984) 'Eros and Syphilization: The Contemporary Horror Film', in Grant 1984, 201–11.

—— (1986) *Power and Paranoia: History, Narrative and the American Cinema, 1940–1950*, New York: Columbia University Press.

Ponder, E. A. (1988) *The American Detective Form in Novels and Film, 1929–1947*, University of North Carolina Ph.D. thesis, 1979, Ann Arbor: UMI Dissertation Information Service.

Porfirio, R. (1985) *The Dark Age of American Film: A Study of the American Film Noir, 1940–1960*, Yale University Ph.D. thesis, 1979, 2 vols, Ann Arbor: UMI Dissertation Information Service.

—— ([1976] 1996) 'No Way Out: Existential Motifs in the Film Noir', in Silver and Ursini 1996, 77–93.

Porteous, K. (1989) 'History Lessons: *Platoon*', in J. Walsh and J. Aulich (eds), *Vietnam Images: War and Representation*, Houndmills: Macmillan, 153–9.

Porter, D. (1981) *The Pursuit of Crime: Art and Ideology in Detective Fiction*, New Haven: Yale University Press.

Powdermaker, H. (1951) *Hollywood the Dream Factory: An Anthropologist Looks at the Movie-Makers*, London: Secker and Warburg.

Powers, R. G. (1983) *G-Men: Hoover's FBI in American Popular Culture*, Carbondale: Southern Illinois University Press.

Prassel, F. R. (1993) *The Great American Outlaw: A Legacy of Fact and Fiction*, Norman: University of Oklahoma Press.

Prats, A. J. (1995) 'The Western, the Eastwood Hero and *Unforgiven*', *Journal of Film and Video* 47, 1–3: 106–23.

Pratt, M. L. (1977) *Towards a Speech Act Theory of Literary Discourse*, Bloomington: Indiana University Press.

—— (1981) 'The Short Story: The Long and the Short of It', *Poetics* 10: 175–94.

Prince, S. (1988) 'Dread, Taboo and *The Thing*', *Wide Angle* 10, 3: 19–29.

Pringle, D. (ed.) ([1996] 1997) *The Ultimate Encyclopedia of Science Fiction*, London: Carlton.

Pryluck, C. (1986) 'Industrialization of Entertainment in the United States', in B. A. Austin (ed.), *Current Research in Film: Audiences, Economics, and Law*, vol. 2, Norwood: Ablex, 117–35.

Purdie, S. (1993) *Comedy: The Mastery of Discourse*, London: Harvester Wheatsheaf.

Purcell, L. E. (1977) '*Trilby* and *Trilby*-Mania: The Beginnings of the Bestseller System', *Journal of Popular Culture* 11, 1: 62–76.

Pye, D. (1996a) 'Introduction, Criticism and the Western', in Cameron and Pye 1996, 9–21.

—— (1996b) 'Masculinity in the Westerns of Anthony Mann', in Cameron and Pye 1996, 167–73.

Quigley Jr., M. (1957) 'Who Goes to the Movies . . . and Who Doesn't', *Motion Picture Herald*, 10 August: 21–2.

Quinn, A. H. ([1927] 1936) *A History of the American Drama: From the Civil War to the Present Day*, 2 vols, New York: Appleton Crofts.

Radway, J. (1984) *Reading the Romance: Women, Patriarchy, and Popular Literature*, Chapel Hill: University of North Carolina Press.

Raeburn, J. (1988) 'The Gangster Film', in Gehring 1988, 47–63.

Rahill, F. (1967) *The World of Melodrama*, Philadelphia: University of Pennsylvania Press.

Reddick, D. B. (1988) *Movies Under the Stars: A History of the Drive-In Theatre Industry, 1933–1983*, Michigan State University Ph.D. thesis, 1986, Ann Arbor: UMI Dissertation Information Service.

Reid, I. (1989) 'When is an Epitaph Not an Epitaph? A Monumental Generic Problem and a Jonsonian Instance', *Southern Review* 22: 198–208.

Reid, M. A. (1995) 'The Black Gangster Film', in Grant 1995, 456–73.

Renov, M. (1988) *Hollywood's Wartime Women: Representation and Ideology*, Ann Arbor: UMI Research Press.

—— (ed.) (1993) *Theorizing Documentary*, New York: Routledge.

Rey, Henri-François (1948) 'Demonstration par l'Absurde: Les Films Noirs', *L'Écran Français* 157.

Reynolds, H. (1992) 'From the Palette to the Screen: The Tissot Bible as Source-book for *From the Manger to the Cross*', in Cosandey, Gaudreault and Gunning 1992, 275–310.

Reynolds, Q. (1955) *The Fiction Factory, or From Pulp Row to Quality Street*, New York: Random House.

Rheuban, J. (1983) *Harry Langdon: The Comedian as Metteur-en-Scène*, Rutherford: Fairleigh Dickinson University Press.

Riblet, D. (1995) 'The Keystone Film Company and the Historiography of Early Slapstick', in Karnick and Jenkins 1995, 168–89.

Richards, J. (1977) *Swordsmen of the Screen: From Douglas Fairbanks to Michael York*, London: Routledge and Kegan Paul.

Richman, L. G. (1991) *Themes and Ideology in the Vietnam Films 1975–1983*,

University of Texas at Dallas Ph.D. thesis, 1984, Ann Arbor: UMI Dissertation Information Service.

Rickard, S. (1996) 'Movies in Disguise: Negotiating Censorship and Patriarchy Through the Dances of Fred Astaire and Ginger Rogers', in R. Lawson-Peebles (ed.), *Approaches to the American Musical*, Exeter: Exeter University Press, 72–88.

Rieupeyrout, J. L. (1953) *Le Western, ou le Cinema Américain par Excellence*, Paris: Editions du Cerf.

Rist, P. (1988) 'Standard Hollywood Fare: The World War II Combat Film Revisited', *CineAction!* 12: 23–6.

Roberts, R. and Olson, J. S. (1995) *John Wayne, American*, New York: The Free Press.

Roberts, S. (1993) '"The Lady in the Tutti-Frutti Hat": Carmen Miranda, a Spectacle of Ethnicity', *Cinema Journal* 32, 3: 3–23.

Roberts, T. J. (1990) *An Aesthetics of Junk Fiction*, Athens: University of Georgia Press.

Roberts, V. M. ([1972] 1974) *On Stage: A History of Theatre*, New York: Harper and Row.

Robinson, D. (1969) *The Great Funnies*, London: Studio Vista.

—— ([1969] 1970) *Buster Keaton*, London: Secker and Warburg.

—— (1986) *Chaplin: His Life and Art*, London: Paladin.

Roddick, N. (1983) *A New Deal in Entertainment: Warner Brothers in the 1930s*, London: British Film Institute.

Rodowick, D. N. ([1982] 1987) 'Madness, Authority and Ideology in the Domestic Melodrama of the 1950s', in Gledhill 1987a, 268–80.

Roffman, P. and Purdy, J. (1981) *The Hollywood Social Problem Film: Madness, Despair and Politics from the Depression to the Fifties*, Bloomington: Indiana University Press.

Rogin, M. (1992) 'Blackface, White Noise: The Jewish Jazz Singer Finds His Voice', *Critical Inquiry* 18, 3: 417–53.

Rollins, P. C. and O'Connor, J. E. (eds) (1998) *Hollywood's Indian: The Portrayal of the Native American in Film*, Lexington: University Press of Kentucky.

Root, J. (1985) 'Film Noir', in Cook 1985, 93–7.

Rose, F. (1995) *The Agency: William Morris and the Hidden History of Show Business*, New York: HarperBusiness.

Rose, M. A. (1993) *Parody: Ancient, Modern and Postmodern*, Cambridge: Cambridge University Press.

Rosow, E. (1978) *Born to Lose: The Gangster Film in America*, New York: Oxford University Press.

Ross, A. (1990) 'Cowboys, Cadillacs and Cosmonauts: Families, Film Genres, and Technoculture', in J. A. Boone and M. Cadden (eds), *Engendering Men: The Question of Male Feminist Criticism*, New York: Routledge, 87–101.

Ross, K. (1996) *Black and White Media: Black Images in Popular Film and Television*, London: Polity Press.

Ross, S. J. (1998) *Working-Class Hollywood: Silent Film and the Shaping of Class in America*, Princeton: Princeton University Press.

Ross, T. J. (1972) 'Introduction' to R. Huss and T. J. Ross (eds), *Focus on the Horror Film*, Englewood Cliffs: Prentice-Hall, 1–10.

Roth, M. ([1977] 1981) 'Some Warners Musicals and the Spirit of the New Deal', in Altman 1981a, 41–56.

Rowe, K. (1995a) *The Unruly Woman: Gender and the Genres of Laughter*, Austin: University of Texas Press.

—— (1995b) 'Comedy, Melodrama and Gender: Theorizing the Genres of Laughter', in Karnick and Jenkins 1995, 39–59.

Rubin, M. (1993) *Showstoppers: Busby Berkeley and the Tradition of Spectacle*, New York: Columbia University Press.

—— (1994) 'MAKE LOVE MAKE WAR: Cultural Confusion and the Biker Film Cycle', *Film History* 6, 3: 355–81.

Ruth, D. E. (1996) *Inventing the Public Enemy: The Gangster in American Culture, 1918–1934*, Chicago: University of Chicago Press.

Ryall, T. (1975/6) 'Teaching through Genre', *Screen Education* 17: 27–33.

—— (1998) 'Genre and Hollywood', in Hill and Church 1998, 327–38.

Ryan, M. (1982) 'The Projection of New Womanhood: The Movie Moderns in the 1920s', in J. E. Friedman and W. G. Shade (eds), *Our American Sisters: Women in American Life and Thought*, Lexington: University of Kentucky Press, 500–18.

Ryan, M. and Keller, D. (1988) *Camera Politica: The Politics and Ideology of Contemporary Hollywood Film*, Bloomington: Indiana University Press.

Ryan, M.-L. (1981) 'Introduction: On the Why, What and How of Generic Taxonomy', *Poetics* 10: 127–47.

Salt, B. ([1983] 1992) *Film Style and Technology: History and Analysis*, London: Starword.

Sampson, R. (1987) *Yesterday's Faces: A Study of Series Characters in the Early Pulp Magazines*, vol. 4, Bowling Green: Bowling Green State University Popular Press.

Sanders, J. (1995) *Another Fine Dress: Role-Play in the Films of Laurel and Hardy*, London: Cassell.

Sanjek R. ([1988] 1996) *Pennies from Heaven: The American Popular Music Business in the Twentieth Century*, New York: Da Capo.

Sante, L. (1991) *Low Life: Lures and Snares of Old New York*, London: Granta.

Sargent, E. W. (1911) 'Technique of the Photoplay', *Moving Picture World*, 2 September, 613–14.

Sarris, A. (1968) *The American Cinema: Directors and Directions 1929–1968*, New York: Dutton.

—— (1977) 'Big Funerals: The Hollywood Gangster, 1927–1933', *Film Comment* 13, 3: 6–9.

Sartelle, J. (1996) 'Dreams and Nightmares in the Hollywood Blockbuster', in Nowell-Smith 1996, 516–26.

Saunders, T. J. (1994) *Hollywood in Berlin: American Cinema and Weimar Germany*, Berkeley: University of California Press.

Saussure, F. de ([1959] 1974) *Course in General Linguistics*, trans. W. Baskin, London: Collins.

Savage, C. (1996) *Cowgirls*, London: Bloomsbury.

Saxton, A. (1990) *The Rise and Fall of the White Republic: Class Politics and Mass Culture in Nineteenth-Century America*, London: Verso.

Saxton, C. (1988) *Illusions of Grandeur: The Representation of Space in the American Western Film*, University of Calfornia-Berkeley, Ph.D. thesis, 1985, Ann Arbor: UMI Dissertation Information Service.

Scarrow, S. (1991) 'The Vietnam Combat Film: The Construction of a Sub-Genre', Unpublished M.Phil. thesis, University of East Anglia.

Schaefer, E. (1992) 'Of Hygiene and Hollywood: Origins of the Exploitation Film', *The Velvet Light Trap* 30: 34–47.

—— (1994) 'Resisting Refinement: The Exploitation Film and Self-Censorship', *Film History* 6, 3: 293–313.

Schatz, T. (1981) *Hollywood Genres: Formulas, Filmmaking and the Studio System*, New York: Random House.

—— (1983) *Old Hollywood/New Hollywood: Ritual, Art, and Industry*, Ann Arbor: UMI Research Press.

Schatz, T. (1988a) *The Genius of the System: Hollywood Filmmaking in the Studio Era*, New York: Pantheon.

—— (1988b) 'The Western', in Gehring 1988, 25–46.

—— (1993) 'The New Hollywood', in J. Collins, H. Radner and A. P. Collins (eds), *Film Theory Goes to the Movies*, New York: Routledge, 8–36.

—— (1996) 'Hollywood: The Triumph of the Studio System', in Nowell-Smith 1996, 220–34.

Schindler, C. (1979) *Hollywood Goes to War: Films and American Society 1939–1952*, London: Routledge.

Schneider, T. (1998) 'Finding a New *Heimat* in the Wild West: Karl May and the German Western of the 1960s', in Buscombe and Pearson 1998, 141–59.

Schoell, W. (1985) *Stay Out of the Shower: Twenty-Five Years of Shocker Films Beginning with Psycho*, New York: Dembner.

—— (1991) *Comic Book Heroes of the Screen*, New York: Citadel Press.

Schrader, P. ([1972] 1996) 'Notes on Film Noir', in Silver and Ursini 1996, 53–63.

Screen (1986) Special Issue on 'Body Horror', 27, 1.

Searles, B. (1990) *Epic! History on the Big Screen*, New York: Abrams.

Segrave, K. (1992) *Drive-In Theaters: A History from their Inception in 1933*, Jefferson: McFarland.

—— (1997) *American Films Abroad: Hollywood's Domination of the World's Movie Screens from the 1890s to the Present*, Jefferson: McFarland.

Seidman, S. (1981) *Comedian Comedy: A Tradition in the Hollywood Film*, Ann Arbor: UMI Research Press.

Selby, S. (1984) *Dark City: The Film Noir*, Jefferson: McFarland Press.

Sennett, T. ([1973] 1985) *Lunatics and Lovers: The Golden Years of Hollywood Comedy from Dinner at Eight to The Miracle of Morgan's Creek*, New York: Limelight.

Sergi, G. (1998) 'A Cry in the Dark: The Role of Post-Classical Film Sound', in Neale and Smith 1998, 156–65.

Shadoian, J. (1977) *Dreams and Dead Ends: The American Gangster/Crime Film*, London: MIT Press.

Shain, R. E. (1976) *An Analysis of Motion Pictures About War Released by the American Film Industry, 1930–1970*, New York: Arno Press.

Sharratt, B. (1980) 'The Politics of the Popular? – From Melodrama to Television', in Bradby, James and Sharratt 1980, 275–95.

Shepherd, J. (1982) *Tin Pan Alley*, London: Routledge and Kegan Paul.

Sherry, M. S. (1995) *In the Shadow of War. The United States since the 1930s*, New Haven: Yale University Press.

Shohat, E. ([1991] 1997) 'Gender and the Culture of Empire: Toward a Feminist Ethnography of the Cinema', in M. Bernstein and G. Studlar (eds), *Visions of the East: Orientalism in Film*, London: I. B. Tauris, 19–66.

Shohat, E. and Stam, R. (1994) *Unthinking Eurocentrism: Multiculturalism and the Media*, London: Routledge.

Short, J. R. (1991) *Imagined Country: Society, Culture and Environment*, London: Routledge.

Shumway, D. R. (1991) 'Screwball Comedies: Constructing Romance, Mystifying Marriage', *Cinema Journal* 30, 4: 7–23.

Siegel, J. E. (1972) *Val Lewton: The Reality of Terror*, London: Secker and Warburg.

Sikov, E. (1989) *Screwball: Hollywood's Madcap Comedies*, New York: Crown.

—— (1994) *Laughing Hysterically: American Screen Comedy of the 1950s*, New York: Columbia University Press.

Silver, A. and Ursini, J. (eds) (1996) *Film Noir Reader*, New York: Limelight.

Silver, A. and Ward, E. ([1979, 1988] 1992) *Film Noir: An Encyclopedic Reference to the American Style*, Woodstock: The Overlook Press.

Silverman, K. (1992) *Male Subjectivity at the Margins*, New York: Routledge.

Silverman, S. M. (1978) 'Hollywood Cloning: Sequels, Prequels, Remakes and Spin-Offs', *American Film* 3, 9: 24–30.

Simmon, S. (1990) 'Review of *American Film Melodrama: Griffith, Vidor, Minnelli*, by Robert Lang', *Film Quarterly* 43, 4: 45–6.

—— (1993) *The Films of D. W. Griffith*, Cambridge: Cambridge University Press.

Simon, J.-P. and Percheron, D. (1976) 'Gag', in J. Collet, M. Marie, D. Percherson, J.-P. Simon and M. Vernet, *Lectures du Film*, Paris: Albatros, 105–7.

Simonet, T. (1987) 'Conglomerates and Content: Remakes, Sequels, and Series in the New Hollywood', in B. A. Austin (ed.), *Current Research in Film: Audiences, Economics, and Law*, vol. 3, Norwood: Ablex, 154–62.

Singer, B. (1990) 'Female Power in the Serial-Queen Melodrama: The Etiology of an Anomaly', *Camera Obscura* 22: 91–129.

—— (1992) '"A New and Urgent Need for Stimuli": Sensational Melodrama and Ultra Modernity', Unpublished conference paper.

—— (1993) 'Fiction Tie-ins and Narrative Intelligibility', *Film History* 5, 4: 489–504.

Siska, W. (1976) 'Modernism in the Narrative Cinema: The Art Film as Genre', Unpublished Ph.D. thesis, Northwestern University.

Sitney, P. A. (1979) *Visionary Film: The American Avant-Garde 1943–1978*, New York: Oxford University Press.

Skal, D. J. (1990) *Hollywood Gothic: The Tangled Web of Dracula from Novel to Stage to Screen*, New York: W. W. Norton.

—— (1993) *The Monster Show: A Cultural History of Horror*, London: Plexus.

Sklar, R. (1975) *Movie-Made America: A Cultural History of the Movies*, New York: Random House.

Slide, A. (1970) *Early American Cinema*, New York: A. S. Barnes.

—— (1978) *Aspects of American Film History Prior to 1920*, Metuchen: Scarecrow Press.

—— (1980) *The Kindergarten of the Movies: A History of the Fine Arts Company*, Metuchen: Scarecrow Press.

—— ([1986] 1990) *The American Film Industry: A Historical Dictionary*, New York: Limelight.

Sloan, K. (1988) *The Loud Silents: Origins of the Social Problem Film*, Urbana: University of Illinois Press.

Slotkin, R. (1973) *Regeneration Through Violence: The Mythology of the American Frontier*, Middletown: Wesleyan University Press.

—— (1985) *The Fatal Environment: The Myth of the Frontier in the Age of Industrialization*, Middletown: Wesleyan University Press.

—— (1992) *Gunfighter Nation: The Myth of the Frontier in Twentieth-Century America*, New York: Atheneum.

Smith, C. and Litton, G. (1981) *Musical Comedy in America*, New York: Theatre Arts Books.

Smith, D. (1975) *The Mafia Mystique*, New York: Basic Books.

Smith, H. N. ([1950] 1971) *Virgin Land: The American West as Symbol and Myth*, Cambridge, Mass.: Harvard University Press.

Smith, J. (1991) '"It Does Something to a Girl. I Don't Know What": The Problem of Female Sexuality in *Applause*', *Cinema Journal* 30, 2: 47–60.

Smith J. L. (1973) *Melodrama*, London: Methuen.

—— (1974) 'Introduction' to J. L. Smith (ed.), *Victorian Melodramas: Seven English, French, and American Melodramas*, London: Dent. vii–xxii.

Smith, J. P. (1989) '"A Good Business Proposition": Dalton Trumbo, *Spartacus* and the End of the Blacklist', *The Velvet Light Trap* 23: 75–100.

—— (1998) *The Sounds of Commerce: Marketing Popular Film Music*, New York: Columbia University Press.

Smith, M. (1988) 'Film Noir: The Female Gothic and *Deception*', *Wide Angle* 10, 1: 62–75.

—— (1995) *Engaging Characters: Fiction, Emotion and Cinema*, Oxford: Clarendon Press.

—— (1998) 'Theses on the Philosophy of Hollywood History', in Neale and Smith 1998, 3–20.

Smith, P. (1993) *Clint Eastwood: A Cultural Production*, London: UCL Press.

Smith-Rosenberg, C. (1985) 'The New Woman as Androgyne: Social Disorder and Gender Crisis, 1870–1936', in C. Smith-Rosenberg, *Disorderly Conduct: Visions of Gender in Victorian America*, New York: Knopf, 245–96.

Snyder, F. E. (1970) 'American Vaudeville – Theater in a Package – Origins of Mass Entertainment', Unpublished Ph.D. thesis, Yale University.

Sobchack, T. (1988) 'The Adventure Film', in Gehring 1988, 9–24.

Sobchack, V. (1982) 'Genre Film: Myth, Ritual and Sociodrama', in S. Thomas (ed.), *Film/Culture: Explorations of Cinema in its Social Context*, Metuchen: Scarecrow Press, 147–65.

—— (1987) 'Bringing It All Back Home: Family Economy and Generic Exchange', in Waller 1987a, 175–94.

—— ([1980] 1988) *Screening Space: The American Science Fiction Film*, New York: Ungar.

—— (1990) '"Surge and Splendor": A Phenomenology of the Hollywood Historical Epic', *Representations* 29: 24–49.

Sobel, R. and Francis, D. (1977) *Chaplin: Genesis of a Clown*, London: Quartet.

Solomon, M. (unpublished) 'Dime Novels and Early Cinema as the Nickleodeon Period Begins: Outlaw and Detective Stories'.

Solomon, S. J. (1976) *Beyond Formula: American Film Genres*, New York: Harcourt Brace Jovanovich.

Somers, D. A. (1971) 'The Leisure Revolution: Recreation in America', *Journal of Popular Culture* 1, 1: 125–47.

Speer, L. (1998) 'Tuesday's Gone: The Nostalgic Teen Film', *Journal of Popular Film and Television* 26, 1: 24–32.

Springer, C. (1988a) 'Antiwar Film as Spectacle: Contradictions of the Combat Sequence', *Genre* 21, 4: 479–86.

—— (1988b) 'Rebellious Sons in Vietnam Combat Films: A Response', *Genre* 21, 4: 517–22.

Staiger, J. (1980) 'Mass-Produced Photoplays: Economic and Signifying Practices in the First Years of Hollywood', *Wide Angle* 4, 3: 12–27.

—— (1995) *Bad Women: Regulating Sexuality in Early American Cinema*, Minneapolis: University of Minnesota Press.

Stam, R., Burgoyne, R. and Flitterman-Lewis, S. (1992) *New Vocabularies in Film Semiotics: Structuralism, Post-Structuralism and Beyond*, London: Routledge.

Stanfield, P. (1996) 'Country Music and the 1930s Western', in Cameron and Pye 1996, 22–33.

—— (1998) 'Dixie Cowboys and Blue Yodels: The Strange History of the Singing Cowboy', in Buscombe and Pearson 1998, 96–118.

—— (1999) 'Dixie Cowboys: Hollywood and the 1930s Western', unpublished Ph.D. thesis, Southampton Institute.

Stearns M. and Stearns J. ([1968] 1994) *Jazz Dance: The Story of American Vernacular Dance*, New York: Da Capo.

Stephanson, A. (1995) *Manifest Destiny: American Expansion and the Empire of Right*, New York: Hill and Wang.

Sterne, M. (ed.) (1980) *Publishers for Mass Entertainment in Nineteenth Century America*, Boston: G. K. Hall.

Stewart, R. F. (1980) *. . . And Always a Detective: Chapter in the History of Detective Fiction*, Newton Abbot: David and Charles.

Stones, B. (1993) *America Goes to the Movies: 100 Years of Motion Picture Exhibition*, Hollywood: National Association of Theatre Owners.

Strickland, R. (1997) *Tonto's Revenge: Reflections on American Indian Culture and Policy*, Albuquerque: University of New Mexico Press.

Strinati, D. (1993) 'The Taste of America: Americanization and Popular Culture in Britain', in D. Strinati and S. Wragg (eds), *Come on Down? Popular Media Culture in Post-War Britain*, London: Routledge, 46–81.

Studlar, G. and Desser, D. (1990) 'Never Having to Say You're Sorry: *Rambo's* Rewriting of the Vietnam War', in Dittmar and Michaud 1990, 101–12.

Suid, L. (1978) *Guts and Glory: Great American War Movies*, Reading, Mass.: Addison-Wesley.

—— (1979) 'The Pentagon and Hollywood', in J. E. O'Connor and M. Jackson (eds), *American History, American Film*, New York: Ungar. 219–36.

—— (1991) *The Film Industry and the Vietnam War*, Case Western Reserve University Ph.D. thesis, 1980, Ann Arbor: UMI Dissertation Information Service.

Sutherland, J. A. (1978) *Fiction and the Fiction Industry*, London: Athlone Press.

Sweeney, K. (1991) 'The Dream of Disruption: Melodrama and Gag Structure in Keaton's *Sherlock Junior*', *Wide Angle* 13, 1: 104–20.

Symons, J. (1972) *Bloody Murder*, London: Faber and Faber.

Szanto, G. (1987) *Narrative Taste and Social Perspectives: The Matter of Quality*, Houndmills: Macmillan.

Tamborini, R. and Weaver III, J. B. (1996) 'Frightening Entertainment: A Historical Perspective', in Weaver and Tamborini 1996, 1–13.

Tan, L. (1998) 'Gunfighter Gaps: Discourses of the Frontier in Hollywood Movies of the 1930s and 1970s', unpublished Ph.D. thesis, Sheffield Hallam University.

Tarbox, C. H. (1983) *Lost Films, 1895–1917*, Los Angeles: Film Classic Exchange.

Tarnowski, J.-F. (1977) 'Approche et Définition(s) du Fantastique et de la Science-Fiction Cinematographiques [1]', *Positif* 195, 6: 57–65.

Tarratt, M. ([1970] 1995) 'Monsters from the Id', in Grant 1995, 330–49.

Tasker, Y. (1993) *Spectacular Bodies: Gender, Genre and the Action Cinema*, London: Routledge.

Taves, B. (1993a) *The Romance of Adventure: The Genre of Historical Adventure Movies*, Jackson: University of Mississippi Press.

—— (1993b) 'The B Film: Hollywood's Other Half', in Balio 1993, 313–50.

Taylor, E. (1989) *Prime Time Families: Television Culture in Postwar America*, Berkeley: University of California Press.

Telotte, J. P. (1980) 'A Sober Celebration: Song and Dance in the "New" Musical', *Journal of Popular Film and Television* 8, 1: 2–14.

—— (1985) *Dreams of Darkness: Fantasy and the Films of Val Lewton*, Urbana: University of Illinois Press.

—— (1988) 'Arbuckle Escapes: The Pattern of Fatty Arbuckle's Comedy', *Journal of Popular Film and Television* 15, 4: 172–9.

—— (1989) *Voices in the Dark: The Narrative Patterns of Film Noir*, Urbana: University of Illinois Press.

Telotte, J. P. (1995) *Replications: A Robotic History of the Science Fiction Film*, Urbana: University of Illinois Press.

—— (1996) 'Fatal Capers: Strategy and Enigma in Film *Noir*', *Journal of Popular Film and Television* 23, 4: 163–70.

Thomas, D. (1992) 'How Hollywood Deals with the Deviant Male', in Cameron 1992, 59–70.

Thompson, D. (1990) 'A Cottage at Palos Verdes', *Film Comment* 26, 3: 16–21.

Thompson, K. (1985) *Exporting Entertainment: America in the World Film Market, 1907–1934*, London: British Film Institute.

—— (1988) *Breaking the Glass Armor: Neoformalist Film Analysis*, Princeton: Princeton University Press.

Thompson, K. and Bordwell, D. (1994) *Film History: An Introduction*, New York: McGraw-Hill.

Threadgold, T. (1989) 'Talking about Genre: Ideologies and Incompatible Discourse', *Cultural Studies* 3, 1: 101–26.

Thumim, J. (1995) '"Maybe He's Tough But He Sure Ain't No Carpenter": Masculinity and In/competence in *Unforgiven*', in P. Kirkham and J. Thumim (eds), *Me Jane: Masculinity, Movies and Women*, 234–48.

Tibbetts, J. C. (1985) *The American Theatrical Film: Stages in Development*, Bowling Green: Bowling Green State University Popular Press.

Todorov, T. (1975) *The Fantastic: A Structural Approach to a Literary Genre*, trans. R. Howard, Ithaca: Cornell University Press.

—— (1977) *The Poetics of Prose*, trans. R. Howard, Ithaca: Cornell University Press.

—— (1981) *Introduction to Poetics*, trans. R. Howard, Brighton: Harvester Press.

—— (1990) *Genres in Discourse*, trans. C. Porter, Cambridge: Cambridge University Press.

Toll, R. C. (1976) *On With The Show: The First Century of Show Business in America*, New York: Oxford University Press.

—— (1982) *The Entertainment Machine: American Show Business in the Twentieth Century*, New York: Oxford University Press.

Tompkins, J. (1985) *Sensational Designs: The Cultural Work of American Fiction, 1790–1860*, New York: Oxford University Press.

—— (1992) *West of Everything: The Inner Life of Westerns*, New York: Oxford University Press.

Torgovnick, M. (1990) *Gone Primitive: Savage Intellects, Modern Lives*, Chicago: University of Chicago Press.

Trachtenberg, A. (1987) 'Photography/Cinema', in *Before Hollywood: Turn-of-the-Century American Film*, New York: Hudson Hills, 71–9.

Traube, E. G. (1992) *Dreaming Identities: Class, Gender and Generation in 1980s Hollywood Movies*, Boulder: Westview Press.

Traubner, R. ([1983] 1989) *Operetta: A Theatrical History*, Oxford: Oxford University Press.

Truettner, W. H. (ed.) (1991) *The West as America: Reinterpreting Images of the Frontier, 1820–1920*, Washington, DC: Smithsonian Institution Press.

Truffaut, F. ([1954] 1976) 'A Certain Tendency of the French Cinema', trans. uncredited, in B. Nichols (ed.), *Movies and Methods: Anthology*, vol. 1, Berkeley: University of California Press, 224–37.

Tudor, A. (1974a) *Theories of Film*, London: Secker and Warburg.

—— (1974b) *Image and Influence: Studies in the Sociology of Film*, London: Allen and Unwin.

—— (1986) 'Genre', in Grant 1986a, 3–10.

—— (1989) *Monsters and Mad Scientists: A Cultural History of the Horror Movie*, Oxford: Blackwell.

Turim, M. (1989) *Flashbacks in Film: Memory and History*, New York: Routledge.

Turner, F. G. ([1920] 1962) *The Frontier in American History*, New York: Holt, Rinehart and Winston.

Turner, G. E. and Price, M. H. (1979) *Forgotten Horrors: Early Talkie Chillers from Poverty Row*, South Brunswick: A. S. Barnes.

Tuska, J. (1984) *Dark Cinema: American Film Noir in Cultural Perspective*, Westport: Greenwood Press.

Twitchell, J. B. (1985) *Dreadful Pleasures: An Anatomy of Modern Horror*, New York: Oxford University Press.

Tynyanov, J. ([1927] 1978) 'On Literary Evolution', trans. C. A. Luplow, in Matejka and Pomorska 1978, 66–78.

Urrichio, W. and Pearson, R. E. (1993) *Reframing Culture: The Case of the Vitagraph Quality Films*, Princeton: Princeton University Press.

Vance, N. (forthcoming) *The Victorians and Ancient Rome*, Oxford: Blackwell.

Vance, W. L. (1989) *America's Rome. Volume I: Classical Rome*, New Haven: Yale University Press.

Vardac, A. N. (1949) *Stage to Screen: Theatrical Origins of Early Film, David Garrick to D. W. Griffith*, Cambridge, Mass.: Harvard University Press.

Varma, D. (1957) *The Gothic Flame*, London: Arthur Baker.

Vasey, R. (1995) 'Beyond Sex and Violence: "Industry Policy" and the Regulation of Hollywood Movies, 1922–1939', *Quarterly Review of Film and Video* 15, 4: 65–85.

—— (1997) *The World According to Hollywood, 1918–1939*, Exeter: University of Exeter Press.

Vernet, M. (1993) '*Film Noir* on the Edge of Doom', in Copjec 1993, 1–31.

Vianello, R. (1984) 'The Rise of the Telefilm and the Networks' Hegemony Over the Motion Picture Industry', *Quarterly Review of Film Studies* 9, 3: 204–18.

Vincendeau, G. (1992) 'Noir is also a French Word: The French Antecedents of Film Noir', in Cameron 1992, 49–58.

Vincent-Buffault, A. ([1986] 1991) *The History of Tears: Sensibility and Sentimentality in France*, Houndmills: Macmillan.

Viviani, C. ([1979] 1987) 'Who is Without Sin? The Maternal Melodrama in American Film, 1930–39', trans. D. Burdick, in Gledhill 1987a, 83–99.

Vlasopolos, A. (1988) 'The "Woman's Film" Genre and One Modern Transmutation: *Kramer vs Kramer*', in J. Todd (ed.), *Women and Film*, New York: Holmes and Meier, 114–29.

Waldman, D. (1983) '"At Last I Can Tell It to Someone!": Feminine Point of View and Subjectivity in the Gothic Romance Films of the 1940s', *Cinema Journal* 23, 2: 29–39.

Walker, A. (1979) *The Shattered Silents: How the Talkies Came to Stay*, New York: William Morrow.

Walker, M. (1982) 'Melodrama and the American Cinema', *Movie* 29/30: 2–38.

—— (1992) 'Film Noir: Introduction', in Cameron 1992, 8–38.

—— (1996) '*Dances with Wolves*', in Cameron and Pye 1996, 284–93.

Walker, M. E. (1991) *The Representation of the Vietnam Veteran in American Narrative Film*, Northwestern University Ph.D. thesis, 1989, Ann Arbor: UMI Dissertation Information Service.

Wallace, M. (1993) 'Race, Gender and Psychoanalysis in Forties Films: *The Lost Boundaries, Home of the Brave* and *The Quiet One*', in Diawara 1993, 257–71.

Waller, G. A. (1987a) *American Horrors: Essays on the Modern American Horror Film*, Urbana: University of Illinois Press.

Waller, G. A. (1987b) 'Introduction' to Waller 1987a, 1–13.

—— (1990) '*Rambo*: Getting to Win This Time', in Dittmar and Michaud 1990, 113–28.

Walsh, A. S. (1984) *Women's Film and Female Experience, 1940–1950*, New York: Praeger.

Walsh, J. (1982) *American War Literature, 1914 to Vietnam*, Houndmills: Macmillan.

—— (1988) 'First Blood to Rambo: A Textual Analysis', in A. Louvre and J. Walsh (eds), *Tell Me Lies About Vietnam: Cultural Battles for the Meaning of the War*, Milton Keynes: Open University Press, 50–61.

Walters, S. D. (1992) *Lives Together/World's Apart: Mothers and Daughters in Popular Culture*, Berkeley: University of California Press.

Warren, A. and Welleck, R. (1956) *Theory of Literature*, New York: Harcourt, Brace.

Warshow, R. ([1948] 1975a) 'The Gangster as Tragic Hero', in *The Immediate Experience: Movies, Comics, Theatre and Other Aspects of Popular Culture* [1962], New York: Atheneum, 127–33.

—— ([1954] 1975b) 'Movie Chronicle: The Westerner', in *The Immediate Experience: Movies, Comics, Theatre and Other Aspects of Popular Culture* [1962], New York: Atheneum, 135–54.

Wasko, J. (1994) *Hollywood in the Information Age: Beyond the Silver Screen*, Cambridge: Polity Press.

Weales, G. (1985) *Canned Goods as Caviar: American Film Comedy of the 1930s*, Chicago: Chicago University Press.

Weaver, III, J. B. and Tamborini, R. (1996) *Horror Films: Current Research in Audience Preferences and Reactions*, Mahwah: Lawrence Erlbaum Associates.

Weinberg, A. K. ([1935] 1979) *Manifest Destiny: A Study of Nationalist Expansion in American History*, New York: AMS Press.

Welter, B. (1966) 'The Cult of True Womanhood: 1820–1860', *American Quarterly* 18: 151–74.

Wertheim, A. (1979) *Radio Comedy*, New York: Oxford University Press.

Wexman, V. W. (1993) *Creating the Couple: Love, Marriage, and Hollywood Performance*, Princeton: Princeton University Press.

—— (1996) 'The Family on the Land: Race and Nationhood in Silent Westerns', in D. Bernadoni (ed.), *The Birth of Whiteness: Race and the Emergence of U.S. Cinema*, New Brunswick: Rutgers University Press.

Whillock, D. E. (1988) 'Defining the Fictive American Vietnam War: In Search of a Genre', *Literature/Film Quarterly* 16, 4: 244–50.

White, G. E. (1968) *The Eastern Establishment and the Western Experience: The West of Frederic Remington, Theodore Roosevelt, and Owen Wister*, New Haven: Yale University Press.

White, M. (1989) 'Representing Romance: Reading/Writing/Fantasy and the "Liberated" Heroine of Recent Hollywood Films', *Cinema Journal* 28, 3: 41–56.

White, R. (1996) 'The Good Guys Wore White Hats: The B Western in American Culture', in Aquila 1996, 135–59.

White, S. (1988) 'Male Bonding, Hollywood Orientalism, and the Repression of the Feminine in Kubrick's *Full Metal Jacket*', *Arizona Quarterly* 44, 3: 120–44.

Wilder, A. (1972) *American Popular Song: The Great Innovators, 1900–1950*, London: Oxford University Press.

Willemen, P. (1972–3) 'Towards an Analysis of the Sirkian System', *Screen* 13, 4: 128–34.

—— (1981) 'Anthony Mann: Looking at the Male', *Framework* 15/16/17: 16.

Williams, A. (1984) 'Is a Radical Genre Criticism Possible?', *Quarterly Review of Film Studies* 9, 2: 121–5.

Williams, J. (1993) *Deadlines at Dawn: Film Criticism 1980–1990*, London: Marion Boyars.

Williams, L. (1984) 'When the Woman Looks', in M. A. Doane, P. Mellencamp and L. Williams (eds), *Re-Vision: Essays in Feminist Film Criticism*, Frederick: American Film Institute/University Publications of America, 83–99.

—— ([1984] 1987) '"Something Else Besides a Mother" *Stella Dallas* and the Maternal Melodrama', in Gledhill 1987a, 299–325.

Williams, T. (1996) *Hearths of Darkness: The Family in the American Horror Film*, London: Associated University Presses.

Williamson, J. (1993) *Deadline at Dawn: Film Criticism 1980–1990*, London: Marion Boyars.

Willis, S. (1997) *Race and Gender in Contemporary Hollywood Film*, Durham: Duke University Press.

Wilson, G. B. (1973) *Three Hundred Years of American Drama and Theatre*, Englewood Cliffs: Prentice-Hall.

Wilson, T. (1996) 'Celluloid Sovereignty: Hollywood's "History" of Native Americans', in Denvir 1996, 199–224.

Wilt, D. (1991) *Hardboiled in Hollywood: Five* Black Mask *Writers and the Movies*, Bowling Green: Bowling Green State University Popular Press.

Winokur, M. (1995) 'Marginal Marginalia: The African-American Voice in the Nouvelle Gangster Film', *The Velvet Light Trap* 35: 19–32.

—— (1996) *American Laughter: Immigrants, Ethnicity, and 1930s American Film Comedy*, London: Macmillan.

Winston, B. (1995) *Claiming the Real: The Documentary Film Revisited*, London: British Film Institute.

Wittgenstein, L. (1953) *Philosophical Investigations*, Oxford: Blackwell.

Wolfe, C. (1990) 'Vitaphone Shorts and *The Jazz Singer*', *Wide Angle* 12, 3: 58–78.

Wolfstein, M. and Leites, N. ([1950] 1977) *Movies: A Psychological Study*, New York: Atheneum Press.

Woll, A. L. (1983) *The Hollywood Musical Goes to War*, Chicago: Nelson-Hall.

Wood, M. (1975) *America in the Movies; or 'Santa Maria, It Had Slipped My Mind'*, New York: Basic Books.

Wood, R. (1979) 'Introduction' to A. Britton, R. Lippe, T. Williams and R. Wood (eds), *The American Nightmare: Essays on the Horror Film*, Toronto: Festival of Festivals, 7–28.

—— (1986) *Hollywood from Vietnam to Reagan*, New York: Columbia University Press.

Woodiwiss, M. (1988) *Crime Crusades and Corruption: Prohibitions in the United States 1900–1987*, London: Pinter.

—— (1990) *Organized Crime, USA: Changing Perceptions from Prohibition to the Present Day*, Brighton: British Association for American Studies.

Woodward, K. S. (1991) *The Comedy of Equality: Romantic Film Comedy in America, 1930–1950*, University of Maryland Ph.D. thesis, 1988, Ann Arbor: UMI Dissertation Information Service.

Worland, R. (1997) 'OWI Meets the Monsters: Hollywood Horror Films and War Propaganda, 1942 to 1945', *Cinema Journal* 37, 1: 47–65.

Worland, R. and Countryman, E. (1998) 'The New Western American Historiography and the Emergence of the New American Westerns', in Buscombe and Pearson 1998, 182–96.

Wright, J. H. ([1974] 1986) 'Genre Films and the Status Quo', in Grant 1986a, 41–9.

Wright, W. (1975) *Six-Guns and Society: A Structural Study of the Western*, Berkeley: University of California Press.

Wrobel, D. M. (1993) *The End of American Exceptionalism: Frontier Anxiety from the Old West to the New Deal*, Lawrence: University of Kansas Press.

Wyatt, J. (1991) 'High Concept, Product Differentiation, and the Contemporary Film Industry', in B. A. Austin (ed.), *Current Research In Film: Audiences, Economics, and the Law,* vol. 5, Norwood: Ablex, 86–105.

—— (1994) *High Concept: Movies and Marketing in Hollywood*, Austin: University of Texas Press.

—— (1998a) 'The Formation of the "Major Independent": Miramax, New Line and the New Hollywood', in Neale and Smith 1998, 74–90.

—— (1998b) 'From Roadshowing to Saturation Release: Majors, Independents and Marketing/Distribution Innovations', in Lewis 1998a, 64–86.

Wyke, M. (1997) *Projecting the Past: Ancient Rome, Cinema and History,* New York: Routledge.

Yellis, K. A. (1969) 'Prosperity's Child: Some Thoughts on the Flapper', *American Quarterly* 21: 44–64.

Yoggy, G. A. (1996) 'Prime-Time Bonanza! The Western on Television', in Aquila 1996, 160–85.

INDEX